Accounting
for CAPE

Accounting

Harold Randall
Lystra Stephens-James
Cecelia Lamorell
Lennox Francis
Dennis Noel

CAMBRIDGE
UNIVERSITY PRESS

CAMBRIDGE UNIVERSITY PRESS
Cambridge, New York, Melbourne, Madrid, Cape Town,
Singapore, São Paulo, Delhi, Mexico City

Cambridge University Press
The Edinburgh Building, Cambridge CB2 8RU, UK

www.cambridge.org
Information on this title: www.cambridge.org/9780521701167

First published 2007
5th printing 2012

Printed in the United Kingdom by Latimer Trend

A catalogue record for this publication is available from the British Library

ISBN 978-0-521-70116-7 Paperback

Cover designed by Richard Jervis Design
Typeset by Meridian Colour Repro Ltd, Pangbourne-on-Thames, Berkshire

Every effort has been made to trace copyright holders. Should any infringements have occurred,
please inform the publishers who will correct these in the event of a reprint.

Erratum: Apologies that sections 15.18–15.20 are repeated in chapter 17 as 17.5–17.7.

Contents

Preface

This book is adequate for the preparation of students for Advanced Level certification in Accounting. It is particularly beneficial to students of the Caribbean who are preparing for the Caribbean Advanced Proficiency Examination (CAPE). The book addresses areas of Financial and Cost Management Accounting. It is desired to expose students to the concepts, principles and practices of Accounting from both a theoretical and practical approach. The book clearly follows the order of the CAPE syllabus but allows for some flexibility in the sequences in which the topics are studied.

As suggested by the CAPE syllabus, adequate preparation through the topics discussed will provide a good foundation not only for examination purposes but also for further study of Accounting at pre-professional and professional levels.

Many years as examiners (and lecturers/teachers) have made us keenly aware of the difficulties experienced by examination candidates, and the text seeks to address these difficulties as they arise in the topics covered. Particular difficulties are identified as they occur in the chapters; in addition, most chapters have 'Examination hints'. Our approach has been from the dual standpoints of teacher and student. If it is any consolation and encouragement to students, we have experienced the frustration and difficulties that many encounter in their studies, but we hope we have proved that determination to succeed brings its reward.

Students should ask the question 'why' even more times than they ask 'how' because an understanding of the reasons underlying accounting practices makes the rules more memorable. 'How do I do this?' will give way to 'I know how to do this!'

We wish to express our great appreciation to Gaynelle Holdip for reading our manuscript and making helpful suggestions.

To our readers, we send our best wishes for success.

Harold Randall
Lystra Stephens-James
Cecilia Lamorell
Lennox Francis
Dennis Noel

Acknowledgements

Typing and graphics were done by Lisa Budhoo and Vinola Nanan; and additional typing by Abigail Harewood.

Unit One

Module One
Accounting Theory, Recording and Control Systems

1 The nature and scope of financial accounting

Objectives
- discuss the development of accounting
- identify the users of accounting information and their needs
- discuss the significance and limitation of accounting information
- illustrate the accounting cycle

1.1 The development of accounting

Prior to the development of the double-entry system of accounting by Luca Pacoli in 1494, the recording of business activity was performed very crudely. As businesses grew in number and in size, there was also a need for recording procedures to keep pace with these changes. Hence, the initial **stewardship** role of simply securing cash developed into a system of accounting, which involves the recording, summarizing, and analysing of data on which the efficient operation of a business depended.

Even though the number of services in accounting expanded, there was still a need to concentrate on certain aspects of business activities, which give rise to two common branches of accounting, namely financial accounting, and cost and management accounting and tax accounting. The simple stewardship task of securing and recording cash is now encompassed in financial accounting. Cost and management accounting was identified as a tool to help managers in making business decisions.

The data collected by early accountants merely reflected receipts and payments of cash. Today, the practice is to **match** income earned with the expenses incurred (expenses) in earning said income.

In the quest for consistency in how businesses record and present their financial information the accounting profession has developed and instituted organized **rule-making authorities**. The Financial Accounting Standards Board (FASB) and the Securities and Exchange Commission (SEC) are two such regulatory bodies instituted to ensure consistency and understandability of accounting information.

The functions of such agencies deal with all issues in accounting. Their role ensured that they consider public opinion on accounting matters; settle controversies; interpret and clarify accounting policies; set standards and ensure compliance.

The function ranges from creating generally accepted accounting principles (GAAP) and concepts to adhering to state laws. GAAP are broad guidelines, conventions, rules and procedures of accounting designed to promote good accounting practices and reduce illegal or unethical practices. So stringent are standards that there is even an official procedure for instituting them.

As businesses expand and financial relationships with customers and suppliers change, cash basis accounting had to be enhanced with accrual basis accounting. The widespread use of credit facilities demanded that accounting take this aspect of business transactions into consideration.

Even the trend of simple **reports** to determine profit or loss or statements of ownership of property and liability has mushroomed into complicated Income Statements; detailed Balance Sheets; explanatory cash flow statements and summarized statements of owner's equity. The preparation of these reports demand manipulation of basic information and reflect the sophisticated level to which accounting has developed.

So complex is accounting that the efforts of the untrained custodian will not suffice. Today accounting is a profession requiring **accreditation** and **certification** of individuals and is important to the growth and development of businesses. In many countries Accounting Professionals are organized into groups that oversee the practice of accounting.

Examples of professional accounting organizations in the Caribbean are
- Institute of Chartered Accountants of Antigua and Barbuda (ICAAB)
- Bahamas Institute of Chartered Accountants (BICA)
- Institute of Chartered Accountants of Barbados (ICAB)

- Institute of Chartered Accountants of Guyana (ICAG)
- Institute of Chartered Accountants of Jamaica (ICAJ)
- Institute of Chartered Accountants of Trinidad and Tobago (ICATT)
- St. Kitts/Nevis Association of Chartered Accountants

These organizations are part of the Institute of Chartered Accountants of the Caribbean (ICAC) and the International Federation of Accountants (IFAC).

1.2 Users of accounting information

Internal	External				
Management	Those with direct financial interest	Government	Regulatory agencies	Economic planners	Other groups
Owners	Present investors	Inland Revenue	Stock exchanges	Financial advisors	Employees
Partners	Potential investors	Value added tax	Securities and Exchange Commission	Stock brokers	Labour unions
Board of directors	Creditors	Government planners		Financial press	Customers
Managers	Banks				General public
Department heads	Other lending agencies				
Supervisors					

1.3 Questions asked by users

Internal	External
• Can we afford to hire new employees or increase wages? • Is there sufficient cash to honour obligations? • How much does it cost to produce one unit? • Can we invest in new equipment?	• Is the business making profits? • Can the company afford to pay dividends? How much? • Will the business be able to meet its obligations when they fall due? • How is the business performing in comparison to its competitors? • Is this merger, acquisition or takeover of any benefit to us? • Is the company following accepted standards when preparing its financial statement?

1.4 **The significance of accounting information**

The importance of accounting information is to facilitate planning and decision-making. Although the accounting process uses previous economic activities of an entity, the information is still useful in

1. deciding how resources are to be allocated;
2. evaluating the potential of the entity to earn profits; and
3. calculating the risks involved.

1.5 **The limitations of accounting information**

Despite the usefulness of accounting information, there are some limitations:

1. An accounting system can only record items that can be given a monetary value and so fails to give a complete picture of the business.
2. The accounting process uses previous economic activities of the business to form the basis of accounting records.
3. The accounting process cannot reflect the mood of the business.
4. Many items on the financial statement are the result of estimates, e.g. provision for depreciation and doubtful debts.
5. Analysing aggregated information is difficult.
6. Preparation of the financial statement at a particular date may not reflect the trend for the year. For example, a firm may experience low sales throughout the year but in the last month of the year there was a sales increase.
7. Accounting policies differ between firms and this makes comparison difficult.

1.6 **The accounting cycle**

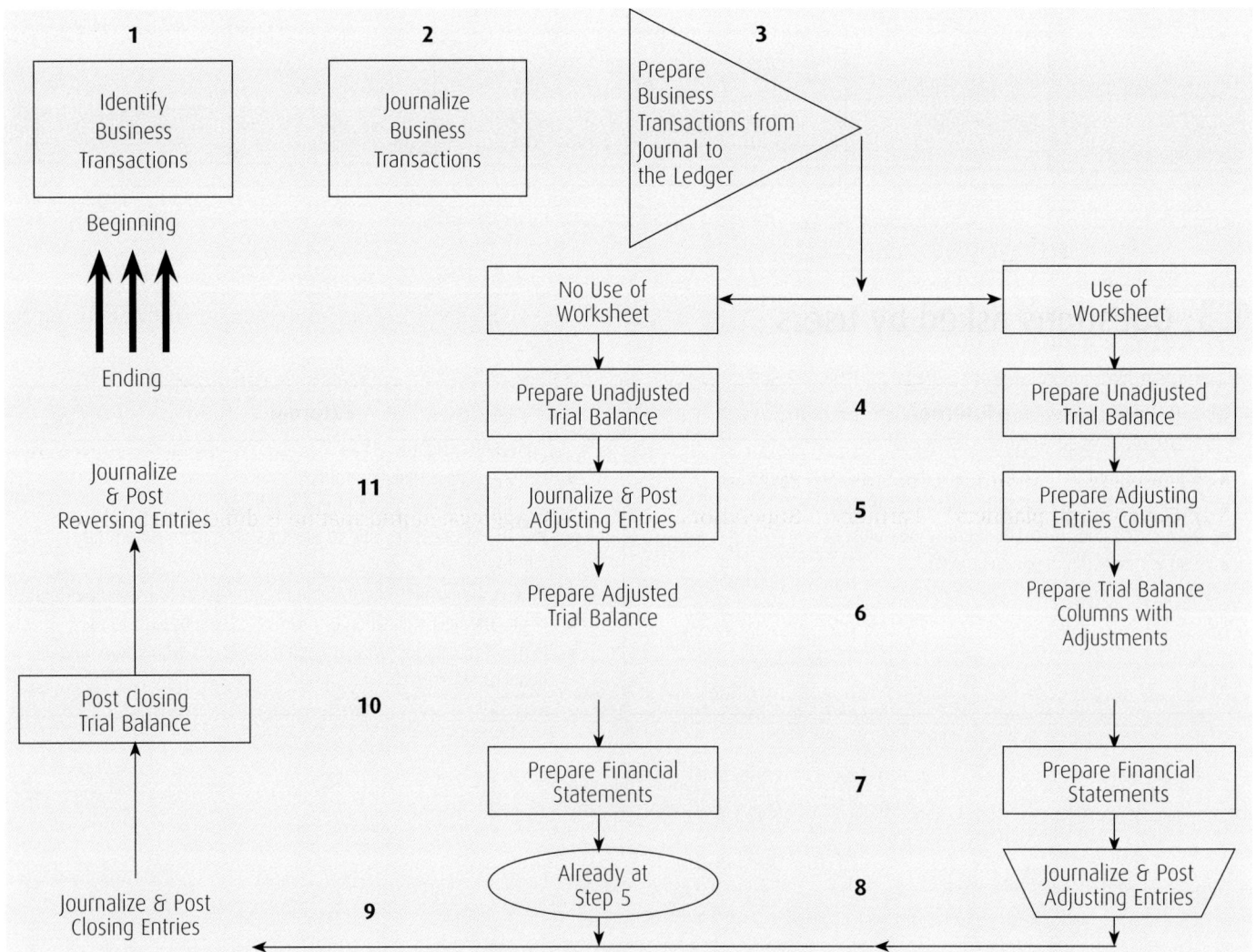

1.7 Explanation of the accounting cycle

During the accounting period	End of the accounting period	Beginning of the accounting period
Steps	**Steps**	**Step**
1. Gathering of information on economic events.	4. Listing all the accounts and their balances to check the equality of debits and credits.	11. Reopening of all real and personal accounts with balances.
2. Condensing the information in chronological order in day books.	5. Recording those economic events not supported by business documents.	
3. Transferring information to the ledger from day books.	6. Making final checks on accuracy before preparing the financial statements.	
	7. Preparing the financial statements for external users.	
	8. Recording adjusting entries in the journal and the ledger.	
	9. Closing the temporary accounts and recording the net income in retained earnings.	
	10. Making a further check on the equality of debits and credits after including the closing entries.	

1.8 Extended questions

1 Which of the following groups has only external users of accounting information?

   (a) Owners   Present investors   Stock Exchange

   (b) Potential investors   Government planners   Stock Brokers

   (c) Managers   Board of Directors   Partners

   (d) Government planners   Partners   Supervisors

2 Which of the following are **not true** about accounting information?

   (a) It reflects the mood of the business.

   (b) Only events with monetary value are recorded.

   (c) Different policies make comparison between companies easy.

   (d) Aggregated information is difficult to analyse.

3 (a) Using the graphic below, enter the users of accounting information.

   (b) Indicate which are external users and which are internal users.

   (c) Indicate the direction of flow of information by using either a one-headed arrow or a two-headed arrow.

   (d) State briefly the purpose of each user-group's interest.

Note. Provide key to diagram.

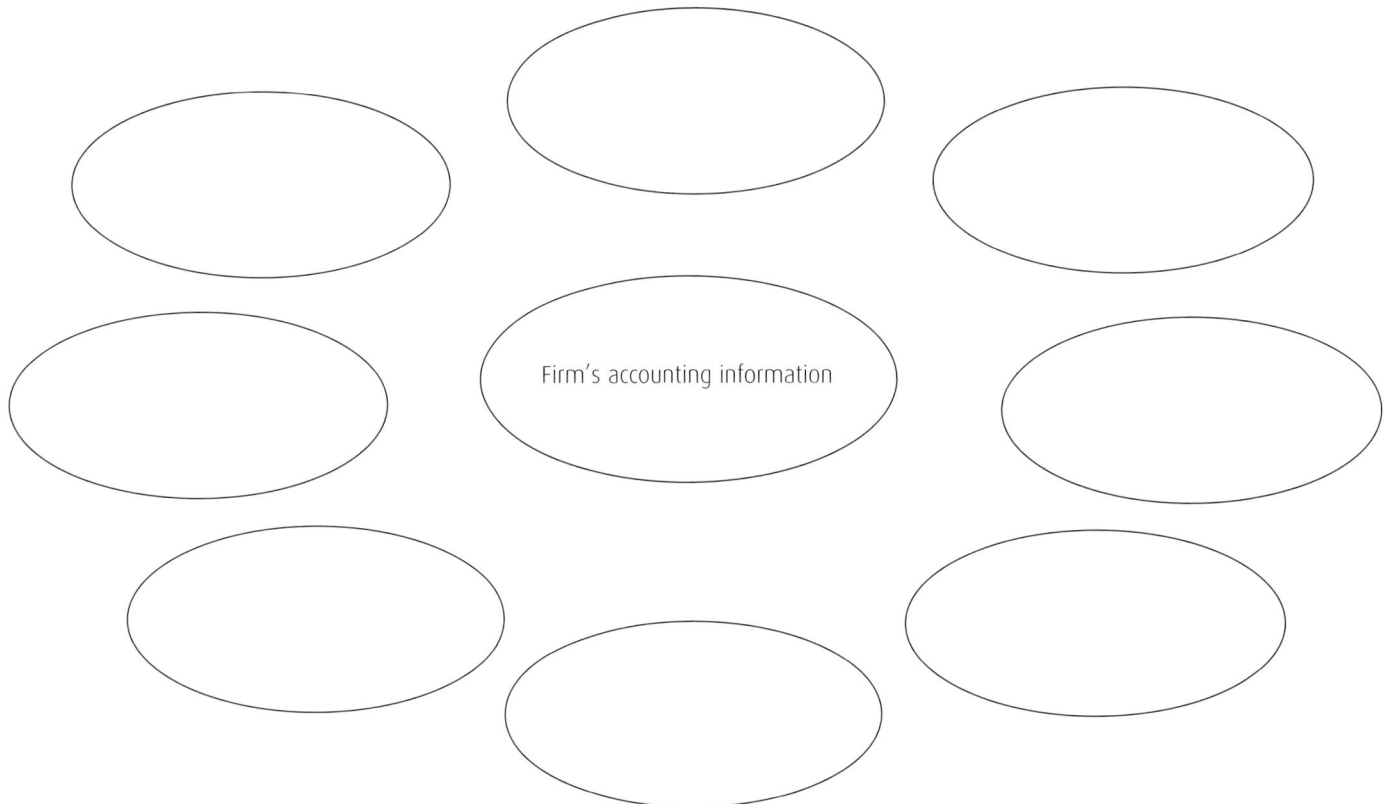

4 Modern day accounting has developed beyond mere stewardship of cash. Discuss.

5 Financial statements are prepared mainly with external users in mind. Discuss.

6 Discuss the statement: 'accounting information is too historical to be of any use'.

7 Discuss some of the limitations of accounting information.

8 Present the accounting cycle in the form of a diagram giving the correct sequence of steps with explanations.

Firm's accounting information

2 The conceptual framework of accounting

Objectives
- describe the Conceptual Framework of Accounting
- list the objectives of financial accounting
- apply the recognition and measurement concepts
- identify the elements of financial statements
- describe the qualitative characteristics of accounting information
- describe the constraints to achieving qualitative characteristics
- describe the development of accounting standards
- justify the use of accounting standards
- outline the standard setting process

2.1 The conceptual framework

The Conceptual Framework of Accounting was developed by the Financial Accounting Standards Board (FASB) and is a system of related objectives. The main purpose of which is to have consistent standard in the preparation of financial statements. The framework provides a basis for resolving disputes, setting standards and outlining fundamental accounting principles. (See diagram below.)

2.2 Objectives of financial reporting

The objective of financial reporting is to provide information that is useful to the users of financial accounting. The information should be useful:
1. For planning and decision making.
2. In the prediction of future cash flows.
3. In identifying economic resources, claims to resources and changes in resourses and claims.

2.3 What are principles or concepts?

Accounting principles are basic rules that are applied in recording transactions and preparing financial statements. They are also known as concepts. These rules are necessary to ensure that accounting records provide reliable information. All businesses should apply the rules in their financial statements. The most important of these rules are now described, and should be learned, understood and applied when preparing financial statements.

2.4 Business entity

Every business is regarded as having an existence separate from that of its owner. This has already been recognized when an owner's capital has been debited in the business Bank account and credited to the owner's Capital account. The credit in the Capital account shows that the owner is a creditor of the business, which owes him the money. This can only be the case if the business is regarded as being separate from the owner as no one can owe himself money. When the owner withdraws money from the business, the amount is debited to his Drawings account. The business accounts do not show if he spends the money on food, clothes, or holidays because these are not business transactions.

(It is important to remember that this is only an accounting concept. Anyone who has a grievance against a business may legally sue a sole trader or a partner in a firm. The business is not a separate entity for that purpose.)

2.5 Money measurement

Only transactions that can be expressed in monetary terms are recorded in ledger accounts. Goods, fixed assets, debtors and creditors etc. may be recorded in ledger accounts because they have resulted from transactions that can be expressed in monetary terms.

Although there are obvious advantages in being able to record things in monetary terms, it has disadvantages. Things which cannot be expressed in monetary terms, such as the skills of workers or their satisfaction with their working conditions, are not recorded in the accounts.

THE CONCEPTUAL FRAMEWORK

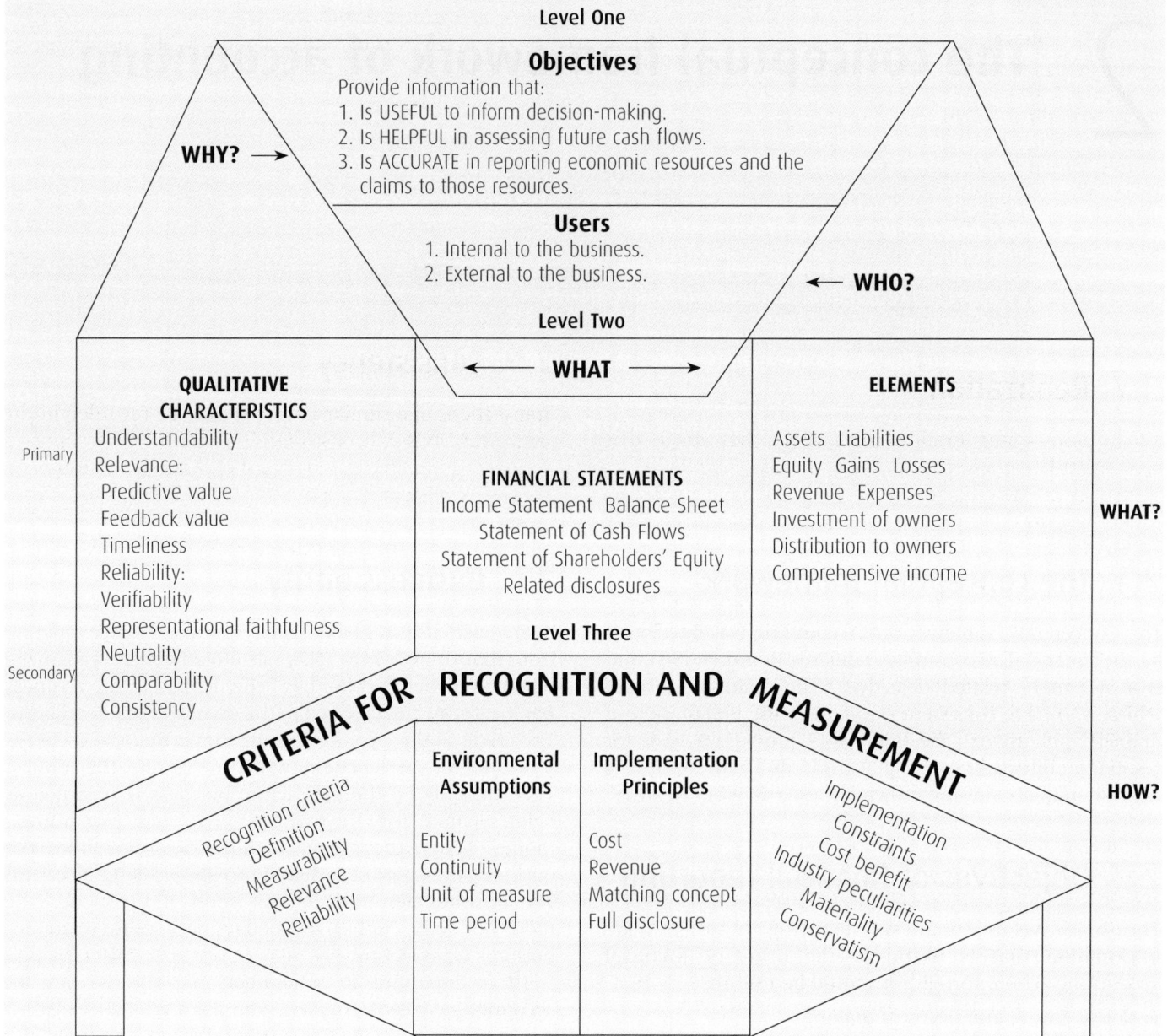

Level One

Objectives

Provide information that:
1. Is USEFUL to inform decision-making.
2. Is HELPFUL in assessing future cash flows.
3. Is ACCURATE in reporting economic resources and the claims to those resources.

WHY? →

← **WHO?**

Users
1. Internal to the business.
2. External to the business.

Level Two

← **WHAT** →

QUALITATIVE CHARACTERISTICS

Primary

Understandability
Relevance:
 Predictive value
 Feedback value
Timeliness
Reliability:
Verifiability
Representational faithfulness
Neutrality

Secondary

Comparability
Consistency

FINANCIAL STATEMENTS

Income Statement Balance Sheet
Statement of Cash Flows
Statement of Shareholders' Equity
Related disclosures

ELEMENTS

Assets Liabilities
Equity Gains Losses
Revenue Expenses
Investment of owners
Distribution to owners
Comprehensive income

WHAT?

Level Three

CRITERIA FOR RECOGNITION AND MEASUREMENT

HOW?

Recognition criteria
Definition
Measurability
Relevance
Reliability

Environmental Assumptions

Entity
Continuity
Unit of measure
Time period

Implementation Principles

Cost
Revenue
Matching concept
Full disclosure

Implementation
Constraints
Cost benefit
Industry peculiarities
Materiality
Conservatism

Some people think it would be useful if these and some other 'non-monetary' items could be included in financial statements.

2.6 Historic cost

Transactions are recorded at their cost to the business. Cost cannot be disputed as invoices or other documentary evidence may be produced to support it. This treatment is said to be objective because it is based on fact and not on opinion.

The opposite of objectivity is subjectivity, which is based upon personal opinion. For example, somebody may give his friend a watch that cost $50. The friend may already have a good watch or perhaps several watches. He would not have paid $50 for another. He would probably value the gift at less than $50. On the other hand, if the friend had not already got a watch and his life depended on him having one, he might value the watch at much more than $50. Values based on personal opinions are said to be subjective and are not reliable bases on which to record transactions.

While the principle of recording transactions at their historic cost has obvious advantages, it has two disadvantages.

- It ignores the changing value of money. A good that was purchased five years ago for $100 might have been sold then for $200 making a profit of $100. If inflation since then has been 25%, today's selling price would be $250 giving an apparent profit of $150. A more realistic calculation of the profit would be to express the original cost at today's prices, $125, giving a profit of $125, which would be enough to buy no more than $100 would have bought five years ago! Historic cost may produce misleading results unless its limitations are understood.
- Like the concept of money measurement, historic cost does not allow things that cannot be expressed in monetary terms to be recorded in accounting.

2.7 Realization

When accountants speak of realization, they mean that something becomes an actual fact, or that something has been converted into money. For example, if a man goes into a shop and says that he will return tomorrow and buy a pair of shoes, there is no sale yet; but if the man returns the next day and buys the shoes, the sale has become a fact. By selling the shoes, the shopkeeper has converted goods into money. The sale has been **realized**. Transactions are realized when cash or a debtor replaces goods or services. This principle is important as it prevents revenue from being credited in the accounts before it has been earned.

Goods on sale or return When a trader sends goods on sale or return to a customer, no sale takes place until the customer informs the seller that he has decided to buy them. The customer has the right to return the goods to the trader. The goods remain the property of the seller until the sale actually takes place. Goods on sale or return when final accounts are being prepared must be treated as stock. If they have been wrongly treated as sold the accounting treatment must be reversed. Sales and debtors must be reduced by the selling price, and closing stock must be increased by the cost price of the goods.

Example

George has sent goods on sale or return to Helen for $500 and treated the transaction as a sale. Helen has not yet accepted the goods. The goods cost George $350. The following balances have been extracted from George's trial balance: Sales $30 000; trade debtors $1000. Stock on hand has been valued at $900. The following adjustments must be made for the final accounts.

2.8 Duality

The concept of **duality** recognizes that there are two aspects for each transaction – represented by debit and credit entries in accounts. The concept is the basis of the accounting equation:

assets = capital + liabilities.

The equation is also expressed in its other form: assets – liabilities = capital. Balance Sheets are prepared in this form.

The accounting equation is a very useful tool for solving some accounting problems.

2.9 Consistency

Transactions of a similar nature should be recorded in the same way (that is, consistently) in the same accounting period and in all future accounting periods. For example, the cost of redecorating premises should always be debited to an expense account for the redecoration of premises and charged to the Profit and Loss Account. It would not be correct, the next time the offices were redecorated, to debit the cost to the Premises (fixed asset) account.

Consistency in the treatment of transactions is important to ensure that the profits or losses of different periods, and Balance Sheets, may be compared meaningfully.

2.10 Materiality

Sometimes a business may depart from the generally accepted principles for recording some transactions. They may do this when the amounts involved are not considered **material** (or significant) in relation to the amounts of the other items in their Profit and Loss Accounts and Balance Sheets.

A company may prepare its Balance Sheet showing all amounts rounded to the nearest $000 or even $m. It would treat the purchase of any asset not exceeding, say, $1000 as revenue expenditure instead of adding it to its fixed assets, as it would not make any noticeable difference to the figure of fixed assets in the Balance Sheet. It would not be considered a material item.

On the other hand, the same amount of expenditure in a small business may be very significant and would need to be treated as capital expenditure in order not to distort profit and the assets in the Balance Sheet.

Sales	$	Debtors	$	Stock	$
Per trial balance	30 000	Per trial balance	1 000	As given	900
Less	500	Less	500	Add	350
Trading Account	29 500	Balance Sheet	500	Trading A/c and Balance Sheet	1 250

An amount may be considered material in the accounts if its inclusion in, or omission from, the Profit and Loss Account or Balance Sheet would affect the way people would read and interpret those financial statements.

2.11 Accruals (matching)

If the final accounts of a business are to give reliable information, the revenue and other income must be no more and no less than the business has earned in the period covered by the Profit and Loss Account. The expenses in the Profit and Loss Account should fairly represent the expenses incurred in earning that revenue. The difference between a Profit and Loss Account prepared on a cash basis and one prepared on an accruals basis will be apparent from the following example:

A business occupies premises at an annual rental of $2000. In one year it has paid $2500 because it has paid one quarter's rent in advance. It has also used $2100 worth of electricity but it has paid only $1200 because it has not paid the latest bill for $900. Its gross profit for the year is $10 000.

Profit and Loss Accounts prepared on (a) a 'cash basis', that is, on the actual payments made, and (b) on an accruals basis, would look as follows:

	(a) Cash basis		(b) Accruals basis	
	$	$	$	$
Gross profit		10 000		10 000
Less Rent	2500		2 000	
Electricity	1200	3 700	2 100	4 100
Net profit		6 300		5 900

The accruals basis is the correct one as it records the actual costs incurred in the period for rent and electricity.

Trading and Profit and Loss Accounts should be prepared on the **accruals**, or matching, basis so that expenses are matched to the revenue earned; that is, expenses should be shown in the Profit and Loss Account as they have been *incurred* rather than as they have been paid.

2.12 Prudence

The prudence concept is intended to prevent profit from being overstated. If profit is overstated, a trader may believe that his income is more than it really is, and he may withdraw too much money from the business. That would lead to the capital invested in the business being depleted. If it happens too often the business will collapse because there will not be enough money to pay creditors

or to renew assets when they are worn out. The principle is sometimes known as the **concept of conservatism**. It is safer for profit to be understated rather than overstated.

The rule is

- profits should not be overstated
- losses should be provided for as soon as they are recognized.

Students often make the mistake of saying that the prudence concept means that profits must be understated. That is not so; the concept is meant to ensure that profits are realistic without being overstated.

2.13 Going concern

A business is a going concern if there is no intention to discontinue it in the foreseeable future. If it is short of working capital and the owner is unable to put more money into it, or to find somebody who will be prepared to lend it money, it may be unable to pay its creditors and be forced to close.

Unless stated to the contrary, it is assumed that the accounts of a business are prepared on a going concern basis. If the business is not a going concern, the assets should be valued in the Balance Sheet at the amounts they could be expected to fetch in an enforced sale, which could be much less than their real worth. Balance Sheets should always show a realistic situation, bearing in mind the weakness of the business.

2.14 Substance over form

These words are used to describe the accounting treatment of something that does not reflect the legal position.

For example, a machine bought on hire purchase remains the property of the seller until the final instalment has been paid. If the purchaser fails to pay the instalments as they become due, the seller may reclaim the machine. That is the legal position, or the 'form'.

However, the machine is being used in the purchaser's business in the same way as the other machines that have not been bought on hire purchase. From an accounting point of view and for all practical purposes, the machine is no different from the other machines; that is the 'substance' of the matter.

The practical view (the substance) is preferred to the legal view (the form) in the accounting treatment. This is known as 'substance over form'.

Example

Antonio bought a machine on hire purchase on 1 January 2003. The cash price of the machine was $50 000. Antonio paid $10 000 on 1 January 2003. The balance was to be settled by four payments of $10 100 (including interest of $100) on 1 April 2003, 1 July 2003, 1 October 2003 and 1 January 2004. The following entries should appear in Antonio's final accounts at 31 December 2003.

Profit and Loss Account: Interest on hire purchase $400

Balance Sheet: Fixed assets $50 000 (the cash price although only $40 000 has been paid)

Current liabilities $10 100 (including the final instalment of $10 000 and accrued interest of $100 not paid until 1 January 2004)

2.15 The elements of financial statements

These are the building blocks that are used to construct financial statements. They focus on items related to the measurement of **financial performance** and reporting **financial position**. The preparation of financial statements is influenced by the economic, legal and social circumstances in each country and also by the needs of the various users of financial statements. These financial statements include Balance Sheet; Income Statement; statement of owners equity and cash flow statement. The following are elements of financial statements:

2.16 Qualitative characteristics of accounting information

An important aspect of accounting information is its usefulness in decision-making. To be useful this information should possess the following qualitative characteristics:

1. Understandability – accounting information should be reported in such a way that it is easily understood by users.
2. Relevance – accounting information should be timely and have the capability to provide feedback and make predictions.
3. Reliability – accounting information should be free of errors and bias and should be:
   a. Verifiable;
   b. A faithful representation;
   c. Neutral.
4. Comparability – accounting information from an entity should be comparable with those of other similar entities.
5. Consistency – the same accounting methods and principles should be used from year to year in the preparation of financial statements.

Balance Sheet	Assets	Probable future economic benefits obtained or controlled by a particular entity as a result of past transactions or events
	Liabilities	Represents obligations to other entities. Most liabilities require future payment of a specified amount of cash at a specified time
	Equity	Also called owner's equity or shareholders' equity; represents the residual interest in the net assets of an entity
Owner's equity	Investments by the owners	Represent increases in equity as a result of fresh injection of funds or the exchange of ownership
	Distributions to owners	Also called capital transactions; represent decreases to equity resulting from dividend payments, transfer of assets to owners as well as the proceeds from the sale of assets
Income statement & cashflow	Revenues	Inflows resulting from the provision of goods and services to customers
	Gains	Net inflows that arise from assets sold above their book values and result in increases in equity
	Expenses	Outflows incurred in the process of generating revenues during the normal operations of a business
	Losses	Decreases in equity resulting from the sale of assets below their book values
	Comprehensive income	Change in equity of an entity during a period from non-owner transactions

2.17 Constraints to achieving quality accounting information

The qualitative characteristics built into the conceptual framework are designed to make accounting information effective and achieve its objectives. This may not be practical at all times. Exceptions due to special situations will arise. There are constraints that exist and influence the reporting of accounting information. These constraints permit entities to change accounting principles without reducing the usefulness of the information. They are:

1. **Cost benefit** constraint influences the accounting choices an entity has to make and thus the reporting of information. The benefits derived by external users should outweigh the costs incurred by the internal preparers.

2. **Materiality** constraint assesses 'the magnitude of an omission or mis-statement of accounting', the omission or inclusion of immaterial facts or inconsequential money amounts is not likely to change or influence the decision-making process of a rational external user.

3. **Conservatism** constraint is applied when there is uncertainty whether the accounting choice should be that of understatement rather than overstatement of income and assets.

4. **Industry peculiarities** constraint comes about when certain accounting policies are peculiar to a particular industry: for instance, some accounting information for the oil industry would not be pertinent to the banking industry.

2.18 The development of accounting standards

The purpose of the standards is to ensure compliance with the true and fair view concept, and they are officially recognized in the Companies Act 1985. All companies are required to comply with the standards, or to publish reasons for departing from them

Company auditors are required to ensure that company accounts are prepared in accordance with the standards and to report any significant departure from the standards to the shareholders. The standards help to increase uniformity in the presentation of company accounts and to reduce the subjective element in the disclosure of information.

2.19 Why standards are important

1. To determine the minimum information to be included in the financial statements.

2. To establish what must be disclosed by different forms of business organizations.

3. To ensure consistency in application of accounting methods.

4. To foster easy comparison.

5. To set a benchmark for understandability.

6. To enable verification by external auditors.

The following diagram illustrates the steps in developing a standard setting process:

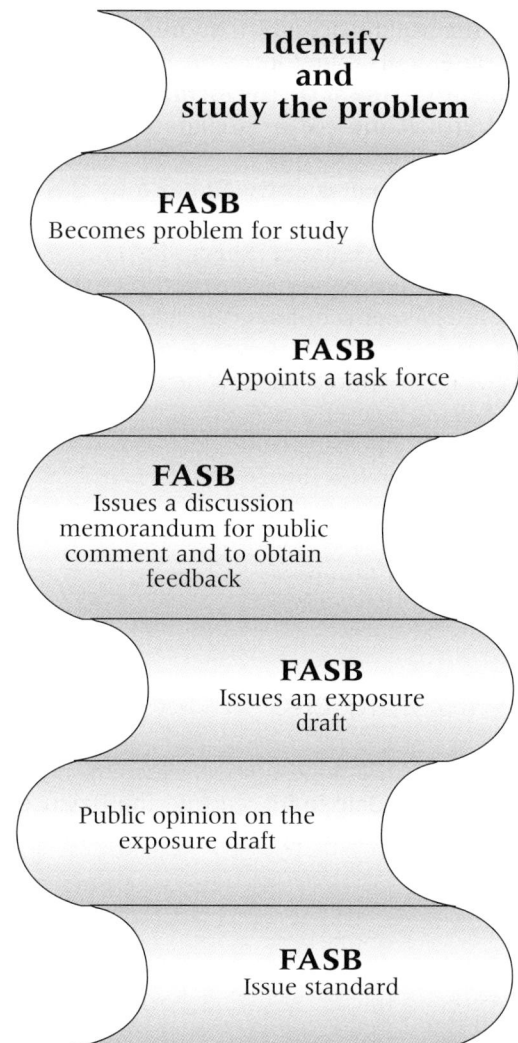

Identify and study the problem

FASB
Becomes problem for study

FASB
Appoints a task force

FASB
Issues a discussion memorandum for public comment and to obtain feedback

FASB
Issues an exposure draft

Public opinion on the exposure draft

FASB
Issue standard

2.20 Examination hints

- Learn all the concepts and make sure you understand them.
- Watch for the application of the concepts when you answer examination questions.
- Make sure you identify the correct concept when asked which one has been applied to a particular situation. (Prudence is not always the right answer!)
- Read questions carefully. Questions may require you to give a definition, or to explain, or to discuss. Each of those requirements must be met with an appropriate response.
- When asked for a definition, do not give an example instead. If asked to define 'substance over form', an answer such as 'substance over form is when an asset is bought on hire purchase' is unlikely to gain any marks because the definition is missing. The following is better: 'Subject over form is the treatment accorded to a transaction so that the real effect on the business is recorded in the accounts, rather than the strictly legal position. For example, an asset bought on hire purchase is treated as though it already belongs to the purchaser although it legally remains the property of the seller until the final instalment has been paid.' This answer gives a definition as required. (The example develops the answer further and may gain an additional mark.)

  'Explain...' requires an explanation of the way a concept is applied and an explanation as to why it is necessary or important.

  'Discuss...' invites an answer which includes a discussion of the advantages **and** disadvantages of a concept.

Examiners choose their words carefully and expect candidates to take note of the wording of questions.

2.21 Multiple-choice questions

1 A trader who sells food does not include food that is past its 'sell by' date in his stock in the Balance Sheet. Which concept has he applied in valuing his stock?

A matching

B prudence

C realization

D going concern

2 A business is about to be closed down as it has insufficient funds to pay its creditors. The owner places a very low value on his stock in the Balance Sheet. Which concept is being applied?

A going concern

B materiality

C money measurement

D subjectivity

3 The owner of a business paid his private telephone bill from the business bank account. The amount was debited to his Drawings account. Which concept was applied?

A business entity

B matching

C prudence

D realization

4 A trader has included rent which is due but not paid in his Profit and Loss Account. Which accounting concept has been applied?

A historic cost

B matching

C money measurement

D prudence

5 The balances in a sales ledger total $16 000. A debtor who owes $800 is known to be in financial difficulty. The figure of debtors shown in the Balance Sheet is $15 200. Which concept has been applied?

A matching

B prudence

C realization

D substance over form

6 A trader sends goods on sale or return to a customer. When the trader prepares his Balance Sheet at 31 March 2004, the customer has still not indicated that he has accepted the goods. Which concept should the trader apply when he prepares his accounts at 31 March 2004?

A consistency

B matching

C prudence

D realization

2.22 Additional exercises

1 Fill in the blanks

1. The accounting body that developed the Conceptual Framework was the _____.

2. The Conceptual Framework is a system of _____ _____.

3. The Conceptual Framework was formulated to ensure financial statements had a _____ standard.

4. The information provided by financial reporting should facilitate _____, predict _____ and identify _____.

5. Financial statements measure _____ _____ and report _____.

6. Liabilities, investments by owners and expenses are _____ of financial statements.

2 Classify each of the statements below as true or false

(a) Financial accounting has to follow the guidelines of GAAP.

(b) Reports of Management accounting are prepared for internal use only.

(c) Management accountants prepare general purpose financial statements.

(d) Financial accounting provides information for internal use.

(e) Financial accounting is not concerned with planning and controlling.

(f) External users must go to Management accountants for their information.

(g) Internal and external users can use the information provided by financial accounting.

(h) Creditors, stock brokers and labour unions are only interested in the data provided by financial accounting.

(i) The reports of Management accounts can be used to predict cash flows.

(j) Auditing is strictly to check the work of the management accountant.

(k) Management accountants provide data for both internal and external users.

(l) External users do not usually make demands on Management accountants for reports.

Match each term on the left with appropriate statement on the right

1. Assets	Residual interest in the net assets of an entity
Equity	Sale of asset above book value
Distribution to owners	Future economic benefits
Gains	Dividends and share of profits
2. Losses	Obligations to other entities
Expenses	Inflows from sale of goods and provision of services
Liabilities	Cause reduction in equity
Investments by owners	Used to generate revenue
Revenue	Fresh injection of funds
3. Reliability	Capability to provide feedback
Comparability	Users are able to comprehend the information
Relevance	The absence of errors and biases
Understandability	Same methods and principles are used annually
Consistency	Comparison with similar entities
4. Cost benefit	Accounting policies used differently in a particular industry
Materiality	Influences accounting choices made by an entity
Conservatism	Does not influence decision making process in an organization
Industry peculiarities	Used when there is an uncertainty of the accounting choice to be used

2.23 Questions

1 A vegetable supplier enters into a contract with HYCO Food Stores Supermarket Ltd on January 8 to deliver limes in February. The limes are delivered on February 14 at a price of $2000, $1000 payable on March 1 and $1000 on April 1. When should the supplier record the $2000 as revenue?

A January 8

B February 14

C $1000 March 1 and $1000 April 1

D When the supermarket receives the limes

Short responses

1. Reliability is a characteristic of accounting information. Explain what it means.

2. Explain the characteristics of accounting information labelled as 'consistency'.

3. Explain comparability as a characteristic of accounting information.

4. Using an appropriate example, discuss how relevance relates to the needs of the users of an entity.

5. Discuss the matching principle using an example.

6. Revenue recognition is an important concept in accounting. Discuss using an example.

7. Discuss the importance of materiality.

8. Discuss how the concept of business entity affects financial reporting.

9. Discuss the importance of comparability of accounting information to the needs of the users of financial statements.

10. State what is the Conceptual Framework of accounting?

11. What is the purpose of Financial accounting?

12. Define three factors that are used to recognize and measure accounting information.

13. State three non-quantifiable characteristics that accounting information should have.

14. Describe three factors that may be considered before reports are attempted.

15. Describe the route to be followed if a 'new' standard in accounting is to be set.

16. Explain why standards are necessary in accounting.

Extended responses

1. Using an appropriate example, discuss how relevance relates to the needs of the users of an entity's financial statements.

2. Describe any three changes that moulded the development in accounting.

3. A business can operate without accounting standards. Discuss.

3 Accounting and administrative control systems

Objectives
- identify the social and ethical issues in financial reporting
- define control systems
- state what are the objectives of control systems
- determine the effectiveness of an internal control system
- identify the principles of internal control systems
- describe and illustrate control systems for
  - Inventory (stock)
  - Cash
  - Accounts receivable (debtors)
  - Accounts payable (creditors)
- describe the control necessary in the electronic data processing environment
- state the role of the internal auditor
- state the role of the external auditor
- discuss ethics in accounting

3.1 Introduction

An internal control system includes all the procedures and policies taken by an entity to safeguard assets and ensure accuracy of financial records. The system also ensures compliance with company policies and government statutes (law) with the ability to evaluate performance of company personnel in order to promote efficiency of operation.

3.2 Objectives of the control system in the organization

- To identify the social and ethical issues in financial reporting.
- To comply with company's policies, regulations and government laws.
- To provide reasonable assurance that the company's goals and objectives are achieved.
- To assess the operating effectiveness of the organization and its structure.
- To discourage occurrence of errors or irregularities.

General

- Segregation of duties – A fundamental principle of internal control requires that the person who is responsible for an asset should not maintain the accounting records of that asset. When this principle is observed, the custodian of the asset cannot misappropriate the asset; and the record keeper has no reason for falsifying the record.
- Adequate documentation – Good records provide a means of control. Poor records invite laxity and often theft. Documents verify that a transaction took place. Therefore documents must be adequate to provide assurances that all the assets are accounted for and are the basis for accounting records. These are relevant principles that determine the use and design for the documents. Documents should be
  pre-numbered;
  - prepared on the date of transaction;
  - clear and simple;
  - designed for multiple use.
- Independent internal verification – Work should be divided among individuals or departments. The transactions are related and divided in such a manner that the work of one acts as a check on that of another.

- Proper authorization – Transactions are executed in accordance with management's general or specific authorization. General authorizations are policies made by management for their employees to use daily. Specific authorization will be used according to the particular situation: for example, payment for the maintenance of a motor vehicle.
- Competent personnel with clear responsibilities – Good internal control demands that responsibility must be established. Where there are shared duties, one person should be made responsible, so that if something goes wrong, it may not be difficult to determine who is at fault.
- Physical safeguard of assets – There are physical, mechanical and electronic devices to safeguard assets. They are essential and used whenever practicable: for example, physical controls are used to safeguard essential assets whereas mechanical and electronic controls safeguard assets and enhance the accuracy and reliability of accounting records.
- Other controls (Rotation of employees) – This principle requires that all physical assets should be insured as a means to recover loss. Employees should be rotated frequently so as to prevent them from becoming too comfortable or attempting to cover up fraud.

Inventory

Security guards. They are used to prevent the unauthorized removal of goods from business premises. Persons taking goods from the compound should have documents indicating the permission to do so. Without documentation one can consider the activity illegal.

Perimeter fence. This is particularly necessary where bulky goods are kept in a stockyard. It prevents easy access by unauthorized persons and vehicles to such material. The transfer of stock from this area should have the necessary documentation.

Administration. This is the unit that is responsible for the preparation and storage of documents and data. The purchasing department places the order, the receiving section accepts the invoice and the accounting department when reliably informed pays for the order. Reports from each of these areas when matched will ensure that all stock is accounted for.

Identity badges. In large organizations when persons in administration have to enter factories and warehouses they usually have to produce some form of identification. This may give them the right to audit but not transfer goods into or out of these areas. The movement of goods is the portfolio of the authorized agent only. Such restricted entry will minimize pilfering.

Locked warehouse. The transfer of goods into warehouses is usually monitored and documented by administration and verified by the stores manager. When materials are transferred to the factory to be used in production the manager of stores becomes accountable for the issue of such material which will be verified by the factory manager. The report on material used by the factory should match the report prepared by the warehouse manager. Stock levels are further monitored by physical stock checks and eventually by stock reports.

See Chapter 25 for methods used for determining stock (inventory) on hand.

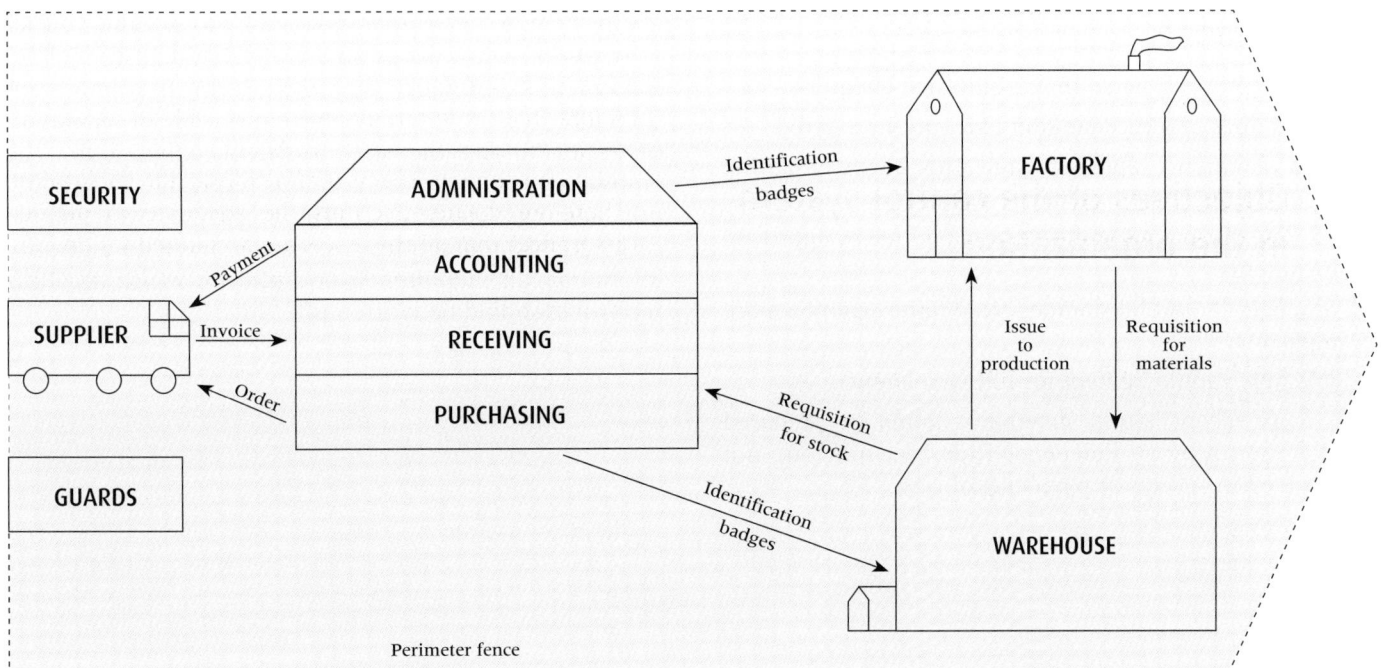

3.3 Controlling cash

Cash includes currency, coins and notes as well as money orders and the amounts in chequing and savings accounts. IOUs are generally not considered as cash as are notes receivable and postage stamps.

With regards to cash, management attempts to:

1. Account for all cash transactions accurately.
2. Ensure there is sufficient to pay bills and obligations when they fall due.
3. Avoid holding too much idle cash since excess cash can be invested elsewhere to generate additional revenue.
4. Prevent loss of cash due to theft and/or fraud.

Procedures to control cash receipts

Although all assets must be protected from theft, cash requires additional protection. Cash is easily concealed, not readily identifiable and more desirable than most assets. It is because of these reasons that most businesses invest heavily in the prevention and protection of cash against theft and loss. These are some basic principles for controlling cash that an entity can use:

1. Records of cash receipts are prepared as soon as cash is received.
2. Cash receipts should be deposited immediately or placed in a vault for safekeeping.
3. Cash payments should not be made out of cash receipts but only by cheques and petty cash.
4. Ensure that the person who handles cash receipts is not the same person handling cash disbursements.

Procedures for controlling cash disbursements

1. Only authorized personnel should sign cheques.
2. All cheques and receipts should be pre-numbered.
3. Cash payments approval and the cheque signing should be assigned to separate persons.
4. Each cheque payment should be supported by approved documents.
5. Vouchers should be stamped 'paid' after payments are made.
6. Vouchers should be kept for future reference.
7. A bank reconciliation statement should be prepared each month by an independent person, someone not involved in receipt or payments of cash.

Reconciliation

A bank reconciliation statement is prepared to account for the differences between the bank statement balance and the cash book bank column balance. This is an internal control tool that is used to detect fraud and/or theft of cash.

Steps to reconciliation:

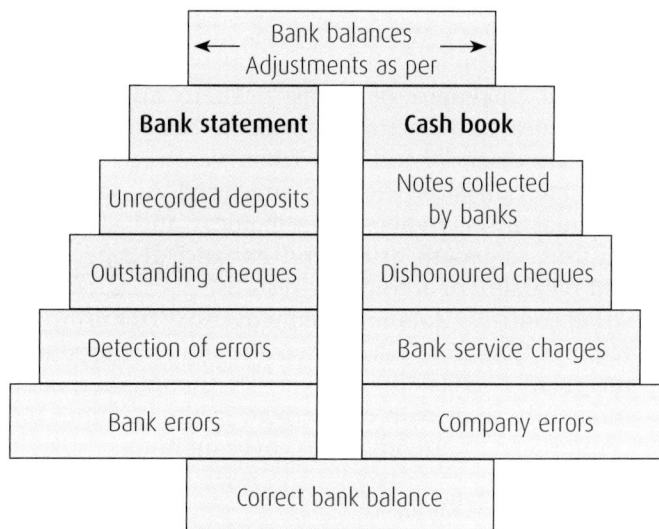

Bank balances Adjustments as per	
Bank statement	**Cash book**
Unrecorded deposits	Notes collected by banks
Outstanding cheques	Dishonoured cheques
Detection of errors	Bank service charges
Bank errors	Company errors
Correct bank balance	

3.4 Controlling accounts receivable

Credit sales created the reality of bad debts or uncollectable accounts receivable. A well-managed company will screen its potential credit customers by obtaining information about them, to determine their ability to pay their debts.

Accounts receivable is an asset which is susceptible to fraudulent interference within the firm. It is important therefore that the internal control principle of separation of duties among the staff is strictly adhered to. The employees who maintain accounts receivable files should not have custody of cash. The employees who handle cash receipts and accounts receivable have no authority to issue credit memoranda or authorize which accounts receivable should be written off.

3.5 Procedures for controlling accounts receivable

A summary of internal control systems for accounts receivable should include:

1. Interview potential credit customers and ascertain information to ensure creditworthiness and ability to repay debts.

2. Authorization of credit to customers only by the credit supervisor.

3. Sale of goods on credit only with proper documentation by sales personnel; i.e. sales invoice.

4. Entry of debt into the accounts receivable book by the accounts receivable clerk, using the sales invoice received from the sales department.

5. Collection by the sales return department of goods returned by credit customers, and the issue of a credit note document to the accounts department.

6. Collection of cash by cashier from credit customers and the issue of receipt to customer and copy to accounts receivable clerk.

7. Entry of receipt in the accounts receivable book, only by the accounts receivable clerk.

8. Checking of documents and books by internal auditor to verify accuracy and consistency of information among departments.

INTERNAL CONTROL RELATING TO ACCOUNTS RECEIVABLE

INDEPENDENT INTERNAL VERIFIER
Reviews activities of individuals and departments to ensure prescribed internal controls are being followed.

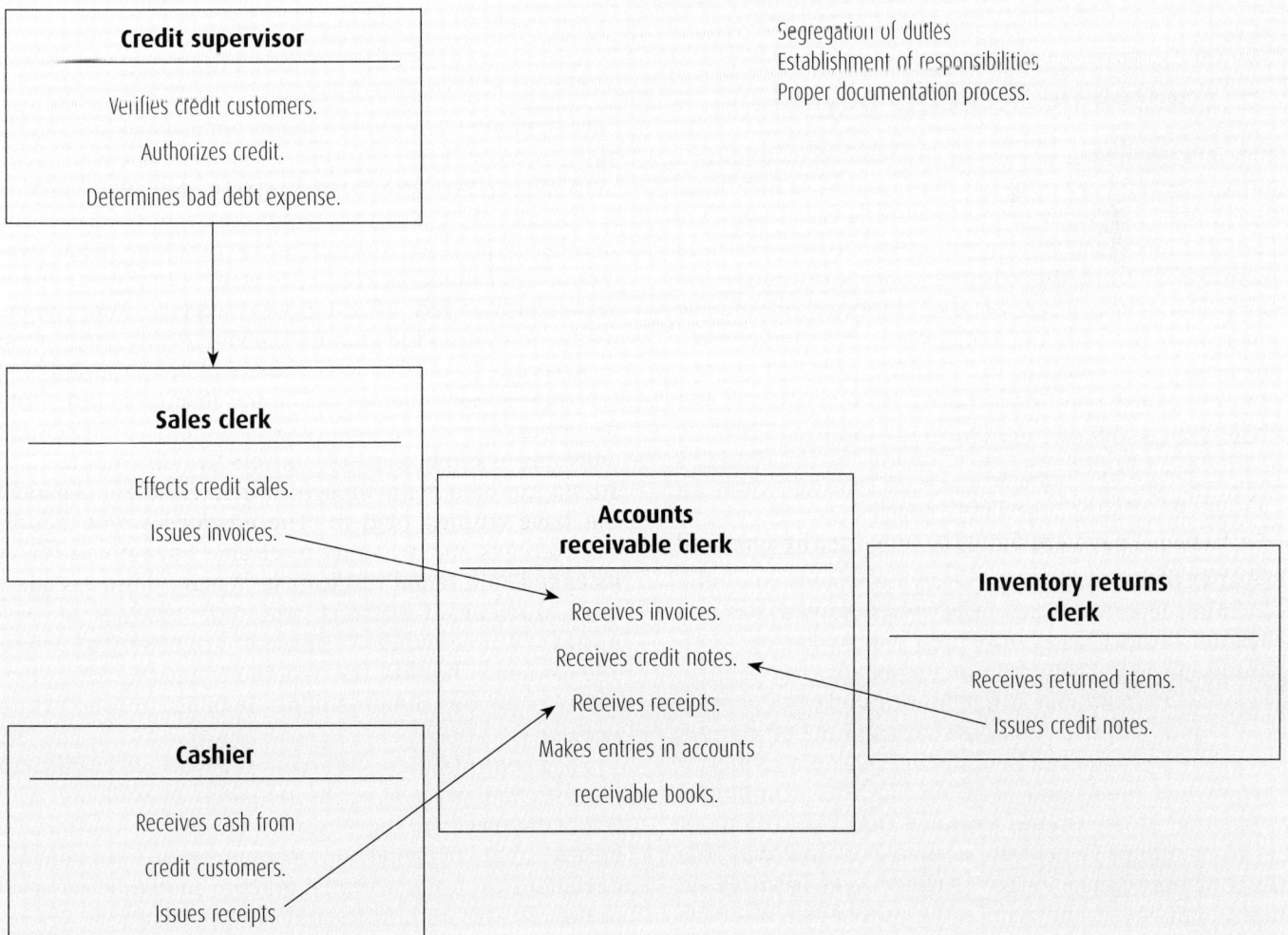

Segregation of duties
Establishment of responsibilities
Proper documentation process.

Credit supervisor

Verifies credit customers.

Authorizes credit.

Determines bad debt expense.

Sales clerk

Effects credit sales.

Issues invoices.

Accounts receivable clerk

Receives invoices.

Receives credit notes.

Receives receipts.

Makes entries in accounts receivable books.

Inventory returns clerk

Receives returned items.

Issues credit notes.

Cashier

Receives cash from credit customers.

Issues receipts

The control systems for accounts payable (creditors)

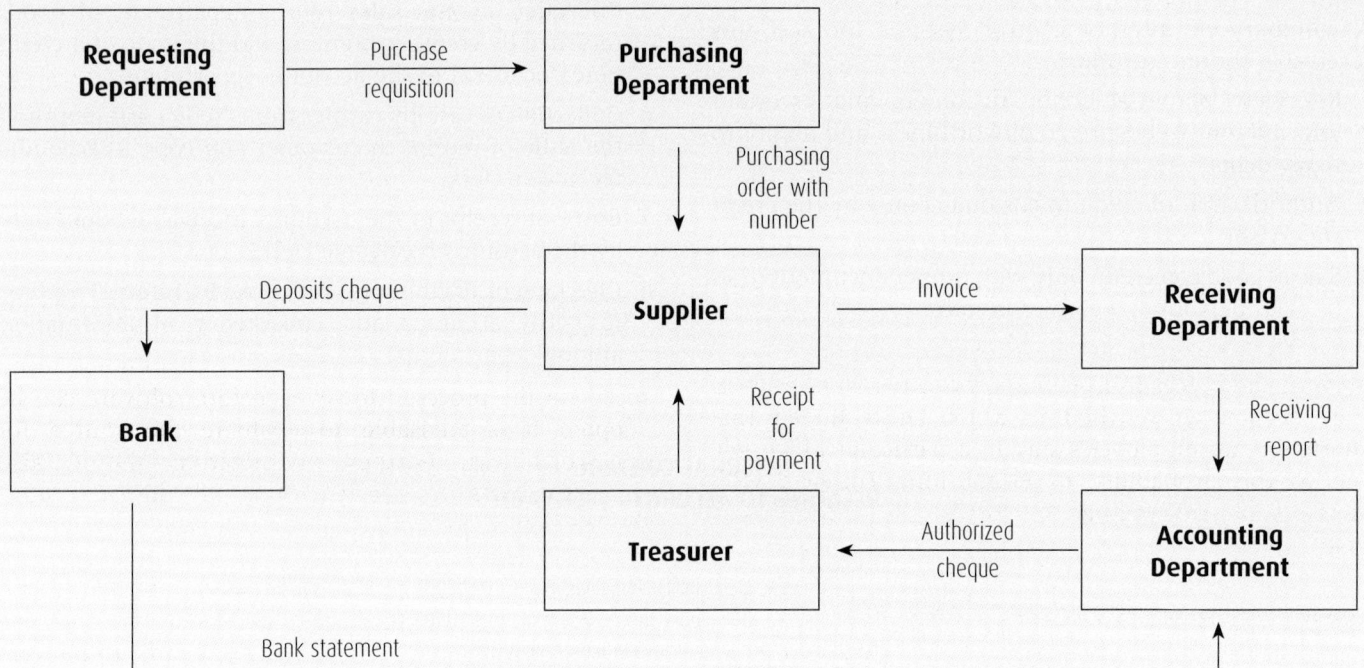

```
┌──────────────┐   Purchase      ┌──────────────┐
│ Requesting   │  requisition    │ Purchasing   │
│ Department   │ ──────────────> │ Department   │
└──────────────┘                 └──────────────┘
                                         │
                                   Purchasing
                                   order with
                                     number
                                         │
                                         ▼
            Deposits cheque    ┌──────────────┐   Invoice    ┌──────────────┐
        ┌───────────────────── │   Supplier   │ ───────────> │  Receiving   │
        │                      └──────────────┘              │  Department  │
        ▼                             ▲                       └──────────────┘
┌──────────────┐              Receipt                                │
│              │                 for                          Receiving
│    Bank      │              payment                          report
│              │                 │                                  │
└──────────────┘              ┌──────────────┐  Authorized  ┌──────────────┐
        │                     │  Treasurer   │ <─────────── │ Accounting   │
        │                     └──────────────┘   cheque     │ Department   │
        │    Bank statement                                  └──────────────┘
        └──────────────────────────────────────────────────────────┘
```

3.6 Controlling accounts payable

Competent personnel. One of the first steps in instituting a control system for accounts payable is to ensure that those charged with particular responsibilities have a high level of ethical conduct developed either from personal experience or from the business code practiced by the entity. The competence of the employee should be supported by the ability to keep information confidential. The employee's competence is often reflected in the degree to which the worker can be objective in the execution of his duties. The unwillingness to compromise integrity goes a long way in testifying for the worker's ability. The system can become very effective when an employee is responsible for a single task.

Separation of duties. From the receiving department to the accounting department no one person is charged with two or more distinct responsibilities when dealing with accounts payable. This is ideal for an effective control system, as it would take a significant number of persons and a host of different positions to corrupt the procedure. Effectiveness is achieved by assigning related activities to different individuals and ensuring that the recording of information on an asset is separated from the custody of the asset. When duties are separated in this way the efforts of one employee act as checks and balances on another employee and reduce the possibilities of errors and irregularities.

Documentation. The written word supported by authorized authentic signatures if proof is required that an activity took place. The purchasing department will have a statement of what was requested and ordered. The supplier will have documentary proof of what was ordered and supplied. The accounts department will have a purchase report of what was received and cheque (stubs) indicating the amount paid.

Accounting records tend to be more accurate and reliable when documents are pre-numbered. The paperwork for accounts is more efficient in preventing omission or duplication of entries. Should there be any attempt to breach the control system the greater part of the paper trail will have to be interrupted.

Independent internal verification. When a business has a large number of persons and organizations to pay, mistakes can be frequent. Hence it is necessary to review and compare reports the workers prepare. Very often there will be disagreement making reconciliation necessary.

For a control system for accounts payable to be efficient it must entail periodic verification done by someone who is not involved in the performance of the routine. To ensure that irregularities are arrested immediately deviations from the accepted practice should be reported to the relevant authorities and action taken.

Proper authorization. In its simplest form this can range from giving employees clear responsibilities to having two signatures to a document to confining an employee to signing a document up to a certain amount in value. Depending on the size of the enterprise the amounts for accounts payable can range from two to six digits. Small amounts can be overseen by clerks and larger amounts by clerks and managers, each providing a signature. This arrangement serves to prevent the clerk being overwhelmed by the figures and the manager compromising his integrity.

Rotation of employees. The positive side to rotating employees is that they will become knowledgeable about other departments of the business. A second reason is to prevent employees from falling prey to temptation when they become entrenched in a job. It is hoped that shortening an employee's stay in a particular office will reduce the probability of establishing contacts with creditors or accountants to defraud the enterprise of cash.

IMPACT OF TECHNOLOGY ON ACCOUNTING

	Computerize	Manual
1. Accuracy	Errors are minimized	Tendency to make errors
2. Subjectivity	Lower level of subjectivity	Higher level of subjectivity
3. Detecting mistakes	Easily detected	Difficult and time-consuming
4. Information storage and retrieval	Software available to hasten process	Time-consuming
5. Security of information	Protected by password, encryption code, firewalls etc.	Limited to physical security
6. Skill needed	Must know computer basics	Training in the field
7. Recording frequency	Less frequently	To be done daily to avoid backlog
8. Processing volume	Short completion time	Heavy workload
9. Processing speed	Analyses quickly	Needs more time
10. Cost	High initial cost that reduces over time	High constant costs because of manual labour

3.7 Describe the control necessary in the electronic data processing environment

Physical security. This is the most common form of security and its purpose is merely to prevent unauthorized persons from having access to the equipment. It can range from simple lock and key to using security guards with an electronic security system, e.g. passwords/passnumbers.

Software to create documents. The activities at the business place might range from letter writing to analysis of financial information. There is software to simplify and speed up the process. However, before software can be adopted it is advisable to evaluate the source for trustworthiness. Further investigation should also determine if it is bug-infected as this may ultimately affect the creation of documents.

Direct data security. Information must be tailored to suit the profile of the user. For example, whereas the purchasing manager might need to have information on sales, it will be unnecessary for him to have data on accounts receivable. Hence he may be denied access to such information.

Access level. How much information should the accounts clerk be allowed to have access to? The wages and salaries clerk may be able to see the salaries up to supervisory level but not be allowed to view the salaries of managers.

View rights. An important decision that must be made is whether the viewer of the information should have the right to add or delete data on himself or others.

Back-ups. The possibility of accidents or natural disasters dictates that there be alternative ways for securing information. A hard copy must be kept to ensure that data on the hard drive is not lost. Data can also be stored at an off-site venue to prevent total loss of information.

Archiving. Electronic filing systems can store a great amount of information and there might be the tendency to retain even that which is obsolete. A decision must be made as to how long to keep any set of data and to ensure that relevant data are not deleted.

3.8 Investigating the effectiveness of an internal control system

The presence of fraud, overlapping authority and job specification stated ambiguously may signal the need to revisit the internal control system. The following investigation procedure may be useful in identifying weak areas in the system.

Identifying laws and regulations

Laws and regulations define the legal status of business organizations. Business entities in the preparation of financial statements are expected to adopt international accounting standards. The person judging the effectiveness of an internal control system should look at the degree of compliance with applicable laws. The greater the deviation from the guidelines, the greater the chances are that the control system will not achieve the desired results.

Checking documents

Documents in an organization provide important information on the formal structure of that entity. The data can range from the mission statement and goals of the business to the organizational chart to operational procedure in the form of a manual. What is of interest to the investigator is how these things gel to make the entity a smooth-running unit.

Examining the level of security

The security measures implemented in a business tell the level of control exercised in protecting lives, information and physical property. An enquiry here should examine the extent to which duties are separated. Limiting access to information and separating duties into smaller activities of the entire operation render control systems more effective in achieving the purpose intended.

Conducting interviews

A more intimate way to test the effectiveness of an internal control system would be to interview staff members. Information gathered would reveal what employees do on a daily basis and can easily be compared with what was stated as their duties. These interviews can be formalized into internal and/or external audits of the control system. Reports on these audits will give managers grounds for tightening areas in the control system that have lapsed.

Observing workers

A less active way to test the internal control system would be to get documentary evidence of and to observe the competences of the employees. The observer can also form an opinion on whether stated business policies are adhered to or ignored. Controls are not going to have the desired effect if employees have too much sway in the furtherance of business policies.

3.9 Role of the auditors

One of the most effective forms of administrative control that an organization can pursue is that of financial audits. These are detailed examinations of the relevant documents and financial statements of the organization at the end of the period. They include tests which will verify the reliability and validity of the accounting principles used in producing the financial reports.

These financial audits are conducted by mandate, through independent external auditors.

Prior to the external auditor's examination, most organizations would have conducted ongoing internal audits, whereby the company's operations are reviewed by independent internal auditors to ensure compliance to management's policies, and an overall assessment of the efficiency of the company's operation. Their tasks will also include ensuring that an effective internal control system is maintained.

The features of an organization's internal and external auditors can be compared and summarized using the following table:

THE INTERNAL AND EXTERNAL AUDITORS COMPARED

	INTERNAL	EXTERNAL
Appointment	Hired by manager.	Hired by shareholders through the board of directors.
Relationship	Usually an employee of the company hired on a permanent basis.	Hired for the special assignment and may use the work of the internal auditors.
Scope of work	Looks at efficiency and effectiveness and allegations of fraud.	Examines records to ensure that appropriate laws, regulations and policies are followed.
Rules to follow	Responsibilities decided by management.	Application of international accounting standards and guidelines.
Type of report	Strengths and weaknesses of the system and makes recommendations.	Expresses an opinion of presentation and control based on a fixed format.
Frequency	Quarterly or as needed.	Annually.
Qualification	Can be trained internally.	Qualified professionals.
Accountable to	Board of directors.	Shareholders.
Responsibility	Decided by management.	Fixed by company law and legislation and not responsible for preventing and detecting fraud.
Operations	Works objectively and independently of employees but dependent on the organization.	Works independently of the corporation and management.

3.10 Ethics in accounting

In all walks of life there is a code of conduct that helps us determine whether actions are wrong or right. This moral code is called ethics. In the business world the accountant by reason of his training is expected to be competent in the execution of his duties. Under no circumstances must he accept a job that he is incapable of doing. Behaviour of the accountant is further defined by the watchwords integrity, objectivity and independence.

Many accounting bodies have a code of professional ethics to ensure that members understand their responsibilities and that the interest of the organization is at the heart of every decision taken. In the absence of ethics the information furnished by accountants will have no credibility. Similarly, dishonest and illegal practices in accounting will make the information grossly unreliable.

The field of auditing serves not only to attest that accounting principles have been adhered to but also to give a limited opinion that the code of ethics was not violated. When accountants deviate from their professional ethics the penalty can range from disciplinary action taken against them (suspension from practice) to large fines and/or imprisonment where the fraudulent activity is material.

The alleged status and power that money carries are there eternally to test the allegiance of the accountant to his profession. All businesses should therefore have a model to investigate significant irregularities and nip them in the bud before they can escalate into embarrassing situations. This is a suggested model to handle ethical dilemmas.

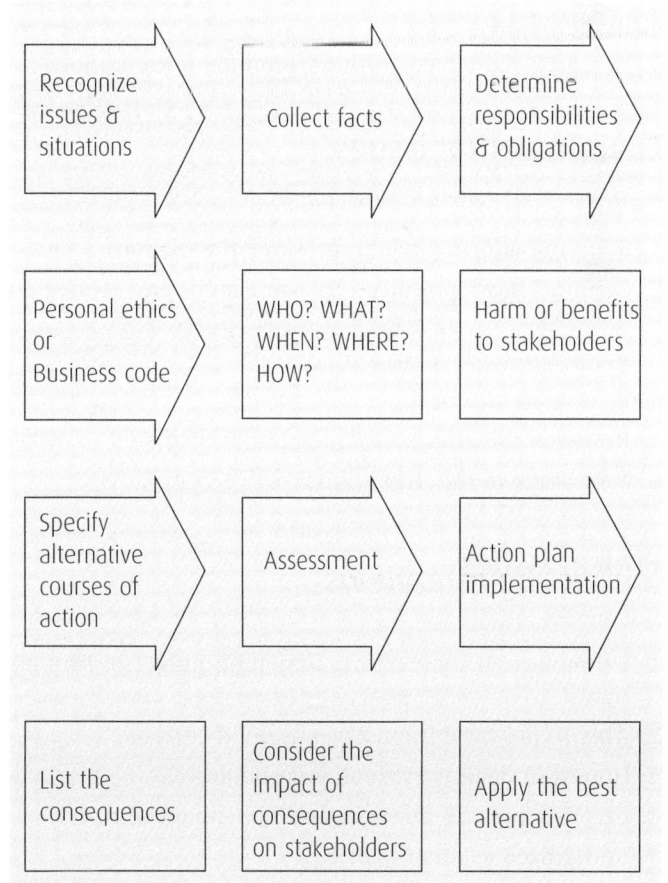

3.11 Social, environmental

Many companies when presenting financial reports are also trying to discuss how they addressed certain social, environmental and ethical issues. There is now a growing trend for businesses to place a value and report the impact their existence has on the society in which they operate. This is the realm of social accounting.

Some of the issues that have surfaced are listed below:

Social issues

Companies have to

1. Define their responsibilities as corporate citizens.
2. Report on the extent to which they have undertaken their duties.
3. State their involvement in the local community.
4. Outline their contribution to wellness.
5. Make a contribution to promoting culture.
6. Develop positive relationships with stakeholders.
7. Promote further education and learning.
8. Be innovative.
9. Research the effects of their 'product' presentation.

Environmental issues

Businesses are further expected to

1. State the efforts made to preserve the planet.
2. Outline how pollution of air, land and water is handled.
3. Reduce noise level to a minimum.
4. Plan waste disposal.
5. Research the effects on animals and plants.
6. Take stock of the 'friendliness' of their products.

Ethical issues

Businesses should be

1. Exemplary in their efforts to defend universal human rights.
2. Able to promote themselves as good citizens.
3. Honest in dealing with all stakeholders.
4. Fair in reporting financial and non-financial issues.
5. Recognized as a fair dealer.
6. Truthful about quality.
7. Dignified in their treatment of the workforce.

3.12 Conclusion

Additional guiding principles given by the ACCA for social reporting include that companies should pursue the commitments they make to the society they operate in and be pacesetters for social improvement.

Adherence to the standard of social accounting is rewarded with membership in the Financial Times Security Exchange for good index series, a body that recognizes and advertises the organizations that conform.

Of even greater importance is the reputation of being a protector of the environment, a supporter of human rights and a positive investor for stakeholders.

3.13 Short response questions

1. What is an internal control system? Define internal control.
2. Describe the features or principles of an internal control system.
3. State the objectives of the control system in an organization.
4. How can the effectiveness of an internal control system be determined?
5. Explain the term 'separation of duties'.
6. State the purpose of bank reconciliation.
7. State why the documents such as cheques, invoices and receipts should be pre-numbered.
8. Explain the procedures that should be used for controlling cash disbursement.
9. Identify five principles of an effective internal control system.
10. How does the principle of segregation of duties differ from that of independent verification?
11. State three examples of physical internal control which an organization may adopt.
12. Effective control in an organization's electronic data processing environment is of extreme necessity. List five control measures used in this environment. Explain the effectiveness of any one of the measures chosen.
13. Indicate seven procedures which can be used for controlling cash disbursements in organizations.
14. Describe the principles of internal control that are usually required when dealing with cash receipts.
15. State why a bank reconciliation statement is prepared.
16. List four control systems which should be applied to accounts receivables.

17. State three ways in which the roles of the internal auditor differ from that of the external auditor.

18. Identify two social and ethical issues with which companies must contend.

3.14 Multiple-choice questions

1 Procedures put in place to protect assets of an organization have the purpose of
   A Regulating movement of cash
   B An internal control system
   C Arranging for an external audit
   D Fixed assets not being over-depreciated

2 A broad objective of the control system in the organization is to
   A Comply with company's policies, regulations and government law
   B Assess the operating effectiveness of the organization and its structure
   C Discourage occurrence of errors or irregularities
   D All of the above

3 Segregation of duties, independent internal verification, adequate documentation and physical safeguard of assets are examples of
   A Principles of internal control system
   B Methods of effective filing system
   C Policies to enhance time efficiency
   D Human resource management

4 Related activities being assigned to different individuals is an example of
   A Adequate documentation
   B Segregation of duties
   C Independent internal verification
   D Proper authorization

5 Reviewing, checking and comparison of data prepared by other employees in an organization is an example of
   A Segregation of duties
   B Independent internal verification
   C Proper authorization
   D Adequate documentation

6 The principle of documentation in internal control ensures that
   A Different individuals in the firm receive cash, record cash and keep cash
   B Only designated personnel are authorized to handle cash receipts

   C Invoices, receipts and cheque stubs are provided as proof that transactions occur
   D Persons with responsibility are highly ethical

7 All of the following are examples of physical internal control except
   A Identity badges
   B Petty cashier
   C Locked warehouse
   D Perimeter fence

8 Which of the following is not considered to be an effective method of electronic control?
   A Secret phone tapping devices
   B Computer back-up devices
   C Password and screening device
   D Access control

9 Procedures to control and monitor cash received by the organization do not include
   A Ensuring personnel who receive cash are not responsible for cash disbursement
   B Depositing cash in the bank or a vault as soon as possible
   C Preparing cash receipt records as soon as cash is received

10 Which of the following items is not considered as cash?
   A Coins
   B Notes receivables
   C Money order
   D Notes

11 An effective internal control system for accounts receivable will ensure that the person who handles cash receipts
   A Should not determine which accounts receivable should be written off as uncollectable
   B Should be a senior manager in the firm with more than 10–15 years dealing with accounts receivables
   C Should be the same person who records data in the accounts receivable books
   D Should only issue a receipt when payment is received within the agreed date

12 Internal control system for accounts receivable should include
   A Authorization of credit to customers only by the credit supervisor
   B Entry of debt into the accounts receivable book using sales invoices from the sales department

C Collection of cash by cashier alone and the issue of receipts to customers

D Collection of cash by personnel who maintains the accounts receivable files

13 Which principles of internal control are associated with the events listed below?

A The company's cheques are pre-numbered

B Only cashiers may operate cash registers

C Only the treasurer or assistant may sign cheques

D Reconciliation of bank statements monthly

E Storage of blank cheques in safe

F Different individuals approve and make payments

14 Indicate which of the following activities relate to the internal auditor and which to the external auditor

A Employment full time by the firm

B Reports to the shareholders

C Must be professionally qualified; i.e. ACCA, CPA etc.

D Responsibilities determined by management

E Responsibilities determined by company, laws, accounting standards, government legislation

F Works independent of company and management

G Discrepancies and exceptions reported to management for action to be taken

3.15 Case study

Joan Felix is an accountant with a local manufacturing company. Joan's good friend Randy Sandy has been operating a retail sports and games business for about a year. The store has been moderately successful, and Randy needs a bank loan to help finance the next stage of his store's growth. He has asked Joan to prepare financial statements that the banker will use to help decide whether or not to grant the loan. Randy has proposed that the fee he will pay for Joan's accountancy work should be contingent upon his receiving the loan.

Required

What factors should Joan consider when making her decision about whether or not to prepare the financial statements for Randy's store?

4 Control accounts

Objectives
- define Control accounts
- state uses and limitations of Control accounts
- prepare Control accounts
- reconcile Control accounts with the ledgers
- calculate revised net profit

4.1 What is a Control account?

A **Control account** contains the totals of all postings made to the accounts in a particular ledger.

Control accounts are usually maintained for the sales and purchase ledgers. The totals are the periodic totals of the books of prime entry from which postings are made to the ledger.

The balance on a Control account should equal the total of the balances in the ledger it controls. Because the entries in the Control accounts are the totals of the books of prime entry they are also known as Total accounts. Control (or Total) accounts are kept in the nominal (or general) ledger.

Just as a trial balance acts as a check on the arithmetical accuracy of *all* the ledgers, a Control account checks the arithmetical accuracy of a single ledger. A difference between a Control account balance and the total of the balances in the ledger it controls shows where a cause of a difference on a trial balance may be found. Any difference between the Control account and the total of the balances in the ledger must be found without delay. The Sales Ledger Control account is also known as the Accounts Receivable Control account, and the Purchase Ledger Control account is also known as the Accounts Payable Control account.

The following examples show how postings are made from the books of prime entry to the ledgers and the Control accounts, and how the balances on the Control accounts should equal the totals of the balances on the accounts in the ledgers.

4.2 The purchase ledger and its Control account

Books of prime entry

Purchases journal		Purchases returns journal		Cash book		
	$		$			$
AB	100	PQ	8		AB	80
PQ	50	XY	10		PQ	40
XY	240		18		XY	200
	390					320

Purchase ledger
AB

		$			$
Cash book		80	Purchases		100
Balance	c/d	20*			——
		100			100
			Balance b/d		20

PQ

		$			$
Purchases returns		8	Purchases		50
Cash book		40			
Balance	c/d	2*			——
		50			50
			Balance b/d		2

XY

		$			$
Purchases returns		10	Purchases		240
Cash book		200			
Balance	c/d	30*			——
		240			240
			Balance b/d		30

Nominal (general) ledger
Purchase Ledger Control account

		$			$
Purchases returns journal		18	Purchases journal		390
Cash Book		320			
Balance	c/d	52 =	*20 + 2 + 30		——
		390			390
			Balance b/d		52

*Balancing figure

4.3 How to prepare a Purchase Ledger Control account

Enter items in the Control account as follows:

Debit side	Credit side
Total of purchase ledger debit balances (if any) brought forward from the previous period	Balance on the account brought forward from the previous period
Total of goods returned to suppliers (from purchases returns journal)	Total of purchases on credit (from purchases journal)
Total of cash paid to suppliers (from cash book)	Refunds from suppliers (from cash book)
Cash discounts received (from discount column in cash book)	Interest charged by suppliers on overdue invoices (from purchases journal)
Purchase ledger balances set against balances in sales ledger (from journal)	Total of debit balances (if any) at end of period in purchase ledger, carried forward
Balance carried forward (to agree with total of credit balances in purchases ledger)	

Note. Debit balances in the purchase ledger must *never* be netted against (deducted from) the credit balances.

❖ Warning. Only credit purchases are entered in the Purchase Ledger Control account. Do not enter cash purchases in it.

4.4 The Sales ledger and its Control account

Books of prime entry

Sales journal			Sales returns journal			Cash book		
		$			$		$	$
Bali		300				Bali	180	
Carla		520	Bali		50	Carla	480	
Paula		140	Paula		10	Paula	100	—
		960			60		760	

Sales ledger
Bali

		$				$
Sales		300	Sales returns			50
			Cash book			180
		—	Balance		c/d	70*
		300				300
Balance	b/d	70				

Carla

		$				$
Sales		520	Cash book			480
		—	Balance		c/d	40*
		520				520
Balance	b/d	40				

Paula

		$				$
Sales		140	Sales returns			10
			Cash book			100
		—	Balance		c/d	30*
		140				140
Balance	b/d	30				

*Balancing figure

Nominal (general) ledger
Sales Ledger Control account

		$			$
Sales journal		960	Sales returns journal	60	
			Cash book	760	
		—	Balance c/d	140 = *70 + 40 + 30	
		960		960	
Balance	b/d	140			

4.5 How to prepare a Sales Ledger Control account

Enter items in the Control account as follows.

Debit side	Credit side
Balance brought forward from previous period	Total of sales ledger credit balances (if any) brought forward from previous period
Credit sales for period (total of sales journal)	Sales returns for the period (total of sales returns journal)
Refunds to credit customers (from cash book)	Cash received from credit customers (from cash book)
Dishonoured cheques (from cash book)	Cash discounts allowed (discount columns in cash book)
Interest charged to customers on overdue accounts (sales journal or cash book)	Bad debts written off (journal)
Bad debts previously written off, now recovered (journal)	Cash from bad debts recovered, previously written off (cash book)
Total of credit balances (if any) in sales ledger at end of period carried forward	Sales ledger balances set against balances in purchase ledger (journal)
	Balance carried forward to agree with total of debit balances in sales ledger

Note. Do not 'net' credit balances in the sales ledger against the debit balances.

4.6 Control accounts and the double-entry model

Control accounts duplicate the information contained in the purchase and sales (personal) ledgers. Control accounts *and* personal ledgers cannot both be part of the double-entry model. It is usual to treat the Control accounts as part of the double entry and to regard the personal ledgers as memorandum records containing the details which support the Control accounts.

Example

The following information has been extracted from the books of Useful Controls Ltd.

		$
At 1 June 2004 Purchase ledger balances brought forward	- debit	900
	- credit	16 340
Sales ledger balances brought forward	- debit	30 580
	- credit	620
Month to 30 June 2004		
Purchases journal total		65 000
Purchases returns journal total		3 150
Sales journal total		96 400
Sales returns journal total		1 980
Cash book: payments to suppliers		59 540
cheques received from customers (see note below)		103 900
purchases discounts		2 670
sales discounts		4 520
Dishonoured cheques		3 300
Journal: Bad debts written off		1 220
Sales ledger balances set against purchase ledger balances		4 800
At June 30 Debit balances on purchase ledger accounts		600
Credit balances on sales ledger accounts		325

Note. The cash received from customers includes $800 relating to a bad debt previously written off.

Required

Prepare a Purchase Ledger Control account and a Sales Ledger Control account for Useful Controls, for the month of June 2004.

Answer

Purchase Ledger Control account

2004		$	2004		$
Jun 1 Balance	b/d	900	Jun 1 Balance	b/d	16 340
30 Purchases returns journal		3 150	30 Purchases journal		65 000
Cash book		59 540	30 Balance	c/d	600
purchases discounts		2 670			
Sales ledger – contra		4 800			
Balance c/d					
(Balancing figure)		10 880			
		81 940			81 940
Jul 1 Balance	b/d	600	Jul 1 Balance	b/d	10 880

Sales Ledger Control account

2004		$	2004		$
Jun 1 Balance	b/d	30 580	Jun 1 Balance	b/d	620
30 Sales journal		96 400	30 Sales returns journal		1 980
Bad debt recovered		800	Cash book		103 900
Bank – dishonoured cheques		3 300	Sales discounts		4 520
Balance	c/d	325	Bad debts written off		1 220
			Purchase ledger – contra		4 800
			30 Balance c/d (Balancing figure)		14 365
		131 405			131 405
Jul 1 Balance	b/d	14 365	Jul 1 Balance	b/d	325

Exercise 1

The following information has been obtained from the books of Byit Ltd.

		$
At 1 March 2004 Purchase ledger balances brought forward (credit)		10 000
	(debit)	16
In the month to 31 March 2004		
Total of invoices received from suppliers		33 700
Goods returned to suppliers		824
Cheques sent to suppliers		27 500
Purchases discounts		1 300
At 31 March 2004 Debit balances in purchase ledger		156
Credit balances in purchase ledger		?

Required

Prepare the Purchase Ledger Control account for the month of March 2004.

Exercise 2

Information extracted from the books of Soldit Ltd is as follows.

		$
At 1 May 2004 Sales ledger balances brought forward (debit)		27 640
(credit)		545
In the month to 31 May 2004		
Total of invoices sent to customers		109 650
Goods returned by customers		2 220
Cheques received from customers		98 770
Sales Discounts		3 150
Cheque received in respect of bad debt previously written off (not included above)		490
Sales ledger balance set against balance in purchase ledger		2 624
At 31 May 2004 Credit balances in sales ledger		800
Debit balance carried down		?

Required
Prepare the Sales Ledger Control account for the month of May 2004.

4.7 Uses and limitations of Control accounts

Uses

- They are an important system of control on the reliability of ledger accounts.
- They warn of possible errors in the ledgers they control if the totals of the balances in those ledgers do not agree with the balances on the Control accounts.
- They may identify the ledger or ledgers in which errors have been made when there is a difference on a trial balance.
- They provide totals of accounts receivable and accounts payable quickly when a trial balance is being prepared.
- If a business employs several accounting staff, the Control accounts should be maintained by somebody who is not involved in maintaining the sales or purchase ledgers. This increases the likelihood of errors being discovered and reduces the risk of individuals acting dishonestly. This division of duties is called **internal check**. For this reason Control accounts are kept in the general ledger and not in the sales and purchase ledgers.

Limitations

- Control accounts may themselves contain errors. (See (1) and (2) in §4.8.)

- Control accounts do not guarantee the accuracy of individual ledger accounts, which may contain compensating errors, for example items posted to wrong accounts.

4.8 How to reconcile Control accounts with ledgers

When there is a difference between the balance on a Control account and the total of the balances in the ledger it controls, the cause or causes must be found and the necessary corrections made. This is known as reconciling the Control accounts.

It is helpful to remember the following.

1. If a transaction is omitted from a book of prime entry, it will be omitted from the personal account in the sales or purchase ledger *and* from the Control account. Both records will be wrong and the Control account will not reveal the error.

2. If a transaction is entered incorrectly in a book of prime entry, the error will be repeated in the personal account in the sales or purchase ledger *and* in the Control account. Both records will be wrong and the Control account will not reveal the error.

3. If an item is copied incorrectly from a book of prime entry to a personal account in the sales or purchase ledger, the Control account will *not* be affected, and it will reveal that an error has been made.

4. If a total in a book of prime entry is incorrect, the Control account will be incorrect *but* the sales or purchase ledgers will not be affected. The Control account will reveal that an error has been made.

Example

The following information has been extracted from Duprey's books at 31 December 2003.

	$
Total of sales ledger balances (debit)	17 640
(credit)	110
Balance on Sales Ledger Control account (debit)	18 710
Total of purchase ledger balances (credit)	6 120
(debit)	80
Balance on Purchase Ledger Control account (credit)	6 330

The following errors have been discovered.

1. A sales invoice for $100 has been omitted from the sales journal.

2. A credit balance of $35 in the sales ledger has been extracted as a debit balance in the list of sales ledger balances.

3. The sales journal total for December has been overstated by $1000.

4. A balance of $250 on a customer's account in the sales ledger has been set against the amount owing to him in the purchase ledger but no entries have been made for this in the Sales and Purchase Ledger Control accounts.

5. A supplier's invoice for $940 has been entered in the purchases journal as $490.

6. An item of $340 in the purchases returns journal has been credited in the supplier's account in the purchase ledger. There was a credit balance of $800 on the customer's account at 31 December.

7. Purchases discounts in December amounting to $360 have been credited to the Purchase Ledger Control account.

Further information

Duprey's draft accounts for the year ended 31 December 2003 show a net profit of $36 000. He makes a provision for doubtful debts of 6%.

Required

(a) Calculate the following at 31 December 2003:
   (i) the revised sales ledger balances
   (ii) the revised purchase ledger balances.
(b) Prepare the amended Sales Ledger and Purchase Ledger Control accounts.
(c) Prepare a statement of the revised net profit for the year ended 31 December 2003.
(d) Prepare an extract from the Balance Sheet at 31 December 2003 to show the trade accounts receivable and trade accounts payable.

Answer

(a) (i) Revised sales ledger balances

	Debit	Credit
	$	$
Before adjustment	17 640	110
Invoice omitted from sales journal	100	
Credit balance listed as a debit	(35)	35
Revised balances	17 705	145

(ii) Revised purchase ledger balances

	Debit	Credit
	$	$
Before adjustment	80	6120
Error in purchases journal $(940 − 490)		450
Adjustment of return credited to supplier $(340 × 2)*	⸺	(680)
Revised balances	80	5890

* An adjustment for an item placed on the wrong side of an account must be twice the amount of the item.

(b)

Amended Sales Ledger Control account

2003		$	2003		$
Dec 31	Balance brought forward	18 710	Dec 31	Correction of sales journal total	1 000
	Invoice omitted from S J	100		Contra to purchase ledger ¢	250
	Balance c/d	145		Balance c/d	17 705
		18 955			18 955
2004			2004		
Jan 1	Balance b/d	17 705	Jan 1	Balance b/d	145

Amended Purchase Ledger Control account

2003		$	2003		$
Dec 31	Contra to sales ledger ¢	250	Dec 31	Balance brought forward	6330
	Correction of discounts $(360 × 2)	720		Error in purchase journal	450
	Balance c/d	5890		Balance c/d	80
		6860			6860
Balance	b/d	80	Balance	b/d	5890

(c) Revised net profit for the year ended 31 December 2003

	Decrease	Increase	
	$	$	$
Net profit per draft accounts			36 000
Sales invoice omitted from sales journal		100	
Overcast of sales journal	1000		
Purchase invoice understated	450		
Increase in provision for doubtful debts			
6% of (17 705 − 17 640)	4	⸺	
	1454	100	(1 354)
Revised net profit			34 646

(d) Balance Sheet extracts at 31 December 2003

	$	$
Trade accounts receivable		
Sales ledger	17 705	
Deduct provision for doubtful debts	1 062	
	16 643	
Purchase ledger	80	16 723
Trade creditors		
Purchase ledger	5 890	
Sales ledger	145	6 035

Notes
- Accounts receivable should never be deducted from accounts payable, or accounts payable from accounts receivable in a Balance Sheet.
- Do not provide for doubtful debts on debit balances in the purchase ledger

Exercise 3

The following information has been extracted from the books of Rorre Ltd at 31 December 2003.

	$
Total of purchase ledger balances	64 (debit)
	7 217 (credit)
Total of sales ledger balances	23 425 (debit)
	390 (credit)
Purchase Ledger Control account	7 847 (credit)
Sales Ledger Control account	22 909 (debit)

Draft accounts show a net profit of $31 000 for the year ended 31 December 2003. The following errors have been discovered.

1. An invoice for $100 has been entered twice in the purchases journal.
2. A total of $84 has been omitted from both the Discounts Received account and the Purchase Ledger Control account.
3. A debit balance of $50 has been entered in the list of purchase ledger balances as a credit balance.
4. An amount of $710 owing to Trazom, a supplier, has been offset against their account in the sales ledger, but no entry has been made in the Control accounts.
5. An invoice in the sales journal for $326 has been entered in the sales ledger as $362.
6. The sales journal total for December has been understated by $800.

Required
(a) Prepare a statement to show the corrected purchase and sales ledger balances.

(b) Prepare corrected Purchase and Sales Ledger Control accounts.
(c) Calculate the amended net profit for the year ended 31 December 2003.
(d) Prepare a Balance Sheet extract at 31 December 2003 to show the debtors and creditors.

4.9 Examination hints

- Give the Control accounts their correct title and head the money columns with $ signs.
- Check carefully that the entries are on the correct sides of the accounts.
- Enter the dates for the entries, distinguishing between the start and end of the period.
- Make sure that you enter the total of any credit balances in the sales ledger into the Sales Ledger Control account and the total of any debit balances in the purchase ledger into the Purchase Ledger Control account.
- Calculate the other closing balances if necessary.
- Bring down the closing balances on the first day of the next period.
- Assume that Control accounts, when they are kept, are part of the double entry and that the personal ledgers contain memorandum accounts, unless the question indicates otherwise. If Control accounts are not maintained, the double entry is completed in the personal ledger accounts.
- Enter bad debts recovered on the debit side of the Sales Ledger Control account as well as showing the cash received for them on the credit side.
- Enter 'contra' items (balances in the sales ledger set off against balances in the purchase ledger) in *both* Control accounts. The entries will always be credited in the Sales Ledger Control account and debited in the Purchase Ledger Control account.

4.10 Multiple-choice questions

1 The debit balance on a Sales Ledger Control account at 30 September 2003 is $104 000. The following errors have been discovered.

	$
Total of sales journal overstated	1300
Sales discounts omitted from Sales Ledger Control account	870
Bad debts written off not recorded in Sales Ledger Control account	240
Increase in provision for doubtful debts	600

What is the total of the balances in the sales ledger?

A $100 990 **B** $101 590 **C** $102 070
D $103 330

2 The credit balance on a Purchase Ledger Control account at 31 October is $28 000. The following errors have been found.

	$
Amount transferred from Calif's account in the sales ledger to his account in the purchase ledger not recorded in the Control accounts	1 400
A debit balance in the purchase ledger at 31 October not carried down in the Purchase Ledger Control account	300
A refund to a cash customer debited in Purchase Ledger Control account	150

What is the total of the credit balances in the purchase ledger?

A $26 450

B $26 750

C $27 050

D $28 950

3 A Purchase Ledger Control account has been reconciled with the purchase ledger balances as shown.

	$
Balance per Control account	76 000
Total of purchases journal for one month not posted to general ledger	4 000
Cash paid to creditors not posted to purchase ledger	5 000
Total of balances in purchase ledger	85 000

Which figure for creditors should be shown in the Balance Sheet?

A $75 000

B $77 000

C $80 000

D $85 000

4.11 Additional exercises

1 The following information was taken from Peter's books.

2004		$	
March 1	Sales Ledger Control account balance	55 650	Dr
	Purchase Ledger Control account balance	34 020	Cr
31	Sales for March	47 700	
	Purchases for March	21 840	
	Cheques received from credit customers	36 900	
	Payments to accounts payable	24 300	
	Customers' cheques returned unpaid	1 920	
	Bad debts written off	2 250	
	Purchases discounts	600	
	Sales discounts	930	
	Returns inwards	580	
	Returns outwards	330	
	Credit balance in purchase ledger transferred from sales ledger	810	

Required

Prepare the Sales Ledger Control account and the Purchase Ledger Control account for the month of March 2004.

2 The following information was extracted from the books of Colombo for the year ended 30 April 2004.

	$
Purchase ledger balances at 1 May 2003	64 680
Credit purchases	1 236 210
Credit purchases returns	18 600
Cheques paid to accounts payable	1 118 970
Cash purchases	13 410
Purchase discount on credit purchases	47 100
Credit balances transferred to sales ledger accounts	7 815

Required

(a) Prepare the Purchase Ledger Control account for the year ended 30 April 2004.

The total of the balances extracted from Colombo's purchase ledger amounts to $101 490, which does not agree with the closing balance in the Control account. The following errors were then discovered.

1. The total of discount received had been overstated by $1500.

2. A purchase invoice for $3060 had been completely omitted from the books.

3. A credit balance in the purchase ledger account had been understated by $150.
4. A credit balance of $1275 in the purchase ledger had been set off against a contra entry in the sales ledger, but no entry had been made in either Control account.
5. A payment of $2175 had been debited to the accounts payable account but was omitted from the bank account.
6. A credit balance of $4815 had been omitted from the list of accounts payable.

Required

(b) (i) Extract the necessary information from the above list and draw up an amended Purchase Ledger Control account for the year ended 30 April 2004.

   (ii) Beginning with the given total of $101 490, show the changes to be made in the purchase ledger to reconcile it with the new Control account balance.

3 At 31 December 2003 the balance on Sellit's Sales Ledger Control account was $17 584 (debit). It did not agree with the total of balances extracted from the sales ledger. The following errors have been found.

1. The total of the discount allowed column in the cash book has been overstated by $210.
2. A receipt of $900 from P. Ford, a customer, has been treated as a refund from B. Ford, a supplier.
3. An invoice for $1200 sent to P. Williams, a customer, has been entered in the sales journal as $1020.
4. The total of the sales journal for December has been understated by $600.
5. Goods with a selling price of $578 were sent to Will Dither, a customer, in December, and he has been invoiced for that amount. It has now been discovered that the goods were sent on sale or return and the customer has not yet indicated whether he will purchase the goods.
6. An invoice for $3160 sent to W. Yeo, a customer, has been entered correctly in the sales journal but has been entered in the customer's account as $3610.

Required

(a) Prepare the Sales Ledger Control account showing clearly the amendments to the original balance.
(b) Calculate the total of the balances extracted from the sales ledger before the errors listed above had been corrected.
(c) Prepare the journal entries to correct the sales ledger accounts. Narratives are required.

4 At 31 May 2004 the debit balance on a Sales Ledger Control account was $18 640. This balance did not agree with the total of balances extracted from the sales ledger. The following errors have now been found.

1. Cash received from accounts receivable entered in the Control account included $400 in respect of a debt which had previously been written off. This fact had not been recognized in the Control account.
2. A debit balance of $325 in the sales ledger had been set off against an account in the purchase ledger. This transfer had been debited in the Sales Ledger Control account and credited in the Purchase Ledger Control account.
3. Cash sales of $1760 had been recorded in the cash book as cash received from accounts receivable.
4. Cash received from K. Bali, $244, had been entered in the account of B. Kali in the sales ledger.
5. Credit balances in the sales ledger totalled $436.

Required

Prepare the corrected Sales Ledger Control account at 31 May 2004.

5 (a) Outline *three* reasons for keeping control accounts.

   (b) The following information was extracted from the books of William Noel for the year ended 30 April 2001.

	$
Purchase Ledger Balance at 1 May 2000	43 120
Credit purchases for the year	824 140
Credit purchases returns	12 400
Cheques paid to accounts payable	745 980
Cash purchases	8 940
Purchase discount on credit purchases	31 400
Credit balances transferred to sales ledger accounts	5 210

Draw up the Purchase Ledger Control account for the year ended 30 April 2001.

The total of the balances in William Noel's purchase ledger amounts to $67 660, which does not agree with the closing balance in the Control account.

The following errors were then discovered.

1. Purchase discount had been overstated by $1000.
2. A credit purchases invoice for $2040 had been completely omitted from the books.
3. A purchases ledger account had been understated by $100.
4. A credit balance of $850 in the purchases ledger had been set off against a contra entry in the sales ledger, but no entry had been made in either Control account.
5. A payment of $1450 had been debited to the accounts payable account but was omitted from the bank account.

6. A credit balance of $3210 had been omitted from the list of accounts payable.

   (c) (i) Extract the necessary information from the above list and draw up an amended Purchase Ledger Control account for the year ended 30 April 2001.

   (ii) Beginning with the given total of $67 660, show the changes to be made in the Purchase Ledger to reconcile it with the new Control account balance.

(UCLES, 2001, AS/A Level Accounting, Syllabus 8706/2, October/November)

5 Bank reconciliation statements

Objectives
• explain the purpose of a bank reconciliation statement
• prepare a bank reconciliation statement
• state the uses of a bank reconciliation statement

5.1 What is a bank reconciliation statement?

A **bank reconciliation statement** shows the correct balance on a bank account. The balance on the bank account in a cash book may not agree with the balance on the bank statement at any particular date. This may be because of

- timing differences (the delay between items being entered in the cash book and their entry on the bank statement)
- items on the bank statement that have not been entered in the cash book (for example, bank charges and interest, direct debits and other items).

Note. A bank statement is a copy of a customer's account in the books of a bank. Consequently items debited in the customer's own cash book appear as credits in the bank statement, and items credited in the cash book are debited in the bank statement. A debit balance in the cash book will appear as a credit balance in the bank statement. If a bank account is overdrawn the customer owes the bank money. The bank is now a creditor represented by a credit balance in the cash book; the customer is the bank's debtor and is shown as a debit balance on the bank statement.

When the balances in the cash book and bank statement do not agree, the correct balance must be found by preparing a bank reconciliation statement.

5.2 How to prepare a bank reconciliation statement

Follow these three steps.

1. Compare the entries in the cash book with the bank statements. Tick items that appear in both the cash book *and* the bank statement. Be sure to tick them in both places.

2. Enter in the cash book any items that remain unticked in the bank statement. Then tick those in both places. Calculate the new cash book balance.

3. Prepare the reconciliation statement. Begin with the final balance shown on the bank statement and adjust it for any items that remain unticked in the cash book. The result should equal the balance in the cash book.

The cash book balance will now be the correct balance of cash at bank.

Example 1

After step 1 has been completed, A.J. Belstrode's cash book and bank statement appear as follows at 31 March 2004. (Note the items which have been ticked.)

Cash book
Bank account

2004		$	2004	Cheque no.		$	
Mar 1	Balance brought forward	1250	Mar 8	1022	Electricity	300	✓
7	Cash banked	700 ✓	10	1023	Wages	600	✓
12	P. Witte	200 ✓	11	1024	Rent	400	✓
15	Cash banked	600 ✓	14	1025	T. Bone	920	✓
20	T. Bagge	430 ✓	15	1026	Wages	440	✓
31	T. Cake	594	28	1027	A. Cape	120	
			29	1028	F. Goode	96	
			31	1029	H. Ope	300	
			31		Balance c/d	598	
		3774				3774	
April 1	Balance b/d	598					

Bank statement

THE REDDYPAY BANK

Account: A.J. Belstrode

			Money out $	Money in $	$
March	1	Balance brought forward			1250 Cr
	7	Paid in		700 ✓	1950 Cr
	10	Paid by cheque 1023	600 ✓		1350 Cr
	11	Paid by cheque 1022	300 ✓		1050 Cr
	12	Paid in		200 ✓	1250 Cr
	14	Direct debit: I. Taikeit	227		1023 Cr
	15	Paid in		600 ✓	1623 Cr
		Paid by cheque 1026	440 ✓		1183 Cr
	6	Paid by cheque 1024	400 ✓		783 Cr
		Paid by cheque 1025	920 ✓		137 Dr
	20	Paid in		430 ✓	293 Cr
	25	Bank Giro credit – Invest dividend		200	493 Cr
	31	Bank charges	112		381 Cr

Step 2 The unticked items in the bank statement are entered in the cash book and ticked.

Cash book
Bank account

2004		$	2004		$
Apr 1	Balance b/d	598	Mar 14	D/d I. Taikeit	227 ✓
Mar 25	Invest – dividend	200 ✓	Mar 31	Bank charges	112 ✓
		‾‾‾	Mar 31	Balance c/d	459
		798			798
April 1	Balance b/d	459			

Note. Do not re-write the whole cash book to enter the new items.

Step 3 A bank reconciliation statement is prepared commencing with the bank statement balance which is adjusted for the items remaining unticked in the cash book.

Bank reconciliation statement at 31 March 2004

		$	$
Balance per bank statement			381
Add: Item not credited in bank statement			594
			975
Deduct cheques not presented:	1027	120	
	1028	96	
	1029	300	516
Balance per cash book			459

The correct bank balance, $459, has been calculated and, if a Balance Sheet at 31 March 2004 is prepared, $459 will be the amount included in it as the bank balance.

Example 2

At 30 June 2004 Eliza's bank statement shows a balance at bank of $1000. When Eliza checks her cash book she finds the following.

- A payment of $200 into the bank on 30 June does not appear in the bank statement.
- Cheques totalling $325 sent to customers on 29 June do not appear in the bank statement.

- The bank statement shows that Eliza's account has been debited with bank charges of $40. These have not been recorded in the cash book.

Required

(a) Prepare Eliza's bank reconciliation at 30 June 2004.

(b) Calculate Eliza's cash book balance at 30 June 2004 before it was corrected.

Answer

		$
(a)	Bank reconciliation statement at 30 June 2004	
	Balance per bank statement	1000
	Add amount paid in not credited	200
		1200
	Deduct cheques not presented	325
	Balance at 30 June 2004	875
(b)	Cash book balance before correction	
	Correct balance at bank at 30 June 2004	875
	Add bank charges not debited in cash book	40
	Cash book balance before it was corrected	915

5.3 Uses of bank reconciliation statements

- They reveal the correct amount of the cash at bank. Without a reconciliation, the cash book and bank statement balances may be misleading.
- They ensure that the correct bank balance is shown in the Balance Sheet.
- They are an important system of control:
  - unintended overdrawing on the bank account can be avoided
  - a surplus of cash at bank can be highlighted and invested to earn interest
  - if reconciliations are prepared regularly, errors are discovered early
  - if the reconciliation is prepared by somebody other than the cashier, the risk of fraud or embezzlement of funds is reduced. This division of duties is called **internal check**.

Exercise 1

The balance on a bank statement at 31 January 2004 was $1220 Credit. The following items had been entered in the cash book in January but did not appear on the bank statements:

(i)   amount paid into the bank $300

(ii) cheques sent to customers $1045.

Required

Calculate the cash book balance at 31 January 2004.

Exercise 2

The bank balance in a cash book at 31 July 2004 was $310 (debit). The following items did not appear in the bank statement at that date:

(i)   cheques totalling $1340 which had been paid into the bank on 31 July 2004

(ii) cheques sent to customers in July, totalling $490.

Required

Calculate the bank statement balance at 31 July 2004.

Exercise 3

At 31 March 2004 a cash book showed a balance of $80 at bank. On the same date the bank statement balance was $650 (credit). When the cash book was compared with the bank statement the following were found:

(i)   a cheque sent to a supplier for $1000 had not been presented for payment

(ii) a cheque for $220 paid into the bank had not been credited on the bank statement

(iii) bank charges of $210 were omitted from the cash book.

Required

(a) Calculate the corrected cash book balance at 31 March 2004.

(b) Prepare a bank reconciliation statement at 31 March 2004.

Exercise 4

The following balances were extracted from the trial balance of a business at 31 December 2003.

	$	$
Trade accounts receivable	1055	
Trade accounts payable		976
Rent	800	
Bank	1245	

When the bank statement for December was received it was discovered that the following items had not been entered in the cash book.

	$
Payment to a supplier by direct debit	360
Amount received from a customer by bank giro	420
Rent paid by standing order	200
Customer's cheque returned, dishonoured	323

Required

Prepare the adjusted trial balance to include the items omitted from the cash book.

5.4 Examination hints

- Remember the three steps required to reconcile a bank account.
- Note carefully if the balances given for the cash book or bank statement are overdrafts.
- Complete the double entry for all items entered in the cash book. Amend the other balances in the trial balance.
- Show bank overdrafts as current liabilities in Balance Sheets, never as current assets.

5.5 Multiple-choice questions

1 At 30 April 2004 the balance in X's cash book was $1740. At the same date the balance on his bank statement was $2240. Comparison of the cash book and bank statement showed the following:

(i) a dividend, $200, credited to X in the bank statement had not been entered in the cash book

(ii) cheques totalling $300 sent to suppliers in April had not been entered in the bank statement.

Which amount should be shown in the Balance Sheet at 30 April 2004?

A $1640 **B** $1740 **C** $1940 **D** $2240

2 A cash book balance at 31 October 2003 was $1600. When the bank statement was received the following were discovered:

(i) a cheque for $425 sent to a customer had been entered in the cash book as $452

(ii) a cheque for $375 sent to a customer had not been presented for payment

(iii) a cheque for $400 paid into the bank had not been credited in the bank statements.

What was the balance on the bank statement at 31 October 2003?

A $1548 **B** $1575 **C** $1602 **D** $1652

3 Y's bank statement showed a credit balance of $2170 at 31 May 2004. An examination of the statement showed the following:

(i) a direct debit for $300 had been debited twice in the bank statement

(ii) a cheque for $1015 sent to a customer had not been presented for payment

(iii) a cheque for $600 paid into the bank had not been credited in the bank statement.

What was the cash book balance at 31 May 2004?

A $1455 **B** $2055 **C** $2285 **D** $2885

4 A bank statement at 31 January 2004 showed a balance of $1000 Dr. The following did not appear on the statement:

(i) cheques not presented for payment, $230

(ii) a cheque for $400 banked on 31 January 2004

(iii) bank charges of $200 had not been entered in the cash book.

What was the original balance in the cash book at 31 January 2004 before it was amended?

A $630 Cr **B** 630 Dr **C** $970 Cr **D** $970 Dr

5 A bank statement showed an overdraft of $360 at 31 July 2004. The following discoveries were made:

(i) cheques totalling $2100 banked in July had not been credited in the bank statement.

(ii) cheques drawn for $875 in the cash book in July had not been entered on the bank statement.

What was the balance in the cash book at 31 July 2004?

A $865 Cr **B** $865 Dr **C** $1585 Cr

D $1585 Dr

5.6 Additional exercise

The following balances have been extracted from a trial balance at 30 June 2004.

	$	$
Trade accounts receivable	400	
Trade accounts payable		380
Rent receivable		750
Bank charges	100	
Bank	990	

After the preparation of the trial balance a bank statement was received and revealed that the following had not been entered in the cash book.

	$
Bank interest receivable credited to account	10
Bank charges	130
Standing order payment to supplier	298
Amount received from customer by direct debit	78
Rent received by bank giro	150

Required
Prepare an amended trial balance extract at 30 June 2004 to take account of the amounts not entered in the cash book.

6 Recording financial information

6.1 Cash basis versus accrual basis

The recording of financial information is influenced by whether the business is operating on a cash basis or a credit basis.

Cash basis

The cash basis of accounting involves recording the immediate receipt and payment of cash. To measure revenue for the period one has to simply total the cash inflows from sales and services rendered to customers. Similarly, expenses can be found by determining the total cash paid for the goods sold and services received from providers. Under this arrangement cash received will be equal to revenue earned and cash paid will be equal to expenses for the period under review.

Accrual basis

In reality businesses hardly ever limit their activities to cash transactions. Many assets and services are acquired through loans and other credit arrangements. The accrual basis of recording allows revenue and expenses to be measured regardless of whether cash was received or paid. An elaborate system is put in place to ensure that a complete recording of financial information is maintained.

Cash basis

Period 1		Period 2	
Services received	$ 800		
Cash paid	$ 800	No outstanding debt	
Expenses	$ 800		

Accrual basis

Period 1		Period 2	
Services received	$ 800		
Cash paid	$ 600	Outstanding debt	$200
Expenses	$ 200		

6.2 General Journal

All transactions should be recorded in one of the books of prime entry before being posted to ledger accounts. The journal is the book of prime entry for transactions for which there is no other book of prime entry. Items which will require entries in the journal are

- corrections of posting errors
- adjustments to accounts (which are dealt with later)
- transfers between accounts
- purchase and sale of items other than stock-in-trade (e.g. machinery, delivery vans, etc. used in the business)
- opening entries in a new set of ledgers (e.g. when there is no more room in the existing ledgers and the balances on the accounts are transferred to new ledgers).

Each journal entry shows the account to be debited, and the account to be credited. It follows that the debits should always equal the credits. The journal is ruled as follows:

Date	Accounts	Dr* $	Cr* $

* Dr is short for debit and Cr is short for credit.

Always state the account to be debited before the one to be credited. Every entry should have a brief but informative explanation of the reason for the entry; this is called the **narrative**.

Example

1 Jonah discovered that he had credited $100 that he had received from A. Burger on 1 April to an account for L. Burger in error. The journal entry to correct the error will be:

Date	Accounts	Dr $	Cr $
April 1	L. Burger	100	
	A. Burger		100

Correction of an error. A remittance from A. Burger on this date was posted incorrectly to L. Burger's account.

2 On 4 May Jonah bought office furniture from A. Whale on credit for $400.

Date	Accounts	Dr $	Cr $
May 4	Office Furniture	400	
	A. Whale		400

Purchase of office furniture from A Whale. See A.Whale's invoice no. 123 dated 4 May.

Note. The narrative gives Jonah the information he needs to enable him to check on the details later if needs be.

3 On 13 May Jonah bought a delivery van for $3000 and paid by cheque.

(The book of prime entry for this cash transaction is the cash book but, by also entering the purchase in the journal, Jonah will be able to see more detail about this important item than if he had entered it in the cash book only.)

Date	Accounts	Dr $	Cr $
May 13	Delivery Van account	3000	
	Bank		3000

Purchase of delivery van, registration no. G1234PYD. See Wheeler's invoice no. 6789 dated 13 May.

Exercise 1

Prepare journal entries in proper form to correct the following.

1 Credit note no. 964, for $120, received from A & Co., a supplier, has been posted to A. Cotter's account in error.

2 Invoice no. 104, for $400, received from Hussain, a supplier, has not been entered in the purchases journal.

3 Invoice no. 6789, for $150, sent to Maya, a customer, has been entered in the sales journal as $105.

4 The purchase of a machine for use in the business, and costing $2300, has been debited to Purchases account in error.

5 Credit note no. 23, for $68, sent to Hanife, a customer, has been omitted from the sales returns journal.

6.3 Recording of information

The following are the basic steps in the recording process.

Step 1. Study the transaction carefully. The purpose is first to identify the types of account involved.

Step 2. Determine the classification of the accounts involved:

i.e. Assets, Liabilities, Owner's Equity, Revenues and Expenses.

Step 3. Determine whether the accounts affected increased or decreased.

Step 4. Debit or credit the accounts affected.

Illustration – Using the September transactions of T. Wyte Cyber Café. Its accounting period is for a month.

Transactions/economic events

2005

September   1   T. Sloane invests $150 000 cash in Cyber Café and Computer repairs Business. The name of the company is T. Wyte Cyber Café.

            1   Office equipment costing $8000 is purchased by signing a 3 month, 10% $8000 note payable.

            5   Office rent for September is paid in cash $1800.

          18   Cyber Café provided computer service repairs on account to Trinmar Limited $8000

          20   Received $28 000 as a result of signing a contract that requires Cyber Café to provide advice and maintenance to BP Gas over the coming year.

          30   T. Sloane introduced additional capital to the business $130 000.

          30   Received $8000 from Trinmar Limited for full settlement on account.

          30   Received $20 000 cash from Petrotrin for computer services provided in September.

          30   Conducted a real estate deal with Benjamin's Real Estate Limited for $200 000. The price consists of Land $80 000, Building $100 000 and Equipment $20 000. $150 000 was paid in cash. The balance to be paid in 30 days.

Analysis of entries

Economic events	Assets	Liabilities	Equity	Income	Expenses
T. Sloane invests $150 000 to start Cyber Café	+		+		
Office equipment costing $8000 is purchased by signing a 3 month 10% $8000 note payable	+	+			
Office rent for September is paid in cash $1800	-				+
Cyber Café provided computer service repairs on account to Trinmar Ltd. $8000	+			+	
Received $28 000 as result of signing a contract that requires Cyber Café to provide advice and maintenance to BP Gas for the coming year	+			+	
T. Sloane introduced $130 000 as additional capital	+		+		
Received $8000 from Trinmar Ltd. for full settlement on account.	+ -				
Received $20 000 cash from Petrotrin for computer services provided in September	+			+	
Conducted a real estate deal with Benjamin's Realty for $200 000. The price consists of Land $80 000, Building $100 000 and Equipment $20 000. $150 000 was paid in cash. The balance to be paid in 30 days.	+	+			

Journal entries

DATE 2005 September	DETAILS	Dr. $	Cr. $
1	Cash	150 000	
	T. Sloane		150 000
	Owner's cash investment in business		
1	Office equipment	8 000	
	Notes Payable		8 000
	Issued 3 month 10% note for office equipment		
5	Rent expense	1 800	
	Cash		1 800
	Paid September rent		
18	Accounts receivable – Trinmar Ltd.	8 000	
	Service revenue		8 000
	For service provided to Trinmar Ltd.		
20	Cash	28 000	
	Unearned revenue		28 000
	For contract signed that requires Cyber Café to provide advice to BP Gas over the coming year.		
30	Cash	130 000	
	T. Sloane, Capital		130 000
	T. Sloane introduced additional capital		
30	Cash	8 000	
	Accounts receivable		8 000
	Cash received from Trinmar Ltd for full settlement of account		
30	Cash	20 000	
	Service revenue		20 000
	Received cash for services provided		
30	Land	80 000	
	Building	100 000	
	Equipment	20 000	
	Cash		150 000
	Accounts payable		50 000
	Purchased assets. $150 000 was paid in cash. The balance to be paid in 30 days		

6.4 Adjustments

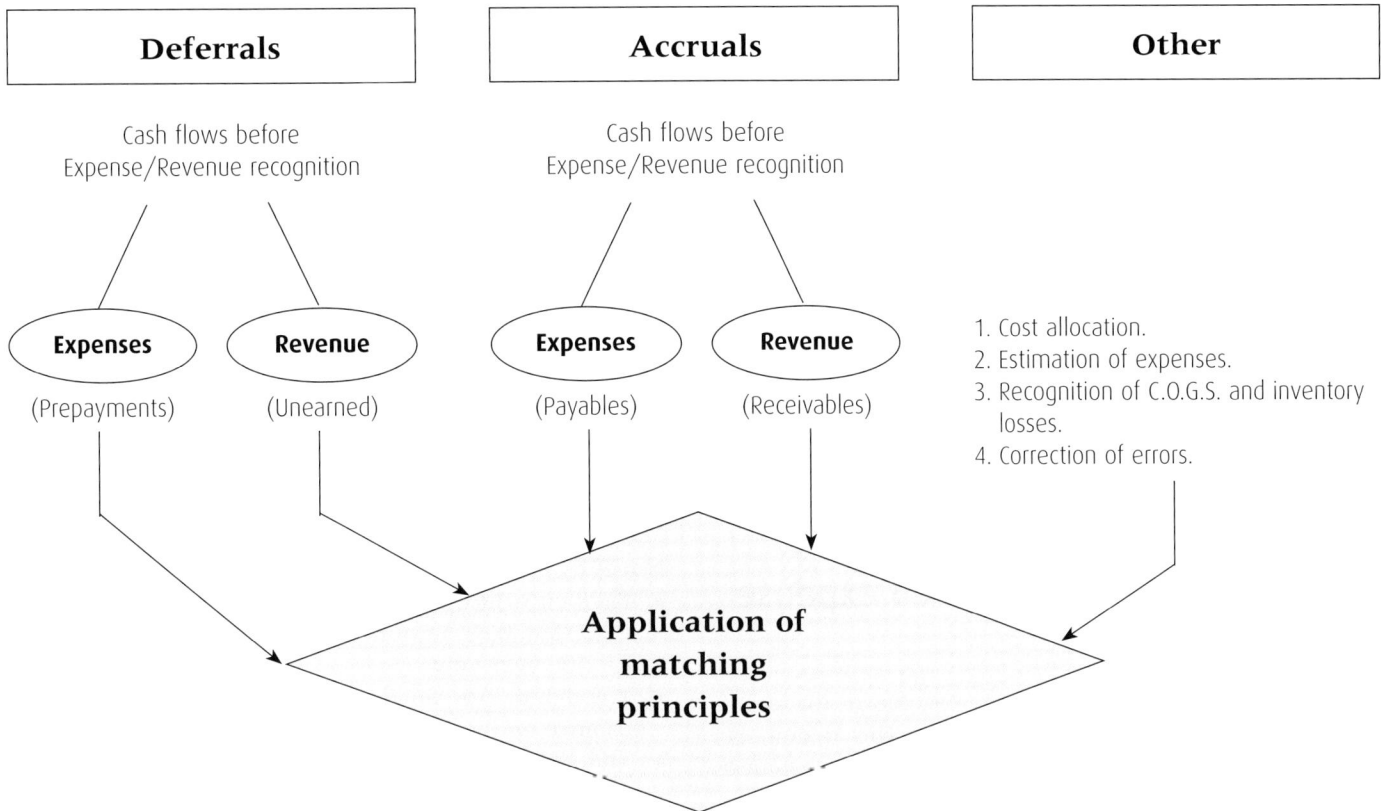

Deferrals	Accruals	Other

Cash flows before Expense/Revenue recognition

Cash flows before Expense/Revenue recognition

Expenses (Prepayments)

Revenue (Unearned)

Expenses (Payables)

Revenue (Receivables)

1. Cost allocation.
2. Estimation of expenses.
3. Recognition of C.O.G.S. and inventory losses.
4. Correction of errors.

Application of matching principles

6.5 What are accruals and deferrals?

Accruals are expenses that have been incurred but not paid for. For example, an unpaid electricity bill is an accrued expense; the electricity has been consumed (the cost has been incurred), but not paid for.

Deferrals (prepayments) are payments made in advance of the benefits to be derived from them. Rent is an example because it usually has to be paid in advance.

6.6 How to treat an accrued expense in an account

An accrued expense is an amount that is owed to somebody; that somebody is a creditor. The creditor must be represented in the accounts either as a credit balance carried down on the account or as a separate liability account at period end.

Example – credit balance carried down

The accounting year of a business ended on 31 December 2003. In the 11 months ended 30 November 2003 payments for electricity amounted to $900. At 31 December 2003 there was an unpaid electricity bill for $130. That amount is carried down on the account as a credit balance.

Notes

- Only $900 has been paid but the Profit and Loss Account has been debited with the full cost of electricity for the year, $1030.
- A creditor for the amount owing for electricity has been created on the account by a credit balance carried down.
- The creditor will be shown in the Balance Sheet under current liabilities as an 'accrued expense' or as an 'expense creditor' to distinguish it from trade creditors.

Electricity			
2003	$	2003	$
Jan – Nov Sundry payments	900	Dec 31 Profit and Loss A/c	1030
Dec 31 Electricity owing c/d	130		
	1030		1030
		2004	
		Jan 1 Balance b/d	130

Example – separate liability account prepared after journal entry

Journal

	$	$
Electricity	130	
Accured electricity		130
Adjustment of expense account for accrued electricity		

When this method is used, at the start of a new period, a reversing entry is made to acknowledge payment of the expense outstanding.

Journal

	$	$
Accured electricity	130	
Electricity		130
To reverse adjusting entry for accrued electricity		

6.7 How to treat a deferred expense in an account

The person to whom a payment has been made in advance is a debtor of the business. The debtor is represented on the expense account by a debit balance carried down or a separate asset account is established.

Example – debit balance carried down

Yousif occupies premises at a rental of $2000 per annum, the rent being payable in advance on 1 January, 1 April, 1 July and 1 October. In 2003, Yousif paid the rent on each of those dates, but on 31 December he paid the rent due on 1 January 2004. At 31 December, the landlord is a debtor for the amount of the prepayment.

Rent payable

2003		$	2003		$
Jan 1	Bank	500	Dec 31	Profit and Loss A/c	2000
Apr 1	Bank	500	Dec 31	Rent paid in advance c/d	500
Jul 1	Bank	500			
Oct 1	Bank	500			
Dec 31	Bank	500			
		2500			2500
2004					
Jan 1	Balance b/d	500			

Example – separate liability account prepared after journal entry

Journal

	$	$
Deferred rent	500	
Rent		500
Adjustment of expense account for prepayment		

When this method is used, at the start of a new period, a reversing entry is made to acknowledge payment of the expense.

Journal

	$	$
Rent	500	
Deferred rent		500
To reverse adjusting entry for prepaid rent		

Notes

- Payments during the year amount to $2500, but the Profit and Loss Account has been debited with the rent for one year only.
- The debtor (the landlord) is represented by the debit balance on the account.
- The debit balance will be included in the Balance Sheet under current assets as a prepayment to distinguish it from trade debtors.

6.8 Adjustments for revenues

How to treat accured revenue in an account

An accrued revenue is an amount that has been earned but not yet collected from a customer or debtor. The debtor must be represented in the accounts either as a debit balance carried down on the account OR as a separate asset account at period end.

Example – debit balance carried down

Shelia Ng, a lawyer, has collected only $10 300 in probate fees from customers. She claims a total revenue earned of $12 000 for the year ended 31 December 2006.

Notes

- The full revenue earned of $12 000 will be credited to the Income Statement.
- The uncollected or accured amount will be shown as a debit balance brought down.
- The debtor will be shown as accured revenue under current assets in the Balance Sheet.

Probate fees

	$		$
Income Statement	12 000	Jan–Nov Bank-sundry payments	10 300
		Accrued fees c/d	1 700
	12 000		12 000
Accured fees b/d	1 700		

Probate fees

	$		$
Income Statement	12 000	Jan–Dec Bank-sundry payments	15 000
Deferred rent revenue c/d	3 000		
	12 000		12 000
		Deferred rent revenue b/d	3 000

Example – separate asset account prepared after journal entry

Journal

	$	$
Accured Probate fees	1 700	
Probate fees		1 700
Adjustment of revenue account for accrued revenue		

When this method is used, at the start of a new period, a reversing entry is made to acknowledge the revenue outstanding.

Journal

	$	$
Probate fees	1 700	
Accured Probate fees		1 700
To reverse adjusting entry for accrued fees		

Example – separate liability account prepared after journal entry

Journal

	$	$
Rent	3 000	
Deferred Rent		3 000
Adjustment of revenue account for prepayment		

When this method is used, at the start of a new period, a reversing entry is made to acknowledge prepayment of the expense.

Journal

	$	$
Deferred Rent	3 000	
Rent		3 000
To reverse adjusting entry for prepaid rent		

How to treat a deferred (prepaid, unexpired) revenue in an account

Where a business collects revenue in advance of the period of earning, a credit balance is carried down on the revenue account OR a separate liability account is established.

Example – credit balance carried down

Shelia Ng collects $3000 per year rent from tenants quarterly in advance. At the end of the accounting year 31 December 2006, Shelia had collected $15 000.

Notes

- The full revenue earned of $12 000 will be credited on the Income Statement.
- The prepaid amount will be shown as a credit balance brought down.
- The creditors will be shown as deferred revenue under current liabilities in the Balance Sheet.

6.9 Further examples of accounting for deferrals and accruals

	Recognition	Transactions	Adjustments	Journal entries	Income statement	Balance sheet
DEFERRALS: EXPENSES	Cash flows before the expense recognition	1. Pre-paid insurance at the beginning of the period $1500 by cheque 2. Service applicable to the period was valued at $1200	Prepayments	DR. Prepaid Insurance $1500 CR. Bank $1500 Dr. Insurance Expense $1200 CR. Prepaid Insurance $1200	Payment expired or expense for the period Payment – Expired = $1500 – $1200 Unexpired = $300	Unexpired portion as a current asset $300
REVENUE	Cash flows before the revenue recognition	1. Collected rent $4000 cash 2. Rent earned for the period, $3600	Unearned revenue	DR. Cash $4000 CR. Rent revenue $4000 Dr. Rent revenue $400 CR. Rent revenue collected in advance $400	Earned revenue Receipt – Unearned = $4000 – $400 Earned = $3600	Unearned portion as a current liability $400

	Recognition	Transactions	Adjustments	Journal entries	Income statement	Balance sheet
ACCRUALS: EXPENSES	Cash flows after the expense recognition	1. Paid wages by cheque $100 000 2. Wages unpaid $20 000	Payables	DR. Wages expense $100 000 CR. Bank $100 000 DR. Wages expense $20 000 CR. Wages payable $20 000	Value of benefits (service) obtained Payment + Payable = $100 000 + $20 000 Benefits Obtained = $120 000	The payable portion as a current liability $20 000
REVENUE	Cash flows after the revenue recognition	1. Fees collected $1600 cash 2. Fees still to be collected $400	Receivables	DR. Cash $1600 CR. Fees revenue $1600 DR. Fees receivable $400 CR. Fees revenue $400	Value of benefits given Receipts + receivables = $1600 + $400 = $2000	The receivable portion as a current asset $400

6.10 Accounts receivable

The creation of Accounts Receivable resulted from the necessity to sell all types of goods and services on credit. Allowing customers the benefit of making payments some time after they have received the goods and services can increase sales and profits. Receivables are the expected future receipts from customers for goods sold on credit. These future receipts are usually small in amount and the term of maturity is short (usually 30 to 60 days). Larger future receipts over a longer credit term are usually transacted by means of Notes Receivables. These are written promises to pay specified sums of money with interest at a definite future date.

Accounts Receivables are shown as current assets on the Balance Sheet.

6.11 Credit sales and collection of receivables

When goods are sold on credit, the Accounts Receivable (debtor) is debited and Sales Revenue is credited. When the debtor pays, cash is debited and the account receivable is credited.

For example Bob Yates Ltd sold $36 000 worth of goods to retailers on 2 Oct. The journal entry in Yates books will be:

| 2 Oct | Accounts Receivable | $36 000 | |
| | Sales Revenue | | $36 000 |

Assuming that by 31 Dec., $29 000 was received from the retailers the journal entry will be:

| 31 Dec | Cash | $29 000 | |
| | Accounts Receivable | | $29 000 |

6.12 Accounting for bad debts – the allowance approach

This is the practice of reporting accounts receivable in the balance sheet at its net realizable value.

As long as goods are sold on credit, the situation of bad debt arises. Bad debt can be seen as a necessary expense associated with generating credit sales.

From the above example, the accounts receivable ending balance is now $7000 (36 000 – $29 000). However, it may be that the company will not collect the full $7000, because some customers for various reasons will not pay their debts. Thus the accounts receivable balance is not to be shown in the balance sheet as $7000 i.e. at the face value.

Suppose Bob Yates Ltd estimates that 15% of the $7000 ($1050) will not be collected, then the Accounts Receivable in the balance sheet will be shown at the Net Realizable Value of $5950 ($7000–$1050).

		$
Thus:	Accounts receivable	7000
	Less allowance for doubtful accounts	1050
	Net realizable value of receivables	5950

6.13 Uncollectable accounts

The $1050 of accounts receivable which is determined to be uncollectable is considered a loss to the company, and is called uncollectable accounts expense. The following adjusting entry is made in the journal:

| Uncollectable accounts expense | $1050 | |
| Allowance for doubtful accounts | | $1050 |

When a specific customer's account is determined to be uncollectable, the amount should be written off, since it is no longer a part of the account receivable. For example a customer who owes $450 has become bankrupt and is unable to pay his debt:

| Allowance for doubtful accounts | $450 | |
| Accounts receivable | | $450 |

To write off the receivable from a customer as uncollectable.

Since an allowance for doubtful account has already been created and an uncollectable account of $1050 has already been declared an expense, it will be wrong to record the $450 as an expense again. Only the allowance for doubtful account and the accounts receivable will be affected. This development will not alter the uncollectable account expense or the net realizable value.

6.14 Methods of estimating bad debt expense

1. Percentage of credit sales method

This method matches the firm's credit sale figures usually over two or three years, with the bad debt losses incurred during the same period. The average bad debt rate is calculated by dividing the total bad debt losses by total credit sales, and a percentage average is found.

E.g.	Year	Bad Debts	Credit Sales
	2001	$ 500	$140 000
	2002	700	180 000
	2003	1 000	200 000
	TOTAL	2 000	520 000

Average Loss Rate for the three years = (2200 / 520 000) x 100 = 0.42 %

In this example 0.42 % is the average bad debt rate for this firm. If in the following year i.e. 2004, the credit sales figure is $240 000, then the estimated bad debt expense will be $240 000 x 0.42 % = $1008.

This figure of $1008 is directly recorded as bad debt expense in the income statement and the allowance for doubtful accounts.

2. Ageing of Accounts receivable – Balance Sheet approach

This method uses the length of time the accounts receivable have been outstanding, to estimate the bad debt expense. The concept is that older accounts are less likely to be collectable. The accounts receivable are classified according to their ages.

Fyzo Trading Agency
Analysis of accounts receivable by age
December 31, 2003

Accounts Receivable	Not Yet Due $	1-30 days Past Due $	1-60 days Past Due $	61-90 days Past Due $	Over 90 days Past Due $	Total $
A. Candy				3 000	1 200	4 200
B. Buttercup	5 000	2 000	800			7 800
C. Vanilla	1 000	800				1 800
D. Chocolate			2 500	1 000	800	4 300
E. Strawberry	2 000					2 000
	8 000	2 800	3 300	4 000	2 000	20 100

Based on the above ageing schedule, the estimated amount of uncollectable accounts can be calculated. The **estimated percentage of credit losses** for each age group of Accounts receivable can be determined from past experience. This estimated percentage loss could then be applied to the dollar amount for each group:

	Age group total $		Percentage considered uncollectable		Estimated uncollectable accounts $
Not yet due	8 000	X	1 %	=	80
1-30 days past due	2 800	X	4 %	=	112
31-60 days past due	3 300	X	12 %	=	396
61-90 days past due	4 000	X	25 %	=	1 000
Over 90 days past due	2 000	X	60 %	=	1 200
	20 100				2 798

Thus out of a total accounts receivable of $20 100, it is estimated that $2798 will be uncollectable. In this respect the allowance for doubtful accounts is to be increased to a new figure of $2798. So that if the opening balance in the allowance for doubtful debt was $2200, and the ending balance calculated above is $2798, the difference $598 i.e. ($2798 – $2200) is the amount of bad debt expense.

6.15 Credit card sales

Non-bank credit cards

Many sales are transacted by means of credit cards: e.g. Visa, MasterCard etc. These credit card companies may be (I) banking institutions or (II) non-banking institutions. When retailers accept credit card payments, the credit card companies pay the retailers almost immediately and they collect the amounts from the customers who made the purchases.

The retailer records credit card sales of $6000 as follows:

Accounts receivable	Dr $6000	
Sales revenue		Cr $6000
To record sales to customers using credit card.		

Credit card companies take the burden of debt collection and bad debt expenses from the retailer, and benefit by retrieving a discount from the retailers. Thus when the retailer receives cash from the credit companies it will be less than the value of sales, and recorded as follows:

Cash a/c	Dr $5700	
Credit card discount expense	$ 300	
Accounts receivable		Cr $6000
To record collection of accounts receivable from card company less 5 % discount.		

Bank credit card

When the credit card company is a bank, the credit card drafts, prepared by the retailer through credit card sales, are deposited directly to the bank concerned. These drafts are accepted as deposits to the bank and the credit card transactions are recorded by the retailers as cash sales.

6.16 The worksheet

Column one

The names and balances of accounts in the ledger or a given trial balance should occupy the first column. Ensure that totals are equal.

Column two

Enter the adjustments ensuring that each one is recorded as a debit and a credit. If an account is to be used and it is not given then add that item to the last of accounts.

Column three

This is the preparation of the adjusted trial balance. When accounts have been adjusted, they should usually have a balance different from the original trial balance. The new balances are calculated as follows:

Original balances	Adjustment	Action
Debit	Debit	Add the balances
Credit	Debit	Find the difference
Credit	Credit	Add the balances
Debit	Credit	Find the difference

Column four

This is the preparation of the Income Statement. All temporary accounts that are used in the calculation of net income or net loss are recorded appropriately under debits or credits. A balancing figure is added to make the total of the debits equal to the total of the credits or vice versa. If the balancing figure is added to the debit column (revenue exceeds expenses) a net profit is recorded. If the balancing figure is added to the credit column (expenses exceed revenue) a net loss is recorded.

Column five

The balance sheet is prepared in the column. The permanent accounts remaining in the adjusted trial balance are transferred to the column. Remember to include net profit in the credit column or net loss in the debit column. The totals of both columns should be equal.

The preparation of the worksheet is not a replacement for the journal entries for the adjustments or the financial statements. These must be written up to form part of the official records of the entity.

Worksheet

	Trial balance		Adjustments		Adjusted trial balance		Income statement		Balance sheet	
Sales		30 600				30 600		30 600		
Purchases	16 000				16 000		16 000			
Returns outwards	600				600		600			
Opening stock	4 000				4 000		4 000			
Warehouse wages expense	7 000				7 000		7 000			
Office wages expense	6 000		(a) 1 200		7 200		7 200			
Rent expense	1 000				1 000		1 000			
Insurance expense	3 000			(b) 500	2 500		2 500			
Building	24 000				24 000				24 000	
Furniture	5 000				5 000				5 000	
Bank	30 000				30 000				30 000	
Cash	10 000				10 000				10 000	
Capital		76 000				76 000				76 000
$	106 600	106 600								
Office – wages accrued				(a)1 200		1 200				1 200
Prepayments			(b) 500		500				500	
Depreciation expense			(c) 2 400		2 400		2 400			
Provision for depreciation				(c) 2 400		2 400				2 400
Closing stock							(c) 2 900	(c) 2 900		
Net Loss								7 200	7 200	
			4 100	4 100	110 200	110 200	40 700	40 700	79 600	79 600
Adjustments										
(a) Office wages unpaid $1200										
(b) Insurance paid in advance 500										
(c) Depreciation on building 2 400										
(d) Closing stock 2 900										

6.17 The worksheet and the accounting cycle

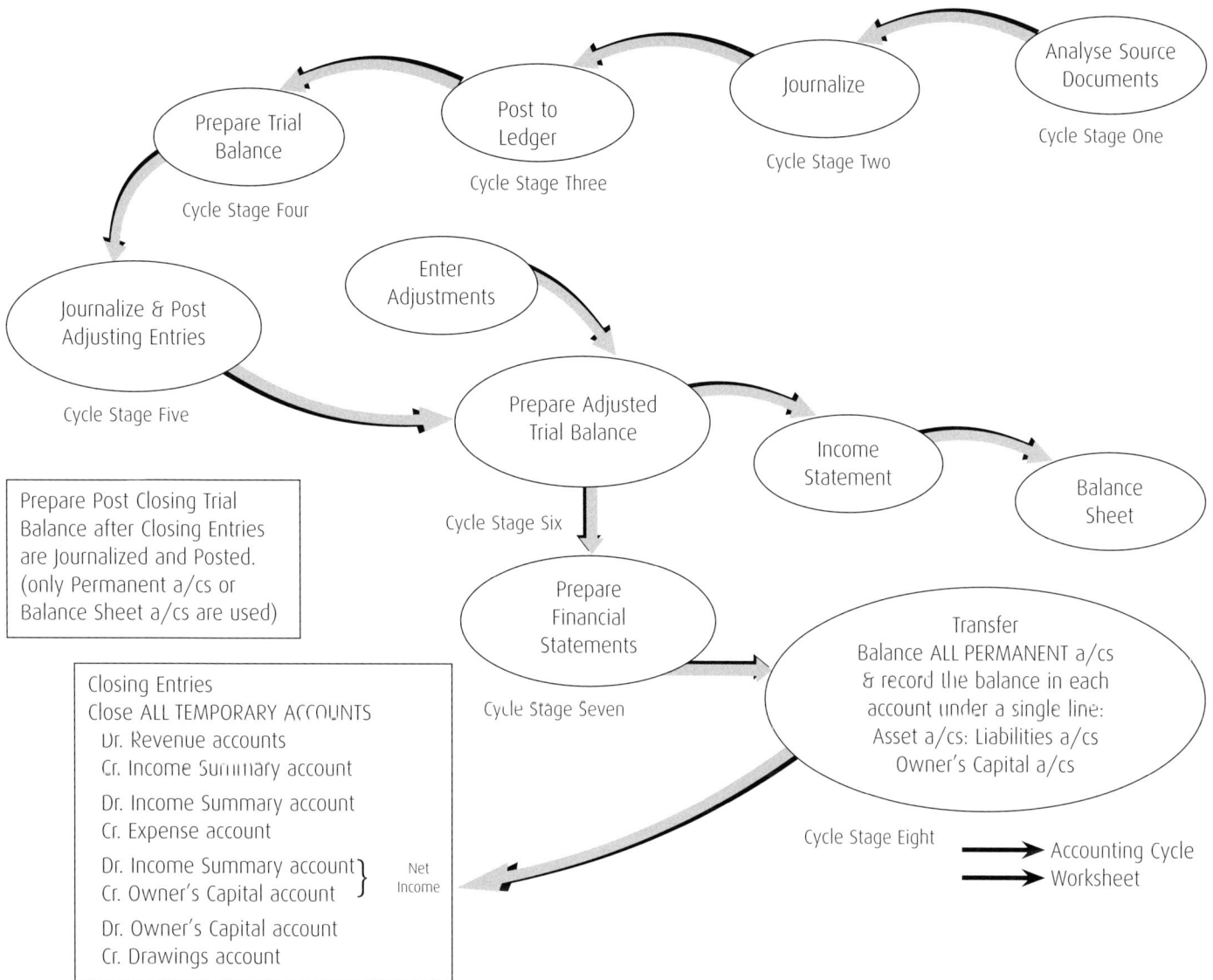

Prepare Trial Balance — Cycle Stage Four

Post to Ledger — Cycle Stage Three

Journalize — Cycle Stage Two

Analyse Source Documents — Cycle Stage One

Journalize & Post Adjusting Entries — Cycle Stage Five

Enter Adjustments

Prepare Adjusted Trial Balance — Cycle Stage Six

Income Statement

Balance Sheet

Prepare Post Closing Trial Balance after Closing Entries are Journalized and Posted. (only Permanent a/cs or Balance Sheet a/cs are used)

Prepare Financial Statements — Cycle Stage Seven

Transfer Balance ALL PERMANENT a/cs & record the balance in each account under a single line: Asset a/cs: Liabilities a/cs Owner's Capital a/cs — Cycle Stage Eight

Closing Entries
Close ALL TEMPORARY ACCOUNTS
Dr. Revenue accounts
Cr. Income Summary account

Dr. Income Summary account
Cr. Expense account

Dr. Income Summary account
Cr. Owner's Capital account } Net Income

Dr. Owner's Capital account
Cr. Drawings account

→ Accounting Cycle
→ Worksheet

6.18 Questions

1 Prepare journal entries with suitable narratives to record the following:

(a) Received from Mumtaz invoice no. 506 dated 3 March for $10 000. This was in respect of the purchase of a machine on credit.

(b) Invoice no. 495 dated 6 March for $675 for goods sold to Wayne. The invoice has been entered twice in the sales journal.

(c) Invoice no. 998 dated 7 March for $4250 in respect of a delivery van purchased from Younas and paid for by cheque.

(d) Credit note no. 103 dated 10 March for $190 sent to Browne.

(e) Invoice no. 854 dated 15 March for $1300 for goods purchased from Sandra.

2 Desmond's trial balance at 31 March 2004 was as follows.

	$	$
Plant and Machinery	36 000	
Motor Vehicles	17 000	
Stock	9 000	
Trade Debtors	7 060	
Bank	5 400	
Trade Creditors		3 950
Capital		70 000
Drawings	22 088	
Sales		219 740
Purchases	100 100	
Sales Returns	17 420	
Purchases Returns		8 777
Wages	67 000	
Rent Payable	8 000	
Rent Receivable		2 600
Interest Receivable		840
Discounts Allowed	2 826	
Discounts Received		1 040
Carriage Inwards	5 170	
Carriage Outwards	7 920	
Sundry Expenses	1 963	
	306 947	306 947

Further information

1. Stock at 31 March 2004 was valued at $11 000.
2. Expenses owing at 31 March 2004 were: rent payable $2000; carriage inwards $330; carriage outwards $280.
3. Sundry expenses of $200 had been paid in advance; interest receivable of $160 had accrued.
4. At 31 March 2004, rent receivable of $200 had been received in advance.

Required

(a) Prepare Desmond's Trading and Profit and Loss Account for the year ended 31 March 2004.
(b) Prepare the Balance Sheet at 31 March 2004.

3 Saul is a trader and his trial balance at 31 May 2004 was as follows.

Account	$	$
Freehold Property at cost	180 000	
Provision for Depreciation of Freehold Property		45 000
Plant and Machinery at cost	97 000	
Provision for Depreciation of Plant and Machinery		53 000
Motor Vehicles at cost	41 000	
Provision for Depreciation of Motor Vehicles		27 000
Trade debtors	34 600	
Provision for Doubtful Debts		1 200
Trade creditors		5 720
Bank	11 374	
Sales		700 000
Sales Returns	6 670	
Purchases	410 890	
Purchases Returns		3 112
Wages	137 652	
Rent Payable	10 000	
Rent Receivable		1 020
Heating and Lighting	4 720	
Telephone and Postage	3 217	
Stationery	6 195	
Repairs to Machinery	17 600	
Discounts Allowed	3 220	
Discounts Received		2 942
Carriage Inwards	4 240	
Carriage Outwards	1 819	
Stock	40 000	
Drawings	28 797	
Capital		200 000
	1 038 994	1 038 994

Further information

1. Stock at 31 May 2004 cost $58 000.
2. Depreciation is to be calculated as follows: freehold property at 4% per annum, straight line; plant and machinery at 15% per annum; motor vehicles at 30% per annum on the reducing balance.
3. Included in trade debtors is a bad debt of $1800; the provision for doubtful debts is to be 5% of trade debtors.
4. $400 was owing for heating and lighting, and $220 for stationery. The stock of stationery at 31 May 2004 had cost $450.

5. Rent paid in advance was $2000; rent receivable was owing in the sum of $280.

6. Saul had taken goods for his own use. The goods had cost $2400. No entries for this had been made in the books.

Required

(a) Prepare Saul's Trading and Profit and Loss Account for the year ended 31 May 2004.

(b) Prepare the Balance Sheet at 31 May 2004.

4 (a) Budwise, a distributor to boutiques for teenage clothing, has recorded $295 000 in credit sales in year 2. The current balance in the allowance for bad debts account is $5900 which represents 10% of accounts receivable. On the last day of the accounting year, a debt of $800 was written off using the allowance method. Calculate the net realizable value of the accounts receivable before and after the write-off of the debt.

(b) In year 3, Budwise has total credit sales of $320 000 and maintains that the same percentage of its credit sales will be uncollectable. Prepare the journal entry to adjust the allowance for uncollectable accounts on 31 December.

(c) Assume Budwise retained in year 3 the same percentage of credit sales as accounts receivable. After the ageing of debtors schedule has been prepared, it is estimated that 8% of the accounts receivable will not be collected. Prepare the adjusting journal entry if Budwise had chosen to use the percentage of receivables method to estimate its allowance for uncollectable accounts.

5 Explain how the following events are to be treated and exemplify your answer with the appropriate journal entries.

(a) At 30 November 2007, the end of the financial year, Vitra owes $1200 to Marian Power and Light for services received.

(b) Leston, a photocopier, has agreed to pay for stationery, half yearly in advance to ensure a continuous supply. He estimates that he will use $18 000 in stationery supplies on an annual basis. By the end of the financial year 30 September, his records show that Leston has paid the appropriate amount to his supplier.

(c) Masterson prefers to pay his rent in advance but his rates in arrears. As at 31 March 2007 his bank statements show that he had made total payments of $28 000 towards his annual rent of $24 000 and his rates of $2000. He owes a further $500 in rates for the year.

6 Explain how the following events are to be treated and exemplify your answer with the appropriate journal entries.

(a) Jeffrey, a service repairman, earned $4500 in fees last month but has collected only four-fifths of it.

(b) Golda, an accountant, earns fees at the rate of $250 per hour. Each client is advised to pay a retainer fee representing 4 hours work in advance to ensure her attention. As at 31 October 2007, the end of the financial year, three clients had paid the retainer fee required.

(c) Laura rents out four offices on a floor of her building for $1500 per month per office. Her rental contracts state that tenants are to pay rent quarterly in advance. At year end 30 June 2007 three tenants have kept their agreement but one tenant was six months in arrears.

7 Trial balance: preparing trial balance income statements and balance sheets for sole traders

Objectives
- state the purpose of a trial balance
- prepare a trial balance
- state the limitations of a trial balance
- prepare income statement accounts
- state what is the purpose of the inventory account
- define balance sheet?
- state why a balance sheet is prepared
- prepare a balance sheet

7.1 What is a trial balance?

A **trial balance** is a list of all the balances extracted from the ledgers at a particular date, and its purpose is to check that the total of the debit balances equals the total of the credit balances. The principle of double entry ensures that the two totals should agree. If the totals do not agree there must be an error somewhere in the bookkeeping.

7.2 How to prepare a trial balance

First balance all the ledger accounts including the cash book. Then list the balances with the debit balances and credit balances in separate columns. The total of the debit balances should equal the total of the credit balances. If the totals are equal, the trial balance agrees.

Example

The following trial balance has been extracted from the books of Zabine at 31 March 2003.

Account	Debit balances $	Credit balances $
Premises	70 000	
Machinery	10 000	
Office Furniture	5 000	
Sales		100 000
Sales Returns	700	
Purchases	6 900	
Purchases Returns		1 000
Trade debtors*	1 100	
Trade creditors**		1 575
Rent Payable	1 600	
Wages and Salaries	4 080	
Heating and Lighting	960	
Sundry Expenses	1 430	
Cash	500	
Bank	12 600	
Loan from Ludmilla		2 000
Capital – Zabine		13 000
Drawings	2 705	
	117 575	117 575

* The balances on the accounts in the sales ledger are listed and totalled separately; the total is entered in the trial balance as trade debtors.

** The balances on the accounts in the purchase ledger are listed and totalled separately; the total is entered in the trial balance as trade creditors.

7.3 Opening inventory

One year's closing inventory is the next year's opening inventory and it must be included in the cost of sales for that year. The debit balance on the inventory account is transferred by journal entry to the Trading Account.

Example

When Andrew prepares his Trading Account for the year ended 31 December 2004 the opening inventory will be transferred from the Inventory account to the Trading Account:

Journal

		$	$
31 Dec 2004	Trading Account	5000	
	Inventory		5000

Inventory

		$			$
31 Dec 2003	Trading Account	5000	31 Dec 2004	Trading Account	5000

In the year ended 31 December 2004 Andrew's sales totalled $150 000 and his purchases were $62 000. Inventory at 31 December 2004 was $8000. Andrew's Trading Account will be as follows.

Andrew
Income Statement for the year
ended 31 December 2004

	$	$
Sales		150 000
Less Cost of sales		
Opening inventory	5 000	
Purchases	62 000	
	67 000	
Less Closing inventory	8 000	59 000
Gross profit		91 000

Note. In almost every case, inventory shown in a trial balance is opening inventory. The exception occurs when the trial balance has been extracted from the books *after* a Trading Account has been prepared, in which case the trial balance will not include Sales, Sales Returns, Purchases or Purchases Returns accounts.

7.4 What is an Income Statement?

Most people carry on business in order to make a living. They depend upon the profit of the business for their income to enable them to buy food, clothes and other necessities. They compare the revenue earned by the business with its expenses. If the revenue exceeds expenses the business has made a profit. On the other hand, if the expenses exceed the revenue the business has made a loss and the trader has no income. Profit or loss is found by the preparation of an Income statement covering a period of time, usually one complete year. Until now, double-entry bookkeeping may have seemed a tiresome and largely pointless exercise, but it is the only system that enables Income Statements to be prepared.

7.5 How to prepare an Income Statement for a sole trader

Income statements are prepared in two formats. They are single steps and multiple steps.

Single-step format

In this method the format is used to match total expenses with total revenues to determine net income or loss from operations. The primary advantage of this format is that it is simple.

Example

Solange is a manicurist. Her revenues and expenses for the year ending 31 December 2003 are as follows:

	$
Revenue for services rendered	100 000
Rent	10 000
Cleaning supplies	500
Wages	8 000
Stationery	2 000
Supplies for the store	20 000
Telephone services	2 000
Electricity	2 000

Prepare a single-step income statement for Solange.

Solange
Income Statement
For the year ending December 31, 2003

	$	$
Revenue		100 000
Less expenses:		
Rent	10 000	
Cleaning supplies	500	
Wages	8 000	
Stationery	2 000	
Supplies	20 000	
Telephone	2 000	
Electricity	2 000	44 500
Net income		55 500

Note: The expenses are grouped together and deducted from the total revenues.

All ledger accounts must be balanced and a trial balance prepared at the date to which the Income statement is to be prepared.

Example

Andrew commenced business on 1 January 2003. The following trial balance has been extracted at 31 December 2003 from his books.

Account	$	$
Sales		126 000
Sales Returns	2 000	
Purchases	55 200	
Purchases Returns		2 200
Purchases Discount		2 340
Sales Discount	3 260	
Wages	28 000	
Rent	16 000	
Heating and Lighting	3 400	
Postage and Stationery	1 070	
Motor Van Expenses	9 830	
Interest on Loan	800	
Sundry Expenses	920	
Premises	40 000	
Motor Vans	18 000	
Office Furniture	5 000	
Trade Accounts Receivable	7 400	
Trade Accounts Payable		3 420
Bank	2 160	
Loan from Marie (repayable in 2005)		10 000
Andrew – Capital		60 000
Drawings	10 920	
	203 960	203 960

Income statements are part of the double-entry model. Balances on the nominal (revenue, income and expense) accounts are transferred to them by journal entries.

Multiple-step format

The advantage of this method is that it provides subtotals not shown in the single-step format. These subtotals allow comparison of period to period profits which are useful for assessing performance and predicting future cash flows.

Vertical

Andrew
Income Statement
For the year ended 31 December 2003

	$	$
Sales		126 000
Sales returns		(2 000)
Sales discount		(3 260)
		120 740
Less Cost of Sales		
Purchases	55 200	
Purchases Returns	(2 200)	
Purchases Discount	(2 340)	
	50 660	
Closing Inventory	(5 000)	
		45 600
Gross profit		75 080
Wages	28 000	
Rent	16 000	
Heating and lighting	3 400	
Postage and stationery	1 070	
Motor van expenses	9 830	
Sundry expenses	920	
Interest on loan	800	
		60 020
Net Income		15 060

Andrew
Income Statement
For the year ended 31 December 2003

	$			$
Purchases	55 200		Sales	126 000
Purchases returns	(2 200)		Sales Returns	(2 000)
Purchases discount	(2 340)		Sales Discounts	(3 260)
	50 660			120 740
Closing inventory	(5 000)			
	45 660			
Gross Profit	75 080			
	120 740			120 740
Wages	28 000		Gross Profit b/d	75 080
Rent	16 000			
Heating and lighting	3 400			
Postage and stationery	1 070			
Motor van expenses	9 830			
Sundry expenses	920			
Interest on loan	800			
Net Income	15 060			
	75 080			75 080

7.6 Carriage inwards and carriage outwards

When goods are purchased, the supplier may make an additional charge to cover the cost of delivery. This charge is carriage inwards and adds to the cost of the goods. Carriage inwards is added to the cost of purchases in the Trading Account.

The cost of delivering goods to a customer is carriage outwards and is debited in the Profit and Loss Account as an overhead. Carriage inwards and carriage outwards are both expense items but it is important to treat them correctly in Income Statements.

Example

A. Trader
Income Statement for the year
ended 31 December 2003

	$	$	$
Sales		93 000	
Less Sales returns		2 700	90 300
Less Cost of sales			
Inventory at 1 January 2003		3 000	
Purchases	45 200		
Less Purchases returns	3 400		
	41 800		
Carriage inwards	4 000	45 800	
		48 800	
Less Inventory at 31 December 2003		7 000	41 800
Gross profit			48 500
Less Overheads			
Wages		12 000	
Rent		5 600	
Carriage outwards		2 220	
Sundry		1 760	21 580
Net profit			26 920

7.7 What is a Balance Sheet?

A **Balance Sheet** is a list of the assets and liabilities of a business at a particular date. A trader needs to know if his business will continue to provide an income for the foreseeable future. A Balance Sheet can provide a good indication of the answer to this question.

Unlike an Income Statement, a Balance Sheet is not part of the double-entry model. After the nominal account balances have been transferred to the Income Statement, the only balances left in the ledger are those for assets and liabilities. The Balance Sheet is a list of these balances.

Although a Balance Sheet is not an account, the Income Statement and Balance Sheet are known collectively as the **final accounts** of a business.

7.8 How to prepare a Balance Sheet

List and group the assets and liabilities of the business under the headings:

Current assets

Long-term investments

Property, plant and equipment

Intangible assets

Current liabilities

Long-term liabilities

Owner's equity

Example

The following is the Balance Sheet for Andrew's business at 31 December 2003. It is prepared from the trial balance given in §7.5 and lists all the balances remaining in the ledger after the Income Statement has been prepared.

Andrew
Balance Sheet at 31 December 2003

	$	$
Fixed assets		
Premises		40 000
Motor vans		18 000
Office furniture		5 000
		63 000
Current assets		
Inventory	5 000*	
Trade Accounts receivable	7 400	
Bank	2 160	
	14 560	
Less Current liabilities		
Trade Accounts payable	3 420	11 140
		74 140
Less Long-term liability		
Loan from Marie		10 000
		64 140
Represented by:		
Capital at 1 January 2003		60 000
Add net profit for the year		15 060
		75 060
Deduct drawings		10 920
		64 140

* Stock: see page 60.

Notes

- A Balance Sheet is a 'position' statement showing the position of a business at a particular moment in time. It is not a period statement like an Income Statement. The date at which the Balance Sheet is prepared must be included in the heading 'Balance Sheet at ....'.
- The Balance Sheet has been prepared in vertical form. Study it carefully until you are quite familiar with it and prepare all your Balance Sheets in similar style.

- Current assets are grouped next in an inner column and totalled. They are listed in the reverse order of **liquidity**. A **liquid asset** is one which is in the form of cash (cash in hand) or nearly so (cash at bank). Inventory is not a liquid asset because it has not been sold and no money has been, or will be, received for it until it is sold. Accounts receivable should soon become a liquid asset. The order in the Balance Sheet is: inventory, accounts receivable, bank and cash (if any).
- The current assets are not added to the fixed assets at this stage.
- Current liabilities are those that are due to be settled within one year of the date of the Balance Sheet. They are deducted from the total of current assets to give the **working capital**. In the example above, the working capital is $11 140.
- Working capital is a very important item in the Balance Sheet. The liquid current assets should exceed the current liabilities and show that the business resources adequately cover the payments it must make to its creditors. If the current assets are insufficient to meet the current liabilities, the trader may be forced to sell property, plant and equipment to pay his creditors and that could be the beginning of the end of the business.
- Long-term liabilities are those which are not due to be settled within one year of the date of the Balance Sheet. They are deducted from the total of property, plant and equipment and working capital.
- The assets less the liabilities are represented by the owner's equity. The capital shown in the trial balance is the balance on the Capital account brought forward from the previous year. The net profit shown by the Profit and Loss Account is added to the opening capital, but a net loss must be deducted. Profit increases capital and losses reduce capital. When the drawings are deducted, the balance on the Capital account will be carried forward as the opening capital next year.

- At the end of the year, the balances on the Profit and Loss Account and Drawings account are transferred to the Capital account (by journal entry) as shown.
- The total of the property, plant and equipment and current assets $(63 000 + 14 560) less the total of the current and long-term liabilities $(3420 + 10 000) equals the closing balance on the Capital account, $64 140. This is always true, and the formula 'assets – liabilities = capital' is known as the **accounting equation**.
- At the end of the year, the balances on the Profit and Loss Account and Drawings account are transferred to the Capital account (by journal entry) as shown.
- Other examples of current assets:
  Short-term investment
  Supplies
  Prepaid insurance
- Examples of current liabilities:
  Notes payable
  Accounts payable
  Salaries payable
  Interest payable
  Unearned revenue
- Examples of long-term liabilities:
  Notes payable
  Mortgage payable

Andrew – Capital

2003		$	2003		$
Dec 31	Drawings	10 920	Jan 1	Balance brought down	60 000
	Balance carried down	64 140	Dec 31	Profit and Loss	15 060
		75 060			75 060
			2004		
			Jan 1	Balance brought down	64 140

7.9 Multiple-choice questions

1 The purchase of an office computer has been debited to Office Expenses instead of to Office Equipment.

What effect will this have on the Balance Sheet?

	Fixed assets	Profit	Capital
A	no effect	understated	no effect
B	no effect	understated	understated
C	understated	no effect	understated
D	understated	understated	no effect

2 The owner of a business has taken goods for his own use but no entry has been made in the books to record this. What is the effect of this on the Balance Sheet?

	Stock	Capital
A	no effect	no effect
B	no effect	overstated
C	overstated	no effect
D	overstated	overstated

3 The following information has been extracted from a Balance Sheet at 31 December 2003.

	$
Fixed assets	300 000
Working capital	30 000
Long-term loan	20 000
Profit for the year	35 000
Drawings	25 000

What was the balance on Capital account at 31 December 2003?

A $300 000   **B** $320 000   **C** $340 000
D $350 000

4 Which of the following statements is incorrect?

A assets = liabilities + capital
B capital = assets – liabilities
C capital – liabilities = assets
D liabilities = assets – capital

5 Which of the following does not appear in a Profit and Loss Account?

A Carriage inwards
B Carriage outwards
C Discounts allowed
D Discounts received

6 The following information has been extracted from the trial balance of a business:

	$
Sales	100 000
Purchases	60 000
Wages	21 000

Closing stock was $3000 more than opening stock.

One-third of the wages was charged to cost of sales in the Trading Account.
What was the gross profit?

A $30 000
B $33 000
C $36 000
D $37 000

7 The Carriage inwards of a business amounted to $6000, and the Carriage outwards was $7000.

The Carriage outwards was charged in the Trading Account in error, and the Carriage inwards was debited in the Profit and Loss Account.
What has been the effect of these errors?

	Gross profit	Net profit
A	understated by $1000	understated by $1000
B	overstated by $1000	overstated by $1000
C	understated by $1000	not affected
D	overstated by $1000	not affected

7.10 Exercises

Exercise 1

Corrine began trading on 1 January 2003. The following trial balance as at 31 December 2003 has been extracted from her books.

Account	$	$
Sales		200 000
Sales Returns	6 300	
Purchases	86 500	
Purchases Returns		5 790
Rent Received		3 000
Discounts Received		3 210
Discounts Allowed	5 110	
Wages	61 050	
Rent Paid	12 000	
Electricity	5 416	
Insurance	2 290	
Motor Van Expenses	11 400	
Sundry Expenses	3 760	
Loan Interest	1 000	
Land and Buildings	84 000	
Plant and Machinery	22 000	
Motor Van	19 000	
Trade debtors	12 425	
Trade creditors		4 220
Bank	5 065	
Loan (repayable in 2004)		20 000
Drawings	25 904	
Capital at 1 January 2003	_____	127 000
	363 220	363 220

Corrine had unsold stock of $10 000 at 31 December 2003.

Required

Prepare Corrine's Trading and Profit and Loss Account for the year ended 31 December 2003 in good form.
  Save your answer; it will be required again.

Exercise 2

The following balances have been extracted from Khor's books at 31 December 2003.

	$	$
Sales		48 000
Sales Returns	1 600	
Purchases	21 000	
Purchases Returns		900
Stock at 1 January 2003		4 000

Stock at 31 December 2003 was $7500.

Required

Prepare Khor's Trading Account for the year ended 31 December 2003.

Exercise 3

Sara's trial balance at 31 March 2004 was as follows.

Account	$	$
Sales		40 000
Stock	5 000	
Purchases	20 500	
Wages	6 000	
Rent	10 000	
Electricity	2 600	
Carriage Inwards	1 320	
Carriage Outwards	1 080	
Sundry Expenses	1 250	
Plant and Machinery	8 000	
Office Equipment	1 000	
Trade Debtors	1 900	
Trade Creditors		800
Bank	820	
Drawings	6 330	
Capital	_____	25 000
	65 800	65 800

Stock at 31 March 2004 was $3000.

Required

Prepare Sara's Trading and Profit and Loss Account for the year ended 31 March 2004.

Exercise 4

Prepare a Balance Sheet at 31 December 2003 for Corrine from the trial balance given in exercise 1.

Exercise 5

Prepare a trial balance from the following balances that have been extracted from the books of Achilles, a grocer, at 31 December.

Account	$
Premises	50 000
Motor Vans	8 000
Office Furniture	2 000
Computer	3 000
Sales	60 000
Sales Returns	700
Purchases	4 000
Purchases Returns	500
Motor Vehicle Running Expenses	4 200
Wages	1 800
Rent	2 000
Bank	1 650
Capital	20 000
Drawings	3 150

Exercise 6

The following trial balance has been extracted from the books of Perkins, a sole trader, at 31 March 2004.

Account	$	$
Premises	60 000	
Plant and Machinery	12 000	
Sales		104 000
Sales Returns	3 700	
Purchases	59 000	
Purchases Returns		2 550
Stock at 1 April 2003	6 000	
Wages	13 000	
Rent Payable	2 000	
Rent Receivable		1 800
Heating and Lighting	2 700	
Repairs to Machinery	4 100	
Interest on Loan	750	
Discounts Allowed	1 030	
Discounts Received		770
Trade debtors	1 624	
Trade creditors		1 880
Bank	5 000	
Drawings	10 096	
Long-term Loan		15 000
Capital		55 000
	181 000	181 000

Stock at 31 March 2004 was $10 000.

Required

Prepare Perkin's Trading and Profit and Loss Account for the year ended 31 March 2004.

Exercise 7

Prepare a Balance Sheet at 31 March 2004 for Perkins from the trial balance given in exercise 6.

Exercise 8

The following trial balance has been extracted from Hadlee's books at 31 December 2003.

	$	$
Plant and Machinery	25 000	
Office Furniture	6 000	
Inventory at 1 January 2003	11 000	
Trade Accounts receivable	4 740	
Trade Accounts payable		1 976
Bank	3 327	
Loan, repayable in 2005		5 000
Sales		72 800
Purchases	28 540	
Sales Returns	1 600	
Purchases Returns		2 144
Wages	3 100	
Rent	4 000	
Heating and Lighting	5 120	
Advertising	2 400	
Sundry Expenses	2 010	
Loan Interest	250	
Drawings	4 833	
Capital		20 000
	101 920	101 920

Inventory at 31 December 2003 cost $9000.

Required

Prepare Hadlee's Trading and Profit and Loss Account for the year ended 31 December 2003.

Exercise 9

Prepare the Balance Sheet at 31 December 2003 for Hadlee from the trial balance given in exercise 8.

Exercise 10

The trial balance extracted from Tikolo's books at 31 March 2004 is as follows.

Account	$	$
Sales		204 000
Sales Returns	3 600	
Purchases	120 000	
Purchases Returns		4 440
Inventory at 1 April 2003	18 000	
Carriage Inwards	5 000	
Carriage Outwards	3 724	
Purchases discount		3 160
Sales discount	5 020	
Wages	36 800	
Rent	8 000	
Heating and Lighting	6 450	
Sundry Expenses	1 143	
Fixtures and Fittings	9 000	
Office Furniture	2 000	
Trade accounts receivable	1 970	
Trade accounts payable		2 130
Bank	2 496	
Drawings	20 527	
Capital		30 000
	243 730	243 730

During the year, Tikolo had taken goods costing $2000 for his own use. This had not been recorded in the books.

Inventory at 31 March 2004 cost $20 000.

Required

Prepare Tikolo's Trading and Profit and Loss Account for the year ended 31 March 2004.

Exercise 11

Prepare the Balance Sheet at 31 March 2004 for Tikolo from the trial balance given in exercise 10.

7.11 Examination hints

- Marks may be awarded in an examination for good presentation of Income Statements.
- Give all Income Statements proper headings.
- Include in the heading the name of the trader or business.
- State the period covered by the account.
- Include the words 'Cost of sales', 'Gross profit' and 'Net profit' (or 'Net loss').
- Copy the vertical layouts of the accounts given in the examples in this chapter as far as possible.
- Make sure you copy accurately all the nominal accounts included in the trial balance into your Income Statement.
- Deduct inventory taken by the trader for personal use from purchases and add to drawings at cost price.
- Include *carriage inwards* as an addition to purchases in the Trading Account, but *carriage outwards* as an overhead in the Profit and Loss account.
- Do not prepare journal entries for the Income Statements unless you are specifically asked to do so. They have been shown in this chapter simply to help you understand how balances are transferred from ledger accounts to the Income Statements.
- Marks may be awarded in an examination for good presentation of Balance Sheets.
- Give every Balance Sheet a proper heading which should include the name of the business and the date. (If the Balance Sheet follows an Income Statement which is headed with the name of the business, the name need not be repeated for the Balance Sheet.)
- Prepare Balance Sheets as shown in this chapter. Show the total of each group.
- Show the working capital clearly.

8 Correction of errors

8.1 What is a Suspense account?

Suspense accounts are sometimes used when transactions are recorded in the books before any decision has been made about their proper accounting treatment. For example, an invoice may contain a mixture of capital and revenue expenditure. The expenditure may be recorded in a Suspense account until it is decided how much is capital expenditure and how much revenue.

This chapter is concerned with Suspense accounts that are opened when the causes of differences on trial balances cannot immediately be found and corrected.

8.2 When a Suspense account should be opened

A Suspense account should be opened only when attempts to find the cause of a difference on a trial balance have been unsuccessful. The following checks should be carried out before opening a Suspense account.

1. Check the additions of the trial balance.
2. If the difference is divisible by 2, look for a balance of half the difference which may be on the wrong side of the trial balance. (Example: a difference of $1084 may be caused by 'discounts allowed $542' being entered on the credit side of the trial balance.)
3. If the difference is divisible by 9, look for a balance where digits may have been reversed. (Example: a difference of $18 may be caused by $542 entered in trial balance as $524.)
4. Check the totals of sales ledger balances and purchase ledger balances to the Control accounts, if these have been prepared.

5. Check the extraction of balances from the ledgers.

If the cause of the difference has still not been found, and a Profit and Loss Account and Balance Sheet are required urgently, a Suspense account may be opened.

8.3 How to open a Suspense account

A Suspense account is opened in the general ledger with a balance on whichever side of the account will make the trial balance agree when the balance is inserted in it. For example, if the total of the credit side of a trial balance is $100 less than the total of the debit side, the Suspense account will be opened with a credit balance of $100. When the Suspense account balance is inserted in the trial balance, the latter will balance. A Balance Sheet may then prepared.

8.4 When a Suspense account has been opened

The cause or causes of the difference on the trial balance must be investigated at the earliest opportunity and the errors corrected.

In real life, if there is still a small balance on a Suspense account after all reasonable attempts have been made to find the difference, a business may decide that the amount involved is not material. It will save further time and expense in searching for errors by writing the balance off to the Profit and Loss Account. However, there may be a danger that a small difference hides large errors which do not quite cancel each other out.

8.5 How to correct errors

The correction of errors will require journal entries which will be posted to the Suspense (and other) accounts *unless* they are errors that do *not* affect the trial balance, which are as follows.

- errors of omission
- errors of commission
- errors of principle
- errors of original entry
- errors caused by the complete reversal of entries
- compensating errors.

(These types of error have been explained more fully in §6.3.)

To decide how to correct an error, ask the following three questions.

(i)   How has the transaction been recorded?

(ii) How should the transaction have been recorded?

(iii) What adjustments are required to correct the error?

Remember the following.

- An item on the wrong side of an account must be corrected by an adjustment equal to *twice* the amount of the original error (once to cancel the error and once to place the item on the correct side of the account).

- Some errors do not affect the double entry; an example would be a balance on a sales ledger account copied incorrectly onto a summary of balances for inclusion in the trial balance. The summary of balances should be amended and a one-sided entry in the journal prepared to correct the Suspense account. Such errors do not require to be corrected by debit *and* credit entries.

8.6 Questions

Exercise

Lee's trial balance at 30 June 2004 fails to agree and he places the difference in a Suspense account. Lee then discovers the following errors.

1. The total of the sales journal for one month was $5430. This had been posted to the Sales account as $5340.

2. An invoice for $150 for the purchase of stock from Bilder had been entirely omitted from the books.

3. A cheque for $75 from Doyle, a customer, had been credited to his account as $57.

4. A debt of $50 in the sales ledger had been written off as bad but no entry had been made in the Bad debts account.

5. An improvement to a machine at a cost of $400 had been debited to Machinery Repairs account. (Lee depreciates machinery by the straight-line method over 10 years; a full year's depreciation is calculated for the year of purchase.)

Required

(a) Prepare the Suspense account in Lee's ledger showing clearly the difference on the trial balance at 30 June as the first entry and the entries required to adjust the errors.

(b) Prepare journal entries for errors 2 and 5. (Narratives are *not* required.)

Lee's draft Profit and Loss Account for the year ended 30 June 2004 showed a net profit of $3775.

Required

(c) Calculate the corrected net profit for the year ended 30 June 2004.

8.7 Examination hints

- Remember the six types of error that do not affect the trial balance. These are not corrected through the Suspense account.
- Prepare correcting journal entries in proper form. (Revise §3.10.) Note whether narratives are required.
- The first entry in a Suspense account is the difference on the trial balance. Enter it on the same side of the account as it will be entered in the trial balance.
- Post the Suspense account from journal entries. If these have not been required by the question it may be helpful to prepare them in rough.
- The Suspense account should not have a balance on it when you have posted the journal entries to it.
- Calculate revised profit or loss from the nominal account entries in the journal.
- Calculate revised working capital from the journal entries affecting current assets and current liabilities.
- Do not make journal entries to other books of prime entry. Postings from the journal should always be to named accounts in the ledgers.

8.8 Multiple-choice questions

(In each of the following cases, a trial balance has failed to agree and the difference has been entered in a Suspense account.)

1 A credit balance in the sum of $93 has been omitted from the list of balances extracted from the sales ledger.

What is the effect on the trial balance?

A The credit side is understated by $93

B The credit side is overstated by $93

C The debit side is understated by $93

D The debit side is overstated by $93

2 A credit note for $46 sent to A. Moses has been debited to A. Mason's account in the sales ledger.

What effect will this have on the trial balance?

	Debit total	Credit total
A	none	none
B	$46 overstated	$46 understated
C	none	$92 understated
D	$92 overstated	none

3 The total of the sales journal for one month is $9160. It has been entered in the Sales account as $9610. Which entries are required to correct the error?

	Debit		Credit	
A	Sales account	$450	Sales journal	$450
B	Sales journal	$450	Sales account	$450
C	Sales account	$450	Suspense account	$450
D	Suspense account	$450	Sales account	$450

4 An invoice for repairs to machinery, $500, has been entered in the Machinery at Cost account.
Which entries are required to correct the error?

	Debit		Credit	
A	Machinery at Cost account	$500	Repairs to Machinery account	$500
B	Repairs to Machinery account	$500	Machinery at Cost account	$500
C	Repairs to Machinery account	$500	Suspense account	$500
D	Suspense account	$500	Machinery at Cost account	$500

5 Which of the following will cause a difference on a trial balance?

A An invoice omitted from the sales journal

B An invoice for $415 entered in the Sales journal as $451

C An invoice for $600 entered in the sales journal not included in the monthly total

D A credit note entered in the sales journal

6 After which error will a trial balance still balance?

A Wages paid, $1500, was entered correctly in the bank account but debited to the wages account as $2500.

B Rent receivable of $200 was debited to the Rent Payable account.

C Goods returned to supplier, $150, were entered in purchases returns journal as $105.

D The sales journal was undercast by $200.

7 A trial balance failed to agree and a Suspense account was opened. It was then found that rent received of $500 had been debited to the Rent Payable account. Which entries are required to correct this error?

	Rent Received account		Rent Payable account		Suspense account	
	$		$		$	
A	credit	500	credit	500	debit	1000
B	credit	500	debit	500	no entry	
C	debit	500	credit	500	debit	1000
D	debit	500	credit	500	no entry	

8.9 Additional exercises

1 Bastien does not maintain Control accounts. His trial balance does not balance and he has opened a Suspense account. The following errors have now been discovered.

1. Discount received from Veeraj, amounting to $70, has been included in the discount column of the cash book but has not been posted to Veeraj's account.

2. Goods have been sold on credit to Bernard for $1400 less 25% trade discount. Correct entries have been made in the sales journal but $1000 has been posted to Bernard's ledger account.

3. A cheque for $400 received from Rodney has been debited in the cash book and also debited in Rodney's ledger account.

4. A motor vehicle costing $12 000 has been bought on credit from Nedof Motors. The Purchases account has been debited and Nedof Motor's account credited.

5. $60 spent by Bastien on his personal expenses has been posted to the Sundry Expenses account.

Required

Prepare the entries in Bastien's journal, with suitable narratives, to correct the above errors.

2 Boulder's trial balance at 31 March 2004 did not balance and the difference was entered in a Suspense account. Boulder does not maintain Control accounts. The following information was later discovered.

1. A receipt of $313 from Head, a customer, has been entered correctly in the cash book but has been debited to Head's account in the sales ledger as $331.

2. Goods sold to Joey for $100 have been returned by him and entered correctly in the Sales Returns account. No entry has been made for the return in Joey's account in the sales ledger.

3. The purchase of a second-hand motor vehicle costing $3000 has been debited to the Motor Vehicle Expenses account.

4. The total of the Discount Allowed column in the cash book has been overcast by $300.

5. A dishonest employee has stolen $700 from the business and the cash will not be recovered. No entry to record the theft has been made in the accounts.

Required

(a) Prepare journal entries to correct errors 1 to 5. Narratives are required.

(b) Prepare a Suspense account commencing with the trial balance difference.

The working capital shown in the Balance Sheet at 31 March 2004 before the errors were corrected was $2400.

Required

(c) Calculate the working capital after the errors have been corrected.

3 Amber's trial balance at 31 December 2003 failed to agree and the difference was entered in a Suspense account. The total of the purchase ledger balances had been entered as creditors in the trial balance but it did not agree with the credit balance of $5419 on the Purchase Ledger Control account. The following errors were found.

1. No entry had been made in the books to record a refund by cheque of $90 from Victor, a supplier.

2. A cheque for $420 sent to Shah, a supplier, had been entered correctly in the cash book but debited to General Expenses account as $240.

3. Goods returned, $900, by Amil, a customer, had been credited in Amil's account and debited in the Purchases account.

4. Goods which cost $350 had been returned to Hussein, a supplier. No entry had been made in the books for this.

5. The discount received column in the cash book had been undercast by $600.

Required

(a) Prepare journal entries to correct errors 1 to 5. Narratives are *not* required.

(b) Prepare the Suspense account commencing with the difference on the trial balance.

(c) Explain how a balance which is not considered material in amount may be treated in the accounts.

4 Logan has prepared the following trial balance at 31 March 2004.

	$	$
Sales		131 940
Purchases	33 000	
Sales returns	260	
Purchase returns		315
Opening stock	6 900	
Debtors Control	14 125	
Creditors Control		16 070
Discount allowed	700	
Discount received		614
Wages and salaries	20 600	
Advertising	1 000	
General expenses	2 340	
Bank	13 710	
Premises	70 000	
Motor vehicles	5 000	
Equipment	3 500	
Capital		25 000
Drawings	3 000	
Suspense		196
	174 135	174 135

Logan is unable to find the difference on the trial balance and has entered the difference in the Suspense Account. The following errors have been made in the accounts.

1. Discount allowed of $55 has been posted to the credit of Discount received.

2. Purchase returns of $108 have been posted to the debit of Sales returns.

3. A cheque for $400 from a debtor has been dishonoured, but no record has been made of this in the accounts. There is no reason to believe that payment will not be made in April 2004.

4. Equipment bought during the year for $4400 has been debited to Purchases account.

5. During the year Logan had taken stock which cost $800 for his own personal use.

6. $90 of the general expenses related to an amount paid out of the business bank account for one of Logan's private expenses. In his attempt to correct the accounts, Logan made another debit entry of $90 in the General Expenses account, with no other entry being made.

Required

(a) Prepare journal entries to correct errors 1 to 6 (narratives are not required).

(b) Prepare the Suspense account to show the correcting entries.

(c) Prepare a corrected trial balance at 31 March 2004.

The net profit per the draft accounts, prepared before the above errors were corrected, was $25 000.

Required

(d) Prepare a statement of corrected net profit showing the effect of each error on the net profit per the draft accounts.

8.10 Correction of errors (trial balance balancing)

Errors	How the error was accorded	The correct journal entry should have been	The adjusting journal entry to be made
OMISSION An invoice sent to Singh had been completely omitted from the books	Not recorded	Dr. Cash a/c 2 000 Cr. Sales a/c 2 000	Dr. Cash a/c 2 000 Cr. Sales a/c 2 000
ORIGINAL A sale to a customer on credit for $820 was recorded as $208	Dr. Debtor a/c 208 Cr. Sales a/c 208	Dr. Debtor a/c 820 Cr. Sales a/c 820	Dr. Debtor a/c 612 Cr. Sales a/c 612
PRINCIPLE The purchase of some office equipment for $1 180 cash had been debited to the office expenses account	Dr. Office Expenses a/c 1 180 Cr. Cash a/c 1 180	Dr. Office Equipment a/c 1 180 Cr. Cash a/c 1 180	Dr. Office Equipment a/c 1 180 Cr. Office Expenses a/c 1 180
COMMISSION $60 received by cheque from W. Augustus was recorded in S. Augustus' account	Dr. Bank a/c 60 Cr. S. Augustus a/c 60	Dr. Bank a/c 60 Cr. W. Augustus a/c 60	Dr. S. Augustus a/c 60 Cr. W. Augustus a/c 60

8.11 Correction of errors using suspense accounts

Errors	Balancing the ledger with the error	The correct journal entry should have been	The adjusting journal entry to be made
1. Posting the Subsidiary Books (a) A creditor for $85 was posted as $58	Dr. (Assumed correct) 85 Cr. Creditor a/c 58 Cr. Suspense a/c 27	Dr. (Assumed correct) 85 Cr. Creditor a/c 85	Dr. Suspense a/c 27 Cr. Creditor a/c 27
(b) The total of the Sales day book of $384 was posted as $483	Dr. (Assumed correct) 384 Dr. Suspense a/c 99 Cr. Sales a/c 483	Dr. (Assumed correct) 384 Cr. Sales a/c 384	Dr. Sales a/c 99 Cr. Suspense a/c 99
2. Recording in the Day Book and one Ledger Account (a) Sales Returns of $360 was recorded in the day book and the Sales Returns account only	Dr. Sales Returns a/c 360 Cr. Suspense a/c 360	Dr. Sales Returns a/c 360 Cr. Debtors a/c 360	Dr. Suspense a/c 360 Cr. Debtors a/c 360
(b) Discounts received $90 had been posted to the Purchase ledger but not to the Discounts received account	Dr. (Assumed correct) 90 Cr. Suspense a/c 90	Dr. (Assumed correct) 90 Cr. Discounts received 90	Dr. Suspense a/c 90 Cr. Discounts received 90
3. Recording two debits or two credits (a) A cheque for $124 received from X and Co. had been posted to the debit side of their account	Dr. X and Co. a/c 124 Dr. (Assumed correct) 124 Cr. Suspense a/c 248	Dr. (Assumed correct) 124 Cr. X and Co. a/c 124	Dr. Suspense a/c 248 Cr. X and Co. a/c 248
(b) Rent expense of $100 was recorded twice on the same side of the cash account	Dr. Suspense a/c 200 Cr. Cash a/c 100 Cr. Cash a/c 100	Dr. (Assumed correct) 100 Cr. Cash a/c 100	Dr. Cash a/c 100 Cr. Suspense a/c 200
4. Recording unequal debits and credits $800 cash withdrawn for private use was credited as $80	Dr. (Assumed correct) 800 Cr. Cash a/c 80 Cr. Suspense a/c 720	Dr. (Assumed correct) 800 Cr. Cash a/c 800	Dr. Suspense a/c 720 Cr. Cash a/c 720
5. Balancing an account wrongly (a) A credit balance of $30 in the Purchases ledger had been omitted from the list of balances extracted from the ledger. The total of the list had been included in the ledger	Dr. (Assumed correct) Cr. Creditor a/c Cr. Suspense a/c 30	Dr. (Assumed correct) Cr. Creditor a/c	Dr. Suspense a/c 30 Cr. Creditor a/c 30
(b) Cash a/c Sales 80 | Purchases 90 Sales 50 | Balance 30	Dr. Cash a/c 30 Dr. Suspense a/c 10 Cr. (Assumed correct)	Dr. Cash a/c (Dr. Balance) 40 Cr. (Assumed correct)	Dr. Cash a/c 10 Cr. Suspense a/c 10

6. Posting to the wrong columns in the Trial Balance			
Sales account of $10 was placed in the debit column of the trial balance	Cr. Suspense a/c 20	Sales in the credit column as $10	Dr. Suspense a/c 20
7. Wrong additions of the columns in the trial balance			
8. Complex Wrong Entries (a) Sales of $795 Cash was correctly recorded in the Cash book and was debited to the Sales Return account as $957	Dr. Cash a/c 795 Dr. Sales Returns a/c 957 Cr. Suspense a/c 1 752	Dr. Cash a/c 795 Cr. Sales a/c 795	Cancel the entry (error) Dr. Suspense a/c 1 752 Cr. Cash a/c 795 Cr. Sales Returns a/c 957 Record the correct entry Dr. Cash a/c 795 Cr. Sales a/c 795
(b) Same error as (a)	Dr. Cash a/c 795 Cr. Sales Returns a/c 957	Dr. Cash a/c 795 Cr. Sales a/c 795	Cancel the error Dr.Sales Returns a/c 957 Dr. Cash a/c 795 Record the correct entry Dr. Cash a/c 795 Cr. Sales a/c 795

FOR CONTROL ACCOUNTS:	Affects	
	Control Accounts	Individual Accounts
Omission from the day book	Yes	Yes
Wrong entry in the day book	Yes	Yes
Wrong posting of individual entry from day book	No	Yes
Wrong posting of the total from the day book	Yes	No

Example

Kadriye extracted a trial balance from her ledgers on 31 December 2003. The trial balance totals were $23 884 (debit) and $24 856 (credit). She placed the difference in a Suspense account so that she could prepare a draft Profit and Loss Account for the year ended 31 December 2003, and a Balance Sheet at that date.

Kadriye then found the following errors.

1. The debit side of the Telephone account had been overstated by $200.

2. An invoice sent to Singh for $240 had been completely omitted from the books.

3. A cheque for $124 received from X and Co. had been posted to the debit of their account.

4. The purchase of some office equipment for $1180 had been debited to Office Expenses account.

5. Discounts received, $90, had been posted to the purchase ledger but not to the Discounts Received account.

6. Rent paid, $800, had been credited to Rent Receivable account.

7. A refund of an insurance premium, $60, had been recorded in the cash book but no other entry had been made.

8. A purchase of office stationery, $220, had been debited to Purchases account in error.

9. A credit balance of $30 in the purchase ledger had been omitted from the list of balances extracted from the ledger. The total of the list had been included in the trial balance.

10. Goods returned to Speedsel had been credited to Speedsel's account and debited to Purchases Returns account. The goods had cost $400.

Required

(a) Prepare journal entries to correct errors 1 to 10. (Narratives are required.)

(b) Prepare the Suspense account showing the opening balance and the correcting entries.

The draft Profit and Loss Account showed a net profit for the year ended 31 December 2003 of $8400 and the Balance Sheet at that date showed working capital (current assets less current liabilities) of $1250.

Required

(c) Calculate the revised net profit for the year ended 31 December 2003.
(d) Calculate the revised working capital at 31 December 2003.

Answer

(a)

Journal entries

	$	$
1. *Note. The debit side of the Telephone account is overstated by $200. Reduce this by crediting the account and debiting the Suspense account with $200*		
Suspense account	200	
Telephone account		200
Correction of the overcast of $200 of the Telephone account.		
2. *Note. This transaction has been omitted from the books entirely. It has not affected the trial balance and the Suspense account is not involved..*		
Singh	240	
Sales		240
Recording invoice for $240 sent to Singh but omitted from books.		
3. *Note. $124 has been posted to the wrong side of X and Co's account. This is corrected by crediting their account with double that amount.*		
Suspense account	248	
X and Co. account		248
Correction of $124 received from X and Co. debited to their account in error.		
4. *Note. This is an error of principle; do not adjust through the Suspense account.*		
Office Equipment (asset) account	1180	
Office Expenses account		1180
Purchase of office equipment treated as revenue expense in error.		
5. *Note. This is not an error of complete omission; correct through the Suspense account.*		
Suspense account	90	
Discounts Received account		90
Discounts received, $90, omitted from Discounts Received Account.		
6. *Note. Rent Receivable account must be debited to cancel error; Rent Payable must be debited to record payment correctly. Note separate debit entries must be made.*		
Rent Receivable account	800	
Rent Payable account	800	
Suspense account		1600
Correction of rent paid incorrectly treated as rent received.		

7. *Note. This refund has not been completely omitted from the books. Adjust through the Suspense account.*

Suspense account	60	
Insurance account		60

Refund of insurance premium omitted from the Insurance account.

8. *Note. This is an error of commission. Do not adjust through the Suspense account.*

	$	$
Office Stationery account	220	
Purchases account		220

Purchase of office stationery treated as stock for re-sale in error.

9. *Note. This not a double-entry error but it has affected the trial balance. The list of balances must be corrected and a one-sided entry in the Suspense account is required*

Suspense account	30	

10. *Note. This is a complete reversal of entries. The correcting entry is twice the original amount and the Suspense account is not involved.*

Speedsel Ltd	800	
Purchases Returns account		800

Goods returned to Speedsel Ltd, $400, credited to their

account and debited to Purchases Returns account in error.

(b)

Suspense account

	$		$
Difference on trial balance	972	Rent receivable	800*
Telephone	200	Rent payable	800*
X and Co.	248		
Discounts received	90		
Insurance	60		
Correction of trade creditors	30		
	1600		1600

*These two entries should be shown separately as the double entry is completed in different accounts.

Note. The Suspense account is opened with the difference on the trial balance and then posted from the journal entries in (a).

(c)

Calculation of corrected net profit for the year ended 31 December

	Decrease (Dr)	Increase (Cr)	
	$	$	$
Net profit per draft Profit and Loss Account			8400
(1) Decrease in telephone expense		200	
(2) Increase in sales		240	
(4) Decrease in office expenses		1180	
(5) Increase in discounts received		90	
(6) Reduction in rent receivable	800		
Increase in rent payable	800		
(7) Reduction in insurance premium		60	
(8) No effect on net profit			
(10) Increase in purchases returns		800	
	1600	2570	
		(1600)	970
Revised net profit			9370

Note. Set the calculation out as shown above. Untidy, 'straggly' calculations do not commend themselves to examiners. Debit entries to nominal accounts in the journal decrease profit, and credit entries to nominal accounts increase profit.

(d)

Calculation of working capital at 31 December			
	Increase (Dr)	Decrease (Cr)	
	$	$	$
Working capital per draft Balance Sheet			1250
(2) Singh invoice omitted	240		
(3) X and Co. $124 cheque misposted		248	
(9) Credit balance omitted		30	
(10) Goods returned to Speedsel	800	—	
	1040	278	
	(278)		762
Revised working capital			2012

Note. The layout of the answer given above is a good one and should be followed whenever possible. Adjust working capital by journal postings to personal accounts and by personal accounts omitted from the trial balance.

8.12 Exercises

Exercise

When Jayesh extracted a trial balance from his books at 31 December 2003 he found that it did not balance. He entered the difference in a Suspense account and then prepared a draft Profit and Loss Account which showed a net profit of $2500. Jayesh later found the following errors.

1. The balance of opening stock $8500 had been entered in the trial balance as $5800.
2. The stock at 31 December 2003 had been understated by $2000.
3. Repairs to a machine, $3500, had been posted to Machinery at Cost account as $5300.
4. An invoice in the sum of $800 for the sale of goods to Bane had been posted to Bane's account but had not been entered in the sales journal.
5. A credit balance of $63 in the sales ledger had been extracted as a debit balance. Jayesh does not maintain Control accounts.

Required
(a) Prepare the journal entries to correct the errors. (Narratives are *not* required.)
(b) Prepare the Suspense account showing the trial balance difference and the correcting entries.

Jayesh's draft Balance Sheet at 31 December 2003 showed working capital of $3200.

Required
(c) Calculate Jayesh's corrected working capital at 31 December 2003.

9 Accounting for non-current or long-lived assets

Objectives
- discuss the methods of depreciation
- identify types of non-current or fixed assets
- determine the value of tangible and intangible assets
- distinguish between short-term and long-term investments
- prepare journal entries to record acquisition, interest revenue and sale of investments
- state how investments are valued and reported on final statements

9.1 What is depreciation?

Depreciation is the part of the cost of a fixed asset that is consumed during the period it is used by a business. For example, a motor car purchased for $10 000 may be worth only $8000 one year later because it is not as good as new after a year's use. The asset has suffered depreciation of $(10 000 – 8000) = $2000.

Assets may depreciate for a number of reasons.

- **Wear and tear:** assets become worn out through use.
- **Obsolescence:** assets have to be replaced because new, more efficient technology has been developed; or machines which were acquired for the production of particular goods are of no further use because the goods are no longer produced.
- **Passage of time:** an asset acquired for a limited period of time, such as a lease of premises for a given number of years, loses value as time passes. Accountants refer to this as **effluxion of time** and speak of **amortizing** rather than 'depreciating' these assets.
- **Using up, or exhaustion:** mines, quarries and oil wells depreciate as the minerals etc. are extracted from them.

9.2 How does depreciation of fixed assets affect accounts?

The accounting treatment of capital expenditure, which is expenditure on fixed assets, is different from the treatment of revenue expenditure. Revenue expenditure is debited to the Profit and Loss Account as it is incurred. Capital expenditure, on the other hand, is on assets that are intended for use in a business for more than one year, usually for many years. It would be wrong to debit the whole of the cost of a fixed asset to the Profit and Loss Account in the year it was acquired; it would be against the matching principle. Nevertheless, the cost of *using* fixed assets to earn revenue must be charged in the Profit and Loss Account; that cost is the depreciation suffered in the accounting period.

9.3 How to account for depreciation

There are several methods used to calculate depreciation. The three most common are:

- straight line
- reducing balance or diminishing return
- units of production

Straight-line depreciation

With this method the total amount of depreciation that an asset will suffer is estimated as the difference between what it cost and the estimated amount that will be received when it is sold or scrapped at the end of its useful life. The total depreciation is then spread evenly over the number of years of its expected life.

Calculation: (cost – estimated proceeds on disposal) ÷ estimated useful life in years.

Example 1

A machine cost $20 000. It is expected to have a useful life of five years at the end of which time it is expected to be sold for $5000 (its **residual value**). The total depreciation over five years is $(20 000 – $5000) = $15 000. The annual depreciation is $15 000 ÷ 5 = $3000.

Ledger entries for depreciation Debit the Profit and Loss Account and credit a Provision for Depreciation account with the annual depreciation each year.

Disposal of non current assets

When the asset no longer serves the business needs, the firm has the option to dispose of the asset. To account for the disposal of the asset, the cost of the asset must be removed to the Disposal account as well as the accumulated depreciation to date. The journal entries to effect such a transaction will be: Dr. Disposal account, Cr. Asset account; Dr. Accumulated depreciation account, Cr. Disposal account.

9.4 Types of non-current or fixed assets

Unlike current assets, fixed or non-current assets or long lived assets are used in the operations of the business for periods over one year. Their use contributes to the income earning capacity of the firm and therefore much attention is paid to the accounting for the cost of non-current assets.

Non-current or fixed assets can be divided into two groups: tangible assets and intangible assets.

1. Tangible assets such as:
   - Plant
   - Equipment and machinery
   - Land and land improvements
   - Building
   - Natural resources

2. Intangible assets – those without physical substance, such as:
   - Patents
   - Trademarks
   - Copyrights
   - Franchise
   - Brand name
   - Goodwill

9.5 How to value tangible assets

Both categories of non-current assets are recorded on the books. The cost of an asset is the sum of all the costs incurred to bring the asset to its intended location. This may include not only the purchase price, but also legal fees, taxes, commissions and installation costs. Since specific costs differ for the various categories of tangible assets it is worth looking at major groups individually.

Land

The cost of land includes the purchase price, survey fees, legal fees and any property taxes in arrears as well as the cost of clearing the land. The acquisition cost does not however include the cost for fencing, paving or installation of lights. This is known as land improvements and is treated as a separate group of long-lived assets.

Illustration 1

Jo Singh recently purchased 20 acres of land from the Sugar Mill for a new warehouse site. He pays $300 000 cash as well as $10 000 for real estate commission and a further $8000 for land taxes in arrears. Singh also pays $5000 for the demolition and removal of an old building and $26 000 to grade and pave the land, $10 000 was the cost of the surveyor. What is the cost of the land?

	$	$
Purchase		300 000
Add related costs:		
Real estate	10 000	
Taxes	8 000	
Demolition	5 000	
Surveyor	10 000	33 000
Total cost of the land		333 000

The journal entry therefore to record the above transactions would be:

	Debit	Credit
Land	333 000	
Bank		333 000
To record the purchase of land from Sugar Mill		

Machinery and equipment

The cost of machinery and equipment includes not only its purchase price, but also, transportation, insurance, sales tax, installation costs and the cost of test runs. Post installation costs such as insurance and maintenance are charged to the Profit and Loss account as expenses.

Lump-sum basket purchases

Businesses can purchase at any one time several assets for a lump-sum amount, for example, a business can purchase a parcel of land, together with a building and machinery. This is known as a basket transaction. In order to identify the individual cost of each asset, the total cost of the 'basket' must be divided according to the **fair market value of each individual asset**.

Illustration 2

Zanadu Limited purchases land, building and office equipment from a large holding company. The lump-sum charge purchase price was $3800 000. Market appraisal indicates that the land's fair market value is $1300 000 and that the building and office equipment's market value is $1700 000. The table below shows how the cost of each asset is determined using the fair market values.

Asset	Market value	% of total market value	Cost of each asset based on the %
Land	$1300 000	43.3%	$ 1645 400
Building and office equipment	$ 1700 000	56.7%	$ 2154 600

The journal entry for recording this transaction would be:

	Debit	Credit
Land	1645 400	
Building and office equipment	2154 600	
Bank		3 800 000

9.6 Accounting for intangible assets

Intangibles are recorded at cost on acquisition. This cost is then spread over the useful life by the process of amortization. This is the reduction of a lump-sum amount by a systematic process. Each year the amortized expense is debited in the income statement. Amortization is often computed using the straight line basis.

- Patents – Exclusive rights given to the holder to produce and sell an invention.
- Trademarks – A distinctive identification or mark of a product or service.
- Copyrights – Exclusive rights to reproduce and sell a book, music, film or other works of art.
- Franchise – Privileges granted by a private business to sell a product or service with specific conditions.
- Goodwill – The excess of the purchase price of a business over its separable net assets.

9.7 Investments

Investments by a business represent the purchase of shares or bonds in other entities for the purpose of earning income or capital appreciation. Firms make investments when they find that there is surplus cash in the business or there is a need to generate additional income. Some firms use investment to benefit from economies of scale.

Investments are categorized depending on the length of time the corporation is willing to hold on to the security. Securities that are highly liquid and easily converted into cash are categorized as short-term investments. Treasury bills, certificate of deposits and money market certificates are all examples of short-term investments. Long-term investments are those which are not expected to be converted into cash within one year. Bonds, mortgages and long-term loans are all examples of long-term investments.

Accounting for Investments

The way on which a corporation accounts for investments depends on a number of factors:
- The length of the investments
- Whether it is a stock or debt investment
- The percentage of the ownership, if it is a stock investment.

When accounting for investments, entries are required to record:
1. Acquisition
2. Interest revenue
3. Sale.

Investments are recorded at acquisition cost including all expenditures necessary to acquire these investments. However, when recording long-term investments, additional entries are required if the cost of the bonds differ from the face value.

Accounting entries for debt investments:

(a) Recording the acquisition of bonds

    DR. Debt investments

        CR. Cash

(b) Recording interest

    DR. Cash

        CR. Interest revenue

(c) Recording sale

    DR. Cash

        CR. Debt investments

           CR. Gain on sale of debt investments

Accounting for equity investments:

(a) Recording acquisition

    DR. Stock investments

        CR. Cash

(b) Recording dividends

    DR. Cash

        CR. Dividend revenue

(c) Recording sale of equity

    DR. Cash

        CR. Stock investment

9.8 Reporting investments on final statements

Short-term investments are listed immediately below cash in the current assets section on the Balance Sheet. They are reported at fair value.

Long-term investments are generally reported in a separate section of the Balance Sheet immediately below current assets. They are also reported at fair value.

Interest revenue is reported under 'other revenues and gains' in the Income Statement. Any interest accruing is reported as a current asset.

Since the value of debt and stock investments may fluctuate greatly during the time investments are held investments may be valued at the Balance Sheet date at cost, at fair value (market value) or at the lower of cost or market value.

The loss on sale of the investment is reported under 'other expenses and losses' in the Income Statement while a gain on sale is shown under 'Other revenues and gains'.

9.9 Question 1

1 Journalize the following transactions and explain how dividend and the gain (loss) on sale should be reported in the income statement.

The PD Company had the following transactions pertaining to stock investments:

March 1	Purchased 600 shares of TCL common stocks (2%) for $7000 cash plus a brokerage fees of $200
August 1	Received cash dividends of $1 per share on the TCL common stock
October 1	Sold 300 shares of TCL common stock for $4000 less brokerage fee $100
December 1	Received cash dividends of $1 per share on TCL common stock.

2 On January 1, the Kristi Company purchased as a temporary investment a $1000 12% bond for $1050. The bond pays interest on January 1 and July 1. The bond is sold on September 1 for $1100 plus accrued interest. Interest has not been accrued since the last interest payment date.

Prepare the journal entry to record the purchase of the bond as a temporary investment.

Prepare the journal entry to record the receipt of interest on July 1.

Prepare the journal entry to record the sale of the bond on September 1.

Module Two
Preparation of Financial Statements

10 Forms of business organizations

Objectives
- identify the various forms of business organizations
- describe the various forms of business organizations
- distinguish among private, public, state-owned and statutory corporations
- assess critically the advantages and disadvantages of the various forms of business organizations

10.1 Characteristics of the various forms of business organizations

Some of the common types of business organizations in which entrepreneurial skills are exhibited are sole traders, co-operatives, partnerships and corporations. Non-commercial entities in contributing to the welfare of citizens also provide a forum for managers to practice their skills on a voluntary basis.

	Sole traders	Co-operatives	Partnerships	Non-governmental organizations	Corporations
Membership	One	Unlimited shareholders	Two to twenty		Indefinite number of stock holders
Financing	By the proprietor	Investment by the membership	Partners' capital	No share capital	By stockholders
Legal status	Not a separate legal entity	Separate legal entity	Not a separate legal entity	Acts under its own name	Separate legal entity
Accounting treatment	Separate economic entity	Separate economic entity	Separate economic entity	Separate economic entity	Separate economic entity
Ownership	The proprietor	Members	Partners	Incorporated by an Act of Parliament	Stockholders or shareholders
Motive	Profit	Service and self-help	Profit	Service to improve the quality of life	Profit
Risk to owner	Unlimited liability	Limited liability	Unlimited liability	Limited by guarantee	Limited liability

Transfer of ownership	Sale by the owner establishes a new business	Cannot be transferred	New partnership required when the agreement changes	Cannot be transferred	Changes with sale of stock
Life span	Ends at the wishes, death or incapacity of the owner	Indefinite	Ends with a change in agreement – admission, retirement, death.	Indefinite	Indefinite or continuous
Raising additional capital	Restricted by owner's efforts	Restricted by the co-operative's ability to attract new members	Limited to the capabilities of the partners	Government grants and public support	Unlimited capacity to raise funds
Management	Strictly by the owner	Board of directors advised by the membership	By the partners except the sleeping partner (dormant or autonomous)	Board of directors independent of government	An elected Board of Directors (shareholders don't manage)
Regulations	Subject to the rules governing small business	Subject to the rules on co-operatives	Governed by the Partnership Act	Governed by the statutes	Restrictions on stock issue, retirement and reporting
Profit sharing	Subject to owner's discretion	Receives dividends and patronage refund	Shared according to the agreement	Used to further the organization's objectives	Subject to double taxation

10.2 Distinguish among the different types of corporations

The general feature of a corporation is a group of persons pooling their resources for the purpose of undertaking trade. They usually provide the financing and automatically become the owners, called shareholders. By extension, the profits or the losses are shared among them or utilized by the state where the corporation is state-owned.

The following table shows the various types of corporations and the features that distinguish one type from the other.

	Private limited	Public limited	State-owned	Statutory
Formation	Individuals and families	Shares sold to the public on the Stock Exchange	Acquired by the state	Act of Parliament
Legal status	Separate identity	Separate entity	Operates under its own name	Uses its own name
Ownership	Individuals and groups	All persons who buy shares in it	All nationals of that state	The government on behalf of all nationals
Management	Shareholders/Board of directors	Board of directors for general policies; Managing Director for operations (daily)	Board appointed by the State	Minister with overall responsibilities

Financing	Shareholders	Shareholders	Usually self-sustaining and government's help	Government guaranteed funding
Product	Anything that is legal	Goods and services that are legal	Vital service natural resource product	Utilities
Profit sharing	Utilized at owner's discretion	Given as dividends to shareholders	Benefits and non-benefits passed on to the population	Provides low cost service to the population
Employment	Hire and retrench as necessary	Hires the best labour available	Protects jobs	Protects jobs
Protocol	Quick decision-making	Formal procedures for decision-making	Decision made by the Board of directors	Meet red-tape involving parliament and public utilities commission
Accountability	To shareholders periodically	To shareholders annually	Periodically to the Board of directors and the specific ministry	To parliament, usually not on time
Efficiency	Strict management	Usually achievement-oriented to please shareholders	Political interference and lax management	Complacent

10.3 Advantages and disadvantages of the various forms of businesses

All types of organizations make their contributions to the society and economy they are in. Each will have features that can make it advantageous or disadvantageous. The following table identifies the strengths and weaknesses of each organization whereby one can critically assess each.

TYPES	ADVANTAGES	DISADVANTAGES
SOLE TRADER	• Easy and inexpensive to start • Pays only personal income taxes • Efficient with quick decision-making • Enjoys all the profits • Able to supervise all operations • Can access government small business loans easily • Unlimited growth potential • Owner-manager operated • Personal employer-employee relationship	• Usually closes down when the owner dies • Market size limited • Ideas for expansion and variety are limited • Unlimited liability • Long working hours • Raising capital from most sources is difficult
CO-OPERATIVES	• Democratic management • Emphasizes serving members • Members provide the market • Provides employment for members	• Management is voluntary and may be poor • Can run into financial difficulties with bad debts • Expansion dependent on membership • Hardly attracts professionals • Clash of interest may arise when members are also employees

PARTNERSHIP	• Very little legal formalities • Pays only personal income tax • Capital and skills accumulation easier • Professionals in management hired • Specialization results in shared workload • Can easily be dissolved • Has potential to grow larger • Owner-manager operated • Flexibility in operations	• Disagreements can slow down decision making • Liability is unlimited • A partner's decision is binding on the organization • Not easy to transfer ownership • Existence affected with changes in ownership
NON-GOVERNMENTAL (NGO) AND NOT-FOR-PROFIT	• May not have profit as the priority • Concerned with long term social improvement • Only those interested in the goals of the organization would join it • Usually self-reliant • Operates within the constitution of the land • Protects itself against persons operating it for personal gains • Usually staffed by persons who are well off financially	• Service may not be of a high standard as effort is voluntary • Goals are distant and achievement is difficult to measure • People who join the organization are not owners of the organization • Funding is dependent on the generosity of individuals and organizations • Very little reporting to measure performance • Has difficulty attracting membership • Membership dominated by retirees and elders
CORPORATIONS	• Easier capital generation • Professional managers hired • Easy ownership transfer • Separate ownership transfer • Changes in ownership does not affect continuity • Enjoys economies of scale • Risks shared • Legal regulations to protect shareholders interest • All persons can become shareholders	• Restricted by government regulations • Double taxation • Separation of ownership and control • Profits to be distributed as dividends • Growth is slow • Management sometimes limited to family members • When small, there is little involvement in research and development • Shareholders not involved in management • Powerful groups can emerge and dominate the company • Over-expansion can result in inefficiency • Worker alienation • Management becomes complex and bureaucratic • Size may encourage fraudulent activities

10.4 Questions

1 (a) Define three common forms of business organization in your country.

(b) Give five features of any one mentioned in part (a).

(c) Briefly explain three disadvantages of the business organization mentioned in part (b).

2 (a) Briefly describe the following types of organizations:

(i) Non-governmental (NGO) and not-for-profit organizations

(ii) Corporations

(iii) Co-operatives

(b) State two disadvantages which non-governmental (NGO) and not-for-profit organizations have over a co-operative business.

3 Make a survey of all the businesses identified in this chapter in your locality. Identify the characteristics of each. Present the information collected and critically assess the advantages and disadvantages of each type.

11 Incomplete records

Objectives
- calculate profit or loss from statements of affairs
- prepare final accounts from incomplete records
- calculate margin and mark-up
- calculate cost of stock lost by fire or theft

11.1 What are incomplete records?

The term **incomplete records** describes any method of recording transactions that is not based on the double-entry model. Often, only a cash book, or only records of accounts receivable and accounts payable, are kept, so that only one aspect of each transaction is recorded. This is **single-entry bookkeeping**. Incomplete records also describes situations where the only records kept may be invoices for purchases, copies of sales invoices, cheque counterfoils and bank statements. Occasionally, incomplete records result from some event, e.g. fire or theft, which causes partial loss of records. In all these cases, Income Statement Accounts and Balance Sheets cannot be prepared in the normal way.

11.2 How to calculate profit or loss from statements of affairs

When records of transactions are insufficient to enable a Trading and Income Statement Account to be prepared, the profit or loss of a business for a given period may be calculated if the assets and liabilities of the business at both the start and end of the period are known. The method is based upon two principles:

1. the accounting equation, capital = assets – liabilities

2. profit increases capital; losses reduce capital.

The difference between the opening and closing capitals, after making adjustments for new capital introduced and the owner's drawings in the period, will reveal the profit or loss. Capital is calculated by listing the assets and liabilities in a **statement of affairs**.

Example

Fatima is a hair stylist who has been in business for some time. She has never kept records of her takings and payments. She wishes to know how much profit or loss she has made in the year ended 31 December 2003. Her assets and liabilities at 1 January and 31 December 2003 were as follows.

	1 January 2003	31 December 2003
	$	$
Equipment	800	1000
Inventory of hair styling sundries	70	45
Amounts owing from clients	50	70
Rent paid in advance	100	120
Balance at bank	150	160
Creditors for supplies	25	30
Electricity owing	40	50

Fatima has drawn $100 per week from the business for personal expenses.

Required

Calculate Fatima's profit for the year ended 31 December 2003.

Answer

	Statements of affairs at	
	1 January 2003	31 December 2003
	$	$
Equipment	800	1000
Inventory of hair styling sundries	70	45
Amounts owing from clients	50	70
Rent paid in advance	100	120
Balance at bank	150	160
	1170	1395
Less		
Creditors for supplies	25	30
Electricity owing	40 65	50 80
Net assets (= capital)	1105	1315
Add drawings in year to 31 December 2003		
(52 × $100)		5200*
		6515
Deduct capital at beginning of year		1105
Profit for the year ended 31 December 2003		5410

* Drawings have been added back as the capital at 31 December 2003 would have been greater if Fatima had not taken this money out of the business.

Note. When an asset is valued at more or less than cost, it should be included in a statement of affairs at valuation.

Exercise 1

Lian has run a business repairing motor vehicles for some years but has not kept proper accounting records. However, the following information is available.

	at 1 January 2003	at 31 December 2003
	$	$
Premises at cost	4000	4000
Motor van at cost	5000	5000
Motor car at cost	—	3000
Plant and equipment	1100	1300
Inventory of parts	400	200
Accounts Receivable for work done	700	800
Balance at bank	1300	900
Owing to suppliers for parts	170	340

The premises were bought some years ago and were valued at $9000 at 31 December 2003. At the same date, the motor van was valued at $4000. The motor car was Lian's own car, which he brought into the business at its original cost. Lian's weekly drawings were $120.

Required

Calculate Lian's profit or loss for the year ended 31 December 2003.

11.3 How to prepare an Income Statement Account and Balance Sheet from incomplete records

Most businesses keep records of receipts and payments. The records may consist of bank paying-in-book counterfoils, cheque-book counterfoils and bank statements in addition to suppliers' invoices and copies of sales invoices. From these records it may be possible to prepare an Income Statement Account and Balance Sheet. The steps are as follows.

Step 1 Prepare an opening statement of affairs. (This calculates opening capital.)

Step 2 Prepare a Receipts and Payments account.

Step 3 Prepare Control accounts for Accounts Receivable and Accounts Payable, if necessary, to calculate sales and purchases. These will be the amounts required to make the Control accounts balance.

Step 4 Adjust the receipts and payments for accruals and prepayments at beginning and end of the period.

Step 5 Calculate provisions for doubtful debts, depreciation and any other matters not mentioned above.

Step 6 Prepare the Income Statement Account and Balance Sheet from the information now available.

Example

The only records that Aasim has kept for his business are bank paying-in-book counterfoils, cheque-book counterfoils and records of Accounts Receivable and Accounts Payable. From these it is possible to summarize his transactions with the bank in the year ended 31 December 2003 as follows.

Takings paid into the bank: $8000.

Cheques drawn: payments to suppliers $2430; rent $600; electricity $320; postage and stationery $80; purchase of shop fittings $480; cheques drawn for personal expenses $2700.

Aasim banked all his takings after paying the following in cash: Accounts Payable for supplies $400 and sundry expenses $115.

Aasim estimated his assets and liabilities at 1 January 2003 to be: shop fittings $1600; Inventory $1960; Accounts Receivable $240; rent prepaid $80; bank balance $1500; cash in hand $50; Accounts Payable for goods $420; electricity owing $130.

At 31 December 2003 Aasim listed his assets and liabilities as follows: shop fittings $1800; Inventory $1520;

Accounts Receivable $380; rent prepaid $50; bank balance $2640; cash in hand $50; Accounts Payable for goods $390; electricity owing $225.

Required

Prepare Aasim's Income Statement Account for the year ended 31 December 2003 and his Balance Sheet at that date.

Answer

Step 1 Opening statement of affairs

	$	$
Assets		
Shop fittings		1600
Inventory		1960
Accounts Receivable		240
Rent prepaid		80
Bank		1500
Cash in hand		50
		5430
Less Liabilities		
Accounts Payable for goods	420	
Electricity owing	130	550
Capital at 1 January		4880

Step 2 Receipts and Payments account. This includes only those amounts actually received and spent. It is a cash book summary with columns for cash and bank.

	Cash $	Bank $		Cash $	Bank $
Jan 1 Balance b/f	50	1500	Trade accounts payable	400	2430
Takings			Rent		600
(8000 + 400 + 115)	8515		Electricity		320
Cash ¢		8000	Postage and stationery		80
			Shop fittings		480
			Sundry expenses	115	
			Drawings		
			(2700 + 250†)		2950
			Bank ¢	8000	
			Balance c/f	50	2640
	8565	9500		8565	9500

† $250 is money not accounted for and is treated as Aasim's drawings.

Step 3 Accounts Receivable and Accounts Payable Control accounts

Accounts Receivable Control				Accounts Payable Control			
	$		$		$		$
Jan 1 Balance b/f	240	Dec 31 Takings[1]	8515	Dec 31 Bank and cash[2]	2830	Jan 1 Balance b/f	420
Dec 31 Sales[3]	8655	Balance c/f	380	Balance c/f	390	Dec31 Purchases[3]	2800
	8895		8895		3220		3220

1 From Receipts and Payments account.

2 From Receipts and Payments account.

3 Balancing figures.

Step 4 Adjust for prepayment and accruals.

	$		$
Rent paid	600	Electricity paid	320
Add prepaid at 1 Jan	80	Less owing at 1 Jan	(130)
Deduct prepaid at 31 Dec	(50)	Add owing at 31 Dec	225
Rent payable for the year	630	Electricity payable for the year	415

Step 5 Calculate depreciation of shop fittings.

	$
Shop fittings at valuation at 1 Jan	1600
Add fittings purchased in year	480
	2080
Shop fittings at valuation at 31 Dec	1800
Depreciation for the year	280

Step 6

Aasim
Trading and Income Statement Account for the year ended 31 December 2003

	$	$
Sales		8655
Less cost of sales		
Inventory at 1 January	1960	
Purchases	2800	
	4760	
Less stock at 31 December	1520	3240
Gross profit		5415
Less		
Rent	630	
Electricity	415	
Postage and stationery	80	
Sundry expenses	115	
Depreciation of shop fittings	280	1520
Net profit		3895

Balance Sheet at 31 December 2003

	$	$	$
Fixed assets: Shop fittings			1800
Current assets			
Inventory		1520	
Trade accounts receivable		380	
Rent prepaid		50	
Bank		2640	
Cash		50	
		4640	
Current liabilities			
Trade accounts payable	390		
Electricity owing	225	615	4025
			5825
Capital at 1 Jan			4880
Profit for the year			3895
			8775
Less Drawings			2950
			5825

11.4 Margin and mark-up

Ability to calculate margin and mark-up may be necessary to solve some incomplete record problems. **Margin** is gross profit expressed as a percentage or fraction of selling price.

Example

	$
Cost price of goods	100
Profit	25
Selling price	125

The margin is profit/selling price $\times$ 100 = 25/125 $\times$ 100 = 20% = 1/5.

Mark-up is gross profit expressed as a percentage or fraction of cost of sales.

In the above example, mark-up is profit/cost price of goods $\times$ 100 = 25/100 $\times$ 100 = 25% = 1/4.

There is a close relationship between margin and mark-up. In the above examples:

margin = 1/5 (or 1/(4 + 1)); mark-up = 1/4 or (1/(5–1)).

From this, a general rule will be observed:

When margin is a/b, mark-up is a/(b–a) and, when mark-up is a/b, margin is a/(b+a).

Examples

If margin is 1/3, mark-up is 1/(3–1) = 1/2; if mark-up is 1/6, margin is 1/(6+1)= 1/7.

If margin is 2/5, mark-up is 2/(5–2) = 2/3; if mark-up is 2/5, margin is 2/(5+2) = 2/7.

Conversion of percentages to fractions Enter the *rate* percentage as the numerator of the fraction and 100 as the denominator, and reduce to a common fraction, for example 25% = 25/100 = 1/4.

Conversion of fraction to a percentage Multiply the numerator of the fraction by 100, cancel top and bottom of the fraction and add 'per cent' or % sign, for example 2/5 = 200/5 = 40%.

Most useful examples to remember 12.5% = 1/8; 20% = 1/5; 25% = 1/4; 33.3% = 1/3; 40% = 2/5; 50% = 1/2; 66.7% = 2/3; 75% = 3/4; 80% = 4/5.

Examples

1 Cost of sales: $3000. Margin is 25%. Calculate the sales revenue.

> *Answer* Margin is 1/4, mark-up is 1/3, i.e. $3000 × 1/3 = $1000.
>
> Therefore sales revenue = $(3000 + 1000) = $4000.

2 Sales revenue: $7000. Mark-up is 40%. Calculate the gross profit.

> *Answer* Mark-up is 2/5; margin is 2/7.
>
> Therefore gross profit = 2/7 × $7000 = $2000.

3 Maheen provides the following information for the year ended 31 December 2003.

	$
Inventory at 1 January 2003	9 000
Inventory at 31 December 2003	11 000
Sales in the year ended 31 December 2003	84 000

Maheen sells her goods at a mark-up of 33.3%.

Prepare Maheen's Trading Account for the year ended 31 December 2003 in as much detail as possible.

		Answer	This is a typical example of a problem that is solved by working backwards.

Maheen: Trading account for the year ended 31 December 2003

		$	$
	Sales *(given)*		84 000
	Less		
	Inventory at 1 January *(given)*	9 000	
Step 4	Purchases (balancing figure 3)	65 000	
Step 3	(balancing figure 2)	74 000	
	Inventory at 31 December *(given)*	11 000	
Step 2	Cost of sales (balancing figure 1)		63 000
Step 1	Gross profit 1/4 × $84 000		21 000

Exercise 2

Ammar provides the following information for the year ended 30 June 2004.

	$
Opening inventory	4 000
Closing inventory	7 000
Cost of goods sold	28 000

Ammar's margin on all sales is 20%.

Required

Prepare Ammar's Trading account for the year ended 30 June 2004 in as much detail as possible.

11.5 Stock lost in fire or by theft

The methods used for preparing accounts from incomplete records are also used to calculate the value of stock lost in a fire or by theft when detailed stock records have not been kept, or have been destroyed by fire.

Solve this type of problem by preparing a 'pro forma' Trading account. (It is described as 'pro forma' because it is not prepared like a normal Trading account by transferring balances from ledger accounts.)

Example

Shahmir's warehouse was burgled on 10 April 2004. The thieves stole most of the stock but left goods worth $1250. Shahmir supplies the following information.

Extracts from Shahmir's Balance Sheet at 31 December 2003:

	$
Inventory	30 000
Accounts Receivable	40 000
Accounts Payable	20 000

Extracts from cash book, 31 December 2003 to 10 April 2004:

	$
Receipts from accounts receivable	176 000
Payments to suppliers	120 000

Other information:

	$
Accounts Receivable at 10 April 2004	24 000
Accounts Payable at 10 April 2004	26 000

Shahmir sells his goods at a mark-up of 25%.

Required

Calculate of the cost of the stolen goods.

Answer

Shahmir
Proforma Trading Account for the period
1 January to 10 April

	$	$
Sales (see working 1 below)		160 000
Cost of sales: Inventory at 1 January 2004	30 000	
Purchases (see working 2 below)	126 000	
	156 000	
Inventory at 10 April 2004		
(balancing figure)	28 000	128 000
Gross profit (mark-up is 25% so margin is 20%; $160 000 × 20%)		32 000

Cost of Inventory stolen: $(28 000 − 1250) = $26 750

Working 1   Accounts Receivable Total account

		$			$
1 January Accounts Receivable	b/f	40 000	10 April Cash	176 000
10 April Sales (balancing figure)		160 000	A/c Rec o/s	24 000
		200 000		200 000

Working 2   Accounts Payable Total account

	$			$
10 April Cash	120 000	1 January Accounts Payable b/f	20 000
A/c Payable c/d	26 000	10 April Purchases (balancing figure)	126 000
	146 000		146 000

Exercise 3

Neha's warehouse was damaged by fire on 5 November 2003 and most of the inventory was destroyed. The inventory that was salvaged was valued at $12 000.

Neha has provided the following information to enable the cost of the inventory lost to be calculated.

Extracts from Balance Sheet at 30 June 2003:

	$
Inventory	47 000
Accounts Receivable	16 000
Accounts Payable	23 000

Further information for the period 30 June 2003 to 5 November 2003:

	$
Receipts from accounts receivable	122 000
Cash sales	17 000
Payments to suppliers	138 000
At 5 November: accounts receivable	37 000
accounts payable	28 000

Neha's mark-up on goods sold is 33.3%.

Required

Calculate the cost of the Inventory lost in Neha's fire.

11.6 Examination hints

- A question that gives only assets and liabilities requires the preparation of statements of affairs to find the profit or loss of the business. The 'requirement' usually begins with 'calculate'.
- If required to prepare a Trading and Income Statement Account and Balance Sheet, prepare them in as much detail as possible.
- Be careful to distinguish between 'mark-up' and 'margin'. Learn how to convert mark-up to margin, and vice versa.

- Include all your workings with your answer. If your workings are not quite right, you may still gain some marks; but 'no workings – no marks' for a wrong answer.
- Tick each item in the question as you deal with it; check that everything has been ticked before writing your answer to ensure you have not missed anything.
- Incomplete records questions test a whole range of candidates' accounting knowledge and skills. For that reason they are frequently set in examinations. Some candidates fear these questions unnecessarily. Keep calm and follow the steps taught in this chapter carefully. If your Balance Sheet does not balance first time, don't panic. Do not spend valuable time looking for the difference if this time is better spent answering the next question. You have probably done enough to gain useful marks, anyway.

11.7 Multiple-choice questions

1 Jackson commenced business with $10 000 that he had received as a gift from his aunt and $8000 that he had received as a loan from his father. He used some of this money to purchase a machine for $15 000. He obtained a mortgage for $20 000 to purchase a workshop.

How much was Jackson's capital?

A $3000   **B** $10 000   **C** $18 000   **D** $38 000

2 At 1 January 2003 Robert's business assets were valued at $36 000 and his liabilities amounted to $2000. At 31 December 2003 Robert's assets amounted to $57 000 and included his private car which he had brought into the business on 1 November 2003 when it was valued at $9000. His accounts payable at 31 December 2003 totalled $17 000 and his drawings during the year

What was Robert's profit for the year ended 31 December 2003?

A $6000   **B** $14 000   **C** $ 24 000   **D** $33 000

3 At 1 April 2002 Tonkin's business assets were: motor van valued at $5000 (cost $8000), tools $1600, inventory $700, accounts receivable $168, cash $400. His accounts payable totalled $1120. At 31 March 2003 his assets were: workshop which had cost $20 000 and on which a mortgage of $16 000 was still outstanding, motor van $4000, tools $1900, inventory $1000, accounts receivable $240 (of which $70 were known to be bad), cash $500. His accounts payable amounted to $800. During the year Tonkin's drawings amounted to $5200.

What was Tonkin's profit for the year ended 31 March 2003?

A $6222   **B** $6292   **C** $9222   **D** $9292

4 At 1 March 2003 Allen's accounts receivable amounted to $12 100. In the year ended 28 February 2004 he received $63 500 from accounts receivable and allowed them cash discounts of $3426. At 28 February 2004 his accounts receivable totalled $14 625.

How much were Allen's sales for the year ended 28 February 2004?

A $62 599   **B** $64 401   **C** $66 025
D $69 451

5 At 1 October 2003 Maria's accounts receivable amounted to $7440. Of this amount $384 is known to be bad. In the year to 30 September 2004 she received $61 080 from accounts receivable. Her accounts receivable at 30 September 2004 were $8163. How much were Maria's sales for year ended 30 September 2004?

A $60 741   **B** $61 419   **C** $61 803
D $62 187

6 All of Grayson's inventory was stolen when his business was burgled on 4 March 2004. His inventory at 31 December 2003 was $23 000. From 1 January to 4 March 2004 sales totalled $42 000 and purchases were $38 000. Grayson's mark-up on goods is 33.3% to arrive at selling price.

What was the cost of the inventory that was stolen?

A $28 000   **B** $29 500   **C** $33 000
D $40 000

11.8 Additional exercises

1 Seng commenced business on 1 January 2003 when he paid $40 000 into the bank together with $20 000 which he had received as a loan from his brother. At 31 December 2003 Seng's assets and liabilities were as follows.

	$
Shop premises	20 000
Motor van	8 000
Shop fittings	3 000
Inventory	4 000
Accounts Receivable	1 000
Bank balance	5 000
Accounts Payable	6 000
Loan from brother	16 000

Seng's drawings were $100 per week.

Required
(a) Prepare Seng's statements of affairs at (i) 1 January 2003 and (ii) 31 December 2003.
(b) Calculate Seng's profit or loss for the year ended 31 December 2003.

2 Saeed does not keep proper books of account for his business but he has provided the following details of his assets and liabilities.

	At 1 July 2003	At 30 June 2004
	$	$
Land and buildings at cost	60 000	60 000
Fixtures and fittings	10 000	12 000
Office machinery	8 000	7 000
Inventory	17 000	21 000
Trade accounts receivable	4 000	5 000
Rent prepaid	1 000	600
Bank balance	14 000	16 000
Trade accounts payable	3 000	1 600
Wages owing	2 000	1 000

Further information

1. Land and buildings have been revalued at $90 000 at 30 June 2004.

2. Office machinery at 30 June 2004 included a computer costing $1400, which Saeed had paid for from his personal bank account.

3. Saeed had withdrawn $200 per week from the business in cash, and a total of $2000 of goods for his own use during the year to 30 June 2004.

Required

Calculate Saeed's profit or loss for the year ended 30 June 2004.

3 Ahmed carries on business as a general trader. He has not kept proper accounting records and he asks you to help him prepare his Trading and Income Statement Account for the year ended 30 September 2004 and his Balance Sheet at that date. Ahmed's assets and liabilities at 30 September 2003 were as follows.

	$
Premises	60 000
Motor van	8 000
Inventory	6 250
Trade accounts receivable	3 200
Rent paid in advance	400
Balance at bank	9 450
Cash in hand	50
Trade accounts payable	1 800
Electricity owing	600
Interest on loan owing	150
Loan from brother	2 000

The loan carries interest at 10% per annum payable in arrears annually on 31 December each year.

Ahmed's transactions in the year ended 30 September 2004 were as follows.

Bank summary

	$
Receipts	
Receipts from accounts receivable	29 400
Cash banked	17 000
Payments	
Suppliers	23 000
Electricity	2 200
Rent	4 000
Motor van expenses	1 800
Interest on loan	200
Wages	7 400
Telephone and stationery	1 650
Purchase of fixtures and fittings	3 000
Drawings	11 800

Cash summary

	$
Receipts	
Cash sales	21 750
Payments	
Goods for resale	3 140
Stationery	300
Motor van expenses	600
Sundry expenses	400

Further information

1. The balance of cash in hand has been maintained at $50.

2. At 30 September 2004, the closing inventory was $8000. Trade accounts receivable were $1600 and trade accounts payable for supplies were $1300.

3. Bad debts written off in the year were $250.

4. Discounts received from suppliers in the year were $420.

5. At 30 September 2004 electricity owing was $320 and rent of $450 had been prepaid.

6. At 30 September 2004 the motor van was valued at $6000.

7. Fixtures and fittings are to be depreciated on the reducing balance method using the rate of 25% per annum. A full year's depreciation is to be taken in the year ended 30 September 2004.

8. Ahmed does not provide for depreciation on the premises.

9. Ahmed has taken goods costing $800 from the business for his own use during the year.

10. Ahmed states that he paid some private bills out of the cash takings, but cannot remember how much is involved.

Required

(a) Prepare Ahmed's Trading and Income Statement Account for the year ended 30 September 2004.

(b) Prepare Ahmed's Balance Sheet at 30 September 2004.

4 Nurvish, who does not keep proper records for his business, supplies the following information.

	1 July 2003	30 June 2004
	$	$
Inventory of goods	16 000	11 000
Creditors for goods	3 600	5 200

In the year ended 30 June 2004, Nurvish paid suppliers $54 000.

Nurvish sells his goods at a gross profit margin of 40%.

On 17 January 2004, Nurvish's premises were flooded and inventory that cost $5000 was damaged and could only be sold at half cost price.

In the year ended 30 June 2004, Nurvish took goods which cost $1300 for his personal use.

Required

Prepare Nurvish's Trading Account for the year ended 30 June 2004.

5 Nadia was ill when her inventory should have been counted on 31 December 2003. The inventory count did not take place until 8 January 2004 when it was carried out by an inexperienced member of staff. The inventory was valued at $62 040 at 8 January 2004.

Nadia was sure that the inventory had been overvalued and discovered the following errors.

1. The inventory had been valued at selling price instead of at cost. The gross profit margin on all goods sold is 20%.

2. Goods had been sent on sale or return to a customer who had not yet accepted the goods. The customer had been sent an invoice for $2000. This had been treated as a sale.

3. Goods sold to a customer on 3 January 2004 had been overcharged by $240.

4. The following transactions had taken place between 1 January and 8 January 2004 but had not been taken into account in the inventory taking:

   (i) goods costing $4400 had been received from suppliers

   (ii) sales of goods for $12 000 (not including goods sent on sale or return).

Required

Calculate the value of inventory at cost at 31 December 2003.

6 Korn, a retailer, does not keep proper books of account but he has provided the following information about his business.

Balances at	30 April 2003	30 April 2004
	$	$
Land and buildings at cost	60 000	70 000
Fixtures and fittings	8 000	10 000
Motor vehicles	10 000	8 000
Trade accounts payable	7 500	6 900
Trade accounts receivable	20 400	32 000
Rent owing	800	1 000
Wages and salaries owing	800	600
Inventory	22 400	21 923
Bank	39 000	To be calculated

Korn's bank account transactions for the year ended 30 April 2004 were as follows.

	$
Receipts	
Trade accounts receivable	170 430
Cash sales	103 000
Sales of fixed assets (see note (4) below)	2 400
Payments	
Trade accounts payable	227 668
Wages	17 200
Rent	8 000
Electricity	9 670
General expenses	5 150
Purchases of fixed assets (see point 4 below)	27 000

Further information

1. Korn banks his receipts from cash sales after taking $300 each week as drawings.

2. During the year ended 30 April 2004, Korn had taken goods costing $1350 for his own use.

3. Korn normally valued his inventory at cost but on the advice of a friend he decided to value his inventory at 30 April 2004 at selling price. His normal mark-up on inventory was 30%.

4. Korn had borrowed $30 000 from his brother on a long-term basis on 1 May 2003. He had not recorded this transaction. Interest on the loan at 10% per annum is payable on 1 May each year.

During the financial year ended 30 April 2004 the following transactions had taken place.

	$	
Purchases		
Freehold land and buildings	10 000	
Motor vehicles	10 000	
Fixtures and fittings	7 000	
Sales		
Motor vehicles	2 000	(net book value at 30 April 2003 $3500)
Fixtures and fittings	400	(net book value at 30 April 2003 $800)

Required

(a) Prepare Korn's Trading and Income Statement Account for the year ended 30 April 2004.
(b) Prepare the Balance Sheet at 30 April 2004.
(c) Comment on the suggestion by Korn's friend that inventory should be valued at selling price, and refer to any relevant accounting principle.

12 Co-operatives

Objectives
- define co-operatives
- state types, ethics and characteristics of co-operatives
- discuss the principles of co-operatives
- discuss the finances of co-operatives
- prepare the financial statements of co-operatives

12.1 Definition

A co-operative is an association of persons united voluntarily to meet their common economic, social and cultural needs through a jointly owned and democratically controlled enterprise. They are designed to provide economic benefits to their member owners who use their services.

12.2 Co-operative types, ethics and characteristics

Co-operatives worldwide are many and varied. Their existence can be traced back to England in the 1840s. They have now become a special feature in many Caribbean countries. Some types are Agriculture co-ops, Wholesale supply co-ops, Transport co-ops, Credit unions, Health care co-ops, Workers co-ops and Consumer co-ops.

The operations of co-operatives are based on traditional values such as self-help, equality, equity, co-operation, solidarity and fairness. In the tradition of their founders, co-operative members believe in the ethical values of honesty, openness, social responsibility and caring for others.

They have their special characteristic features such as:

I Open membership.

II Low initial investment to join the co-operative.

III Member owner controlled.

IV Focus on member owner needs.

V Earnings returned through patronage.

VI Retained profit supplies the equity and operating capital.

12.3 Co-operative principles

The co-operative principles are guidelines which were first established in Rochdale, England in the 1840s but have been reviewed and updated over time by the International Co-operative Alliance. Through these guidelines the co-operative values are put into practice. To date there are seven operating principles.

1st Principle: Voluntary and open membership
Voluntary organization; open to all persons; no discrimination along gender, social, racial, religious or political lines.

2nd Principle: Democratic member control
Equal voting rights, members participate in policy and decision-making, elected representatives accountable to members.

3rd Principle: Member economic participation
Members control capital of the co-operative, members receive some benefits, members allocate surpluses for various purposes.

4th Principle: Autonomy and independence
Co-operatives are autonomous, self-help organization, democratic control by members ensured, agreement with other organizations must involve maintaining their autonomy.

5th Principle: Education, training and information
Co-operatives provide education and training for their members, elected representatives, managers, and employees so they can contribute effectively to the development of their co-operatives. They inform the general public – particularly young people and opinion leaders – about the nature and benefits of co-operation.

6th Principle: Co-operation among co-operatives
Co-operatives serve their members most effectively and strengthen the co-operative movement by working together through local, national, regional and international structures.

7th Principle: Concern for community
Co-operatives work for the sustainable development of their communities through policies approved by their members.

12.4 Co-operative finances

The capital of the co-operative is provided mainly by members through share deposits, membership fees, savings contributions and surpluses ploughed back into the organization. The shares are owned by the members and are usually returned to them when they cease being a member. Dividends on share capital are usually very small so as to prohibit speculative tendencies on the part of outsiders. Honoraria are usually paid to members of the board, although in larger financial co-operatives, such as credit unions, members of the board are paid salaries. State legislation determines what percentage of the co-operative net income is to be set aside as a statutory reserve, to ensure a strong financial base. Other reserves, for example, education, development fund and investment appropriated from the remaining surplus, will be determined by membership.

12.5 Accounts of co-operatives

The features of the accounts prepared and financial statements presented for co-operatives, will depend on the nature of activities they are involved in. Generally however, most co-operatives will prepare:

1. An income statement or Statement of Operation, which includes a statement of undivided surplus

2. A balance sheet.

Equity Consumer Co-operative statement of operation for the year ended 31 December 2004 (Income and Expenditure account and the Appropriation account)

	$	$
Net sales		4 500 000
Cost of sales		3 000 000
Gross savings		1 500 000
Other income:		
Interest on investment		50 000
Membership fees		30 000
		1 580 000
Less expenses:		
Selling expenses	400 000	
General expenses	230 000	
Admin. expenses	100 000	730 000
Net savings		850 000
+ Balance at start of year		130 000
Net surplus		980 000
Less:		
Statutory reserve	147 000	
Education fund	60 000	
Patronage refund	80 000	
Development fund	100 000	387 000
Balance available for distribution		593 000
Less dividends		310 000
Balance at end of year (Undivided surplus)		283 000

Equity consumer co-operative balance sheet as at 31 December 2004			
	$	$	$
Fixed Assets			
Building			420 000
Equipment			80 000
Machinery			60 000
			580 000
Non-Current Assets			
Investment		120 000	
Loans to Members		200 000	320 000
			880 000
Current Assets			
Inventory		430 000	
Accounts receivables		60 000	
Bank & Cash		640 000	
Prepayment		20 000	
		1 150 000	
Less: Current Liabilities			
Members deposit	250 000		
Accounts payable	110 000		
Dividends payable	310 000	670 000	480 000
			1 360 000
Long Term Liability: Loan			(200 000)
			1 160 000
Members equity			
Share capital			417 000
Reserves			
Statutory			200 000
Education			160 000
Development			180 000
Undivided surplus			283 000
			1 160 000

Questions for co-operatives

1 Describe the principles of co-operatives.

2 What are the financial statements of a co-operative?

3 From the following information of Barbados Fishing Co-operative Society Limited prepare an Income Statement for the year ending 31 December 2005 and a Balance Sheet as at 31 December 2005.

	$000
Premises	2500
Equipment at cost	2450
Motor vehicles	925
Provision for Depreciation:	
Equipment	1125
Motor vehicles	100
Stock	300
Accounts receivable	1500
Prepayments	50
Bank	500
Share capital	5420
Statutory reserve	75
Development fund	75
Honoraria payable	75
Proposed dividends	90
Electricity	35
Stationery	80
Office expense	8
Travelling expense	15
Auditors' fees	150
Repairs	25
AGM expenses	200
Wages and salaries	75
Miscellaneous expenses	25
Motor vehicle expenses	15
Bank charges	10
Interest on members' deposits	25
Insurance	75
Membership dues	450
Interest and dividends received	1250
Other income	118
Undivided surplus at the start of the year	500

4 The following Trial Balance was extracted from the books of El Dorado Co-operative on 31 December 2006. You are required to prepare the financial statements for the year ended 31 December 2006.

	Dr. $	Cr. $
Accounts payable		23 480
Balance at start of the year		114 589
Net savings (surplus/income)		146 931
Fixed assets – buildings	1 300 000	
Education fund		20 000
Statutory reserve		250 000
Accounts receivable	950 000	
Provision for depreciation (fixed asset – building)		30 000
Share capital		1 610 000
Mortgage		55 000
TOTAL	$2 250 000	$2 250 000

Additional information is given as follows:

(a) $10 000 is to be appropriated for the statutory reserve and $15 000 for the Education Fund.

(b) Dividends are to be paid at the rate of 5%.

13 Not-for-profit organizations

Objectives
- identify and describe not-for-profit organizations
- distinguish between profit and not-for-profit organizations
- prepare income and expenditure account for not for profit entities
- prepare balance sheet for not-for-profit entities
- identify and describe non-government organizations (NGOs)

13.1 What are non-profit making organizations (not-for-profit organizations)?

Non-profit-making organizations exist to provide facilities for their members. Examples are sports and social clubs, dramatic societies, music clubs, etc. Making a profit is not their main purpose, although many carry on fund-raising activities to provide more or better facilities for the members. The organization is 'owned' by all of its members and not by just one person or partnership. Records of money received and spent are usually kept by a club member who is not a trained bookkeeper or accountant. Usually no other records are kept. This topic is therefore an extension of the work of the previous chapter, which deals with incomplete records.

It follows from the above that a business which is *meant* to make profits is not a non-profit-making organization, even if it keeps making losses.

13.2 Special features of the accounts of non-profit-making organizations

- An **Income and Expenditure Account** takes the place of the Profit and Loss Account.
- The words **surplus of income over expenditure** are used in place of 'net profit'.
- The words **excess of expenditure over income** are used in place of 'net loss'.
- The term **Accumulated fund** is used in place of 'Capital account'.

- A Trading Account is only prepared for an activity that is in the nature of trading and is carried on to increase the club's funds.

13.3 Distinguish between profit and not-for-profit organizations

Profit	Not-for-profit
1 Provide services to make a profit	**1** Does not provide services to make a profit
2 Organization owned by one person or partnership	**2** Organization owned by all of its members
3 Source of revenue: from services rendered and the owner's capital	**3** Source of revenue: from donations and subscriptions.

13.4 The treatment of income

Income of a club (which is the term that will be used in the rest of this chapter to cover all non-profit-making organizations) should be treated in the club's accounts as follows.

Subscriptions

The amount credited to the Income and Expenditure Account should equal the annual subscription per member multiplied by the number of members. It may be helpful to prepare a Subscriptions account as workings to decide how much should be credited to the Income and Expenditure Account.

Subscriptions in arrears and **subscriptions in advance** should *normally* be treated as accruals and prepayments. However, each club has its own policy for treating subscriptions in arrears or in advance. The two possible policies are as follows.

- **Cash basis**. The amount actually received in the year is credited to the Income and Expenditure Account. This may include subscriptions for a previous year or paid in advance for the next year.
- **Accruals basis**. All subscriptions due for the year, including those not yet received, are credited to the Income and Expenditure Account. It will usually be the club's policy to write off, as bad debts, subscriptions that are not received in the year after they were due.

Life subscriptions and entry fees

Life subscriptions and entry fees are received as lump sums but should not be credited in full to the Income and Expenditure Account when received. The club should have a policy of spreading this income over a period of, say, five years. The amounts received should be credited to a Deferred Income account and credited to the Income and Expenditure Account in equal annual instalments over a period determined by the club committee.

Donations

Donations and legacies to a club are usually made for particular purposes, for example towards the cost of a new pavilion or a piece of equipment. Such donations should be credited to an account opened for the purpose, and expenditure on it debited to the account. Money received for special purposes should be placed in a separate bank account to ensure that it is not spent on other things.

Ancillary activities

Ancillary activities are incidental to a club's main purpose. They raise money to supplement income from subscriptions. If they involve some sort of trading, a Trading Account should be prepared for them as part of the annual accounts, and the profit or loss should be transferred to the Income and Expenditure Account.

Non-trading activities, such as socials, outings and dinner-dances, may be dealt with in the Income and Expenditure Account with the income and costs being grouped together as follows.

	$	$
Annual dinner-dance		
Sale of tickets	600	
Less: hire of band	(100)	
catering	(240)	
Net receipts		260

13.5 How to prepare club accounts

The preparation of club accounts follows the same procedures as those used for businesses whose records are incomplete (see chapter 11).

Example

The Star Sports and Social Club provides recreational activities, refreshments and social events for its members. It sells sports equipment to its members at reduced prices. Its assets and liabilities at 31 December 2003 were as follows.

	$
Fixed assets	
Pavilion	120 000
Club sports equipment	40 000
Motor roller	2 000
Current assets	
Stock of equipment for sale to members	4 000
Annual subscriptions owing	1 200
Bank balance	6 730
Current liabilities	
Creditors for equipment for sale to members	1 300
Annual subscriptions received in advance	800
Life subscriptions fund	1 750

In the year ended 31 December 2003 the club's cash receipts and payments were as follows.

	$
Receipts	
Annual subscriptions	18 000
Proceeds from sale of equipment	12 000
Sale of tickets for dinner-dance	4 400
Refreshment bar takings	2 660
Life member subscriptions	400
Payments	
Caretaker's wages	8 000
Repairs to club equipment	1 700
Purchase of club equipment	2 000
Equipment for sale to members	4 000
Heating and lighting	1 800
Dinner-dance expenses	
Hire of band	200
Catering	1 000
Food for refreshment bar	1 400
Secretary's expenses	840

Further information

1. At 31 December 2004:

   annual subscriptions in arrears were $1400

   annual subscriptions received in advance were $900.

2. Stock of equipment for sale to members: $2000.

3. Creditors for equipment for sale to members: $900.

4. A member donated $5000 to a fund to encourage young people to train for sport. This donation was invested immediately in savings bonds.

5. The club transfers life subscriptions to the Income and Expenditure Account in equal instalments over five years.

6. Depreciation is to be provided on fixed assets by the reducing-balance method as follows.

Pavilion	6%
Sports equipment	20%
Motor roller	20%

Required

(a) Prepare the Star Sports and Social Club's Income and Expenditure Account for the year ended 31 December 2004.

(b) Prepare the club's Balance Sheet as at 31 December 2004.

Note. Often the amount of information given in questions such as this looks terrifying but don't let that worry you. Keep calm. Read the question carefully two or three times, making sure you understand it, and underline important points. Decide what workings are required and which must be shown in your answer. Then proceed as follows.

Step 1 Prepare an opening statement of affairs. This will give the balance on the Accumulated fund at 1 January 2004 and will be the starting point for recording the transactions during the year.

Statement of affairs at 31 December 2003		
		$
Fixed assets		
Pavilion		120 000
Club sports equipment		40 000
Motor roller		2 000
Current assets		
Stock of equipment for sale to members		4 000
Annual subscriptions owing		1 200
Bank balance		6 730
Total assets		173 930
Current liabilities		
Creditors for equipment for sale to members	1300	
Annual subscriptions received in advance	800	
Life subscriptions fund	1750	3 850
Accumulated fund at 1 January 2004		170 080

Step 2 Prepare a Receipts and Payment account. This will summarize all the transactions affecting the Income and Expenditure Account and Balance Sheet and calculate the bank balance at 31 December 2004.

Receipts and Payments account for the year ended 31 December 2004					
		$			$
1 Jan	Balance brought forward	6 730	31 Dec	Caretaker's wages	8 000
31 Dec	Annual subscriptions	18 000		Repairs: club equipment	1 700
	Sales of equipment	12 000		Purchase: club equipment	2 000
	Sale of tickets			Purchase of equipment	
	Dinner-dance	4 400		for resale	4 000
	Takings – refreshments	2 660		Heating and lighting	1 800
	Life membership			Dinner-dance	
	subscriptions	400		hire of band	200
				catering	1 000
				Food for refreshment bar	1 400
				Secretary's expenses	840
				Balance c/f	23 250
		44 190			44 190

Step 3 Prepare workings to adjust for accruals, prepayments, depreciation and any other items. Show these workings with your answer.

You may show your workings as ledger ('T') accounts or as calculations. Decide which method is best for you and practise it in all your exercises. Both methods will be shown here.

'T' accounts					Calculations	
1.	**Purchase of equipment for resale**					$
		$		$	Cash paid	4 000
	Cash paid	4 000	Creditors b/f	1 300	less creditors b/f	(1 300)
	Creditors c/f	900	I & E a/c	3 600		2 700
		4 900		4 900	add creditors c/f	900
					Trading a/c	3 600
2.	**Annual subscriptions**	$		$		$
	Owing at 1 Jan	1 200	Prepaid at 1 Jan	800	Received in year	18 000
	Prepaid at 31 Dec	900	Cash	18 000	less owing 1 Jan	(1 200)
	I & E a/c	18 100	Owing at 31 Dec	1 400	prepaid 31 Dec	(900)
		20 200		20 200		15 900
					add prepaid 1 Jan	800
					owing 31 Dec	1 400
					I & E a/c	18 100
3.	**Life subscriptions**					
		$		$		$
	I & E a/c $\frac{1}{5} \times 2150$	430	B/f	1 750	Balance b/f	1 750
	C/f	1 720	Cash received	400	Cash received	400
		2 150		2 150		2 150
					I & E a/c $\left(\frac{1}{5}\right)$	430
4.	**Club sports equipment**					
		$		$		$
	B/f	40 000	I & E (20%)	8 400	Balance b/f	40 000
	Cash	2 000	c/d	33 600	Cash	2 000
		42 000		42 000		42 000
					I & E a/c (20%)	8 400
					Net book value	33 600

Step 4 The Income and Expenditure Account and Balance Sheet may now be copied out from steps 1, 2 and 3. As the sale of equipment to members is trading, a Trading Account should be prepared even though one is not asked for in the question.

If steps 1, 2 and 3 have been carried out with care, preparing the Income and Expenditure Account and Balance Sheet is now little more than a copying exercise and can be completed in little time.

(a)

Sales of equipment		
	$	$
Sales		12 000
Less cost of sales		
Stock at 1 January 2004	4000	
Purchases (working 1)	3600	
	7600	
Less stock at 31 December 2004	2000	5 600
Profit transferred to Income & Expenditure Account		6 400

Star Sports and Social Club
Income and Expenditure Account for the year ended 31 December 2004

	$	$	$
Annual subscriptions (working 2)			18 100
Life subscriptions (working 3)			430
Profit on sale of equipment			6 400
Dinner/dance*			
Sale of tickets		4 400	
less hire of band	200		
catering	1 000	1 200	3 200
Refreshment bar*			
Takings		2 660	
less cost of food		1 400	1 260
			29 390
Less expenses			
Caretaker's wages		8 000	
Repairs to club equipment		1 700	
Heating and lighting		1 800	
Secretary's expenses		840	
Depreciation: Pavilion (6% of $120 000)		7 200	
Equipment (working 4)		8 400	
Motor roller (20% of $2000)		400	28 340
Surplus of income over expenditure			1 050

*Expenses of dinner-dance and refreshment bar are grouped with the income from those activities to help members see how those activities have contributed to the club's funds.

(b)

Balance Sheet at 31 December 2004		
	$	$	$
Fixed assets at net book value			
Pavilion			112 800
Club equipment			33 600
Motor roller			1 600
			148 000
Current assets			
Stock of equipment for sale to members		2 000	
Subscriptions owing		1 400	
Bank		23 250	
		26 650	
Less Current liabilities			
Creditors	900		
Subscriptions prepaid	900		
Life subscriptions	1 720	3 520	23 130
			171 130
Represented by			
Accumulated fund at 1 January 2004			170 080
Add surplus of income over expenditure			1 050
Accumulated fund at 31 December 2004			171 130
Fund to encourage young people to train for sport			5 000
Represented by savings bonds			5 000

13.6 Non-government organizations (NGOs)

These are made up of a wide number of organizations formed as non-profit making businesses. Some of there organizations are:

- Charitable organizations
- Private foundations and
- Trade Unions.

An NGO is a legal entity incorporated as a company, has no share capital and, is limited by guarantee. Source of funding can be in the form of:

- Donations
- Fund-raising activities e.g. all inclusive fetes
- Sale of publications
- Endowment fund e.g. Scholarship fund.

13.7 Examination hints

- Club accounts often look difficult, but they need not be so. Keep calm and follow carefully the steps taught in this and the previous chapter.

- Always follow carefully whatever instructions are given in an examination question.
- Even if your answer is not perfect, you can earn many useful marks if you show the examiner what you can do.
- Include all your workings with your answer.
- Tick each item in the question as you deal with it; check that everything has been ticked to ensure you have not missed anything.

13.8 Multiple-choice questions

1 Which of the following will *not* be found in the accounts of a club?

 A Accumulated fund

 B Drawings account

 C Receipts and Payments account

 D Balance Sheet

2 The following information for a year is extracted from a sports club's accounts.

	$
Subscriptions received	10 000
Sales of equipment to members	7 000
Opening stock of equipment	1 300
Closing stock of equipment	800
Purchases of equipment	5 000

What was the club's total income for the year?

 A $10 000   **B** $11 500   **C** $12 500

 D $17 000

3 The following information relates to a club for a year.

Number of members	60
Annual subscription	$20
Subscriptions owing at beginning of year	$100
Subscriptions owing at end of year	$60

How much should be credited to the club's Income and Expenditure Account for annual subscriptions for the year?

 A $1100   **B** $1160   **C** $1200   **D** $1260

4 A club's records provide the following information for a year.

	$
Annual subscriptions received in the year	4000
Annual subscriptions received in advance at end of year	50
Balance on Life Subscriptions account at beginning of year	500
Life subscriptions received during the year	100

The club's policy is to credit life subscriptions to the Income and Expenditure Account over five years.

How much should be credited to the Income and Expenditure Account for subscriptions for the year?

 A $4050   **B** $4070   **C** $4150   **D** $4170

5 The Accounting term used for Capital in a Non-profit organization is

 A Surplus

 B Accumulated fund

 C Drawings

 D Share premium

13.9 Additional exercises

1 The Civic Athletics Club's Receipts and Payments account for the year ended 31 May 2004 is as follows.

Receipts	$	Payments	$
Balance at bank 1 June 2003	4 650	Refreshment supplies bought	2 654
Subscriptions received	7 970	Wages	4 000
Sales of tickets for dance	1 897	Rent of rooms	540
Refreshment bar takings	4 112	Purchase of new equipment	1 778
Sale of old equipment	94	Teams' travelling expenses	995
Donation	90	Balance at bank at 31 May 2004	8 846
	18 813		18 813

Further information

1. Refreshment bar stocks were valued at $150 at 1 June 2003, and at $180 at 31 May 2004.

2. Creditors for refreshment bar stocks were: at 1 June 2003 $15; at 31 May 2004 $40.

3. At 1 June 2003, subscriptions owing were $330, of which $310 was paid in the year to 31 May 2004. It is club policy to write off subscriptions if they have not been received by the end of the year following their due date. Subscriptions owing at 31 May 2004 were $275.

4. Of the wages paid, $900 was paid to staff serving refreshments.

5. On 1 June 2003 the club's equipment was valued at £4700. The equipment sold during the year had a book value of $70 at the date of sale. At 31 May 2004, the equipment was valued at $6000.

Required

(a) Calculate the Accumulated fund as at 1 June 2003.
(b) Prepare the refreshments Trading Account for the year ended 31 May 2004.
(c) Prepare the Income and Expenditure Account for the year ended 31 May 2004.
(d) Prepare the club's Balance Sheet as at 31 May 2004.

2 The members of The Howzidun Magic Club meet to demonstrate their conjuring skills and to entertain visitors, who pay an entrance fee at the door. The club also has a shop for the sale of conjuring tricks and props.

The club's Bank account for the year ended 30 June 2004 was as follows:

	$		$
Balance at 1 July 2003	16 800	Purchases of tricks and props	8 220
Subscriptions received	10 730	Shop wages	6 000
Cash taken at door	9 456	Cost of annual dance	2 600
Shop takings	12 348	Purchase of equipment	5 000
Annual dance receipts	3 720	Secretary's expenses	2 125
Grant from local council	4 000	Transfer to Deposit account	20 000
Donations to the Disappeared		Balance at 30 June 2001	13 775
Wizards Memorial Fund	666		
	57 720		57 720

The club has 200 members. The annual subscription was $30 until 1 July 2003 when it was increased to $40.

At 1 July 2003, 20 members had not paid their subscriptions for the year ended 30 June 2003 but, of these, 15 had paid their arrears of subscriptions by 30 June 2004. By 30 June 2004, all members had paid their subscriptions for the year up to date and some had paid their subscriptions for the year to 30 June 2005.

Other assets and liabilities were

	At 1 July 2003	At 30 June 2004
	$	$
Shop stock	1 600	1 850
Creditors for shop purchases	400	210
Equipment at cost	7 000	12 000
Deposit account	10 000	30 000
Disappeared Wizards Memorial Fund	–	666

The equipment at 1 July 2003 had been depreciated for five years by $1400 per annum. The new equipment is to be depreciated at the same annual percentage rate.

The grant from the local council was the first instalment of an annual grant of $8000.

The transfer to the Deposit account was made on 1 January 2004. Interest at 4% per annum is payable on 30 June each year.

Required

(a) Calculate the Accumulated fund at 1 July 2003.
(b) Prepare the Club Shop Trading Account for the year ended 30 June 2004.
(c) Prepare the Club Subscriptions account for the year ended 30 June 2004.
(d) Prepare the Club Income and Expenditure Account for the year ended 30 June 2004.
(e) Prepare the Club Balance Sheet at 30 June 2004.

3 The Taupo Sailing Club provides its members with a number of activities:

(i) hire of boats for members; non-members are charged an extra 20% for boat hire

(ii) yacht racing competitions

(iii) a clubhouse with a refreshment bar which is also used for social functions

(iv) a sailing training school for all age groups.

The following financial information relates to 1 April 2003.

	$
Fixed assets at net book value	
Freehold premises	350 000
Yacht maintenance shop	42 000
Boatyard and launch facilities	74 000
Fixtures and fittings	28 000
Boats and yachts	465 000
Other items	
Members' subscriptions:	
in arrears	3 000
in advance	6 000
Balance at bank	94 000
Stocks of refreshments	1 250
Creditors for refreshments	1 030

The following financial information relates to the year ended 31 March 2004.

(continues)

Receipts	$	Payments	$
Hire of yachts and boats		Repairs and maintenance of yachts	23 400
to members	43 000	Purchase of new boats and yachts	61 000
to non-members	34 000	Wages of training-school staff	16 500
Receipts from training school	34 500	Wages of refreshment-bar staff	14 000
Members' subscriptions	186 000	Purchase of refreshment-bar food	53 000
Refreshments and social events	77 000	Receipts from yacht racing competition	13 000
Expenses of yacht racing competition	28 900	Sundry expenses	26 000

Further information

1. At 31 March 2004, members' subscriptions owing amounted to $2000; members' subscriptions in advance for 2004/2005 were $3400.

2. The club's depreciation policy is as follows.

   - Freehold premises, boatyard and launch facilities, and boats and yachts: 5% per annum on net book value

   - Fixtures and fittings, and yacht maintenance shop: 10% per annum on net book value.

3. Creditors at 31 March 2004 were as follows.

	$
Repairs and maintenance of yachts	1350
Refreshments	970
Wages: training-school staff	700
refreshment bar staff	400

Refreshment bar stock at 31 March 2004 was valued at $1600.

Required

(a) Prepare Taupo Sailing Club's Income and Expenditure Account for the year ended 31 March 2004 in good format. A Trading Account should be prepared for the refreshment bar.

(b) Prepare the club's Balance Sheet as at 31 March 2004.

4 The Abracamagic Club's Bank Current account for the year ended 30 September 2001 was as follows.

	$		$
Balance at 1.10.2000	8 400	Purchases for shop	3 745
Subscriptions received	6 435	Shop wages	4 000
Donations	600	General expenses	1 500
Cash taken at door	3 500	Cost of Annual Dance	1 490
Grant from local council	6 000	Transfer to Deposit account	16 000
Annual Dance receipts	1 400	New equipment	2 000
Shop takings	7 168	Rent	8 000
Balance at 30.9.2001	3 232		
	36 735		36 735

In order to increase funds the club has a shop which sells magic tricks. In addition to an annual membership subscription, members pay $1 each time they visit the club. This is referred to as 'Cash taken at door'.

The annual membership subscription was $40 until 30 September 2001 when it was raised to $45.

There were 150 members at 1 October 2000.

At that date 15 of them had not paid their subscriptions for the year ended 30 September 2000, and 12 had already paid their subscriptions for the year ended 30 September 2001.

By 30 September 2001, all members had paid their due subscriptions, and some had paid in advance for the year ending 30 September 2002, but the Treasurer had not yet calculated how many.

Other balances were as follows.

	At 1 October 2000	At 30 September 2001
	$	$
Shop stock	500	850
Cash float for shop	50	70
Creditors for shop	1 450	1 260
Deposit account	15 000	31 000
Equipment at cost	8 000	10 000

The equipment at 1 October 2000 had been depreciated by $1600 per annum for five years.

The new equipment is to be depreciated at the same annual percentage rate.

The local council's grant was for $10 000 and the remainder of this has yet to be received. This will be treated as revenue income in the final accounts.

Interest of $800 is due on the deposit account for the year ended 30 September 2001.

At 30 September 2001, general expenses of $65 were due and unpaid.

Required

(a) Calculate the Accumulated fund at 1 October 2000.

(b) Prepare the Club Shop Trading Account for the year ended 30 September 2001.

(c) Prepare the Club Subscriptions account for the year ended 30 September 2001.

(d) Prepare the Club Income and Expenditure Account for the year ended 30 September 2001.

Exercise 1

The Wellington Drama Club has 120 members. The annual subscription is $20 per member. Subscriptions not paid in one year are written off if not paid by the end of the next year.

The Club presents two plays a year, each play being performed over ten days. The Club hires a local hall for the performances and the dress rehearsals, which take place over three days before the presentation of each play.
The Club donates half of its net surpluses to the Actors Benevolent Fund.

The receipts and payments of the Club in the year ended 31 December 2004 were as follows.

Receipts	$
Sales of tickets	20 000
Sales of programmes	3 000
Sales of refreshments	3 500
Subscriptions for the year ended 31 December 2004	2 000
Subscriptions for the year ended 31 December 2003	280
Subscriptions for the year ending 31 December 2005	360
Payments	
Hire of hall	2 600
Printing of posters, tickets and programmes	180
Hire of costumes	4 700
Cost of refreshments	2 200
Payments for copyrights	1 400

At 31 December 2003, members subscriptions of $360 were owing.

Required

(a) Prepare The Wellington Drama Club's Income and Expenditure Account for the year ended 31 December 2004.

(b) Prepare a Balance Sheet extract at 31 December 2004 to show the items for subscriptions.

Exercise 2

The Hutt River Dining Club is funded partly by the members' annual subscriptions ($20 per member), partly by restaurant takings and partly from profits from the sale of books on dieting, healthy eating and cooking.

At 31 December 2003, the club's Balance Sheet showed the following.

	$	$
Catering equipment at cost	11 000	
Depreciation of catering equipment	3 000	8000
Stock of food		200
Stock of books		1100
Subscriptions owing		180
Cash at bank		1520
Creditors for supplies of food		40
Subscriptions in advance		60

Receipts and payments for the year ended 31 December 2004 were as follows.

Receipts	$
Annual subscriptions	5 000
Restaurant takings	73 760
Sales of books	12 150
Payments	
Staff wages	39 000
Cost of food	24 980
Purchase of books	4 840
New catering equipment	3 750
Heating and lighting	8 390
Sundry expenses	2 270

Further information

1. Subscriptions owing at 31 December 2004: $40.

2. Subscriptions paid in advance at 31 December 2004: $140.

3. Stocks at 31 December 2004: food $270; books $965.

4. Creditors at 31 December 2004: for food $360; for books $200.

5. Annual depreciation of catering equipment is 10% on cost.

Required

(a) Calculate the Accumulated fund at 1 January 2004.

(b) Prepare a Receipts and Payments account for the year ended 31 December 2004.

(c) Prepare the Members Subscriptions account for the year ended 31 December 2004.

(d) Prepare a Trading Account for the year ended 31 December 2004 for the sale of books.

(e) Prepare a Restaurant account for the year ended 31 December 2004.

(f) Prepare The Hutt River Dining Club's Income and Expenditure Account for the year ended 31 December 2004.

(g) Prepare the Balance Sheet as at 31 December 2004.

14 Statutory corporations

Objectives
- define statutory corporation
- prepare income statement for a statutory corporation
- prepare balance sheet for a statutory corporation

Corporations control vital areas of an economy. Three types of corporations existing in the Caribbean are Private, Public and Statutory.

14.1 Statutory corporations

This is a company incorporated by its own special Act of Parliament: the Government has established a statutory corporation for a particular purpose for example, a public service or utility

Statutory corporations exist in nearly all the Caribbean countries. Some examples are Media houses, Telecommunication services, Water utilities, Transportation services, Insurance services, Financial houses and Bureau of standards.

14.2 Preparation of Income Statement

The application of IAS 1 for the preparation of an Income Statement is the same. However, because of the incorporation of the statutory company by the Act of Parliament, the legislation determines the appropriation of profits: for example, allocation of funds and undistributed profits.

14.3 Preparation of statement as appropriation of earnings

Worked Example 1

Blue Waters Corporation had the following balances as at December 31, 2003:

Balance b/f	$ 700 000
Net income for the year	$ 50 000
Additional information:	
Transfer to statutory reserves	$ 50 000
Transfer to consolidated fund	$ 100 000

Required

Prepare the appropriation of earnings statement for the year ending December 31, 2003.

BLUE WATERS
Appropriation of earnings statement for the year ended December 31, 2003

	$
Statement of retained earnings	
Balance b/f	700 000
Net income	50 000
	750 000
Transfers	
Statutory reserves	(50 000)
Consolidated fund	(100 000)
Retained earnings	(600 000)

14.4 Preparation of the Balance Sheet

IAS 1 requires the corporation to prepare its Balance Sheets in a prescribed format whereas the Act of Parliament stipulates what to do with the appropriated profits. The owner's equity section of the Balance Sheet will differ according due to the type of statutory corporation.

Types of statutory corporations – Balance Sheet

(A) Government-controlled

Worked Example 2

Jamco Bureau of Standards is a Statutory Corporation controlled by the government. At December 31, 2005, the Corporation had the following balances:

	$
Long-term loan	200 000
Retained earnings b/d	600 000
Cash	500 000
Equipment	1 000 000
Accounts receivable	300 000
Furniture	500 000
Funds collected from Government	1 200 000
Bank overdraft	200 000
Accounts payable	100 000

Required

Prepare the Balance Sheet for the period ending December 31, 2005.

Jamco Bureau of Standards
Balance Sheet as at December 31, 2005

	$	$		$	$
Equity:			Assets:		
Paid up by Government	1 200 000		Fixed Assets		
Retained earnings	600 000		Equipment	1 000 000	
Total equity		1 800 000	Furniture	500 000	
			Total fixed assets		1 500 000
Long term liabilities			Current assets		
Long term loan		200 000	Cash	500 000	
			Accounts receivable	300 000	800 000
Current liabilities					
Accounts payable	100 000				
Bank overdraft	200 000	300 000			
Total		2 300 000			2 300 000

(B) Insurance company

Worked Example 3

Zion Insurance Company had the following balances as at December 31, 2004:

Land	$ 500 000
Furniture	$ 300 000
Equipment	$ 700 000
Cash	$ 800 000
Paid up capital	$ 1 300 000

Additional information:	
Transfer to special reserve	$ 400 000
Transfer to compulsory reserve	$ 300 000
Transfer to revaluation surplus	$ 300 000
Insurance collected in advance (still to be recorded)	$ 200 000

Required

Prepare Zion's Balance Sheet for the year ended December 31, 2004.

Zion Insurance Corporation
Balance Sheet as at December 31, 2004

	$		$	$
Equity:		Assets:		
Paid up capital	1 300 000	Fixed assets		
Special reserve	400 000	Land	500 000	
Reserves(Compulsory)	300 000	Equipment	700 000	
Revaluation Surplus	300 000	Furniture	300 000	1 500 000
	2 300 000			
Long term liabilities		Current assets		
Insurance unearned	200 000	Cash		1 000 000
Total	**2 500 000**			**2 500 000**

14.5 Question

1 TLC Media House was incorporated as a Statutory Corporation on January 1, 2001. The balances as at December 31, 2003 are

	$
Net Income b/f	500 000
Transfers: Statutory reserves	100 000
Consolidated fund	200 000
Balance b/d	1 400 000
Paid in by Government	2 000 000
Mortgage payable	500 000
Equipment	3 000 000
Provision for depreciation: Equipment	100 000
Accounts payable	200 000
Bank overdraft	300 000
Furniture	1 000 000
Cash	300 000
Accounts receivable	400 000

Required
Prepare TLC Media House (i) Income statement
(ii) Balance sheet

2 Barbados Mutual Insurance Company Balances at February 2006 were

	$
Net income b/f	900 000
Transfers: Special reserve	200 000
Compulsory reserve	300 000
Current assets	1 000 000
Paid-up capital	2 000 000
Fixed assets:	
Land	800 000
Buildings	500 000
Equipment	300 000
Furniture	300 000

Required
Prepare Barbados Mutual Insurance
(i) Appropriation account
(ii) Balance Sheet

14.6 Multiple-choice question

A statutory company is an entity that has been established by a/an _____.

A Act of Parliament

B Hire Purchase Act

C Companies Act

D Partnership Act

15 Partnership accounting

Objectives
- describe the formation of a partnership
- state the contents of a partnership agreement
- explain the appropriation account
- prepare account for formation of partnership
- state advantages and disadvantages of partnership
- prepare accounts for admission of partners
- prepare accounts for dissolution of partnership
- prepare accounts for incorporation of partnership

15.1 What are partnerships?

A partnership is formed when two or more people carry on business together with the intention of making profit.

Partners must agree on how the partnership is to be carried on, including how much capital each partner is to contribute to the firm and how profits and losses are to be shared. These, and other important matters, are decided in a **partnership agreement**. The agreement will usually be in writing, possibly by deed (a formal legal document), or verbally. If the partners do not make an agreement and a dispute arises regarding their rights and duties as partners, the Court may assume that past practice constitutes an 'implied' agreement, and resolve the dispute according to what the partners have done previously.

Partnership Acts usually govern partnerships and states the rights and duties of partners. The Act includes the following provisions, which are important and apply to partnerships *unless* the partners have agreed to vary the terms.

- All partners are entitled to contribute equally to the capital of the partnership.
- Partners are not entitled to interest on the capital they have contributed.
- Partners are not entitled to salaries.
- Partners are not to be charged interest on their drawings.
- Partners will share profits and losses equally.
- Partners are entitled to interest at 5% per annum on loans they make to the partnership.

The Appropriation account

The Appropriation Account is a continuation of the Profit and Loss Account. It begins with the net profit or loss brought down from the Profit and Loss Account. The following methods of dividing profits between partners must be treated as appropriations of profit in the Appropriation Account.

Partners' salaries A partnership agreement may entitle one or more partners to be paid a salary. This may be paid in addition to a further share of profit. A salary guarantees a partner an income, even if the firm does not make a profit. Partners' salaries are never debited in the Profit and Loss Account.

Interest on capital and drawings Interest on capital recognizes that if partners do not invest their capital in the partnership, their money could earn interest in some other form of investment. The partnership agreement should state the rate of interest to be paid. Interest on capital is payable even if the firm does not make a profit.

Interest charged to partners on their drawings is intended to encourage the partners to leave their shares of profit in the business as additional temporary capital.

Interest on partners' loans to the firm

Interest on a loan made by a partner to a firm is *not* an appropriation of profit – it is an expense to be debited in the Profit and Loss Account, *not in the Appropriation Account*.

Profit/loss sharing

Any balance of profit or loss on the Appropriation Account after charging interest on capitals and partners' salaries is shared between the partners in their agreed profit-sharing ratios. If there is no partnership agreement, the profit or loss will be shared equally.

It is important to remember that interest on capitals and partners' salaries is a method of sharing profit so that a partner's total share of profit includes these items.

Read questions carefully and note what the partners have agreed. If a question does not state what the partners have agreed about any of the matters in the Partnership Act listed above, apply the terms of the Act in your answer to the question.

15.2 How to prepare partnership accounts

Open the following accounts for each partner:

    Capital
    Drawings
    Current

The Current account is used to complete the double entry from the partnership Profit and Loss and Appropriation Accounts for the partner's share of profits, losses, interest and salary. It is also credited with interest on a partner's loan to the firm, if any, from the Profit and Loss Account. At the end of the year, the balance on the partner's Drawings account is transferred to the debit of his Current account.

Note. If partners do not maintain Current accounts, the double entry for interest, their salaries and shares of profit must be completed in their Capital accounts.

Example (No partnership agreement regarding interest, partners' salaries or sharing of profits/losses)

Michael and Charles began to trade as partners on 1 January 2003. Michael introduced $60 000 into the business as capital, and Charles contributed $40 000.

On 1 July 2003, Charles lent $10 000 to the business. The partnership trial balance at 31 December 2003 was as follows.

	$	$
Sales		300 000
Purchases	120 000	
Staff wages	42 000	
Rent	10 000	
Electricity	7 000	
Sundry expenses	5 400	
Premises at cost	60 000	
Fixtures and fittings at cost	28 000	
Trade debtors	5 460	
Trade creditors		2 860
Bank balance	94 000	
Capital accounts: Michael		60 000
Charles		40 000
Drawings Michael	24 000	
Charles	17 000	
Loan from Charles		10 000
	412 860	412 860

Further information

1. Stock at 31 December 2003: $18 000.
2. Depreciation is to be provided as follows.

    Premises: 5% per annum on cost

    Fixtures and fittings: $12\frac{1}{2}$% per annum on cost.

3. The partners had not made any agreement regarding interest on capital and drawings, salaries or sharing of profits and losses.

Required

(a) Prepare the Trading and Profit and Loss and Appropriation Accounts for the year ended 31 December 2003.

(b) Prepare the partners' Current accounts at 31 December 2003.

(c) Prepare the Balance Sheet at 31 December 2003.

Answer

(a)

Michael and Charles
Trading and Profit and Loss and Appropriation Account for the year ended 31 December 2003

		$	$	$
Sales				300 000
Less Cost of sales				
Purchases			120 000	
Less Stock at 31 December 2003			18 000	102 000
Gross profit				198 000
Staff wages			42 000	
Rent			10 000	
Electricity			7 000	
Sundry expenses			5 400	
Depreciation: Premises		3000		
Fixtures and fittings		3500	6 500	
Interest on loan (6 months at 5% p.a.)			250	71 150
Net profit				126 850
Shares of profit	Michael ($\frac{1}{2}$)		63 425	
	Charles ($\frac{1}{2}$)		63 425	126 850

(b)

Partners' Current accounts

		Michael	Charles			Michael	Charles
2003		$	$	2003		$	$
Dec 31	Drawings	24 000	17 000	Dec 31	Interest on loan	–	250
	Balances c/d	39 425	46 675		Share of profit	63 425	63 425
		63 425	63 675			63 425	63 675
				2004			
				Jan 1	Balance b/d	39 425	46 675

(c)

Balance Sheet at 31 December 2003

	Cost $	Dep. $	NBV $
Fixed assets			
Premises	60 000	3 000	57 000
Fixtures and fittings	28 000	3 500	24 500
	88 000	6 500	81 500
Current assets			
Stock		18 000	
Trade debtors		5 460	
Bank		94 000	
		117 460	
Current liabilities: Trade creditors		2 860	114 600
			196 100
Long-term liability: Loan from Charles			10 000
			186 100
Capital accounts: Michael		60 000	
Charles		40 000	100 000
Current accounts: Michael		39 425	
Charles		46 675	86 100
			186 100

Example (Partnership agreement in place)

Data as in example 1 above, with the following additional information.

The partnership agreement includes the following terms.

- Interest on capitals and drawings: 5% per annum.
- Partnership salaries (per annum): Michael $20 000; Charles $10 000.
- The balance of profits and losses is to be shared as follows: Michae 2/3; Charles 1/3.
- Charles is to be credited with interest on his loan to the partnership at a rate of 8% per annum.

Required

(a) Prepare the Trading and Profit and Loss and Appropriation Account for the year ended 31 December 2003.

(b) Prepare the partners' Current accounts at 31 December 2003.

Answer

(a)

Michael and Charles
Trading and Profit and Loss and Appropriation Account for the year ended 31 December 2003

		$	$	$
Sales				300 000
Less Cost of sales				
Purchases			120 000	
Less Stock at 31 December 2003			18 000	102 000
Gross profit				198 000
Staff wages			42 000	
Rent			10 000	
Electricity			7 000	
Sundry expenses			5 400	
Depreciation: Premises		3 000		
Fixtures and fittings		3 500	6 500	
Interest on loan (6 months)			400	71 300
Net profit				126 700
Add Interest on drawings:	Michael		1 200	
	Charles		850	2 050
				128 750
Less Interest on capitals:	Michael		3 000	
	Charles		2 000	
			5 000	
Partners' salaries:	Michael		20 000	
	Charles		10 000	35 000
				93 750
Shares of profit	Michael ($\frac{2}{3}$)		62 500	
	Charles ($\frac{1}{3}$)		31 250	93 750

(b)

Partners' Current accounts

2003		Michael $	Charles $	2003		Michael $	Charles $
Dec 31	Drawings	24 000	17 000	Dec 31	Interest on capital	3 000	2 000
	Interest on drawings	1 200	850		Interest on loan	–	400
					Salary	20 000	10 000
	Balance c/d	60 300	25 800		Share of profit	62 500	31 250
		85 500	43 650			85 500	43 650
				2004			
				Jan 1	Balance b/d	60 300	25 800

Exercise 1 (No partnership agreement)

Tee and Leef are trading in partnership. Their trial balance at 31 March 2004 is as follows.

	$	$
Capital accounts at 1 April 2003: Tee		100 000
Leef		50 000
Current accounts at 1 April 2003: Tee		5 000
Leef		10 000
Drawing accounts: Tee	29 000	
Leef	31 000	
Sales		215 000
Purchases	84 000	
Stock at 1 April 2003	16 000	
Selling expenses	30 000	
Administration expenses	42 000	
Fixtures and fittings at cost	48 000	
Provision for depreciation of fixtures and fittings		8 000
Office equipment at cost	27 000	
Provision for depreciation of office equipment		5 000
Trade debtors	24 000	
Trade creditors		11 000
Bank balance	85 000	
Loan from Leef		12 000
	416 000	416 000

Further information

1. Stock at 31 March 2004: $20 000.
2. Selling expenses prepaid at 31 March 2004: $6000.
3. Administration expenses accrued at 31 March 2004: $4000.

4. Depreciation is to be provided as follows: on fixtures and fittings 10% of cost; on office equipment 20% of cost.
5. Leef made the loan to the business on 1 April 2003.
6. The partners had not made any agreement regarding interest, salaries or profit sharing.

Required

(a) Prepare the partnership Trading, Profit and Loss and Appropriation Account for the year ended 31 March 2004.
(b) Prepare partners' Current accounts at 31 March 2004 in columnar form.
(c) Prepare the partnership Balance Sheet at 31 March 2004.

Exercise 2 (Partnership agreement in place)

The facts are as in exercise 1, but Tee and Leaf have a partnership agreement which includes the following terms.

1. Leef is to be credited with interest on his loan to the partnership at the rate of 10% per annum.
2. The partners are allowed interest at 10% per annum on capitals and are charged interest at 10% per annum on drawings.
3. Leef is entitled to a salary of $4000 per annum.
4. The balance of profit/loss is to be shared as follows: Tee 3/5; Leef 2/5.

Required

(a) Prepare the partnership Trading, Profit and Loss and Appropriation Account for the year ended 31 March 2004.
(b) Prepare the partners' Current accounts at 31 March 2004 in columnar form.
(c) Prepare the partnership Balance Sheet at 31 March 2004.

15.3 Advantages and disadvantages of partnerships

Advantages

- The capital invested by partners is often more than can be raised by a sole trader.
- A greater fund of knowledge, experience and expertise in running a business is available to a partnership.
- A partnership may be able to offer a greater range of services to its customers (or clients).
- The business does not have to close down or be run by inexperienced staff in the absence of one of the partners; the other partner(s) will provide cover.
- Losses are shared by all partners.

Disadvantages

- A partner has not the same freedom to act independently as a sole trader has.
- A partner may be frustrated by the other partner(s) in his or her plans for the direction and development of the business.
- Profits have to be shared by all partners.
- A partner may be legally liable for acts of the other partner(s).

15.4 Formation

Partnerships may be formed by merging the accounts of two sole traders. Initial records are entered in the general journal.

Example

Merging accounts for two sole traders (with the use of the general journal). Adella has been operating a boutique in SAN FERNANDO for the past five years. The sales turnover is very slow. She decided to form a partnership with Susan, a local dressmaker. They decided to share profits and losses equally. Adella's business has the following assets and liabilities.

Cash	$200 000	Inventory	$40 000
Accounts receivable	80 000	Bank	100 000
Furniture & fittings	80 000	Accounts payable	50 000

Susan's assets and liabilities are as follows:

Cash	$300 000	Equipment	$150 000
Land	100 000	Building	500 000
Mortgage	600 000		

Before preparing the journal entries all the assets and liabilities are added together separately.

JOURNAL ENTRY
Dr. Assets
Cr. Liabilities
Cr. Each partnership Capital accounts.

Date	Detail	Dr.	Cr.
		$000	$000
	Cash	500	
	Inventory	40	
	Accounts receivable	80	
	Furniture & fittings	80	
	Bank	100	
	Equipment	150	
	Land	100	
	Building	500	
	Accounts payable		50
	Mortgage		600
	Capital – Adella		450
	Capital – Susan		450

15.5 Recording of non-cash assets at fair market value (in the general journal)

Non-cash assets

Non-cash assets are assets that cannot be readily converted into cash. They are fixed in nature.

Other partnerships are enlarged by the admittance of new partners. Some partners bring non-cash assets; the fair market value must be ascertained.

Fair market value

Non-cash assets should be recorded at the fair market value.

The fair market value (market value) of non-cash assets is the price at which assets can be bought or sold in the market place.

Example

James and John started their partnership company on May 1 2004. They agreed to contribute an equal amount of capital and share profits and losses equally. The total capital will be $800 000 and they will invest any differences in cash. The partners agree to contribute the following non-cash assets:

	Book value	Fair value
	$000	$000
James:		
Machinery	200	300
Furniture	100	90
John:		
Inventory	150	90
Equipment	50	40

Journal entry
Dr. Assets at Fair market value
Dr. Cash (for the difference of capital invested)
Cr. Each partner's capital account (equally for the $800)

Date	Detail	Dr.	Cr.
		$000	$000
	Cash	280	
	Machinery	300	
	Furniture	90	
	Inventory	90	
	Equipment	40	
	Capital – John		400
	Capital – James		400

15.6 Reasons for admission of partners

- For additional funds/resources
- For expansion or reduction of operations
- To inherit a large customer base
- For skills and experience
- To share risk
- To share decision-making

15.7 Admission of a new partner

Example I

Balance Sheet of Jones and James	
Fixed assets	120 000
Current assets	50 000
	$ 170 000
Current liabilities	30 000
Long-term liabilities	40 000
Capital: Jones	40 000
James	60 000
	$ 170 000

John is interested in acquiring 25% of the partnership. He makes a direct payment of $20 000 to each of the partners. The payment is not to be shown in the books. Show the new Balance Sheet.

Admission by interest aquisition

Direct payment to partners not recorded.

1. Calculate the interest acquired from each partner.
   Jones: 25/100 × 40 000 = 10 000
   James: 25/100 × 60 000 = 15 000
2. Record the interest acquired
   Dr. Old partners' capital   Dr. Jones   10 000
                             Dr. James   15 000
   Cr. New partners' capital   Cr. John   25 000
3. Adjust Balance Sheet
   Note: Amount actually paid not shown in the books.

Example 2

Singh and Bynoe are partners with a profit and loss sharing ratio of 33% and 67% respectively. Their balance sheet is as follows:-

Singh and Bynoe
Balance Sheet as at July 31, 2005

Fixed assets	400 000
Current assets	150 000
	$550 000
Liabilities	100 000
Capital: Singh	150 000
Bynoe	300 000
	$550 000

Winston acquired a 25% interest for $200 000 cash. Prepare the journal entries.

Admission-investing activity – bonus method

Payment with bonus recorded

1. Calculate the investment of the new partner.

   Dr. Cash 200 000   Cr. New partner's capital 200 000

2. Calculate the book value of capital after the new investment.

   Old partners' + New partner's capital

   Singh 150 000 + Bynoe 300 000 + Winston 200 000 = 650 000

3. Calculate the new partner's implied capital.

   % interest purchased × book value of capital $\frac{25}{100}$ × 650 000 = 162 500

4. Calculate the bonus

   Capital invested less interest acquired (of new partner) 200 000 – 162 500 = 37 500

5. Distribute the bonus to old partners.

   Singh Y_3 × 37 500 = 12 500 Bynoe $\frac{2}{3}$ × 37 500 = 25 000

6. Record the distribution

   Cr. Singh 12 500   Dr. Winston 37 500

   Cr. Bynoe 25 000

Note: Acquired > Invested > deduct bonus from old partners' capital.

Admission-investing activity – goodwill recorded

Goodwill is the difference between the total value of a business and the total fair value of the separate net assets.

Possible reasons for the creation of goodwill:

- Acquisition of a business may allow easier access to materials or labour markets.
- Business has a good rapport with its existing customers, so that the business can be sold for more than its tangible assets.
- The business is in an excellent location.
- May acquire business that has skilled personnel.

Ways to calculate goodwill

- Value purchase (book value and fair market value)
- Average new partner's share add value introduced
- Number of times x year's profits
- Worth less net tangible assets.

Steps (goodwill method)

- Calculate implied capital (business capital based on new partner's investment).
- Calculate the book value of capital after the new partner's investment.
- Calculate goodwill.
- Allocate goodwill to old partners' capital accounts.
- Calculate the balances in each partner's capital accounts after the admission of the new partner.

Example 3

Chee and Chin are partners and their balance sheet is as follows:

Chee and Chin Balance Sheet
as at October 31, 2005

Fixed assets	200 000
Current assets	100 000
	$300 000
Liabilities	60 000
Capital: Chee	108 000
Chin	132 000
	$300 000

The profit sharing ratio is Chee 60% and Chin 40%. Chow acquired 20% interest in capital for $70 000.
Show: 1. The Capital accounts after admission.
           2. The new Balance Sheet.

Payment with goodwill recorded. (Goodwill recorded as an asset in the balance sheet.)

1. Record the capital invested by the new partner.

   Dr. Cash 70 000   Cr. Capital 70 000.

2. Calculate the implied capital of the business.

   If 20% = 70 000 then 100% = 70 000 × 5 = 350 000.

3. Calculate the book value of capital

Old investment   +   Additional investment

108 000 + 132 000 +   70 000 = 310 000.

4. Calculate goodwill

Implied capital   –   book value of capital

350 000   –   310 000 = 40 000.

5. Allocate goodwill (in old profit sharing ratio)

Chee $\frac{60}{100} \times 40\,000 = 24\,000$

Chin $\frac{40}{100} \times 40\,000 = 16\,000$

6. Record goodwill

Dr. Goodwill 40 000 Cr. Capital (Old partners) Chee 24 000 Chin 16 000.

7. Other assets. If other assets are revalued

Dr. The assets   Cr. Capital (Old partners)

with the amount of the revaluation.

New Balance Sheet	
Goodwill	40 000
Fixed assets	200 000
Current assets	170 000
	$410 000
Liabilities	60 000
Capital: Chee	132 000
Chin	148 000
Chow	70 000
	$410 000

Admission-investing activity – goodwill not recorded

Justification for leaving out goodwill

1. Valuation was negotiated or derived from a formula (not objective).
2. Value may change with business conditions.
3. Opinion divided on its amortization.
4. No charge to reduce profits.

Example 4

Ram and Persad are in partnership sharing profits and losses 6:4 respectively. After admitting Singh the ratio charged to 5:3:2.

Singh introduced capital of $38 000 of which $16 000 was for goodwill which will not be shown on the books.

If Ram's capital was $56 000 and Persad's was $32 000 show:

(a) the partners' Capital accounts
(b) the Goodwill account.

Payment with goodwill not recorded (only the effects of goodwill reflected in the Capital accounts).

1. Show the Capital accounts of each partner: Ram 56 000, Persad 32 000.

Make entries.

2. Record the capital invested by the new partner:

Dr. Cash 38 000

Cr. Capital Singh 38 000.

3. Calculate the value of goodwill.

If Singh paid $16 000 for $\frac{2}{10}$ or $\frac{1}{5}$ of goodwill

then goodwill was valued at (16 000 × 5) $ 80 000.

4. Allocate goodwill in the old profit sharing ratio.

Ram $\frac{6}{10} \times 80\,000 = 48\,000$

Persad $\frac{4}{10} \times 80\,000 = 32\,000$.

5. Shared goodwill: Dr. Goodwill 80 000

Cr. Ram (Capital a/c) 48 000

Cr. Persad (Capital a/c) 32 000

6. Write down goodwill (new profit/loss sharing ratio)

Dr. Ram (Capital a/c)   40 000

Dr. Persad (Capital a/c) 24 000

Dr. Singh (Capital a/c)   16 000

Cr. Goodwill   80 000.

Capital accounts							
	R	P	S		R	P	S
Goodwill	40 000	24 000	16 000	Balance b/d	56 000	32 000	—
Balance c/d	64 000	40 000	22 000	Bank			38 000
				Goodwill	48 000	32 000	—
	104 000	64 000	38 000		104 000	64 000	38 000

Goodwill account			
Ram	48 000	Ram	40 000
Persad	32 000	Persad	24 000
		Singh	16 000
	80 000		80 000

15.8 Apportionment of profit after partnership change

Partnership changes often occur in the middle of a firm's financial year. If a Profit and Loss Account is not prepared at the time of the change, the profit or loss for the financial year must be apportioned between the periods before and after the change.

If the profit is assumed to have been earned evenly throughout the year, it should be divided between the old and new partnerships on a time basis. However, some expenses may not have been incurred on a time basis and these must be allocated to the period to which they belong. Such expenses will be specified in a question. Apportionment of profit or loss is shown in a Profit and Loss Account prepared in columnar form as in the following example.

Example

Old and New are partners sharing profits and losses equally after allowing Old a salary of $10 000 per annum. On 1 January 2004 their Capital and Current account balances were as follows.

	Old	New
	$	$
Capital accounts	25 000	20 000
Current accounts	7 500	5 000

On 1 July 2004, the partners agree to the following revised terms of partnership.

1. Old to transfer $5000 from his Capital account to a Loan account on which he would be entitled to interest at 10% per annum.
2. New to bring his private car into the firm at a valuation of $12 000.
3. New to receive a salary of $5000 per annum.
4. Profits and losses to be shared: Old $\frac{3}{5}$, New $\frac{2}{5}$

Further information for the year ended 31 December 2004 is as follows.

	$
Sales (spread evenly throughout the year)	200 000
Cost of sales	87 500
Rent	25 000
Wages	35 000
General expenses	15 000

Of the general expenses, $5000 was incurred in the six months to 30 June 2004.

New's car is to be depreciated over four years on the straight-line basis and is assumed to have no value at the end of that time.

All sales produce a uniform rate of gross profit.

Required

(a) Prepare the Trading and Profit and Loss and Appropriation Accounts for the year ended 31 December 2004.
(b) Prepare the partners' Current accounts for the year ended 31 December 2004.

Answer

Old and New
Trading and Profit and Loss and Appropriation Account for the year ended 31 December 2004

		$
Sales		200 000
Less Cost of sales		87 500
Gross profit carried down		112 500

	6 months to 30 June 2004		6 months to 31 December 2004		Year to 31 December 2004	
	$	$	$	$	$	$
Gross profit brought down		56 250		56 250		112 500
Rent	12 500		12 500		25 000	
Wages	17 500		17 500		35 000	
General expenses	5 000		10 000		15 000	
Interest on loan	–		250		250	
Depreciation – car	–		1 500		1 500	
		35 000		41 750		76 750
Net profit		21 250		14 500		35 750
Less						
Salary: Old		5 000		–	5 000	
New		–		2 500	2 500	7 500
		16 250		12 000		28 250
Share of profit: Old ($\frac{1}{2}$) 8 125	($\frac{3}{5}$) 7 200			15 325		
New ($\frac{1}{2}$) 8 125	16 250	($\frac{2}{5}$) 4 800	12 000	12 925	28 250	

(b)

Partners' Current accounts

	Old $	New $		Old $	New $
2004			2004		
Dec 31 Balance c/d	27 825	20 425	Jan 1 Balance b/d	7 500	5 000
			Dec 31 Salary	5 000	2 500
			Share of profit	15 325	12 925
	27 825	20 425		27 825	20 425
			2005		
			Jan 1 Balance b/d	27 825	20 425

Exercise 3

Hook, Line and Sinker have shared profits and losses in the ratio 3 : 2 : 1 for a number of years. On 1 July 2004, the partners agreed that, from that date,

1. Hook will be entitled to a salary of $6000 per annum
2. profits and losses will be shared equally.

Information extracted from their books for the year ended 31 December 2004 was as follows.

	$
Sales	129 500
Cost of sales	66 500
Wages	14 000
General expenses	5 250
Depreciation of fixed assets	1 750

Two-thirds of the General expenses were incurred in the six months ended 31 December 2004.

On 1 April 2004, Hook made a loan of $8000 to the partnership. Interest on the loan is at a rate of 10% per annum.

Sales have accrued evenly throughout the year and all sales have earned a uniform rate of gross profit.

Required

Prepare a Trading and Profit and Loss Account for the year ended 31 December 2004 in columnar form to show the appropriation of profit before and after the change.

15.9 Partnership dissolution

This is the formal closure of a partnership company.

Reasons for dissolution

Bankruptcy of a partner.

Partners found guilty of misconduct.

Death of partner.

Partners no longer want to continue in business.

Where no time limit has been agreed.

It is illegal for the business to continue.

When a partner becomes mentally ill.

When on of the partners becomes permanently incapable of handling matters.

When there is a breach of the partnership agreement.

When the business can only be run at a loss (continuing trading losses).

Retirement of a partner.

Disagreement among the partners.

Completion of purpose.

15.10 Dissolution (liquidation)

(A) Dispose of assets

1. Transfer all assets (except Cash/Bank) To Realization:
   Dr. Realization a/c
   Cr. Asset (s) a/c

2. Sell assets individually
   Dr. Cash/Bank a/c
   Cr. Realization a/c

3. Pay partners with assets
   Dr. Partners' capital a/c
   Cr. Realization a/c
      or
   Sale of the going concern assets:
   Dr. Cash a/c
   Cr. Realization a/c
   with the purchase consideration

(B) Dispose of assets

1. Payment
   Dr. the Liability a/c
   Cr. Cash/Bank a/c

2. Gain on settlement
   Dr. Liability a/c
   Cr. Realization a/c

3. Loss on settlement
   Dr. Realization a/c
   Cr. Liability a/c

4. Loans by partners
   Dr. Loan a/c
   Cr. Cash/Bank a/c
      or
   Sale of the going concern liabilities:
   Dr. Liabilities
      (taken over)
   Cr. Realization a/c

(C) Dispose of assets

Realization a/c			Capital a/c	
Loss on disposal	Gains on disposal	Shared losses	Bals b/f	
Loss on settlement	Gain on settlement		Shared gains	
Dissolution expenses				
Gains (Cr. Balance)	Losses (Dr. Balance)			
Shared in P/L/ Ratio	Shared in P/L/ Ratio			

Example

Jill and Joan are partners and share profits and losses equally. The partners have agreed to dissolve the partnership. The balance sheet book values are

Cash	$250 000
Non cash assets	$400 000
Other liabilities	$150 000
Capital, Jill	$200 000
Joan	$300 000
Additional information	
Liquidation expenses	$10 000
Sale of non cash assets	$300 000
Liabilities settled	$100 000

Solution

Realization a/c

Non current assets	$400 000	Cash	$300 000
Cash – realization expenses	10 000	Liabilities	50 000
		Jill, Capital	30 000
		Joan, Capital	30 000
	$410 000		$410 000

Cash a/c

Balance b/d	$ 250 000	Realization expenses	$ 10 000
Realization	300 000	Liabilities	100 000
		Capital, Jill	170 000
		Capital, Joan	270 000

Non-cash assets a/c

Balance b/d	$400 000	Realization	$400 000

Other liabilities a/c

Cash	$100 000	Balance b/d	$150 000
Gain	50 000		

Capital – Jill

Realization	$ 30 000	Balance b/d	$200 000
Cash	170 000		

Capital – Joan

Realization	$ 30 000	Balance b/d	$ 300 000
Cash	270 000		

15.11 Liquidation and safe payment plan

This occurs when the partnership is not liquidated at once but in stages.

Format of liquidation and safe payment schedule:

Liquidation schedule

	Cash	Non–cash assets	Liabilities	Capital of partner(s)
	$	$	$	$
Balance b/d	xxx	xxx	(xxx)	(xxx)
Sale of assets	xxx	(xxx)		xxx
Balance	xxx	xxx	xxx	xxx
Pay liabilities	(xxx)		(xxx)	
Balance	xxx	xxx		xxx
Cash payment	(xxx)			xxx
Balance	xxx	xxx		xxx

Safe payment schedule

	Capital
Balance after payment of liabilities	xxx
Allocation of possible loss	
(balance b/d from liquidation schedule)	xxx
Balance	xxx
Allocation of partners deficit (using partners ratio)	xxx
Balance	xxx

NOTE: Allocation of loss can be for anything: for example, the sale of a non-current asset.

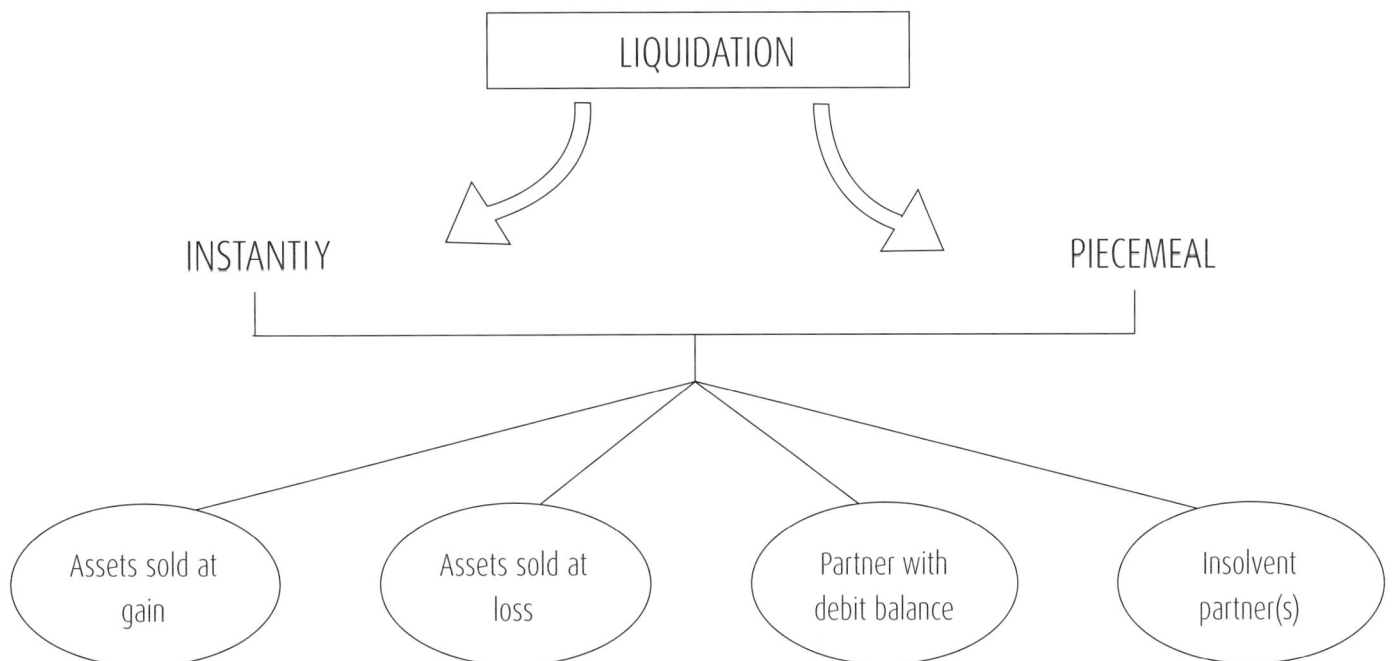

15.12 Retirement of a partner

A partner may retire voluntarily (by selling equity) or involuntarily by reaching retirement age or by dying. The latter will dissolve the partnership. Payments on either occasion may be from partners' personal assets or partnership assets.

Payment from partners' personal assets

Procedure:

1. The cash contribution will not be entered in the books.
2. Journal entry to be made for the transfer of capital from the retired partner to an existing partner.

> Dr. Retired partner capital a/c
>
> Cr. Existing partner capital a/c.

When a partner leaves a firm, or a new partner joins, it marks the end of one partnership and the beginning of a new one. As in the case of a simple change in profit-sharing ratios, a change in partners may occur at any time in a firm's financial year, and no entries may be made in the books to record the change until the end of the year.

Account must be taken of

- asset revaluation
- goodwill
- changes in the profit/loss-sharing ratios.

If a partnership change occurs on the first day of a firm's financial year, the procedure is so straightforward that it is unlikely to form the basis of an examination question. There is no reason why partners should join on the first day of a firm's financial year, or why one should leave on the last day of the financial year. In practice, changes usually occur during a financial year and the accounting records are continued without interruption; final accounts are not produced until the end of the year.

Example (Admission of new partner)

Grey and Green have shared profits and losses in the ratio of 3 : 2. On 1 October 2004 they decided to admit Blue as a partner. No entries to record Blue's admittance as a partner were made in the books before the end of the financial year on 31 December 2004.

Information extracted from the books for the year ended 31 December 2004 included the following:

	$	
Turnover	400 000	
Cost of sales	240 000	
Wages	40 000	
Rent	8 000	
General expenses	9 600	
Depreciation of fixed assets:		
1 January to 30 September 2004	6 000	
1 October to 31 December 2004	4 350	(based on asset revaluation as shown below)

At 31 December 2003 the balances on Grey and Green's Capital and Current accounts were as follows:

	Capital accounts	Current accounts
	$	$
Grey	50 000	2000
Green	30 000	3000

On 1 October 2004, the partnership assets were revalued as follows:

	$	
Freehold premises	50 000	increase
Other fixed assets	14 000	decrease
Current assets	3 000	decrease

The partners agreed the value of goodwill at 1 October 2004 at $40 000 and decided that no Goodwill account should be opened in the books.

On 1 October 2004 Blue paid $20 000 into the firm's bank account as capital. On the same day, Grey lent the partnership $20 000. He is entitled to interest at a rate of 10% per annum on the loan.

The balances on the partners' Drawings account at 31 December 2004 were as follows:

	$
Grey	23 000
Green	17 000
Blue	3 000

The new partnership agreement provided for the following as from 1 October 2004:

(i) Interest was allowed on the balances on Capital accounts at 31 December each year at a rate of 5% per annum.

(ii) Green was entitled to a salary of $12 000 per annum.

(iii) The balance of profits and losses were to be shared: Grey $\frac{2}{5}$; Green $\frac{2}{5}$: Blue $\frac{1}{5}$.

Required

(a) Prepare the Capital accounts of Grey, Green and Blue at 31 December 2004.

(b) Prepare the Partnership Trading, Profit and Loss and Appropriation Account for the year ended 31 December 2004.

(c) Prepare the partners' Current accounts at 31 December 2004.

Answer

Working: Goodwill		Before 1.10.04		After 1.10.04	Capital accounts
		$		$	$
Grey $\left(\frac{3}{5}\right)$		24 000	$\left(\frac{2}{5}\right)$	16 000	8000 credit
Green $\left(\frac{2}{5}\right)$		16 000	$\left(\frac{2}{5}\right)$	16 000	no change
Blue		–	$\left(\frac{1}{5}\right)$	8 000	8000 debit

(a)

Partners' Capital accounts

2004		Grey $	Green $	Blue $	2004		Grey $	Green $	Blue $
Oct 1	Green – Goodwill			8 000	Jan 1	Balance b/d	50 000	30 000	–
Dec 31	Balance c/d	77 800	43 200	12 000	Oct 1	Bank	–	–	20 000
						Profit on			
						revaluation	19 800	13 200	–
						Goodwill	8 000		
		77 800	43 200	20 000			77 800	43 200	20 000
					2005				
					Jan 1	Balance b/d	77 800	43 200	12 000

(b)

Grey, Green and Blue
Trading and Profit and Loss and Appropriation Accounts for the year ended 31 December 2004

					$
Turnover					400 000
Less Cost of sales					240 000
Gross profit carried down					160 000

		9 months to 30 June 2004		3 months to 31 December 2004		Year to 31 December 2004	
		$	$	$	$	$	$
Gross profit brought down			120 000		40 000		160 000
Wages		30 000		10 000		40 000	
Rent		6 000		2 000		8 000	
General expenses		7 200		2 400		9 600	
Interest on loan		–		500		500	
Depreciation		6 000	49 200	4 350	19 250	10 350	68 450
Net profit			70 800		20 750		91 550
Interest on capitals:	Grey			973			
	Green			540			
	Blue			150			
				1 663			
Salary: Green				3 000	4 663		4 663
					16 087		86 887
Profit shares:	Grey $\left(\frac{3}{5}\right)$ 42 480		$\left(\frac{2}{5}\right)$ 6 435		48 915	
	Green $\left(\frac{2}{5}\right)$ 28 320		$\left(\frac{2}{5}\right)$ 6 435		34 755	
	Blue – 70 800		$\left(\frac{1}{5}\right)$ 3 217 16 087		3 217 86 887	

(c)

Partners' Current accounts

2004		Grey $	Green $	Blue $	2004		Grey $	Green $	Blue $
Dec 31	Drawings	23 000	17 000	3 000	Jan 1	Balance b/d	2 000	3 000	–
Dec 31	Balance c/d	29 388	24 295	367	Dec 31	Loan interest	500	–	–
						Interest on			
						capital	973	540	150
						Salary	–	3 000	–
						Profit	48 915	34 755	3 217
		52 388	41 295	3 367			52 388	41 295	3 367
2005					Jan 1	Balance b/d	29 388	24 295	367

Exercise 4

Bell and Booker have been partners for some years, making up their accounts annually to 31 December. The partnership agreement contained the following provisions.

- Interest was allowed on capitals at 10% per annum.
- Booker was entitled to a salary of $15 000 per annum.
- Profits and losses were to be shared: Bell $\frac{2}{3}$; Booker $\frac{1}{3}$.

At 31 December 2003 the partners' Capital and Current account balances were as follows:

	Capital	Current accounts
	$	$
Bell	100 000	16 000
Booker	60 000	12 000

On 1 September 2004, Bell and Booker admitted their manager, Candell, as a partner. Candell had been receiving a salary of $24 000.

The revised partnership agreement provided as follows.

- Partner's salary: Booker $18 000 per annum.
- Interest on capitals at 10% per annum.
- Profits and losses shared: Bell $\frac{2}{5}$, Booker $\frac{2}{5}$, Candell $\frac{1}{5}$.

The partnership's fixed assets at cost at 31 December 2003 were as follows:

	At cost	Depreciation to date	Net book value
	$	$	$
Freehold premises	180 000	45 000	135 000
Plant and machinery	90 000	60 000	30 000
Motor cars	30 000	27 000	3 000
Office equipment	21 000	14 000	7 000

No additions to, or disposals of, fixed assets had taken place between 31 December 2003 and 31 August 2004.

The assets were revalued at 1 September as follows:

	$
Freehold premises	210 000
Plant and machinery	27 000
Motor cars	3 000
Office equipment	6 000

Depreciation of fixed assets is calculated on cost and is provided as follows: freehold premises 4% per annum; plant and machinery 20% per annum; motor cars 25% per annum; office equipment 10% per annum.

Goodwill was valued at $60 000, but no Goodwill account was to be opened in the books.

On 1 September 2004, Candell paid $50 000 into the firm's bank account as capital, and also brought his private car, valued at $9000, into the business. On the same day, Bell transferred $20 000 from his Capital account to a loan account on which interest is to be paid at a rate of 12% per annum.

The following information is available from the partnership books for the year ended 31 December 2004:

	$
Turnover	600 000
Cost of sales	330 000
Wages and salaries	106 000
Rent	42 000
Heating and lighting	6 000
Sundry expenses	12 000

Note. Sales were spread evenly throughout the year and earned a uniform rate of gross profit.

Drawings in the year ended 31 December 2004 were: Bell $30 000; Booker $40 000; Candell $4000.

Required

(a) Prepare a Trading, Profit and Loss and Appropriation Account for the year ended 31 December 2004.

(b) Prepare the partners' Capital and Current accounts for the year ended 31 December 2004.

Example (Partner retires)

Norman, Beard and David have traded in partnership for some years. Norman decided to retire on 30 September 2004 but no accounts were prepared for the partnership until the end of the financial year on 31 December 2004.

The following balances have been extracted from the trial balance at 31 December 2004:

	$	$
Sales		720 000
Purchases	400 000	
Stock at 1 January 2004	20 000	
Wages	100 000	
Rent	26 000	
Heating and lighting	21 000	
Sundry expenses	120 000	

Further information

1. Stock at 31 December 2004 cost $24 000.

2. At 31 December 2004 rent of $2000 had been prepaid and $1200 had accrued for heating and lighting.

3. Fixed assets at 1 January 2004 at cost were as follows:

	$
Plant and machinery	80 000
Office equipment	10 000

Additional machinery was purchased on 1 October 2004 for $12 000.

4. Depreciation of fixed assets is to be provided at 10% per annum on cost.

5. Goodwill was valued at $45 000, but no Goodwill was to be recorded in the books.

6. The partners' Capital and Current account balances at 1 January 2004 were as follows:

	Capital accounts	Current accounts
	$	$
Norman	50 000	8 000 (Cr)
Beard	40 000	9 000 (Cr)
David	20 000	3 000 (Cr)

7. The partners' drawings were as follows:

	$
Norman (up to 30 September 2004)	30 000
Up to 31 December 2004:	
Beard	50 000
David	32 000

8. Norman left $60 000 of his capital in the business as a loan with interest at 10% per annum. The interest was payable on 30 June and 31 December each year.

9. The partnership agreement up to 30 September 2004 allowed for the following.

> Interest on capitals: 8% per annum (based on balances on Capital accounts at 1 January 2004).
>
> Salary: David $6000 per annum.
>
> Profit and losses to be shared: Norman $(\frac{1}{2})$, Beard $(\frac{1}{3})$, David $(\frac{1}{6})$.

The agreement was amended on 1 October 2004 as follows:

> Interest on capitals: 10% per annum (based on balances on Capital accounts at 1 October 2003).
>
> Salary: David $10 000 per annum.
>
> Profits and losses to be shared: Beard $(\frac{3}{5})$, David $(\frac{2}{5})$.

10. The assets were not revalued at 30 September 2004.

11. It is assumed that gross profit has been earned evenly throughout the year.

Required

(a) Prepare the partners' Capital accounts.

(b) Prepare the partnership's Trading, Profit and Loss and Appropriation Accounts for the year ended 31 December 2004.

(c) Prepare the partners' Current accounts for the year ended 31 December 2004.

Answer

(a)

Partners' Capital accounts

2004		Norman $	Beard $	David $	2004			Norman $	Beard $	David $
Sep 30	Goodwill		12 000	10 500	Jan 1	Balance	b/d	50 000	40 000	20 000
	Loan a/c	60 000			Sep 30	Goodwill		22 500		
	Bank	46 750				Current a/c		34 250*		
Dec 31	Balance c/d		28 000	9 500						
		106 750	40 000	20 000				106 750	40 000	20 000
2005										
					Jan 1	Balance b/d			28 000	9 500

* The balance on the outgoing partner's Current account is transferred to Capital account.

(b)

Norman, Beard and David
Trading and Profit and Loss and Appropriation Accounts for the year ended 31 December 2004

	$	$
Sales		720 000
Less Cost of sales		
Stock at 1.1.04	20 000	
Purchases	400 000	
	420 000	
Less Stock at 31.12.04	24 000	396 000
Gross profit		324 000

		9 months to 30.9.04		3 months to 31.12.04		Total	
		$	$	$	$	$	$
Gross profit			243 000		81 000		324 000
Wages		75 000		25 000		100 000	
Rent (26 000 – 2000)		18 000		6 000		24 000	
Heating and lighting (21 000 + 1200)		16 650		5 550		22 200	
Sundry expenses		9 000		3 000		12 000	
Depreciation: Plant and machinery		6 000		2 300		8 300	
Office equipment		750		250		1 000	
Interest on loan		–	125 400	1 500	43 600	1 500	169 000
Net profit			117 600		37 400		155 000
Interest on capital:	Norman	3 000		–		3 000	
	Beard	2 400		700†		3 100	
	David	1 200		238†		1 438	
		6 600		938		7 538	
Salary	David	4 500	11 100	2 500	3 438	7 000	14 538
			106 500		33 962		140 462
Shares of profit	Norman	53 250		–		53 250	
	Beard	35 500		20 377		55 877	
	David	17 750	106 500	13 585	33 962	31 335	140 462

† On capitals of $28 000 and $9500 respectively.

(c)

Partners' Current accounts

		Norman	Beard	David				Norman	Beard	David
2004		$	$	$	2004			$	$	$
Sep 30	Drawings	30 000			Jan 1	Balance b/d		8 000	9 000	3 000
	Capital a/c	34 250*			Sep 30	Int. on Capital		3 000		
						Profit		53 250		
Dec 31	Drawings		50 000	32 000	Dec 31	Int. on Capital			3 100	1 438
	Balance c/d		17 977	10 773		Salary				7 000
						Profit		____	55 877	31 335
			64 250	67 977	42 773			64 250	67 977	42 773
					2005					
					Jan 1	Balance b/d			17 977	10 773

* The balance on the outgoing partner's Current account is transferred to Capital account.

Exercise 5

Wilfrid, Hide and Wyte were partners sharing profits and losses in the ratio of 3 : 2 : 1 after charging interest on capitals at 10% per annum. Their Capital and Current account balances at 1 July 2003 were as follows:

	Capital a/cs	Current a/cs
	$	$
Wilfrid	80 000	12 000
Hide	50 000	3 000
Wyte	30 000	4 000

Wilfrid decided to retire on 31 December 2003. He left $75 000 of the balance on his Capital account as a loan to the firm, with interest at 10% per annum. The balance on his Capital account was paid to him by cheque.

At 31 December 2003, Goodwill was valued at $60 000 but Goodwill was not to be shown in the books. It was also agreed that the partnership assets should be revalued at $21 000 less than their current book values.

Hide and Wyte continued in partnership from 1 January 2004, with interest allowed on capitals at 10% per annum and with profits and losses being shared equally.

The partners' drawings in the year ended 30 June 2004 were as follows:

	$
Wilfrid (6 months to 31 December 2003)	23 000
Hide (12 months to 30 June 2004)	28 000
Wyte (12 months to 30 June 2004)	18 000

Further information

1.

	$
Gross profit for the year ended 30 June 2004	187 000 (assumed to have been earned evenly throughout the year)
Expenditure for the year ended 30 June 2004:	
Wages	91 000
Rent paid	14 000
Electricity paid	7 000
Sundry expenses	9 000

2. At 30 June 2004, rent of $2000 had been paid in advance, and electricity in the amount of $1400 had accrued.

Required

(a) Prepare the partnership Profit and Loss and Appropriation Account for the year ended 30 June 2004.

(b) Prepare the Capital and Current accounts of the partnership for the year ended 30 June 2004.

15.13 Incorporation

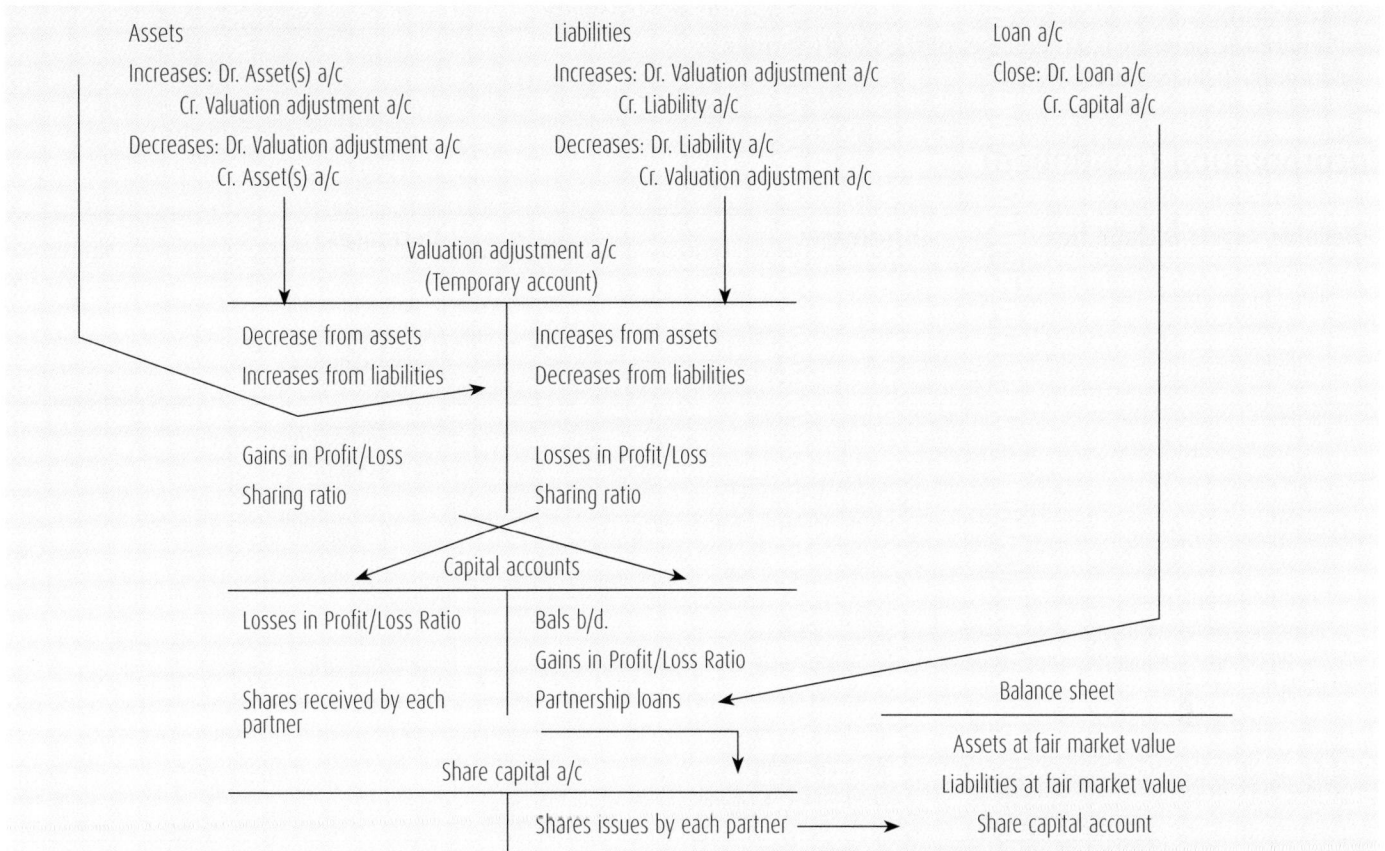

Assets	Liabilities	Loan a/c
Increases: Dr. Asset(s) a/c	Increases: Dr. Valuation adjustment a/c	Close: Dr. Loan a/c
Cr. Valuation adjustment a/c	Cr. Liability a/c	Cr. Capital a/c
Decreases: Dr. Valuation adjustment a/c	Decreases: Dr. Liability a/c	
Cr. Asset(s) a/c	Cr. Valuation adjustment a/c	

Valuation adjustment a/c
(Temporary account)

Decrease from assets	Increases from assets
Increases from liabilities	Decreases from liabilities
Gains in Profit/Loss	Losses in Profit/Loss
Sharing ratio	Sharing ratio

Capital accounts

Losses in Profit/Loss Ratio	Bals b/d.
	Gains in Profit/Loss Ratio
Shares received by each partner	Partnership loans

Balance sheet

Assets at fair market value

Share capital a/c

Shares issues by each partner ⟶

Liabilities at fair market value

Share capital account

Example

Ivy and Flora are partners in a beauty salon. They decided to convert the beauty salon into a beauty school and supplies company. The new name of the company is Classy Care Company. They needed to acquire additional funding so they decided to incorporate business on January 1st 2005. The authorized share capital of the company is 200 000 shares at $5 par value. The following is the balance sheet of the partnership before incorporation.

IVY AND FLORA
Balance Sheet as at December 31 2004

	BOOK VALUE	FAIR VALUE
Current assets		
Cash	$ 20 000	$ 20 000
Accounts receivable	50 000	50 000
Inventories	100 000	80 000
Investments	5 000	10 000
Fixed assets		
Land and building	100 000	150 000
Equipment	150 000	140 000
Current liabilities		
Accounts payable	20 000	20 000
Long term liabilities		
Mortgage payable	50 000	45 000
Capital		
Ivy	200 000	
Flora	155 000	

Additional Information

Ivy and Flora share profits and losses equally.

The new company will issue 50 000 shares with a par value of $5 to Ivy and Flora.

Required

1. Journalize the entry to record the incorporation of the partnership.
2. Prepare the opening balance sheet of the newly formed company (Classy Care).

Incorporation (continued)

Revalue Assets & Liabilities	Increases	Decreases
1. Adjust to fair market value – Assets – Liabilities	New > Old – Gain Old > New – Gain	Old > New – Loss New > Old – Loss
2. Accumulate Gains/Losses in the Valuation Adjustments a/c – Assets – Liabilities	Dr. Asset a/c Cr. Valuation a/c Dr. Valuation Cr. Provision a/c	Dr. Valuation a/c Cr. Asset a/c Dr. Provision a/c Cr. Valuation a/c
3. Share the balance in the Valuation a/c (in the P/Ls Ratio) and transfer to the capital accounts	Credit balance: Dr. Valuation a/c Cr. Capital a/c	Debit balance: Dr. Capital a/c Cr. Valuation a/c
4. Transfer partner's loan to capital accounts	Debit loan account Credit partner's capital a/c	
5. Close capital accounts to share capital a/c	Shares > Capital: Dr. Capital a/c Cr. Share Capital a/c Cr. Premium a/c Capital > Shares: Dr. Capital a/c Dr. Premium a/c Cr. Share Capital a/c	

Solution: Step 1

Before journalizing entries you must calculate the change (the difference between the book value and fair market value of all the assets and liabilities). This is done in order to adjust the accounting entries.

Inventories	100 000 –	80 000	= 20 000
Investment	5 000 –	10 000	= 5 000
Land & Building	100 000 –	150 000	= 50 000
Equipment	150 000 –	140 000	= 10 000
Mortgage payable	50 000 –	45 000	= 5 000

If you had to make accounting entries in the journal, a temporary account is opened known as the valuation adjustment account. The journal entries would look as follows:

DATE	DETAILS	Dr.	Cr.
	Valuation adjustment	20 000	
	Inventories		20 000
	Investment	5 000	
	Valuation adjustment		5 000
	Land and Building	50 000	
	Valuation adjustment		50 000
	Valuation adjustment	10 000	
	Equipment		10 000
	Mortgage payable	5 000	
	Valuation adjustment		5 000

Step 2

In order to determine the amount each partner will receive due to the incorporation, the valuation account must be closed off and the balances will be transferred to the partner's capital accounts using the old profit sharing ratio. The entries of the valuation adjustment account will look as this:

Valuation adjustment account

Inventories	$20 000	Investment	$ 5 000
Equipment	10 000	Land and Building	50 000
Capital: Ivy	15 000	Mortgage payable	5 000
Flora	15 000		
	60 000		60 000

The journal entry for the above will be as follows:

DATE	DETAILS	Dr.	Cr.
	Valuation adjustment	30 000	
	Capital: Ivy		15 000
	Flora		15 000

In order to record the distribution of shares, the capital accounts must be adjusted and the amount of share capital to issue to Ivy and Flora must be calculated as well.

Adjustment of capital account amounts

Ivy	200 000 + 15 000	= 215 000
Flora	155 000 + 15 000	= 170 000
		385 000

Calculation of share capital total
Number of shares to be issued * par value
50 000 * $5 = $250 000

Journal entry to record the distribution of shares (this signifies the incorporation and the official closure of the partnership company)

DATE	DETAILS	Dr.	Cr.
	Capital: Ivy	215 000	
	Flora	170 000	
	Share capital		250 000
	Capital paid in (share premium)		135 000

* This is the difference between the sum total of Ivy and Flora's capital accounts and the shares distributed to them as share capital.

Balance Sheet of Classy Care after the incorporation

CLASSY CARE
Balance Sheet as at January 1st 2005

Current assets			
Cash	2 000		
Accounts receivable	50 000		
Inventories	80 000		
Investment	10 000	160 000	
Current liabilities			
Accounts payable		20 000	140 000
Fixed assets			
Land and Building		150 000	
Equipment		140 000	290 000
			430 000
Financed by			
Long term liabilities			
Mortgage payable			45 000
Authorized share capital			
(Ordinary shares 100 000 x $5.00)	500 000		
Issued capital			
Ordinary shares (50 000 x $5.00)		250 000	
Share premium		135 000	385 000
			430 000

15.14 Questions

1 Sugar and Cane are in partnership sharing profits and losses in the ratio 2:3 respectively. Their existing capital balances are $65 000 and $105 000 respectively. They have agreed to allow Arrow into the partnership.

(a) Prepare journal entries to record the admission of Arrow into the partnership in each of the following options.

(b) Calculate the new capital balances after the admission of Arrow in each of the following independent situations:

   (i) Arrow purchases $\frac{1}{3}$ of Cane's interest in the partnership for $60 000.

   (ii) Arrow purchases a $\frac{1}{4}$ share in the partnership paying $95 000 cash.

2 On January 1, 2002 the capitals of L&J were as follows: Lois $26 000 and Jay $24 000. In 2002 the partnership reports net income of $30 000. The income ratio provides for salary allowances of $12 000 for Lois and $10 000 for Jay. The remainder is to be shared equally. Neither partner had any drawings in 2002.

Prepare:

(a) A schedule showing the distribution of income in 2002.

(b) Journalize the division of 2002 net income to the partners.

3

Cash	$ 60 000
Non – Cash Assets	$180 000
Accounts Payable	$ 40 000
D. Tall – Capital	$100 000
I. High, Capital	$100 000

Required: (a) Prepare a liquidation schedule for the partnership. Assume that the non-cash assets are sold for $200 000.

(b) Prepare journal entries to record the liquidation of the firm.

15.15 Partnership case study

Three Bakers

In a small town called Plenty there were three bakers all sole proprietors struggling to run their individual businesses. Baker Joe was a marketing expert but was not good at baking. Baker Ben was a very skilful baker but lacked marketing skills and his bakery needed an upgrade. Baker Ann recently came into some cash and wanted to purchase new machinery but was afraid she did not have the market to sell extra goods.

1 Identify the type of business organization that will benefit these bakers.

2 What are the benefits to be gained by the bakers coming together and pooling their resources?

3 What are the drawbacks?

4 Assuming the bakers decided to pool their resources, list some conditions required to make this organization a success.

15.16 How to make journal entries in the books of a company to record the purchase of a business

Before any entries for the purchase of a business are made in a company's ledger accounts, the transaction must be recorded in the journal. The entries should include the Bank and Cash accounts if these are taken over. However, the bank and cash balances of the business being acquired are not usually taken over unless a sole trader or a partnership converts their business into a limited company.

Example

Bortit Ltd purchased the business of A. Sellit, a sole trader, on 1 October 2004. Sellit's Balance Sheet at that date was

	$	$
Fixed assets		
Land and buildings		60 000
Plant and machinery		35 000
Motor vehicles		21 000
		116 000
Current assets		
Stock	7 000	
Debtors	4 000	
Bank	5 000	
	16 000	
Less Current liabilities		
Creditors	2 000	14 000
		130 000
Capital		130 000

The assets were taken over at the following values:

Land and buildings	80 000
Plant and machinery	28 000
Motor vehicles	16 000
Stock	5 000
Debtors	3 000
Creditors	2 000

Bortit Ltd did not take over Sellit's Bank account.

Bortit Ltd paid A. Sellit $150 000, made up as follows: cash $20 000 and 100 000 ordinary shares of $1 each.

Required

Prepare the journal entries in Bortit Ltd's books to record the purchase of A. Sellit's business.

Answer

	Dr	Cr
	$	$
Land and buildings	80 000	
Plant and machinery	28 000	
Motor vehicles	16 000	
Stock	5 000	
Debtors	3 000	
Goodwill	20 000[1]	
Creditors		2 000
Cash		20 000
Ordinary share capital		100 000
Share Premium account	_____	30 000[2]
	152 000	152 000

The purchase of the business of A. Sellit on 1 October 2004 for the sum of £150 000 payable as follows: cash $20 000 and by the issue of 100 000 ordinary shares of $1 at $1.30 per share.

1 Goodwill = purchase consideration ($150 000) less value of net assets acquired ($130 000).

2 The shares were valued at $(150 000 – 20 000) = $130 000. $30 000 is the share premium.

Bortit Ltd's Balance Sheet at 1 October 2004 before it acquired the business of A. Sellit was as follows:

	$	$
Tangible fixed assets		
Land and buildings		200 000
Plant and machinery		75 000
Motor vehicles		40 000
		315 000
Current assets		
Stock		21 000
Debtors	16 000	
Bank	32 000	
	69 000	
Current liabilities		
Creditors	7 000	62 000
		377 000
Capital and reserves		
Ordinary share capital		300 000
Retained profit		77 000
		377 000

Required

Prepare Bortit Ltd's Balance Sheet immediately after the purchase of the business of A. Sellit.

Answer

Add the journal entries to Bortit Ltd's assets, liabilities, share capital and reserves.

Bortit Ltd Balance Sheet at 1 October 2004 after the acquisition of A. Sellit's business

		$	$
Intangible fixed asset			
Goodwill			20 000
Tangible fixed assets			
Land and buildings	(200 000 + 80 000)		280 000
Plant and machinery	(75 000 + 28 000)		103 000
Motor vehicles	(40 000 + 16 000)		56 000
			439 000
Total fixed assets			459 000
Current assets			
Stock	(21 000 + 5000)	26 000	
Debtors	(16 000 + 3000)	19 000	
Bank	(32 000 – 20 000)	12 000	
		57 000	
Current liabilities			
Creditors	(7000 + 2000)	9 000	48 000
			507 000
Capital and reserves			
Ordinary share capital (300 000 + 100 000)			400 000
Share premium			30 000
Retained profit			77 000
			507 000

Exercise 6

Hamil Ltd purchased the business of Abdul, a sole trader, on 30 June 2004. The Balance Sheets of both businesses at that date were as follows.

	Abdul $	Abdul $	Hamil Ltd $	Hamil Ltd $
Fixed assets				
Freehold property		40 000		100 000
Plant and machinery		15 000		60 000
Office equipment		–		14 000
Office furniture		7 000		–
		62 000		174 000
Current assets				
Stock	4 000		10 000	
Debtors	6 000		7 000	
Bank	1 000		25 000	
	11 000		42 000	
Current liabilities				
Creditors	3 000	8 000	6 000	36 000
		70 000		210 000
Capital account		70 000		
Share capital and reserves				
Ordinary shares of $1				150 000
Share Premium account				20 000
Retained profit				40 000
				210 000

It was agreed that Abdul's assets should be valued as follows.

	$
Freehold property	70 000
Plant and machinery	12 000
Office furniture	4 000
Stock	2 500
Debtors	5 500

Hamil Ltd did not acquire Abdul's bank account. The consideration for the sale was $120 000 and was satisfied by the payment to Abdul of $20 000 in cash and the issue to him of 80 000 ordinary shares in Hamil Ltd.

Required

(a) Prepare the journal entries in Hamil Ltd's books to record the purchase of Abdul's business.
(b) Prepare Hamil Ltd's Balance Sheet immediately after the acquisition of Abdul's business.

15.17 Purchase of a partnership business

The purchase of a partnership business by a company follows a similar procedure to that for the purchase of a sole trader's business. When one of the partners has made a loan to the firm and the company takes the loan over, it is usual for the company to issue a debenture to the partner concerned. If the rate of interest on the debenture is different from the rate previously received by the partner on the loan, the amount of the debenture will usually ensure that the partner continues to receive the same amount of interest each year as previously. To calculate the amount of the debenture, find the capital sum which, at the new rate, will produce the same amount of interest. Multiply the amount of the loan by the rate paid by the partnership and divide by the rate of interest on the debenture, as shown in the following example.

(i) Partner's loan to partnership: $100 000 at 8% interest per annum. Annual interest = $8000.
A 10% debenture producing annual interest of $8000 will be $100\,000 \times \frac{8}{10} = \$80\,000$.

(ii) If in (i) the rate of interest on the debenture is 5% the amount of debenture is: $100\,000 \times \frac{8}{5} = \$160\,000$. (Interest on $160\,000 at 5% per annum = $8000.)

Exercise 7

Carol has lent $60 000 at 5% interest per annum to the firm in which she is a partner. A company has offered to buy the partnership business. Part of the purchase price consists of a debenture to be issued to Carol to ensure that she continues to receive the same amount of interest annually as she had been receiving from the partnership.

Required

(a) Calculate the amount of the debenture to be issued to Carol if the debenture carries interest at 8% per annum.
(b) Calculate the amount of the debenture if it carries interest at 4% per annum.

Exercise 8

Spaid and Shuvell are partners in a business and their Balance Sheet at 31 December 2004 is as follows.

	$	$
Fixed assets		
Land and buildings		50 000
Fixtures and fittings		18 000
Office machinery		12 000
		80 000
Current assets		
Stock	17 000	
Debtors	8 000	
Bank	4 000	
	29 000	
Current liabilities		
Creditors	12 000	17 000
		97 000
Long-term liability		
Loan from Spaid at 10% per annum		12 000
		85 000
Capitals		
Spaid		50 000
Shuvell		35 000
		85 000

The partners have accepted an offer from Digger Ltd to purchase the business for $118 000. The company will take over all the assets and liabilities of the partnership except the bank account. The partnership assets are to be valued as follows.

	$
Land and buildings	60 000
Fixtures and fittings	14 000
Office machinery	10 000
Stock	15 000
Debtors	6 000

Digger Ltd will settle the purchase price as follows:

- a payment of cash, $28 000
- an 8% debenture issued to Spaid to ensure that he continues to receive the same amount of interest annually as he has received from the partnership
- the balance to be settled by an issue of ordinary shares of $1 in Digger Ltd at $1.25 per share.

Digger Ltd's Balance Sheet at 31 December 2004 is as follows.

	$	$
Fixed assets		
Land and buildings		90 000
Fixtures and fittings		30 000
Office machinery		15 000
		135 000
Current assets		
Stock	20 000	
Debtors	5 000	
Bank	60 000	
	85 000	
Current liabilities		
Creditors	16 000	69 000
		204 000
Share capital and reserves		
Ordinary shares of $1		200 000
Retained profit		4 000
		204 000

Required

Prepare Digger Ltd's Balance Sheet immediately after the company has acquired the partnership business.

15.18 Return on investment

It is important that a company purchasing another business succeeds in making the new business as profitable as its existing business. Profitability is measured by expressing profit as a percentage of capital invested. If a company has purchased a business for $100 000 and the business has made a profit of $12 000 in the first year, the profitability is 12%. This is the **return on capital invested**. If it is equal to, or more than, the return on capital the company was earning on its existing business, the investment may be considered to have been worthwhile. If it is less, overall profitability of the business will be **diluted** (or decreased). However, it is better to measure the profitability over a number of years to get a reliable picture.

The new business may have been merged with the existing business so closely that separate results for the new business are not available. In such a case, the incremental (that is, the additional) profit is measured against the additional capital invested in the business.

Example

X Ltd had a capital of $300 000. Its average annual profit was $54 000. Its return on capital was

$$\frac{\$54\,000}{\$300\,000} \times 100 = 18\%.$$

X Ltd purchased another business on 1 January 2004 for $100 000 which was settled by the issue to the vendor of shares in X Ltd. X Ltd's profit for the year ended 31 December 2004 was $84 000. The profitability of X Ltd has increased by 3% to 21%:

$$\frac{\$84\,000}{\$400\,000} \times 100.$$

A more reliable picture is obtained if the additional profit of $30 000 is calculated as a percentage of the price paid for the new business:

$$\frac{\$30\,000}{\$100\,000} \times 100 = 30\%.$$

X Ltd has benefited from the purchase of the new business.

15.19 Examination hints

- Goodwill is the difference between the values of the net assets acquired and the purchase price.
- Show goodwill as an intangible fixed asset, even if it is negative goodwill.
- When a debenture is issued to a partner, and the partner is to receive the same amount of annual interest as he/she received before the sale of the firm; check that you have calculated the amount of the debenture correctly.
- If you are required to prepare journal entries in a company's books to record the purchase of a business, do *not* show the entries in the books of the business being taken over.
- Make sure you prepare the journal entries in good form.
- Show all workings when preparing the company's Balance Sheet after the new business has been acquired.

15.20 Multiple-choice questions

1 The following is information about the assets and liabilities of a business.

	Book value	Market value
	$	$
Tangible fixed assets	90 000	101 000
Current assets	32 000	29 000
	122 000	
Current liabilities	(14 000)	14 000
	108 000	

Goodwill is valued at $50 000.

What should be paid for the net assets of the business?

A $116 000

B $119 000

C $166 000

D $169 000

2 A company paid $1.8 million to acquire the business of a sole trader. The sole trader's assets and liabilities were valued as follows.

	$
Fixed assets	700 000
Current assets	300 000
Current liabilities	50 000
Long-term loan	100 000

How much was paid for goodwill?

A $650 000

B $750 000

C $850 000

D $950 000

3 The Balance Sheet of a sole trader is as follows.

	$
Fixed assets	
Intangible: Goodwill	30 000
Tangible	100 000
Net current assets	50 000
	180 000

A company purchased the business, paying for the tangible fixed assets and the net current assets at the valuations shown above.

The company settled the purchase price by issuing 200 000 ordinary shares of $1 at $1.50 per share.

How much did the company pay for goodwill?

A $30 000

B $50 000

C $120 000

D $150 000

16 Corporations

Objectives
Prepare journal entries for:
- the issue and redemption of Common Stock, Treasury Stock and Preferred Stock
- the issue and retirement of bonds
- mortgage loans payment of interest and repayment of principal
- the accounting treatment of lease liability

16.1 Corporations

A corporation is a separate legal entity that can be the result of the formation of an entirely new entity; the conversion of a partnership or the expansion of an existing business.

Registrar of companies

When such an entity is to be formed an application must be made to the relevant authorities indicating:

- The name of the corporation.
- The authorized capital (the name, type, number of shares and the amount in value).
- The bye-laws and procedures for conducting affairs.
- The powers of shareholders, directors and officers.

Methods of financing

Because of their size, corporations need and command large sums of money which may originate from:

- The issue of shares, both common and preferred stock.
- The issue of treasury stock.
- The issue of bonds.
- Long term notes payable (mortgage loans).
- Lease liabilities.

16.2 Characteristics of common stock

1. It represents ownership of a corporation.
2. Common stock represents the most fixed part of the capital structure.
3. Common stock holders are the last to be refunded in liquidation.

RAISING CAPITAL: ISSUE OF SHARES

AUTHORIZED
The value of shares that the corporation has permission to sell

REGISTERED

NOMINAL

ISSUED
The value of shares offered for sale to the public

APPLICATION
The amount that shareholders pay when applying for shares

ALLOTMENT
The value of shares that are assigned to shareholders by the corporation

FIRST CALL & **FINAL CALL**
The request for shareholders to pay any amounts owing for shares

CALLED-UP CAPITAL
The amount shareholders have been asked to pay by a particular date

PAID-UP CAPITAL
The actual amount collected from shareholders at a particular date

SHARE CAPITAL ACCOUNT
Sale of shares at par or stated value

PREMIUM ACCOUNT
Sale of shares in excess of par or stated value

COMMON STOCK
Capital that forms the backbone of the corporation and yields a variable rate of return

PREFERRED STOCK
Capital that carries a fixed rate of return

CUMULATIVE
Guaranteed fixed rate of return on the investment

NON-CUMULATIVE
Guaranteed fixed rate of return only when dividend is declared

SHARES

REDEEMABLE
Agreement that the corporation can purchase at a later date

NON-REDEEMABLE
No agreement for the corporation to buy back

BONDS ISSUE
Increase in the number of shares but decrease in the value per share

RIGHTS ISSUE
Increase in the number of shares at the expense of the shareholder

Issue of common stock

The following table defines the different values of common stock and provides the journal entries for recording the relevant data.

VALUATION	DEFINITIONS AND EXAMPLES	JOURNAL ENTRIES	
NO PAR	Stock with no assigned value at incorporation. Example: Issued 1 000 shares at $5.00 each. These are no par shares and have no stated value.	Dr. Cash/Bank Cr. Common stock	5 000 5 000
PAR	Stock that have assigned a value at incorporation. Example: Issued at 20 000 shared of $2.00 par value common stock at par and received cash.	Dr. Cash Cr. Common stock	40 000 40 000
ABOVE PAR	Stock issued at a value above that which was given at incorporation. Example: Issued 8 000 shares of $2.00 par value common stock at $5.00 each and received cash.	Dr. Cash Cr. Common stock *Cr. Premium	40 000 16 000 24 000
BELOW PAR	Stock issued at a value below that which was given at incorporation. Example: Issued 2 000 shares at $2.00 par value common stock at $1.50 each and received cheque.	Dr. Bank *Dr. Premium Cr. Common stock	3 000 1 000 4 000
STATED VALUE	This is the value that the board of directors may assign to no-par-stock. Example: Blue Jays Corporation has $3.00 stated value no par stock and issued 10 000 shares at $5.00 per share for cash.	Dr. Cash Cr. Common stock *Cr. Premium	50 000 30 000 20 000
FOR SERVICES	Organizational expenses in setting up a corporation paid for through the issuance of shares. Example: Lawyer and consultants fees were settled in shares, 20 000 shares at $3.50 each.	Dr. Organizational Expenses Cr. Common stock *Cr. Premium	80 000 70 000 10 000
FOR NON-CASH ASSETS	Buying assets by using an issue of shares. Example: Office building valued at $100 000 were bought by issuing 15 000 shares at $5.00 each, having a par value of $3.00.	Dr. Office building Cr. Common stock *Cr. Premium	75 000 45 000 30 000

*Also called Paid-in-Cash in excess of par – Common stock

Effect on financial statement presentation

FINANCIAL STATEMENT PRESENTATION
Balance Sheet (Extract)

STOCKHOLDERS EQUITY		
Paid in capital:		
Common stock	210 000	
Premium	94 000	
Total paid in capital		304 000
Retained earnings		100 000
Total stockholders' equity		404 000

	Cash dividend	**Stock dividend (Rights Issue)**	**Stock split (Bonus Issue)**
Declaration	Dr. Retained earnings Cr. Dividend payable	Dr. Retained earnings Cr. Common stock Dividend distributable	No journal entry necessary
Payment	Dr. Dividend payable Cr. Cash	Dr. Common stock dividend distributable	No journal entry necessary. (No cash flow)
Total Effects	Reduces total assets and stockholders' equity	Reduces retained earnings and increases paid-in-capital	No effect on total paid-in-capital, retained earnings and total shareholders' equity Number of shares increase and *****value per share decreases The AIM should be to give the reserve the most flexible status

Bonus (Script) Issue

	Before	Adjustment	After
Fixed assets	80 000	NIL	80 000
Current assets	24 000	NIL	24 000
Current liabilities	<4 000>	NIL	<4 000>
	100 000	–	100 000
Share capital & reserves			
Ordinary shares	10 000	+ 40 000	50 000
Premium	20 000	– 20 000	NIL
Retained earnings			
(Profit + Loss)	70 000	– 20 000	50 000
	100 000		100 000

1. Four additional shares for every one held.
   Hence, 40 000 shares @ $1.00 issued:
   Total 40 000 + 10 000 = 50 000

2. Payment for these shares made from:
   Premium account 20 000 – 20 000 = NIL
   (Profit + Loss)
   Retained Earnings 70 000 – 20 000 = 50 000

This enables the business to keep the reserves very flexible.

Rights Issue

	Before	Adjustment	After
Fixed assets	80 000	NIL	80 000
Current assets	24 000	+ 6 000	30 000
Current liabilities	<4 000>	NIL	<4 000>
	100 000	-	100 000
Share capital & reserves		+ 20 000 [1]	
Ordinary shares	10 000	+ 6 000 [2]	36 000
Premium	4 000	- 4 000	NIL
Asset revaluation reserve	15 000	- 15 000	NIL
Retained earnings	71 000	- 1 000	70 000
	100 000		100 000

1. Two bonus shares for every one held:
    10 000 x 2 + 10 000   = 30 000

2. Payment for these shares made from:
    Premium   4 000
    Asset revaluation reserve   15 000
    Retained earnings   1 000
                                          20 000

3. Rights issue - One for five held:
    Issued 30 000/5   = 6 000

4. Cash (Current asset increase by + 6 000)

Dividends

Common stockholders are rewarded through either cash or stock payment or dividends.

The cash dividend to be paid to common stockholders must first be declared by the board of directors of the corporation. When this is done, a liability is incurred which may vary from year to year. The journal entry to record this declaration is

Debit retained earnings
Credit dividends payable

Dividend payable is a current liability. When the dividend is paid:

Debit dividend payable
Credit cash

16.3 Retained earnings and reserves

Reserves are portions of the capital and net profit set aside for future use. When the amount designated is for a fixed use it is called a **capital reserve**. When usage of the amount is flexible, it is called a **revenue reserve**.

	CAPITAL RESERVE	REVENUE RESERVE
Flexibility	Used only for the purpose designated	Can be used as the need arises
Examples	Plant replacement Capital redemption Premium Asset revaluation	General reserve Income statement balance
Dividends	Not available for dividends	Distributable
Creation	Dr. Retained earnings Cr. Named reserve	Dr. Retained earnings Cr. General reserve

16.4 Preferred stock

Characteristics of preferred stock

1. have priority over common stock in the distribution of the earnings (dividends)
2. have first rights to assets in liquidation
3. do not have voting rights
4. may sometimes contain a cumulative dividend feature.

Issue of preferred stock

The accounting treatment of preferred stock is the same as indicated for common stock.

Example: Chin Ling Car Rental Ltd. Issued 50 000 10% shares of $12 par value preferred stock for $15 per share. The entry to record this would be as follows:

Dr. Cash		750 000
Cr. Preferred stock		600 000
Cr. Paid-In-capital in excess of par value		
	– preferred stock	150 000

Dividends

The name of the share of the amount stated indicates the amount of dividend the stockholder will receive on each share.

Example: A stockholder having 3000 4% preferred shares of $8 par value will receive $940 as dividend. (Calculated as follows: $3000 \times 8 \times \frac{4}{100} = \$960$.)

All preference stockholders will receive their respective amounts before any distribution is made to the common stockholders.

Cumulative dividend

The arrangement to pay preferred stockholders cumulative dividend means that they must receive dividends for the prior years, if unpaid and the current year before common stockholders are paid.

Example: ABL Corporation declared a dividend of 120 000 to be paid to preferred stockholders of 100 000 10% preferred stock of par value $5.00. Dividend for the previous year is unpaid.

Dividend declared	120 000
Prior year dividend for preference shareholders	50 000
	70 000
Current year dividend for Preference shareholders	50 000
Amount available for common shareholders dividend	20 000

16.5 Treasury stock

Characteristics of Treasury stock

1. belong to the corporation
2. have been issued and fully paid for
3. have been reacquired by the entity
4. have not been retired
5. do not affect the original common stock when resold
6. increase total assets and total stockholders equity when resold
7. have no claim to dividends.

Reasons for Treasury stock

Many large corporations have treasury stock:

1. to increase the market value of its shares. The more frequently the share is traded in the securities market, the greater the chances are that its value would be enhanced.
2. to increase the earnings per share. The fewer shares among which to divide the earnings of the corporation the larger the portion of earnings each share will receive.
3. to have more purchasing power for acquisition of other companies. Like cash, the use of shares is also a convenient way to buy additional investments.
4. to motivate and compensate officers and employees in a company. Having shares in an enterprise where one is employed may encourage the worker to give of his best.
5. to prevent shareholder domination in a company. A certain fraction of stockholders, when large enough, can sway the corporation in a particular direction and may even lead to takeover.

VALUATION	DEFINITIONS & EXAMPLES	JOURNAL ENTRIES	
Purchase	Shares reacquired from stockholders (recorded at cost). Example: 60 000 shares of $1.00 par value purchases at $2.50.	Dr. Treasury stock Cr. Cash	150 000 150 000
Sale above cost	Stock sold at a price higher than the cost to acquire them. Example: 18 000 shares of Treasury stock previously acquired at $2.50 are sold at $3.00 per share.	Dr. Cash Cr. Treasury stock Cr. Paid-in-capital from Treasury stock	54 000 45 000 9 000
Sale at cost	Stock sold at the Cost to acquire them. Example: 20 000 shares Treasury stock sold at $2.50 previously acquired at $2.50.	Dr. Cash Cr. Treasury stock	50 000 50 000
Sale below cost	Stock sold at a price lower than the cost to acquire them. Example: 12 000 shares of treasury stock sold at $2.00. These shares were acquired at $2.50 per share.	Dr. Cash Dr. Paid-in-capital from Treasury stock Cr. Treasury stock	24 000 6 000 30 000
Retirement			

Premium

(Paid-In-Capital) from Treasury stock

Once the selling price is greater then the cost price the (Paid-in-capital) premium from Treasury stock account will have a credit balance.

When the credit balance is eliminated the excess of cost over selling price is debited to retained earnings.

Example: 5000 shares of treasury stock purchases at $2.50 each were sold at $1.50 each.

   Balance in Paid-in-capital account $3000 (credit).

Journal Entry

Dr. Cash (5000 x $1.50)	7 500
Dr. Paid-in-capital from Treasury stock	3 000
Dr. Retained earnings	2 000
Cr. Treasury stock (5000 x $2.50)	12 500

Dividends

Treasury stock are not entitled to receive dividends.

Effect on financial statement presentation

Balance Sheet (extract)

STOCKHOLDERS EQUITY	
Paid-in-capital:	
Common stock	210 000
Premium	97 000
Total Paid-In-capital	307 000
Retained earnings	98 000
Total Paid-in-capital and Retained earnings	405 000
Less: Treasury stock (5 000 x 2.50)	12 500
Total stockholders' equity	392 500

16.6 Redemption of preferred stock

When it becomes necessary to reduce fixed cost capital a number of options are available. The table describes and shows how redemption is accounted for.

SOURCES OF FUNDS & VALUATION	DEFINITIONS AND EXAMPLES	JOURNAL ENTRIES	
USING A NEW ISSUE: AT PAR	Buying shares from stockholders at the price stated at incorporation. Example: Issued 100 000 shares of common stock at $2 par value in order to recall 5000 10% preferred stock of $12 par value.	Dr. Cash Cr. Common stock Dr. Preferred stock Cr. Cash	200 000 200 000 60 000 60 000
AT A PREMIUM	Buying shares from stockholders at a price above par value. Example: Issued 100 000 shares of common stock of $2 par value at $3 each in order to recall from stockholders 5000 10% preferred stock of $12 par value at $13 each.	Dr. Cash Cr. Common stock Cr. Premium Dr. Preferred stock Dr. Premium Cr. Cash	200 000 200 000 100 000 60 000 5 000 65 000
CAPITALIZING PROFITS: AT PAR	Using part of the retained earnings to buy shares from preference stockholders at par value. Example: Recalled 10 000 10% shares of preferred stock each having a par value of $12.	Dr. Retained earnings Cr. Capital redemption reserve Dr. Preference stock Cr. Cash	120 000 120 000 120 000 120 000
AT A PREMIUM	Using part of the retained earnings to buy shares from preferred stockholders at a premium. Example: Recalled 5000 10% shares of preferred stock of $12 par value at $13 each.	Dr. Retained earnings Cr. Capital redemption reserve Cr. Premium Dr. Preference stock Dr. Premium Cr. Cash	65 000 60 000 5 000 60 000 5 000 65 000

Financial statement presentation

Balance Sheet		
STOCKHOLDERS' EQUITY		
Paid-in-capital:		
Capital stock		
10% Preferred stock, $12 par value,		
Cumulative 200 000 shares authorized,		
50 000 issued & outstanding		600 000
Common stock, $2 par value 500 000 shares authorized,		
400 000 issued & outstanding		800 000
TOTAL CAPITAL STOCK		1 400 000
Additional Paid-In-capital		
In excess of par value – preferred stock	150 000	
In excess of par value – common stock	400 000	
From Treasury stock	NIL	
Total additional Paid-in-capital		550 000
Total Paid-in-capital		1 950 000
Retained earnings		94 000
Total Paid-in-capital & retained earnings		2 044 000
Less: Treasury stock-common (shares x cost) (5000 × 2.50)		<12 500>
Total stockholders' equity		2 031 500

	BOOK VALUE	FAIR VALUE
Objectivity	Based on historical cost	Subjective evaluation of stockholders and potential investors
Stability	Follows the trend of stockholders per share equity	May exceed the book value
Rate	Used to make contracts because of its fixed nature	Fluctuates depending on market conditions and the economy
Usefulness	Used in court cases to settle the rights of the individual	Too variable to be used in a statement of fact

16.7 Book value of share

When a corporation has only one class of stock the book value per share is calculated as follows:

$$\text{Book value per share} = \frac{\text{Total stockholders' equity}}{\text{Number of common shares outstanding}}$$

When the corporation has preferred and common stock the calculation is varied as follows:

$$\text{Book value per share} = \frac{\text{Total stockholders' equity} - \text{Preferred stockholders' equity}}{\text{Number of common stock}}$$

16.8 Retained earnings and prior period adjustments

Retained earnings is net income that is unused by the corporation and represents stockholders' claim on the assets of the entity.

Prior period adjustment is the correction of a material error made in the net income of a previous year.

Overstated net income:

    Dr. Retained earnings

    Cr. The item causing the overstatement

        (An understated expense/overstated revenue)

Understated net income:

    Dr. The item causing the understatement

        (An overstated expense/understated revenue)

    Cr. Retained earnings

Effect on the financial statements

At the beginning of the accounting period an adjustment is made to the Retained Earnings of the previous year. Hence, a balance sheet at the beginning of the current period will have the following:

Balance sheet at the start of the year

Retained earnings	
Balance as reported Jan 1	xxx
Correction for overstatement	
(Understatement) in prior period	(xxx)
Balance Jan 1, as adjusted	$_____

Balance sheet at year end

Retained earnings (less prior period adjustment).

	CAPITAL RESERVE	REVENUE RESERVE
Creation	Dr. Income statement Cr. Named reserve	Dr. Income statement Cr. General reserve
Examples	Plant replacement, Capital redemption, Additional premium paid in	General reserve Retained earnings
Flexibility	Used only for the purpose named	Can be used for as seen fit

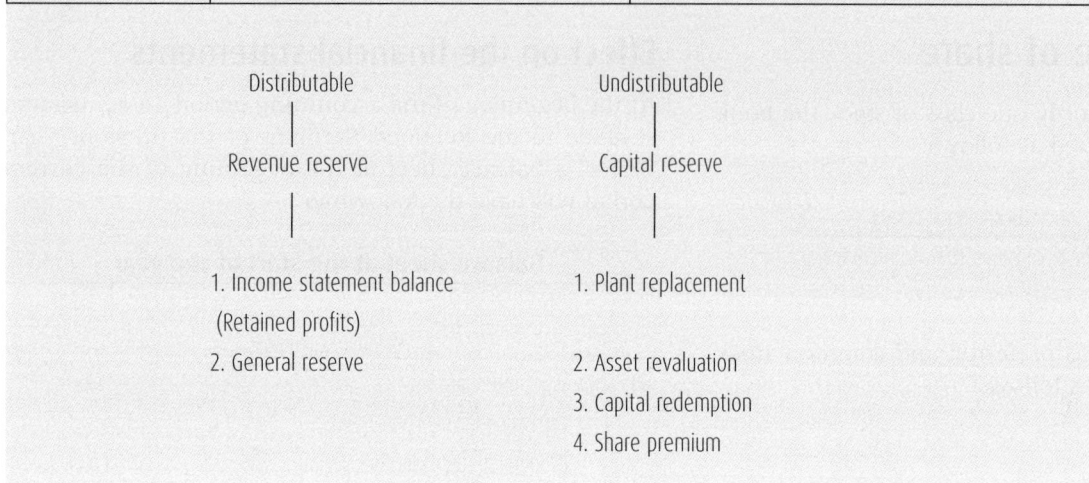

Distributable

Revenue reserve

1. Income statement balance
   (Retained profits)
2. General reserve

Undistributable

Capital reserve

1. Plant replacement

2. Asset revaluation
3. Capital redemption
4. Share premium

16.9 General bond features

A bond is a long-term loan represented by a formal promise made by the issuing company to pay back the principal with interest.

Generally noted in a bond indenture and displayed in the certificate are the face value, the stated interest note, the interest payment dates, the maturity date, and the bond authorization date. Two additional features that affect valuation but do not appear are the market (effective yield) interest rate and the bond issue date. These features are defined in the illustration.

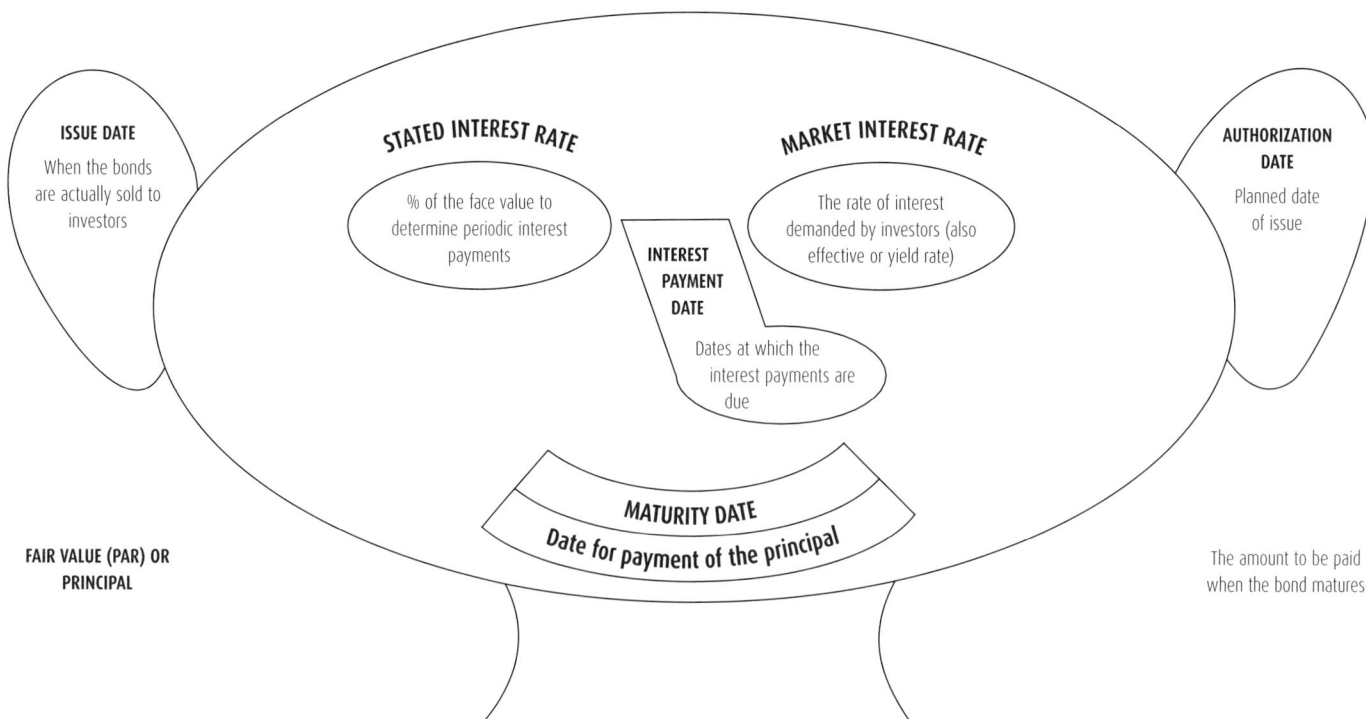

ISSUE DATE
When the bonds are actually sold to investors

STATED INTEREST RATE
% of the face value to determine periodic interest payments

INTEREST PAYMENT DATE
Dates at which the interest payments are due

MARKET INTEREST RATE
The rate of interest demanded by investors (also effective or yield rate)

AUTHORIZATION DATE
Planned date of issue

MATURITY DATE
Date for payment of the principal

FAIR VALUE (PAR) OR PRINCIPAL

The amount to be paid when the bond matures

16.10 Classification of bonds

When people invest they look for investments that satisfy their goals, preferences and prices. Bonds are issued with these criteria in mind, hence the various classifications.

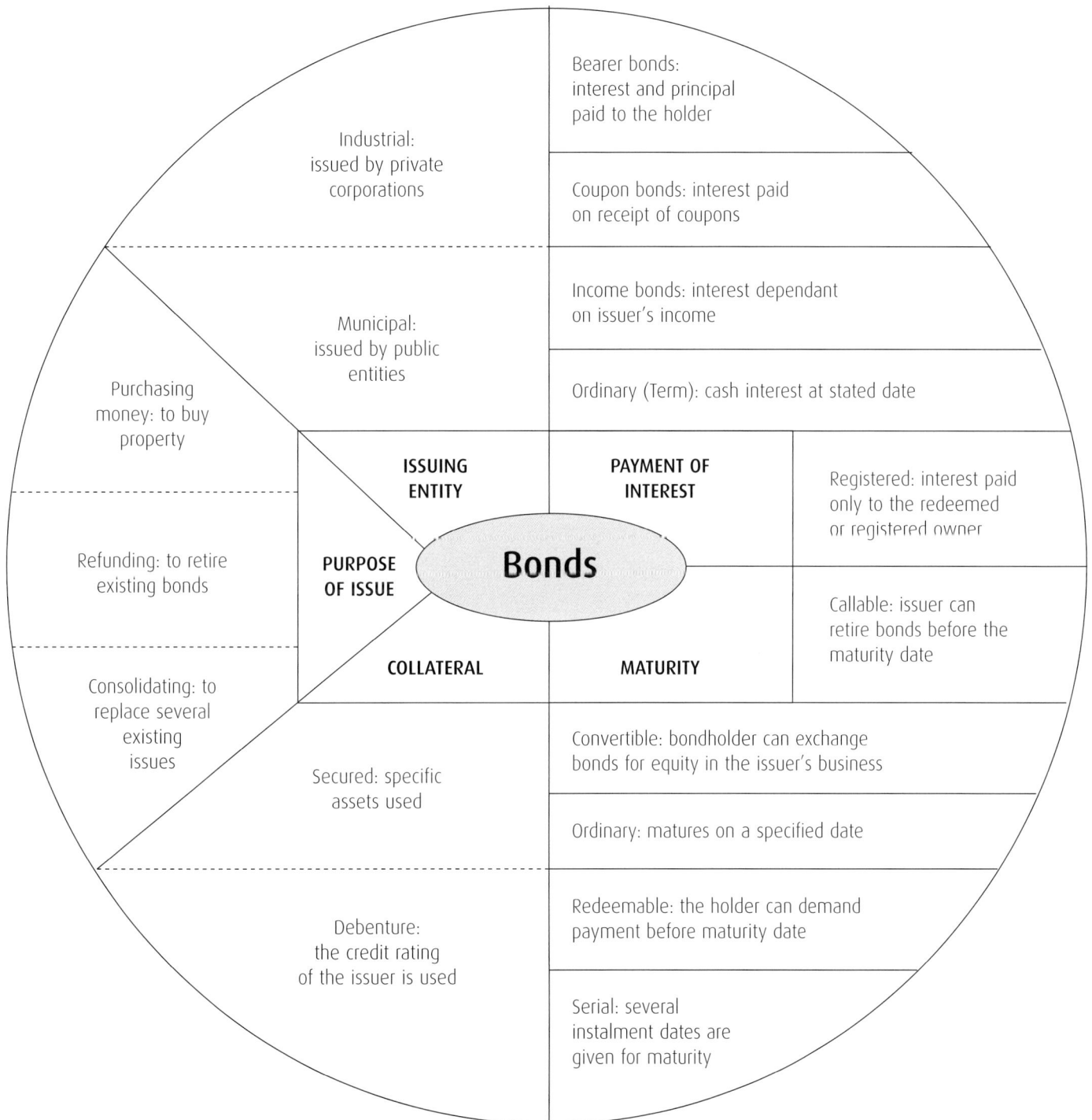

Bonds

ISSUING ENTITY
- Industrial: issued by private corporations
- Municipal: issued by public entities

PAYMENT OF INTEREST
- Bearer bonds: interest and principal paid to the holder
- Coupon bonds: interest paid on receipt of coupons
- Income bonds: interest dependant on issuer's income
- Ordinary (Term): cash interest at stated date
- Registered: interest paid only to the redeemed or registered owner

MATURITY
- Callable: issuer can retire bonds before the maturity date
- Convertible: bondholder can exchange bonds for equity in the issuer's business
- Ordinary: matures on a specified date
- Redeemable: the holder can demand payment before maturity date
- Serial: several instalment dates are given for maturity

COLLATERAL
- Secured: specific assets used
- Debenture: the credit rating of the issuer is used

PURPOSE OF ISSUE
- Purchasing money: to buy property
- Refunding: to retire existing bonds
- Consolidating: to replace several existing issues

16.11 Bonds issue price and rate of return

The issue price of bonds is dependant on the dominant rate. There is the **contractual rate** of interest which is stated on the bond certificate and there is the **market rate** of interest which represents the rate of return demanded by investors.

When the market rate equals the stated rate the bond will issue at face (or par) value.

When the market rate is greater than the stated rate the bond will issue at a **discount**.

If the market rate is less than the stated rate the bond will sell at a premium.

C1. Face value, when the Market rate 10% = Contractual rate 10%

C2. Discount, when the Market rate 12% > Contractual rate 10%

C3. Premium, when the Market rate 10% < Contractual rate 12%

The discount or premium adjustment to the selling price of the bond is necessary to bring the yield rate in line with the market rate of similar bonds.

16.12 Issue of bonds

Bonds may be sold at par (face value), at a premium or at a discount. Since it evokes two kinds of cash flows, the price of the issue will consist of the principal and the interest payments. The price of the issue can be found by using the formula:

Present value of the principal at maturity plus the present value of the interest payments

which can be determined from

Face value * present value of $1: Effective rate, No. of semi-annual interest periods

plus

(Face value) * (Stated Rate) (Present Value Annuity: Effective rate, No. of semi-annual interest periods)

Case 1 At par (face value)	Stated rate	8%
	Effective rate	8%
Case 2 At a discount	Stated rate	8%
	Effective rate	10%
Case 3 At a premium	Stated rate	8%
	Effective rate	6%

Case 1: Bond issued at face value

A bond is said to be issued at face value when the contractual rate equals the market rate.

Example: Scanner Incorporated issued 200, 5 year, 8% $1000 bonds at 100% (100% of face value) with interest payable semi-annually.

Calculation: Semi-annual interest = $200\,000 \times \frac{8}{100} \times \frac{1}{2} = \$8000$

Total interest over 10 periods = 8000 × 10 = $8000

Journal entries

Issue of bonds

Cash	200 000	
To bonds payable		200 000
Being issue of bonds at face value		

Interest incurred

Bond interest expense	8 000	
To Bond interest payable		8 000
Being bond interest accruing semi-annually		

Interest payment

Bond interest payable	8 000	
To cash		8 000
Being semi-annual payment of bond interest		

Retirement of bond

Bond payable	200 000	
To cash		200 000
Being redemption of bond at maturity		

Case 2: Bond issued at a discount

A bond is said to have been issued at a **discount** when the contractual rate is **less** than the market rate.

Example: Scanner Incorporated issued $200 000, 5 year, 10% bonds for $184 576.

Calculation:

Cash interest over 10 periods $= 200\,000 \times \frac{8}{100} \times \frac{1}{2} \times 10$

$\qquad\qquad\qquad\qquad\qquad = \$80\,000$

Total interest expense for bond term:

$\qquad$ = Face value + Cash interest – Issue price

$\qquad$ = 200 000 + 80 000 – 184 576

$\qquad$ = $95 424

Discount on bond:

$\qquad$ = Face value – Issue price

$\qquad$ = 200 000 – 184 576

$\qquad$ – $15 424

Note: Total interest expense is made up of

Total interest (to be) paid	80 000
Plus discount	15 424
	$95 424

Semi-annual interest = 80 000 ÷ 10 = 800

Semi-annual amortization = 15 424 ÷ 10 = 1542

Journal entries

Issue of bonds

Cash	184 576	
Discount on bonds payable	15 424	
To bonds payable		200 000
Being issue of bonds at a discount		

Interest payment (first interest date)

Bond interest expense	8 000	
To cash		8 000
Being payment of bond interest		

Discount amortization

Bond interest expense	1 542	
To discount on bonds payable		1 542
Being discount amortization		

Interest incurred (second period)

Bond interest expense	8 000	
To bond interest payable		8 000
Being accrued bond interest		

Interest payment (second period)

Bond interest payable	8 000	
To cash		8 000
Being payment of bond interest		

Note: The calculation of bond discount amortization is based on the **straight line method**.

See Table A for details.

Bond discount amortization straight-line method

A	B	C	D	E	F
Semi-annual interest periods	Interest to be paid $200\,000 \times \frac{8}{100} \times \frac{1}{2}$	Interest to be recorded (B) + (D)	Discount amortization bond discount / 10	Unamortized premium (E) - (D)	Net bond liability $200\,000$ - E
Beginning 1	–	–	–	15 424	184 576
Ending 1	8 000	9 542	1 542	13 882	186 118
2	8 000	9 542	1 542	12 340	187 660
3	8 000	9 542	1 542	10 798	189 202
4	8 000	9 542	1 542	9 256	190 744
5	8 000	9 542	1 542	7 714	192 286
6	8 000	9 542	1 542	6 172	193 828
7	8 000	9 542	1 542	4 630	195 370
8	8 000	9 542	1 542	3 088	196 912
9	8 000	9 542	1 542	1 546	198 458
10	8 000	9 542	1 542	0	200 000

A – 5 years of semi-annual payments will equal ten periods.

B – Face value of the bond times the semi-annual contractual interest rate each period.

C – Interest paid (B) plus discount amortization (D).

D – Discount amortization divided by the number of interest periods.

E – Unamortized discount amount to be written off: decreases to *****.

F – Net bond liability, the bond payable after deducting the unamortized discount.
(same as the carrying value of the bond); increases to the face value at maturity)

Bond discount amortization effective interest method

Discount amortization	= Bond interest expense Less: Bond interest paid

Bond interest expense
= Net bond liability at beginning of period
multiplied by
the effective interest rate
= $184\,576 \times .05$
= $9229

Bond interest paid
= Face value of bonds multiplied by
the contractual interest rate
= $200\,000 \times .04$
= $8000

Discount amortization
= 9229 – 8000
= $1229

The journal entries will be: Dr. Bond interest payable 8 000. Cr. Cash 8 000 (payment on interest).

First interest payment: Dr. Bond interest expenses $9 229. Cr. Discount on bonds payable $1 229. Cr. Cash $ 8 000 (payment of interest and discount amortization).

Note: In the effective interest method, the calculations are done for each (six months) period.
See Table B for details.

Bond discount amortization effective interest rate method

Table B

A	B	C	D	E	F
Semi-annual interest periods	Interest to be paid $200\,000 \times \frac{8}{100} \times \frac{1}{2}$	Interest expense to be recorded $NBL \times \frac{10}{100} \times \frac{1}{2}$	Discount amortization (C) − (B)	Unamortized discount (E) − (D)	Net bond liability $200\,000 - E$
Beginning 1	–	–	–	15 424	184 576
Ending 1	8 000	184 576 × 0.05 9 229	9 229 − 8 000 1 229	14 195	185 805
2	8 000	185 805 × 0.05 9 290	9 290 − 8 000 1 290	12 905	187 095
3	8 000	187 095 × 0.05 9 355	9 355 − 8 000 1 355	11 550	188 450
4	8 000	188 450 × 0.05 9 423	9 423 − 8 000 1 423	10 127	189 873
5	8 000	189 873 × 0.05 9 494	9 494 − 8 000 1 494	8 633	191 367
6	8 000	191 367 × 0.05 9 568	9 568 − 8 000 1 568	7 065	192 935
7	8 000	192 935 × 0.05 9 647	9 647 − 8 000 1 647	5 418	194 582
8	8 000	194 582 × 0.05 9 729	9 729 − 8 000 1 729	3 689	196 311
9	8 000	196 311 × 0.05 9 816	9 816 − 8 000 1 816	1 906	198 094
10	8 000	198 094 × 0.05 9 906	9 906 − 8 000 1 906	-0-	200 000

A – The number of semi-annual periods over the 5-year life of the bond.

B – Face value times the semi-annual contractual interest rate each period.

C – The net bond liability, (NBL, the carrying value of the bond times) times the semi-annual effective interest rate each period.

D – The amount written off as discount each period.

E – The balance of discount to be written off.

F – Net bond liability or the carrying value of the bonds.

Case 3: Bonds issued at a premium

A bond is said to have been issued at a **premium** when the contractual rate is **greater** than the market rate.

Example: Scanner Incorporated issued $200 000, 5 year, 8% bonds at 6% for $217 040

Calculation:

Cash interest over 10 periods = $200\,000 \times \frac{8}{100} \times \frac{1}{2} \times 10$

= $80 000

Total interest expense for bond term:

= Face value + Cash interest − Issue price

= 200 000 + 80 000 − 217 040

= $62 960

Premium on bond = Issue price − Face value

= 217 040 − 200 000

= $17 040

Note: Total interest expense is made up of

Total interest (to be paid)	80 000
Less premium	17 040
	$62 960

Semi-annual interest = 80 000 ÷ 10 = $8000

Semi-annual amortization = 17 040 ÷ 10 = $1704

Journal entries

Issue of bonds

Cash	217 040	
To bonds payable		200 000
To premium on bonds payable		17 040
Being issue of bonds at a premium		

Interest payment (first interest date)	
Bond interest expense	6 296
To cash	6 296
Being payment of bond interest	

Premium amortization (first period entry)	
Premium on bonds payable	1 704
To cash	1 704
Being premium amortization	

Interest incurred and amortization (second interest date)	
Bond interest expense	6 296
Premium in bonds payable	1 704
To bond interest payable	8 000
Being accrued bond interest and amortization of premium	

Note: The calculation of bond premium amortization is based on the **straight-line method**. See Table C for details.

Bond premium amortization effective interest rate method

Table C

A		B	C	D	E	F
Semi-annual interest periods		Interest to be paid $200\,000 \times \frac{8}{100} \times \frac{1}{2}$	Interest expense to be recorded (B) – (D)	Premium amortization bond premium/10	Unamortized premium (E) – (D)	Net bond liability $200\,000 + E$
Beginning	1	–	–	–	17 040	217 040
Ending	1	8 000	6 296	1 704	15 336	215 336
	2	8 000	6 296	1 704	13 632	213 632
	3	8 000	6 296	1 704	11 928	211 928
	4	8 000	6 296	1 704	10 224	210 224
	5	8 000	6 296	1 704	8 520	208 520
	6	8 000	6 296	1 704	6 816	206 816
	7	8 000	6 296	1 704	5 112	205 112
	8	8 000	6 296	1 704	3 408	203 408
	9	8 000	6 296	1 704	1 704	201 704
	10	8 000	6 296	1 704	0	200 000

A – Five years of semi-annual interest payments will equal ten periods.

B – Face value of the bond times the semi-annual contractual interest rate each period.

C – Interest paid (B) less premium amortization (D).

D – Premium amortization divided by the number of interest periods.

E – Unamortized premium, amount to be written off decreases to 0.

F – Net bond liability (same as the carrying value of the bond); decreases to the face value at maturity.

Bond premium amortization effective interest method

Calculation:

Premium Amortization	= Bond interest paid Less: Bond interest expense
Bond interest paid	= Face value of bonds multiplied by the contractual interest rate
	= 200 000 × 0.04
	= $8000
Bond interest expense	= Net bond liability at beginning of period multiplied by the effective interest rate
	= 217 040 × 0.03
	= $6511
Premium amortization	= 8000 – 6511
	= $1489

See Table D for details.

Bond premium amortization effective interest rate method

Table D

A	B	C	D	E	F
Semi-annual interest periods	Interest to be paid $200\,000 \times \frac{8}{100} \times \frac{1}{2}$	Interest expense to be recorded $NBL \times \frac{6}{10} \times \frac{1}{2}$	Premium amortization (B) – (C)	Unamortized premium (E) – (D)	Net bond liability 200 000 + E
Beginning 1	–	–	–	17 040	217 040
Ending 1	8 000	217 040 × 0.03 6 517	8 000 – 6 511 1 489	15 551	215 551
2	8 000	215 551 × 0.03 6 467	8 000 – 6 467 1 533	14 018	214 018
3	8 000	214 018 × 0.03 6 421	8 000 – 6 421 1 579	12 439	212 439
4	8 000	212 439 × 0.03 6 373	8 000 – 6 373 1 627	10 812	210 812
5	8 000	210 812 × 0.03 6 324	8 000 – 6 324 1 676	9 136	209 136
6	8 000	209 136 × 0.03 6 274	8 000 – 6 274 1 726	7 410	207 410
7	8 000	207 410 × 0.03 6 222	8 000 – 6 222 1 778	5 632	205 632
8	8 000	205 632 × 0.03 6 169	8 000 – 6 169 1 831	3 801	203 801
9	8 000	203 801 × 0.03 6 114	8 000 – 6 114 1 886	1 915	201 915
10	8 000	201 915 × 0.03 6 085	8 000 – 6 085 1 915	0	200 000

A – The number of semi-annual periods over the five-year life of the bonds.

B – The face value times the semi-annual contractual interest rate each period.

C – The net bond liability (the carrying value of the bond) times the semi-annual effective interest rate each period.

D – The amount written off each period as a premium.

E – The balance of premium to be written off.

F – Net bond liability or the carrying value of the bond.

16.13 Accounting for retirement of bonds

Bonds are retired when the issuing corporation redeems them before or at maturity, or when the bondholders convert them to common stock. The following entries are used to record redemption of bonds.

16.14 Before maturity

This is the purchase of bonds before the redemption or retirement date. At the redemption date, the book value of the bond equals to the face value.

Example: Bonds of payable value $5 M with a carrying value of $5.125 M were retired. The cash received was $5.2 M

Steps:
1. Eliminate the carrying value of the bond at the redemption date.
2. Record the cash paid.
3. Recognize the gain or loss on redemption.

$$\text{Gain} = \text{Carrying value} - \text{Cash paid}$$
$$\text{Loss} = \text{Cash paid} - \text{Carrying value}$$
$$= 5.2 \text{ M} - 5.125 \text{ M}$$
$$= \$0.075 \text{ M}$$

4. Calculate the discount or premium

$$\text{Premium} =$$
$$\text{Cash paid} - (\text{Bond payable} + \text{loss on redemption})$$
$$= 5.2 \text{ M} - (5.0 \text{ M} + .075)$$
$$= \$0.125 \text{ M}$$

Journal entry

		$ M
Bonds payable	5.0	
Premium	.125	
Loss on bond redemption	.075	
To cash		5.2

Being redemption of bonds before maturity

16.15 At maturity

This is the payment or conversion of the face value of the bond when it matures. At maturity, the book value of the bond equals its face value.

Example:
Fashion Able Incorporated is redeeming 5000, 8 year, 10%, $1000 bonds at $1000.

Journal entry

		$ M
Bonds payable	5	
To cash		5

Being redemption of bonds at maturity

16.16 Conversion to common stock

Under this arrangement, bonds at maturity are exchanged for common stock instead of cash.

Example: Fashion Able Incorporated redeemed $5000 000 in bonds by issuing 400 000 shares of $10 par value common stock.

Journal entry

		$ M
Bonds payable	5	
To Common stock		4
To Premium		1

Being redemption of bonds at maturity

16.17 Sinking fund for bonds

When the issuing entity sells bonds it tries to ensure that enough cash is available at maturity to redeem the instrument. An amount of cash or other assets is set annually to meet the debt and is called a **sinking fund**.

This pool of cash can be invested thereby becoming a source of investment income for the entity. The investment plus the income is then utilized in paying the interest on the bond and the principal at maturity.

The following table describes how the sinking fund is accounted for.

ACTIVITY	JOURNAL ENTRIES
Sale of bonds	Dr. Cash Cr. Bonds payable
Annual Instalments or amounts added to the fund	Dr. Bond sinking fund Cr. Cash
Income earned from investing the cash	Dr. Cash Cr. Sinking fund investment income
Sale of the investment to pay the bondholder	Dr. Cash Cr. Bond sinking fund
Redemption of the bond	Dr. Bond $^a/_c$ Cr. Cash $^a/_c$

16.18 Financial statement presentation

Bonds Issued at a premium
Balance Sheet Year 1

CURRENT LIABILITIES
Bond interest payable (for 6 months)

LONG-TERM LIABILITIES
Bonds payable
Add: Premium on bonds payable

Bonds Issued at a discount
Balance Sheet Year 1

CURRENT LIABILITIES
Bond interest payable (for 6 months)

LONG-TERM LIABILITIES
Bonds payable
Less: Discount on bonds payable

16.19 Long-term notes payable

Mortgage loans

Characteristics of Long-term notes payable:

1. The terms of the notes exceed one year.
2. When interest rates are fluctuating market rates may be used.
3. The notes stipulated may be adjustable or fixed.
4. Instalment payments are made over the period of the loan.
5. Payments are made on the interest and the principal.
6. They are recorded at face value.

16.20 Accounting for mortgage loans

Journal entries

Obtaining the mortgage loan	Dr. Cash Cr. Mortgage notes payable
Payment of the instalment	Dr. Interest expense Dr. Mortgage notes payable Cr. Cash

16.21 Financial statement presentation

Balance sheet

LONG-TERM LIABILITIES
Mortgage (Unpaid principal)

CURRENT LIABILITY
Reduction of principal for next period

16.22 Lease liability

Characteristics of operating lease

1. The lessee has temporary use of the property.
2. The lessor remains owner of the property.
3. The lessee records rental payments as expense, the lessor as revenue.
4. Other costs related to the lease by the lessee are recorded as expenses.

Accounting treatment of operating lease

Payments towards the lease are recorded as follows:

> Dr. Rental expense
> Cr. Cash

Characteristics of capital lease

1. Ownership rights transferred to the lessee.
2. Payments for the lease are capitalized and recorded as assets.
3. The lessee has an option to purchase.
4. Term >75% of economic life.
5. PV lease payments = 90% of the fair market value.

Accounting treatment for capital lease

When the lease is obtained it is recorded as follows:

> Dr. Lease asset (named)
> Cr. Lease liability

Financial statement presentation

Balance Sheet	
Current liability	
Lease liability (next year)	
Long term liability:	Plant asset:
Bonds	Leased asset – Named
Mortgage	
Lease liability	

16.23 Questions

1. Record the following transactions of Cheshire Corporation in the general journal:
   (a) Bought 2000 shares of its own shares $20 per common stock for $30 per share
   (b) Sold 300 treasury shares for $35 per share
   (c) Sold 300 treasury shares of $32 per share.

2. A company issues 8000 shares of its $10 per value common stock in exchange for equipment valued at $110 000. The entry to record this transaction includes
   (a) Premiums for $35 000
   (b) Retained earnings for $35 000
   (c) Common stock for $105 000
   (d) Equipment for $105 000.

3. What is the main difference between:
   (a) a bond and a share
   (b) notes payable and bonds payable?

4. 'Dividends are paid out of appropriated profits' – this is a statement commonly made by own accountants. Criticize this statement. What is the source of cash dividends?

17 Business purchase

Objectives
- state the difference between the purchase of a business and the purchase of the assets of a business
- calculate goodwill arising on the purchase of a business
- prepare journal entries to record the purchase of a business
- prepare Balance Sheet following the purchase of a business
- calculate the return on an investment in a new business

17.1 What is the difference between the purchase of a business and the purchase of the assets of a business?

It is important to distinguish between a company buying the assets of another business, and the purchase by the company of that other business. Some students get confused between the two different kinds of purchase. A company may buy the assets of another business which may then cease to trade. The customers of that other business must find another supplier. That is very different from a company buying another business; the company takes over the assets and liabilities of that business together with its customers and carries on the trade of the business taken over. The distinction is important because the purchase only of assets does not involve any payment for goodwill; the purchase of a business usually does involve payment for goodwill.

A company often issues shares to the owner of a business as payment. The shares may be issued at a premium.

Sometimes a sole trader or a partnership may decide to convert their business into a limited company. This is done by forming a new company which purchases the partnership business.

Example

Aiisha has traded for some years as a sole trader. On 1 October 2004 she decided to form a limited liability company to take over her business. She will hold ordinary shares of $1 in the company as her capital.

Aiisha's summarized Balance Sheet at 1 October 2004 was as follows:

	$
Fixed assets	20 000
Net current assets	14 000
	34 000
Capital account	34 000

The summarized Balance Sheet of the new company will appear as follows:

Aiisha Ltd

	$
Fixed assets	20 000
Net current assets	14 000
	34 000
Share capital	
Ordinary shares of $1	34 000

17.2 Goodwill

When a company purchases a business, it will usually buy the assets less the liabilities at an agreed valuation. In addition, it usually pays for the advantage of acquiring an established trade. The company does not have to build up a new business from nothing; the business has been built up by the previous owner who will normally expect to be rewarded for his efforts.

Goodwill is the amount paid for the acquisition of a business in excess of the fair value of its separable net assets. The term 'separable net assets' is used to describe the piecemeal sale of the assets of a business and the settlement of its liabilities out of the proceeds.

It is important to distinguish between **purchased goodwill** and **inherent goodwill**. Purchased Goodwill has been paid for. Inherent goodwill has not been paid for and will arise, for instance, if a trader decides that he wants to show the goodwill of his business in his Balance Sheet; he debits a Goodwill account in his books and credits his Capital account with any amount that he wishes to show as goodwill. An Accounting Standard (FRS 10) states that *only purchased goodwill* should be shown in company Balance Sheets and should be shown as an 'intangible' fixed asset. FRS 10 also has some other important things to say about Goodwill, which will be considered in chapter 27.

If the amount paid for a business is less than the fair value of its separable net assets, the difference is called **negative goodwill** (not Badwill!) and must be shown as a negative amount among the intangible fixed assets in the Balance Sheet. (Before December 1997, when FRS 10 was published, negative goodwill had to be shown as a Reserve in the Balance Sheet.)

17.3 How to make journal entries in the books of a company to record the purchase of a business

Before any entries for the purchase of a business are made in a company's ledger accounts, the transaction must be recorded in the journal. The entries should include the Bank and Cash accounts if these are taken over. However, the bank and cash balances of the business being acquired are not usually taken over unless a sole trader or a partnership converts their business into a limited company.

Example

Bortit Ltd purchased the business of A. Sellit, a sole trader, on 1 October 2004. Sellit's Balance Sheet at that date was

	$	$
Fixed assets		
Land and buildings		60 000
Plant and machinery		35 000
Motor vehicles		21 000
		116 000
Current assets		
Stock		7 000
Debtors	4 000	
Bank	5 000	
	16 000	
Less Current liabilities		
Creditors	2 000	14 000
		130 000
Capital		130 000

The assets were taken over at the following values:

Land and buildings	80 000
Plant and machinery	28 000
Motor vehicles	16 000
Stock	5 000
Debtors	3 000
Creditors	2 000

Bortit Ltd did not take over Sellit's Bank account.

Bortit Ltd paid A. Sellit $150 000, made up as follows: cash $20 000 and 100 000 ordinary shares of $1 each.

Required

Prepare the journal entries in Bortit Ltd's books to record the purchase of A. Sellit's business.

Answer

	Dr	Cr
	$	$
Land and buildings	80 000	
Plant and machinery	28 000	
Motor vehicles	16 000	
Stock	5 000	
Debtors	3 000	
Goodwill	20 000[1]	
Creditors		2 000
Cash		20 000
Ordinary share capital		100 000
Share Premium account	_____	30 000[2]
	152 000	152 000

The purchase of the business of A. Sellit on 1 October 2004 for the sum of £150 000 payable as follows: cash $20 000 and by the issue of 100 000 ordinary shares of $1 at $1.30 per share.

1 Goodwill = purchase consideration ($150 000) less value of net assets acquired ($130 000).

2 The shares were valued at $(150 000 – 20 000) = $130 000. $30 000 is the share premium.

Bortit Ltd's Balance Sheet at 1 October 2004 before it acquired the business of A. Sellit was as follows:

	$	$
Tangible fixed assets		
Land and buildings		200 000
Plant and machinery		75 000
Motor vehicles		40 000
		315 000
Current assets		
Stock		21 000
Debtors	16 000	
Bank	32 000	
	69 000	
Current liabilities		
Creditors	7 000	62 000
		377 000
Capital and reserves		
Ordinary share capital		300 000
Retained profit		77 000
		377 000

Required

Prepare Bortit Ltd's Balance Sheet immediately after the purchase of the business of A. Sellit.

Answer

Add the journal entries to Bortit Ltd's assets, liabilities, share capital and reserves.

(Workings are shown in brackets.)

Bortit Ltd Balance Sheet at 1 October 2004 after the acquisition of A. Sellit's business

	$	$
Intangible fixed asset		
Goodwill		20 000
Tangible fixed assets		
Land and buildings (200 000 + 80 000)		280 000
Plant and machinery (75 000 + 28 000)		103 000
Motor vehicles (40 000 + 16 000)		56 000
		439 000
Total fixed assets		459 000
Current assets		
Stock (21 000 + 5000)		26 000
Debtors (16 000 + 3000)	19 000	
Bank (32 000 – 20 000)	12 000	
	57 000	
Current liabilities		
Creditors (7000 + 2000)	9 000	48 000
		507 000
Capital and reserves		
Ordinary share capital (300 000 + 100 000)		400 000
Share premium		30 000
Retained profit		77 000
		507 000

Exercise 1

Hamil Ltd purchased the business of Abdul, a sole trader, on 30 June 2004. The Balance Sheets of both businesses at that date were as follows:

| | Abdul | | Hamil Ltd | |
	$	$	$	$
Fixed assets				
Freehold property		40 000		100 000
Plant and machinery		15 000		60 000
Office equipment		–		14 000
Office furniture		7 000		–
		62 000		174 000
Current assets				
Stock		4 000		10 000
Debtors	6 000		7 000	
Bank	1 000		25 000	
	11 000		42 000	
Current liabilities				
Creditors	3 000	8 000	6 000	36 000
		70 000		210 000
Capital account		70 000		
Share capital and reserves				
Ordinary shares of $1				150 000
Share Premium account				20 000
Retained profit				40 000
				210 000

It was agreed that Abdul's assets should be valued as follows:

	$
Freehold property	70 000
Plant and machinery	12 000
Office furniture	4 000
Stock	2 500
Debtors	5 500

Hamil Ltd did not acquire Abdul's bank account.

The consideration for the sale was $120 000 and was satisfied by the payment to Abdul of $20 000 in cash and the issue to him of 80 000 ordinary shares in Hamil Ltd.

Required

(a) Prepare the journal entries in Hamil Ltd's books to record the purchase of Abdul's business.

(b) Prepare Hamil Ltd's Balance Sheet immediately after the acquisition of Abdul's business.

17.4 Purchase of a partnership business

The treatment of the purchase of a partnership business was dealt with in detail in section 15.17.

17.5 Return on investment

It is important that a company purchasing another business succeeds in making the new business as profitable as its existing business. Profitability is measured by expressing profit as a percentage of capital invested. If a company has purchased a business for $100 000 and the business has made a profit of $12 000 in the first year, the profitability is 12%. This is the **return on capital invested**. If it is equal to, or more than, the return on capital the company was earning on its existing business, the investment may be considered to have been worthwhile. If it is less, overall profitability of the business will be **diluted** (or decreased). However, it is better to measure the profitability over a number of years to get a reliable picture.

The new business may have been merged with the existing business so closely that separate results for the new business are not available. In such a case, the incremental (that is, the additional) profit is measured against the additional capital invested in the business.

Example

X Ltd had a capital of $300 000. Its average annual profit was $54 000. Its return on capital was

$$\frac{\$54\,000}{\$300\,000} \times 100 = 18\%.$$

X Ltd purchased another business on 1 January 2004 for $100 000 which was settled by the issue to the vendor of shares in X Ltd. X Ltd's profit for the year ended 31 December 2004 was $84 000. The profitability of X Ltd has increased by 3% to 21%

$$\left(\frac{\$84\,000}{\$400\,000} \times 100\right).$$

A more reliable picture is obtained if the additional profit of $30 000 is calculated as a percentage of the price paid for the new business:

$$\frac{\$30\,000}{\$100\,000} \times 100 = 30\%.$$

X Ltd has benefited from the purchase of the new business.

17.6 Examination hints

- Goodwill is the difference between the values of the net assets acquired and the purchase price.

- Show goodwill as an intangible fixed asset, even if it is negative goodwill.
- When a debenture is issued to a partner, and the partner is to receive the same amount of annual interest as he/she received before the sale of the firm; check that you have calculated the amount of the debenture correctly.
- If you are required to prepare journal entries in a company's books to record the purchase of a business, do *not* show the entries in the books of the business being taken over.
- Make sure you prepare the journal entries in good form.
- Show all workings when preparing the company's Balance Sheet after the new business has been acquired.

17.7 Multiple-choice questions

1 The following is information about the assets and liabilities of a business.

	Book value	Market value
	$	$
Tangible fixed assets	90 000	101 000
Current assets	32 000	29 000
	122 000	
Current liabilities	(14 000)	14 000
	108 000	

Goodwill is valued at $50 000.

What should be paid for the net assets of the business?

A $116 000

B $119 000

C $166 000

D $169 000

2 A company paid $1.8 million to acquire the business of a sole trader. The sole trader's assets and liabilities were valued as follows.

	$
Fixed assets	700 000
Current assets	300 000
Current liabilities	50 000
Long-term loan	100 000

How much was paid for goodwill?

A $650 000

B $750 000

C $850 000

D $950 000

3 The Balance Sheet of a sole trader is as follows.

	$
Fixed assets	
Intangible: Goodwill	30 000
Tangible	100 000
Net current assets	50 000
	180 000

A company purchased the business, paying for the tangible fixed assets and the net current assets at the valuations shown above.

The company settled the purchase price by issuing 200 000 ordinary shares of $1 at $1.50 per share.

How much did the company pay for goodwill?

A $30 000

B $50 000

C $120 000

D $150 000

17.8 Additional exercises

1 The following is the Balance Sheet of the Erchetai partnership at 30 April 2002.

	$	$
Goodwill		50 000
Tangible fixed assets		928 000
		978 000
Current assets		
Stock	40 000	
Debtors	76 000	
Bank	80 000	
	196 000	
Current liabilities: Creditors	29 000	167 000
		1 145 000
Long-term liability		
Loan (carrying interest at 8% per annum)		100 000
		1 045 000
Partners' capitals		1 045 000

On 30 April 2002, Istaimy plc acquired the business of the Erchetai partnership. The following matters were taken into consideration in fixing the terms of the acquisition.

1. No depreciation had been provided on freehold buildings. It was agreed that a provision of $128 000 should have been made.

2. On 1 April 2002 Erchetai had purchased a machine. The cost was $60 000. $20 000 was paid immediately. The balance is payable by four equal instalments on 1 May, 1 June, 1 July and 1 August, together with interest at the rate of 12% per annum. Only the initial payment of $20 000 had been recorded in the partnership's books. It was Erchetai's policy to depreciate machinery at the rate of 15% per annum on cost, and to provide for a full year's depreciation in the year of purchase.

3. A debtor owing $5000 at 30 April 2002 has since become bankrupt. Erchetai has been advised that a dividend of 20 per cent will be paid.

4. Stock has been valued at cost. Investigation shows that if stock had been valued at net realizable value it would have been valued at $28 000. If separate valuation at the lower of cost and net realizable value had been applied to each item of stock it would have been valued at $30 000.

The purchase consideration was satisfied as follows:

- The long-term loan was satisfied by the issue of $80 of 10% debenture stock 2008/10 for every $100 of the loan.

- The partners were issued, for every $50.00 of capital, with:

  3×8 percent preference shares at $1.20 per share, and 3 ordinary shares of $10.00 each at $12.50.

Required

Prepare the journal entry to record the purchase of the partnership business in the books of Istaimy plc. Your answer should include cash transactions.

(UCLES, 2002, AS/A Level Accounting, Syllabus 9706/4, October/November)

2 On 1 April 2004 Joel Ltd acquired the partnership business of Kay and Ola. The partnership Balance Sheet at 31 March 2004 was as follows.

	$000	$000
Fixed assets		
Land and buildings		150
Plant and machinery		280
		430
Current assets		
Stock	150	
Debtors	141	
Bank	69	
	360	
Current liabilities		
Creditors	130	230
		660
Long-term liability		
Loan from Kay at $12\frac{1}{2}$% per annum		100
		560
Financed by capital accounts: Kay		300
Ola		260
		560

Further information

1. The assets (including the bank account) and current liabilities were taken over at the following valuations.

	$000
Land and buildings	220
Plant and machinery	170
Stock	128
Debtors	105
Creditors	138

2. Kay received sufficient 10% Convertible Loan Stock to ensure that she continued to receive the same amount of interest annually as she had received as a partner. The terms of this issue give Kay the option to have the debenture stock converted to ordinary shares in Joel Ltd on 1 June 2006 at $1.25 per share.

3. The balance of the purchase price was settled by the allocation of 300 000 shares in Joel Ltd to Kay and Ola at $1.50 per share.

Joel Ltd's Balance Sheet at 31 March 2004 was as follows.

	$000	$000	$000
Fixed assets			
Land and buildings			1425
Plant and machinery			803
			2228
Current assets			
Stock		381	
Debtors		519	
Bank		420	
		1320	
Creditors: amounts falling due within one year			
Trade creditors	500		
8% debentures 2004/2005	450	950	
			370
			2598
Share capital and reserves			
Ordinary shares of $1			1350
Profit and Loss Account			1248
			2598

Immediately following the acquisition of the partnership, Joel Ltd redeemed its 8% debentures 2004/2005 at a premium of 4%. In order to preserve the capital structure of the company, a reserve equal to the amount of the debentures redeemed was created.

Required

(a) Prepare Joel Ltd's Balance Sheet as it appeared immediately after it had acquired the partnership of Kay and Ola and redeemed the 8% debentures. (Show all workings.)

(b) Calculate the profit required on Joel Ltd's investment in the partnership business to produce a return of 25% on the investment.

On 1 June 2006 the market price of Joel Ltd's shares was $1.37.

Required

(c) (i) State, with reason, whether Kay should convert her 10% convertible loan stock into ordinary shares in Joel Ltd.

(ii) State the effect that the conversion of Kay's 10% convertible loan stock into shares would have on Joel Ltd's Balance Sheet.

Module Three
Financial Reporting and Interpretation

18 Published company accounts

Objectives
- the financial statements and reports that must be published and sent to shareholders
- reporting standards relating to Income Statement Accounts
- reporting standards relating to Balance Sheets
- the contents of directors' reports
- the importance of auditors' reports
- distinguish between liquidation and receivership
- state the factors which contribute to business failure
- describe the function of the receiver when liquidating a business
- outline the steps in the liquidation and receivership process
- prepare financial statements for a limited company
- apply a given corporation tax rate to the net income

18.1 Introduction to published company accounts

Shareholders are not permitted to manage their company unless they are also directors of the company. The directors act as stewards of the shareholders' investments in the company; they are in a position of trust. Companies Acts ensure that the directors account to the shareholders regularly for their stewardship of the company. The documents which are required to be prepared and published annually are

- Income Statement Account
- Balance Sheet
- cash flow statement
- directors' report
- auditors' report.

These documents must be sent to shareholders in advance of every annual general meeting. They must also be sent to debenture holders. The directors must file an annual return, which includes the annual accounts, with the Registrar of Companies, and the returns may be inspected by any member of the public. Apart from shareholders and debenture holders, other persons who may be interested in a company's accounts are

- trade and other creditors
- providers of long-term finance such as banks and finance houses

- trade unions, representing the company's workforce
- financial analysts employed by the financial press
- fund managers managing clients' investments
- the Stock Exchanges.

18.2 Companies Act

Companies Acts require the Income Statement Account to give a **true and fair view** of the income statement of the company for the financial year, and the Balance Sheet to give a *true and fair view* of the state of affairs of the company as at the end of the financial year. The word *true* may be explained in simple terms as meaning that, if financial statements indicate that a transaction has taken place, then it has actually taken place. If a Balance Sheet records the existence of an asset, then the company has that asset. The word *fair* implies that transactions, or assets, are shown in accordance with accepted accounting rules of cost or valuation.

Window dressing describes attempts by directors of a company to make a Balance Sheet show the financial position of company to be better than it really is. For example, the directors may cause cheques to be drawn and entered in the books of account on the last day of the financial year but not send the cheques to the creditors until the next financial year. This would have the effect of artificially reducing a company's liabilities in the Balance

Sheet, but it would not give a true and fair view because the creditors had not, in fact, been paid. An attempt to inflate the retained profit figure in the Balance Sheet by including unrealized profits in the Income Statement Account would not give a true and fair view. The Companies Act 1985 states that only profits which have been realized at the Balance Sheet date shall be included in the Profit and Loss Account.

The accounting principle of **substance over form** is one accounting principle intended to give a true and fair view.

International accounting standards are guidelines designed to be used in the preparation of financial statements.

18.3 Segmental reporting, IAS 14

Companies that carry on different classes of business, or carry on their business in several geographical areas, are required to prepare their accounts in a form that provides information about each individual class (or segment) of the business or geographical area. **Segmental reporting**, as it is called, provides users of financial statements with information that might not otherwise be available to them. They are then better able to assess a company's past and possible future performance.

In their financial statements, companies should define their separate classes of business and the geographical areas in which they operate. They should give, for each segment:

- turnover
- profit before taxation
- net assets employed.

Other information, such as costs common to all the activities, does not need to be shown separately.

Example

Multido Ltd operates in three distinct industries: aerospace, civil engineering and automotive.

The segmental report for the year ended 31 March 2004 is as follows.

	Aerospace $m.	Civil engineering $m.	Automotive $m.	Total $m.
Turnover	80	120	65	265
Profit before taxation				
Segmental profit	16	23	16	55
Common costs				(30)
				25
Net interest				(3)
Profit before taxation				22

18.4 Reporting financial performance, IAS 8 and 35

IAS 8 and 35 are other standards designed to help users of Income Statement Accounts to make better assessments of a company's past and future performance. It requires

- details of turnover to be shown separately for continuing, new and discontinued businesses owned by the company
- separate operating profits for continuing, new and discontinued businesses
- the following to be shown separately in the Income Statement Account
  - profits or losses on sale or cessation of an operation*
  - costs of fundamental reorganization or restructuring*
  - profits or losses on the disposal of fixed assets*
  - exceptional items
  - extraordinary items
- a statement of total recognized gains and losses
- a reconciliation of movements in shareholders' funds.

Exceptional items are shown with an asterisk (*) above. They are defined in the IAS as material items which derive from events or transactions that fall within the ordinary activities of the company and which, because of the amounts involved, need to be disclosed if the financial statements are to give a true and fair view.

Exceptional items should be shown under their natural heading in the format of the Income Statement Account as prescribed by the Companies Act 1985. They should be identified with the continuing new or discontinued operations as appropriate.

Extraordinary items are now so rare that identifying them causes some difficulty.

Statement of total recognized gains and losses Only realized gains and losses are recognized in the Profit and Loss Account; but the net worth of a company is determined by unrealized gains and losses as well as those that have been realized. An example of an unrealized gain or loss occurs when, for example, an asset is revalued, or shares are issued at a premium.

18.5 Liquidation & receivership

Liquidation

Liquidation refers to the termination of a business by using its assets to discharge liabilities. A limited company may go into 'voluntary' liquidation following a shareholders' decision that the company is no longer solvent, i.e. able to meet its daily obligations or go into liquidation because of a court order. Once in liquidation, a liquidator will be appointed to collect and redistribute all the company's assets using the rules set out in the insolvency laws of the particular country or territory. This is known as winding up of a company. Once the winding up is complete, the liquidator sends the final accounts to the Registrar of Companies and the company is considered to be dissolved (gone out of business) three months later.

Receivership

Receivership is a type of liquidation: a company enters into a business that has performed badly over a prolonged period of time. Creditors can initiate court proceedings and then the court appoints a receiver to run the company. The receiver is often an accountant who specializes in this work. The receiver's job is to preserve what he can of the business so that it can be sold off to obtain money to repay creditors. Receivership is an extraordinary remedy and can be executed with or without the consent of the property owner. Receiverships are usually a less expensive and more flexible alternative than bankruptcy.

The Role of the Receiver includes the following:

- Take control of assets
- Pay creditors
- Carry on the business.

Types of Receivership

1. A creditor may have a receiver appointed either privately or by a court order.

2. Lenders often complete security agreements with borrowers as a condition to loaning money.

3. A secured creditor will generally proceed with a court-appointed receiver, rather than a private appointment.

Reasons why businesses go into receivership

1. Cash shortage

2. Competition

3. Poor internal control

4. Poor liquidity control

5. Lack of a secure customer base

6. Obsolete technology

7. Change in demand

8. Poor management resources.

It is more common for a creditor to proceed by way of liquidation instead of receivership. A creditor generally chooses a liquidation over a receivership to:

1. reverse priorities
   Generally in a receivership, section 109 of the Employment Standards Code gives employee earnings priority over secured creditors. This reverses in a liquidation, where the secured creditors have priority over employee earnings;

or

2. increase authority
   Unlike a receiver, a trustee in a liquidation has extensive powers. This is particularly useful in investigations where fraudulent activity has been alleged.

18.6 Accounting for inventories IAS 2

The basic principle is that inventories should be valued at lower of cost and net realizable value. The cost of inventories should include:

- All cost of purchases
- Costs of conversion
- Other costs incurred in bringing the inventories to their present location and condition.

18.7 IAS 10. Accounting for post balance sheet events and contingencies

Post balance sheet events: definition

Events are activities, transactions or circumstances pertinent to the business, which have financial consequences. These events occur at any time during the trading period.

However, this chapter is concerned only with events that occur after the Balance Sheet has been prepared but before the said financial statements are authorized for issue to shareholders, a review board or to the regulatory body. These events are called Post Balance Sheet events.

The concern here is how should these events, occurring after the Balance Sheet date, be treated in the financial statement.

  i. Should they be accounted for and recognized in the current financial statement by adjusting the original figures?

 ii. Should they just be disclosed by means of a note, without adjusting the financial statement figures? or

iii. Should they be ignored?

Example 1

If at the end of Trading period on Dec 31 2004, the Balance Sheet of Rostant Ltd showed a Net Account Receivable figure of $140 000, then on February 8 2005, two days before the financial statements were authorized for issue, the directors were reliably informed that a major debtor for $80 000 of the $140 000 has been declared bankrupt, how should this post balance sheet event be treated in the current financial statement?

Example 2

After the preparation of the financial statement of Energy Enterprises, but before the financial statements were authorized for issue, a major fire destroyed the firm's warehouse causing losses of $240 000. How should this post balance sheet event be treated?

An examination of International Accounting Standard, 10 (IAS10) would assist in determining the accounting treatment required.

IAS 10 defines Post Balance Sheet Events as 'Those events, favourable and unfavourable, that occur between the balance sheet date and the date when the financial statements are authorized for issue.' It must be noted that the financial statements are authorized for issue by the board of directors or management after they have been reviewed.

Types of events: adjusting and non-adjusting

The accounting treatment of events arising after the balance sheet date will be determined by the nature or types of events.

These events fall into two categories:

i. Those events which provide additional information or evidence of conditions that existed at the balance sheet date, *adjusting events* and

ii. Those events that are indicative of conditions which only arose after the balance sheet date, *non-adjusting* events.

1. Adjusting events

These are post balance sheet events for which adjustments can be made to the original figures in the financial statements. These events provide evidence of conditions that existed at the balance sheet date.

Examples of adjusting events.

a. Bankruptcy of a consumer, requiring the debt which existed at the balance sheet date to be now written off.

b. The determination after the balance sheet date, of the cost of assets purchased, or the proceeds from assets sold, before the balance sheet date.

c. The discovery of fraud or errors that show that the financial statements are incorrect.

d. The settlement after the balance sheet date of a court case that confirms that the firm had a present obligation at the balance sheet date.

e. Sale of stocks at less than cost, requiring a reduction in the valuation of closing stock.

f. Amounts received or receivable in respect of insurance claims which were being negotiated at the balance sheet date.

Example 1 above, Rostant Ltd, should be treated as a post balance sheet adjusting entry and recognized in the financial statements. The amounts should therefore be adjusted.

2. Non-adjusting events

These are events arising after the balance sheet date, but do not concern conditions which existed at the balance sheet date. No adjustments for these events must take place in the financial statements. They have no effect on items in the balance sheet or the income statement.

Disclosure of non-adjusting events If non-adjusting events after the balance sheet date are material, or significant, some form of disclosure is required by way of a note to the financial statement. Non-disclosure of these non-adjusting events could influence the economic decisions of users taken on the basis of financial statements as presented.

When non-adjusting events are disclosed, the information given must include

(a) the nature of the event, and

(b) an estimate of its financial effect, or a statement that such an estimate cannot be made.

Examples of non-adjusting events

(a) Raising of new capital.

(b) Major change in the composition of the business; i.e. acquisition or disposing of a major subsidiary.

(c) Major destruction of fixed assets or inventories as a result of fire or flood or other disaster.

(d) Abnormally large changes after the balance sheet date in asset prices or foreign exchange rates.

(e) The issue of stocks or long-term loans.

(f) Strikes and other labour disputes.

Example 2 above, Energy Enterprises would be treated as a post balance sheet non-adjusting event, and disclosed by way of notes in the financial statements.

18.8 IAS 37. Provisions, contingent assets and contingent liabilities

A provision is a potential liability of uncertain amount or timing. Once a reliable estimate of the amount can be made, provisions are recognized as liabilities because (1) they are present obligations, and (2) it is possible that an outflow of resources (payment) will be required to settle the obligations.

When a provision is recognized the expenditure must be recorded in the financial statements.

A provision is recognized when

(a) The entity has a present obligation (legal or constructive) as a result of past events.

(b) A reliable estimate can be made of the amount of the obligation.

(c) It is probable that an outflow of economic resources will be required to settle the obligation.

If these conditions are not met, no provision shall be recognized.

In this context 'probable' is interpreted to mean 'more likely than not'.

A constructive obligation is one based on past acceptable practices, which lead to future valid expectations.

An example of a provision may be seen in the refund policy of a retail store, that refunds purchases by dissatisfied customers, even though it is under no legal obligation to do so; however the policy of making refunds is generally known.

In this situation the obligating event is the sale of the product, which gives rise to a constructive obligation because the conduct of the store has created a valid expectation on the part of its customers that the store will refund purchases. An outflow of economic resources is probable. Thus the provision is recognized for the best estimate of the cost of refunds.

Other situations which may necessitate provisions include

1. Claims under warranties.

2. Contamination of the environment (clean-up penalties).

3. Removal of an oil rig and restoration of damage caused by setting it up, after the extraction of oil.

18.9 Contingencies

A contingency is a condition which exists at the balance sheet date where the outcome will be confirmed only on the occurrence or non-occurrence of one or more uncertain future events.

Contingencies suggest a *possible* obligation i.e. one which may or may not occur, and not a *probable* obligation, i.e. one which is more likely than not to occur.

A contingency, unlike a provision, must not be recognized. It must only either be disclosed or ignored. Thus 'contingent' is used for assets and liabilities that do not meet recognition criteria.

A contingent asset is a *possible* asset that arises from past events and whose existence will be confirmed only by the occurrence or non-occurrence of one or more uncertain future events not wholly within the control of the entity.

Contingent assets are not recognized in financial statements since they may result in the recognition of income that may never be realized. However, when the realization of income is virtually certain, then the related

asset is no longer a contingent asset and its recognition is now appropriate. A contingent asset is disclosed when an inflow of economic resources is probable.

A contingent liability occurs when conditions for a provision are not met.

18.10 Distinguishing between provisions and contingent liabilities

Provisions are *recognized* as liabilities (assuming that a reliable estimate can be made) because they are present obligation and it is *probable* that an outflow of resources will be required to settle the obligations.

Contingent liabilities are *not recognized* as liabilities because they are either:

i. Possible obligations which may not lead to an outflow of economic resources or

ii. Present obligations which do not meet the recognition criteria, i.e.

   (a) no probable outflow of economic resources,

   (b) a reliable estimate of the amount of the obligation cannot be made.

A contingent liability is *disclosed*, not recognized.

18.11 Treatment of contingencies

1. Do not provide, but disclose the nature of the contingency in a note to the accounts.

   This treatment means that the users of the accounts would be provided with information about the contingency.

2. Do not provide and do not disclose the nature of the contingency in a note to the accounts.

   In this treatment the user of the accounts has no information.

18.12 Disclosure requirements
Events after the balance sheet date

An entity shall disclose

1. the date when the financial statements were authorized for issue,

2. the person who gave the authorization,

3. if the owner or owners have the power to amend the financial statements after issue,

4. information received after the balance sheet date even when the information does not affect the amount that it recognizes in its financial statements,

5. for non-adjusting events (a) the nature of the event and (b) an estimate of its financial effects, or a statement that such an estimate cannot be made.

Provisions

An entity shall disclose

1. the carrying amount at the beginning and the end of the period,
2. additional provisions made in the period, including increasing the existing provision,
3. amounts used (i.e. Incurred and charged against the provision) during the period,
4. unused amounts reversed during the period,
5. a brief description of the nature of the obligation and the expected timing of any resulting outflow of economic benefits.

Contingent liabilities

An entity shall disclose

1. a brief description of the nature of the contingent liability,

2. an estimate of its financial effect (if possible, its best estimate),
3. an indication of the uncertainties relating to the amount or timing of any outflows,
4. the possibility of reimbursement.

Contingent assets

Where an inflow of economic benefits is probable, the entity shall disclose

1. a brief description of the nature of the contingent asset,
2. an estimate of their financial effects.

18.13 **Summary illustration**

An illustration depicting the treatment of contingent liabilities is presented by the International Accounting Standards Board, which serves as an appendix to accompany IAS 37.

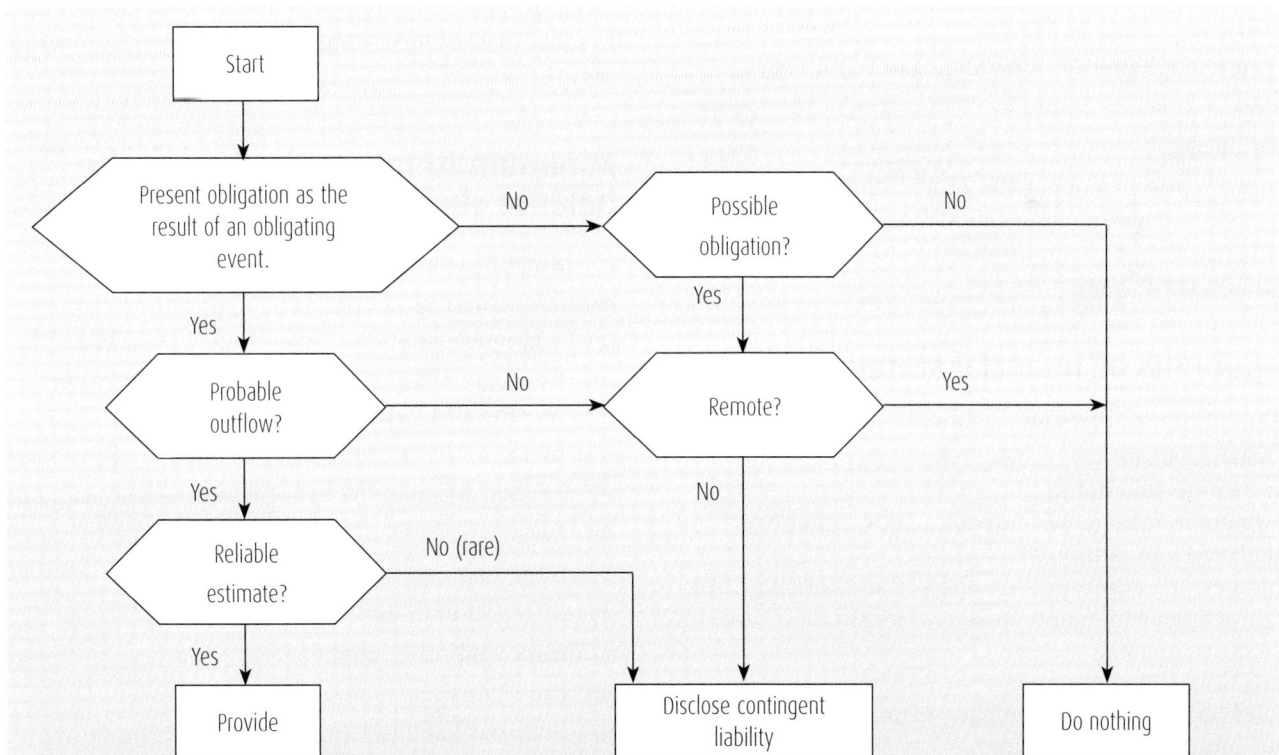

Source: International Accounting Standards

Note: in rare cases, it is not clear whether there is a present obligation. In these cases, a past event is deemed to give rise to a present obligation if, taking account of all available evidence, it is more likely than not that a present obligation exists at the balance sheet date.

18.14 IAS 1. Presentation of financial statements

Objective of IAS 1

The objective of IAS1 (revised 1997) is to prescribe the basis for presentation of general purpose financial statements, to ensure comparability both with the entity's financial statements of previous periods and with the financial statements of other entities. IAS 1 sets out the overall framework and responsibilities for the presentation of financial statements, guidelines for their structure and minimum requirements for the content of the financial statements. Standards for recognizing, measuring, and disclosing specific transactions are addressed in other Standards and Interpretations.

Objectives of financial statements

The objective of general purpose financial statements is to provide information about the financial position, financial performance, and cash flows of an entity that is useful to a wide range of users in making economic decisions. To meet that objective, financial statements provide information about an entity's

- Assets
- Liabilities
- Equity
- Income and expenses, including gains and losses
- Other changes in equity
- Cash flows.

That information, along with other information in the notes, assists users of financial statements in predicting the entity's future cash flows and, in particular, their timing and certainty.

Components of financial statements

A complete set of financial statements should include:

- a balance sheet;
- an income statement;
- a statement of changes in equity showing either;
- all changes in equity, or
- changes in equity other than those arising from transactions with equity holders acting in their capacity as equity holders;
- cash flow statement and,
- notes, comprising a summary of accounting policies and other explanatory notes.

The financial statements must 'present fairly' the financial position, financial performance and cash flows of an entity. Fair presentation requires the faithful representation of the effects of transactions, other events, and conditions in accordance with the definitions and recognition criteria for assets, liabilities, income and expenses set out in the Framework. The applications of IFRSs, with additional disclosure when necessary, is presumed to result in financial statements that achieve a fair presentation.

IAS 1 requires that an entity prepare its financial statements, except for cash flow information, using the accrual basis of accounting [IAS 1.25].

The presentation and classification of items in the financial statements shall be retained from one period to the next unless a change is justified either by a change in circumstances or a requirement of a new IFRS.

Balance sheet

An entity must normally present a classified balance sheet, separating current and non-current assets and liabilities.

Current assets are cash; cash equivalent; assets held for collection, sale or consumption within the enterprise's normal operating cycle; or assets held for trading within the next 12 months. All other assets are non-current.

Current liabilities are those to be settled within the enterprise's normal operating cycle or due within 12 months, or those held for trading, or those for which the entity does not have an unconditional right to defer payment beyond 12 months. Other liabilities are non-current.

Long-term debt expected to be refinanced under an existing loan facility is non-current, even if due within 12 months.

Minimum items on the face of the balance sheet

(a) property, plant and equipment;

(b) investment property;

(c) intangible assets;

(d) financial assets (excluding amounts shown under (e), (h) and (i));

(e) investments accounted for using the equity method;

(f) biological assets;

(g) inventories;

(h) trade and other receivables;

(i) cash and cash equivalents;

(j) trade and other payables;

(k) provisions;

(l) financial liabilities (excluding amounts shown under (j) and (k));

(m) liabilities and assets for current tax, as defined in IAS 12;

(n) deferred tax liabilities and deferred tax assets, as defined in IAS 12;

(o) minority interest, presented within equity; and

(p) issued capital and reserves attributable to equity holders of the parent.

Income statement

All items of income and expense recognized in a period must be included in profit or loss unless a Standard or an Interpretation requires otherwise.

Minimum items on the face of the income statement should include

(a) revenue;

(b) finance costs;

(c) share of the profit or loss of associates and joint ventures accounted for using the equity method;

(d) a single amount comprising the total of (i) the post-tax profit or loss of discontinued operations and (ii) the post-tax gain or loss recognized on the disposal of the assets or disposal group(s) constituting the discontinued operation;

(e) tax expense; and

(f) profit or loss.

Expenses should be analysed either by nature (raw materials, staffing costs, depreciation, etc.) or by function (cost of sales, selling, administrative, etc.) either on the face of the income statement or in the notes. If an enterprise categorizes by function, additional information on the nature of expenses – at a minimum depreciation, amortization, and staff costs – must be disclosed.

Suggested format of the balance sheet: IAS 1		
	$m	$m
Assets:		
Non-current assets:		
Property, plant and equipment	X	
Goodwill	X	
Investments	X	
		X
Current assets:		
Inventories	X	
Trade and other receivables	X	
Prepayments	X	
Cash	X	
	X	
Total Assets		$xx

	$m	$m
Equity and liabilities:		
Capital and reserves:		
Issued capital	X	
Reserves	X	
Accumulated profits	X	
		X
Non-current liabilities:		
Loan notes	X	
Current liabilities:		
Trade and other payables	X	
Overdrafts	X	
Proposed dividends	X	
Tax provision	X	
		X
		$xx

'By function' format	$m
Revenue	X
Cost of sales	(x)
Gross profit	X
Other operating income	X
Distribution costs	(x)
Administrative costs	(x)
Profit from operations	X
Net interest cost	(x)
Profit before tax	X
Income tax expense	(x)
Net profit for period	$x

'By nature' format	$m	$m
Revenue		X
Other operating income		X
Changes in inventories of finished goods and work in progress	X	
Raw materials and consumables used	X	
Staff costs	X	
Depreciation and amortization expense	X	
Other operating expense	X	
		X
Net interest cost	X	X
Profit before tax		X
Income tax expense		X
Net profit for period		$xx

18.15 IAS 7 Cash flow statements

This standard requires that organizations present a cash flow statement as part of their financial statements. It shows the difference between profit and cash so that a user will be able to:

- Assess liquidity
- Obtain additional information on the activities of the business
- Provide information of cash inflow and outflow from the business
- Estimate future cash flows
- Determine cash flows generated from trading.

It is required that the cash flows must be classified under three headings:

- Operating activities
- Investing activities
- Financing activities.

18.16 Directors' report

The Companies Act 1985 requires directors to prepare a report for each financial year. The purpose of the report is to supplement the information given by the financial statements, which, by themselves, cannot convey all the information that users of the accounts need to know to form an assessment of the past and future performance of the business.

The Companies Act states that the directors' report shall contain the following information.

1. A review of the business during the year and its position at the end of the year.

   [The Profit and Loss Account and Balance Sheet only provide information which can be expressed in monetary terms (concept of money measurement). They cannot describe the conditions under which the company has traded.]

2. The accounting statements prepared for IAS 1 cannot explain the activities carried on by the company or give complete information about new and discontinued activities.

3. Particulars of important events that have occurred after the end of the financial year and which affect the company.

   [Post Balance Sheet events take place after the end of a company's financial year and may affect items in the Balance Sheet or Profit and Loss Account (adjusting events).

   Non-adjusting events occur after the date of the Balance Sheet but do not require the Profit and Loss Account or Balance Sheet items to be changed.]

4. Recommended dividends.

   [These must be approved by the members of the company at the annual general meeting.]

5. Names of the directors of the company, their remuneration, pension details and their interests in shares or debentures of the company.

   [Shareholders are entitled to know who have been stewards of their interests during the year and the extent of each director's commitment to the company as a shareholder or debenture holder.]

6. Donations to political parties or charities during the year.

   [Shareholders may not wish their money to be used for political purposes, or may wish that some of the profits be used for charitable purposes.]

7. Arrangements for promoting the health, safety and welfare at work of the employees.

   [Shareholders are entitled to be re-assured that the company is abiding by current legislation concerning health and safety and that it is concerned with the welfare of its employees (good labour relations).]

8. Information about research and development being carried on by the company.

   [Shareholders are able to see the extent of the company's involvement in the development of its product, which may be a guide to the future prospects of the company.]

9. An indication of the future developments in the company's business.

   [An indication of likely future growth and/or diversification) or disposing of non-core activities.]

10. Significant changes in fixed assets during the financial year.

    [Shareholders are informed of any material differences between the Balance Sheet values of fixed assets and their current market values.]

11. Policy regarding the payment of creditors.

    [This requirement arose from the practice of many large companies of improving their cash flows by delaying payments to creditors, whose cash flows suffered in consequence. Many suppliers of large companies are small businesses who are largely reliant upon prompt payments. There is an ethical dimension to the requirement to disclose this information.]

12. Details regarding employment of disabled persons.

    [Companies must not discriminate against disabled persons. They should provide information concerning the provision of facilities for disabled employees.]

18.17 Auditors' report

Directors are stewards of the company in which shareholders have invested their capital. The shareholders are unable to inspect the company's books but they are, along with the debenture holders, entitled to receive copies of the annual accounts. It is important that shareholders and debenture holders can be sure that the directors can be trusted to conduct the company's business well and that the financial statements and directors' report are reliable.

The shareholders appoint auditors to report at each annual general meeting whether

- proper books of account have been kept;
- the annual financial statements are in agreement with the books of account;
- in the auditors' opinion, the Balance Sheet gives a true and fair view of the position of the company at the end of the financial year and the Profit and Loss Account gives a true and fair view of the profit or loss for the period covered by the account;
- the accounts have been prepared in accordance with the Companies Acts and all current, relevant accounting standards.

If auditors are of the opinion that the continuance of a company is dependent on a bank loan or overdraft, they have a duty to mention that fact in their report as it is relevant to the going concern concept.

The auditors' responsibility extends to reporting on the directors' report and stating whether the statements in it are consistent with the financial statements. They must also report whether, in their opinion, the report contains misleading statements.

Auditors must be qualified accountants and independent of the company's directors and their associates. They report to the shareholders and not to the directors; as a result, auditors enjoy protection from wrongful dismissal from office by the directors.

18.18 Examination hints

- Make sure you are familiar with the requirements of the Companies Acts and the accounting standards regarding published company accounts. They link very strongly with what you have already learnt and with the understanding and interpretation of accounts, which will be covered in the next chapter.
- Multiple-choice questions are often based on a knowledge this topic.
- Practise answering discursive type questions based on published accounts. Answers should be clear, concise and relevant.

Prepare an Income Statement for a limited company and apply a given corporation tax rate to net income

Example

Trim Ltd records showed the following balances for March 28, 2004:

	$
Wages and salaries	2 000
Gross profit	30 000
Insurance	2 000
Gain on sale of asset	17 500
Loss due to hurricane	20 000
Transportation out	900
Interest received	300
Repairs	1 500
Mortgage Interest paid	2 000
Telephone	1 000
General administration expenses	1 000
Selling expenses	3 000
Depreciation – Office equipment	1 000
Bad debts	150
Electricity	1 500
Sundry expenses	500
Commissions paid	500

Additional information:

1. Wages and salaries, insurance, telephone and electricity are to be allocated 60% selling and 40% administrative.

2. Sundry expenses are to be allocated 70% selling and 30% administrative.

3. The tax rate is 30%.

Prepare the partial Income Statement for the year ended March 28, 2004.

Answer

Trim Ltd
Partial Income Statement
For the year ending March 28, 2004

	$	$	$
Gross profit			30 000
Operating expenses			
Selling expenses:			
Insurance (2000 × 60%)	1 200		
Transportation out	900		
Repairs	1 500		
Selling expenses	3 000		
Bad debts	150		
Wages and salaries (2000 × 60%)	1 200		
Commissions paid	500		
Telephone (1000 × 60%)	600		
Electricity (1000 × 60%)	900		
Sundry expenses (500 × 70%)	350	10 300	
Administrative expenses:			
Wages and salaries (2000 × 40%)	800		
Insurance (2000 × 40%)	800		
Telephone (1000 × 40%)	400		
General administrative expenses	1 000		
Depreciation – office equipment	1 000		
Sundry expenses (500 × 30%)	150	4 150	14 450
			15 550
Income from operations:			
Other expenses and revenues:			
Gain on sale of assets		17 500	
Interest received		300	
Mortgage interest paid		(2 000)	15 800
Income before tax and extraordinary item			31 350
Income tax expense (31 050 × 30%)			9 315
Income before extraordinary item			22 035
Loss due to hurricane		20 000	
Less income tax saving (20 000 × 30%)		6 000	14 000
Net income			8 035

18.19 Multiple-choice questions

1 IAS 1 (Accounting policies) lists four accounting principles. Which of the following is stated by the standard to be a desirable principle?

  A accruals

  B consistency

  C going concern

  D historical cost

2 IAS 14 (Segmental reporting) requires companies to give separate figures for certain items for each segment. For which of the following are separate figures *not* required?

  A cost of sales

  B net assets employed

  C profit before taxation

  D turnover

3 Which of the following is required to be disclosed by way of a note to the accounts?

  A exceptional items

  B the basis on which depreciation has been calculated

  C the number of shares held by directors

  D the reason for any issue of shares during the year.

4 What should be disclosed by way of a note to the Balance Sheet regarding depreciation of fixed assets?

  A date of acquisition

  B estimated proceeds of disposal

  C estimated net residual value

  D useful economic lives of the assets

5 Which of the following, occurring after the Balance Sheet date, is an adjusting event?

  A a capital reconstruction

  B a debtor at the Balance Sheet date subsequently becoming bankrupt

  C an issue of shares

  D loss of stock in a fire

18.20 Additional exercises

1 Explain what is meant by an adjusting event. Describe the action that needs to be taken when one occurs and explain why the action is necessary.

2 What is segmental reporting and what does it entail? Why is it helpful to the users of financial statements?

18.21 Questions on post balance sheet events and provisions and contingencies

1 What is a post balance sheet?

2 Define adjusting events and give three examples.

3 Define non-adjusting events and give three examples.

4 A material post balance sheet event should be disclosed as a note if it is

  A an adjusting event which is not material

  B a non-adjusting event which is not material

  C a non-adjusting event which is material

  D an adjusting event which is material.

5 Post Balance Sheet events occur

  A after financial statements are prepared but before they are issued for circulation

  B after financial statements are issued for circulation

  C before transactions are posted to the Balance Sheet

  D at the Balance Sheet date.

6 If events occurring after the Balance Sheet date result in a change of the original figures in the financial statement, this is

  A an event to be disclosed by way of note

  B an event to be ignored

  C a non-adjusting event

  D an adjusting event.

7 Adjusting events

  A provide evidence of conditions that existed at the Balance Sheet date

  B do not concern conditions which existed at the Balance Sheet date

  C must occur within two days after the Balance Sheet date

  D must be disclosed by way of notes.

8 An example of an adjusting entry is

  A the issue of stocks or long term loans

  B bankruptcy of a customer

  C a major destruction of fixed assets by fine

  D the raising of new capital.

9 Indicate which events are adjusting and which are non-adjusting:

    i. discovery of fraud or errors in the financial statements

    ii. sale of inventory at less than cost requiring revaluation of closing inventory

    iii. strikes and other disputes

    iv. bankruptcy of a major debtor

    v. disposal or acquisition of a major subsidiary

    vi. issue of long-term loans

    vii. destruction of large amounts of inventory through flooding.

    viii. Raising new capital.

10 Post Balance Sheet non-adjusting events are

  A treated as adjusting events

  B disclosed by way of notes

  C ignored if material

  D altered in the Balance Sheet.

11 A potential liability of uncertain amount or timing is

  A a provision

  B a contingency

  C a bad debt

  D an example of depreciation.

12 A provision is recognized and recorded in the financial statement when

  A the entity has a present obligation as a result of past events

  B a reliable estimate can be made of the amount of the obligations

  C it is almost certain that it will result in an outflow of economic resources

  D the outcome of certain conditions is unlikely to occur.

13 A Contingency

  A suggests a possible obligation which may or may not occur

  B is a definite asset or liability which must be recorded

  C is always recognized

  D must never be disclosed.

14 Contingent assets are not recognized in financial statements since

  A they may result in the recognition of income that may never be realized

  B they are already claimed by the firm

  C these assets are Balance Sheet items

  D they are in fact liabilities.

15 A contingent asset is disclosed when

  A the financial information is reliable

  B the value of the asset can be ascertained

  C the amount is over $5000

  D an inflow of economic resources is probable.

19 Statement of cash flow (IAS 7)

Objectives
- state the purpose of a statement of cash flow
- reproduce an outline of statement of cash flow
- explain the classifications of a statement of cash flow
- convert an accrual account balance to its cash equivalent
- list components under each classification of the cash flow statement
- prepare a statement of cash flow

The statement of cash flow explains how a firm obtained and used cash and cash equivalent during an accounting period. Cash and cash equivalents comprise cash on hand and demand deposits, together with short-term, highly liquid investments that are readily convertible to a known amount of cash. It is a statement which classifies the sources of cash received (cash inflows) and the uses made of the cash through payments (cash outflows). It explains how the cash balance at the beginning of the period becomes the cash balance at the end of the period.

The statement classifies cash receipts and payments into three broad categories:

1. Operating activities
2. Investing activities
3. Financing activities.

The statement of cash flow has become a mandatory and integral part of the financial statements for public limited liability corporations, however private corporations and other types of business organizations are encouraged to prepare them as well. It is in keeping with the requirements of IAS 7, whereby all enterprises that prepare financial statements in conformity with IAS are required to present a cash flow statement.

19.1 Why statement of cash flow?

The income statement summarizes the performance of an enterprise over a period by determining its profitability at the end of the period. Since profitability is calculated on an accrual and not on a cash basis, it does not give an indication of the liquidity position of the enterprise. Profit is not necessarily cash. Profit does not give a meaningful picture of a company's operation. The corresponding balance sheet of the enterprise gives only a snapshot picture of its cash position at the end of the period, and not how cash was generated and disbursed by the enterprise during the period. The statement of cash flow attempts to give users of financial information a clearer picture and better understanding of the movement of cash and cash equivalent.

19.2 Purposes of cash flow

1. To assess the ability of the firm to generate positive net cash flows.
2. To assess the firm's ability to service loans and pay dividends.
3. To determine the reasons for the difference between the firm's reported profit and its cash position at the end of a period.
4. To examine the cash investing and financing transactions during the period.
5. To explain changes in the cash position not explained by the income statement.

IAS 7 sets out the structure of a cash flow statement as well as the minimal level of disclosure. The objective of the standard is to require reporting entities falling within its scope to report on a standard basis their cash generation and cash absorption for a period.

19.3 Structure of statement of cash flows

Report company statement of cash flow for year ended December 31 2004

	$	$
Cash flows from operating activities		
List of inflows	xxx	
Less: List of outflows	(xxx)	
Net increase (decrease) from operating activities		xxx
Cash flows from investing activities		
List of inflows	xxx	
Less: List of outflows	(xxx)	
Net increase (decrease) from investing activities		xxx
Cash flows from financing activities		
List of inflows	xxx	
Less: List of outflows	(xxx)	
Net increase (decrease) from financing activities		xxx
Net increase (decrease) in cash		xxx
Plus beginning cash balance		xxx
Ending cash balance		xxx

19.4 Cash flows from operating activities

These are cash flows derived from operating or trading activities. They relate to income statement items. This section focuses on the firm's ability to generate cash internally through operations and its management of current assets and current liabilities. Firms are allowed two possible methods for cash flow statements in respect to operating activities:

(i) the direct method, (ii) the indirect method.

19.5 Direct method

The direct method looks at the components of cash flows from operating activities which are listed as receipts and payments. This method uses an analysis of the cash book:

Inflows (receipts)	Outflows (payments)
Cash received:	Cash paid:
From customers (sale of goods or services)	for purchase of goods or services to suppliers
As dividends & interest received on Investments	for salaries and wages
	To government for taxes
	To interest on loans
	For other expenses

The difference between the inflows and outflows is called the net cash inflow (outflow) from operating activities. The direct method is usually difficult and costly to implement and is therefore rarely used by companies. However, it is the method encouraged by the FASB, although the indirect method is acceptable.

Example

A summary of the direct method may be

	$	$	$
Cash receipt from customers		732 500	
Dividends received		80 000	
Interest received		23 000	835 500
Payment to suppliers	240 000		
Payment to employees	200 000		
Interest paid	40 000		
Tax paid	30 000		(510 000)
Net cash inflow from operating activities			325 500

19.6 Indirect method

The indirect method adjusts the net income of the firm by eliminating non-cash items such as depreciation, gains or losses on disposal of fixed assets, to arrive at the net cash inflow (outflow) from operating activities. This method starts with the net income computed under the accrual basis concept, and ends, after adjustments, with the cash basis concept. In other words net income previously obtained is converted to net cash provided by operating activities.

Basically there are two steps in the method:

Step 1   Removes non-cash revenues and expenses which were included in the Income Statement.

Step 2   Focuses on changes in working capital items in the Balance Sheet.

Step 1

Depreciation expense, loss on sale of equipment and gain on sale of vehicles are non-cash expenses and revenue which impacted on the net profit but which did not have a coinciding cash movement. The relevant expenses are added back, and revenue deducted in arriving at cash flows from operating activities.

Example

Cash flows from operating activities

	$
Net Income after tax and interest	331 000
Add Depreciation expense	9 000
Add Loss on sale of equipment	3 000
Less Gain on sale of vehicles	(6 000)
	337 000

Step 2

The current asset and current liability accounts are examined for changes between the start of the period and end of the period. Usually the current year's and previous year's balance sheets are used. All account balances except cash and cash equivalents are examined. As the adjustments are made to reflect cash flows, the net income will be realigned to show the net cash flow.

As a rule of thumb, an increase or decrease will result in the following adjustments to the net income:

Change in asset	Cash Flow	Treatment
Increase in asset	Outflow	Subtract from net income
Decrease in liability	Outflow	Subtract from net income
Increase in liability	Inflow	Add to net income
Decrease in asset	Inflow	Add to net income

Example:

Cash flows from operating activities

Net income	$331 000
Depreciation expense (add)	9 000
Loss on sale of equipment (add)	3 000
Gain on sale of vehicles (subtract)	(6 000)
	337 000
Decrease in inventory (add)	5 000
Increase in accounts payable (add)	6 000
Increase in accounts receivable (subtract)	(15 000)
Decrease in prepayments (add)	2 500
Decrease in accruals (subtract)	(10 000)
Net cash inflows from operating activities	325 500

Cash flows from investing activities

Cash flows from investing activities relate to the cash inflows and cash outflows resulting from the sales or purchases of long-term operational assets, including investments.

Example

Cash Inflows from	Cash Outflows for
Sale or disposal of property, plant, equipment, machinery, etc.	Purchase of property, plant, equipment, machinery, etc.
Sale or maturity of investments in securities	Purchase of investments in securities that are not cash equivalents, patents, trademarks.

To determine the net cash flows from investing activities may at times require an analysis of changes in the beginning and ending balances of the non-current assets accounts, together with additional income statement information. For example, the Equipment and machinery account in the Balance Sheet for Credible Manufacturing shows a 1 January 2006 balance of $420 000. The Income Statement information indicates that (1) equipment costing $13 000 was sold, and (2) machinery costing $280 000 was purchased. The 31 December balance is now $687 000 ($420 00 – $13 000 + $280 000).

There are transactions however, which will increase the value of a fixed asset (for example, land) but without any increase in cash: for example, through the issuance of common stock or bonds payable and revaluation. A transaction of this nature would only be disclosed as a separate schedule below the statement of cash flow.

19.7 Financing activities

This section shows cash flows to and from the providers of capital, usually external providers. These activities alter the equity capital and borrowing structure of the enterprise.

Cash inflows will include: receipts from the issue of stocks; receipts from borrowing on notes, mortgages, bonds, etc.

Cash outflows: repayment of loans; payments on repurchasing of stocks; payments of dividends.

It is important to remember that only repayment on the principal of the loan will be entered under financing activities. Any loan interest paid will go under operating activities. To compute cash flows from financing activities one needs at times to review changes in long-term debts and stockholders equity accounts between the opening and closing period.

Having imputed net cash flows from operating activities, investing activities and financing activities, the resulting figure is the net increase or decrease in cash for the period. To this figure is added the beginning cash balance, to end with closing cash balance as seen in the corresponding year's balance sheet.

In order to have a clearer understanding of the process involved in presenting a statement of cash flow, we can now use the balance sheet, income statement and additional information of Credible Manufacturing Company to prepare a cash flow statement for the year ended 31 December 2006.

Credible Manufacturing Company Balance Sheet
As at 31 December 2006

	2006	2005	Change in Account	
	$	$		
Current Assets				
Cash	203 500	60 000	143 500	Increase
Accounts receivable	35 000	20 000	15 000	Increase
Inventory	100 000	105 000	5 000	Decrease
Prepayments	17 000	19 500	2 500	Decrease
Non-Current Assets				
Equipment and Machinery	687 000	420 000	267 000	Increase
Vehicles	200 000	260 000	60 000	Decrease
Long-term investment	60 000	70 000	10 000	Decrease
	1 302 500	954 500		
Liabilities & Stockholder's Equity				
Current Liabilities				
Accounts payable	9 000	3 000	6 000	Increase
Accruals	5 000	15 000	10 000	Decrease
Long-Term Liabilities				
Bond payable	30 000	130 000	100 000	Decrease
Stockholder's Equity				
Common stock	300 000	100 000	200 000	Increase
Retained earnings	958 500	706 500	252 000	Increase
	1 302 500	954 500		

Credible Manufacturing Company Income Statement for the year ending 31 December 2006

	$	$
Revenues		692 000
Gain on sale of vehicles		6 000
		698 000
Cost of goods sold	260 000	
Operating Expenses (excluding depreciation)	80 000	
Depreciation	9 000	
Loss on sale of equipment	3 000	352 000
Income before income taxes		346 000
Income tax expense		15 000
Net income		331 000

Additional Information:

1. Investment costing $10 000 was sold for the same price.
2. Equipment costing $13 000 with net book value of $11 000 was sold for $8 000.
   Machinery costing $280 000 was purchased for cash.
3. Depreciation expenses for the year is $9 000.
4. Vehicle costing $60 000 with a book value of $34 000 was sold for $40 000.
5. The company paid a cash dividend for $60 000.
6. Common stock of $200 000 was issued for cash.
7 Bonds of $100 000 were redeemed for cash.

The complete Statement of Cash Flow may now look like this:

Credible Manufacturing Company Cash Flow Statement for the year ending 31 December 2006 (indirect method)

	$	$
Net Income		331 000
Depreciation expense (add)		9 000
Loss on sale of equipment (add)		3 000
Gain on sale of vehicles (subtract)		(6 000)
		337 000
Decrease in inventories (add)		5 000
Increase in accounts payable (add)		6 000
Decrease in prepayments (add)		2 500
Increase in accounts receivable (subtract)		(15 000)
Decrease in accruals (subtract)		(10 000)
Net cash Inflow from operating activities		325 500
Investing activities:		
Additions to equipment & machinery	(280 000)	
Disposal of vehicles	40 000	
Proceeds from sale of equipment	8 000	
Proceeds from sale of investment	10 000	
Total cash outflow from investing activities		(220 000)
Financing activities:		
Inflow from stock issue	200 000	
Outflow to repay long-term debt	(100 000)	
Outflow for dividends	(60 000)	
Total cash inflow from financing activities		40 000
Net increase in cash		143 500
Add beginning cash balance		60 000
Ending cash balance		203 500

Note: The ending cash balance agrees with the cash balance stated on the balance sheet as at 31st December, 2006

Dividends, taxes and extraordinary items

IAS 7 suggests that interests and dividends received and paid may be classified as operating, investing or financing cash flows, providing that they are classified consistently from period to period (IAS 7.31).

Cash flows arising from taxes on income are normally classified as operating, unless they can be specially identified with investing or financing activities (IAS 7.35), also cash flows relating to extraordinary items should be classified as operating, investing or financing as appropriate and should be separately disclosed (IAS 7.29).

19.8 The concept of cash

The concept of cash is given a broad definition for financial statement purposes. Cash is defined as money or any instrument that banks will accept for deposit and immediate credit to the depositor's account.

Cash includes currency and other items that are payable on demand. These include cheques, money orders and bank drafts. Instruments will include cash equivalents which are investments with financial institutions which will mature within three months and whose value is unlikely to change on conversion to cash. These are treasury bills and bank certificates of deposits.

Notes payable, IOUs and postage stamps are not considered as cash.

For financial reporting purposes, all cash accounts and cash equivalents are usually combined as one.

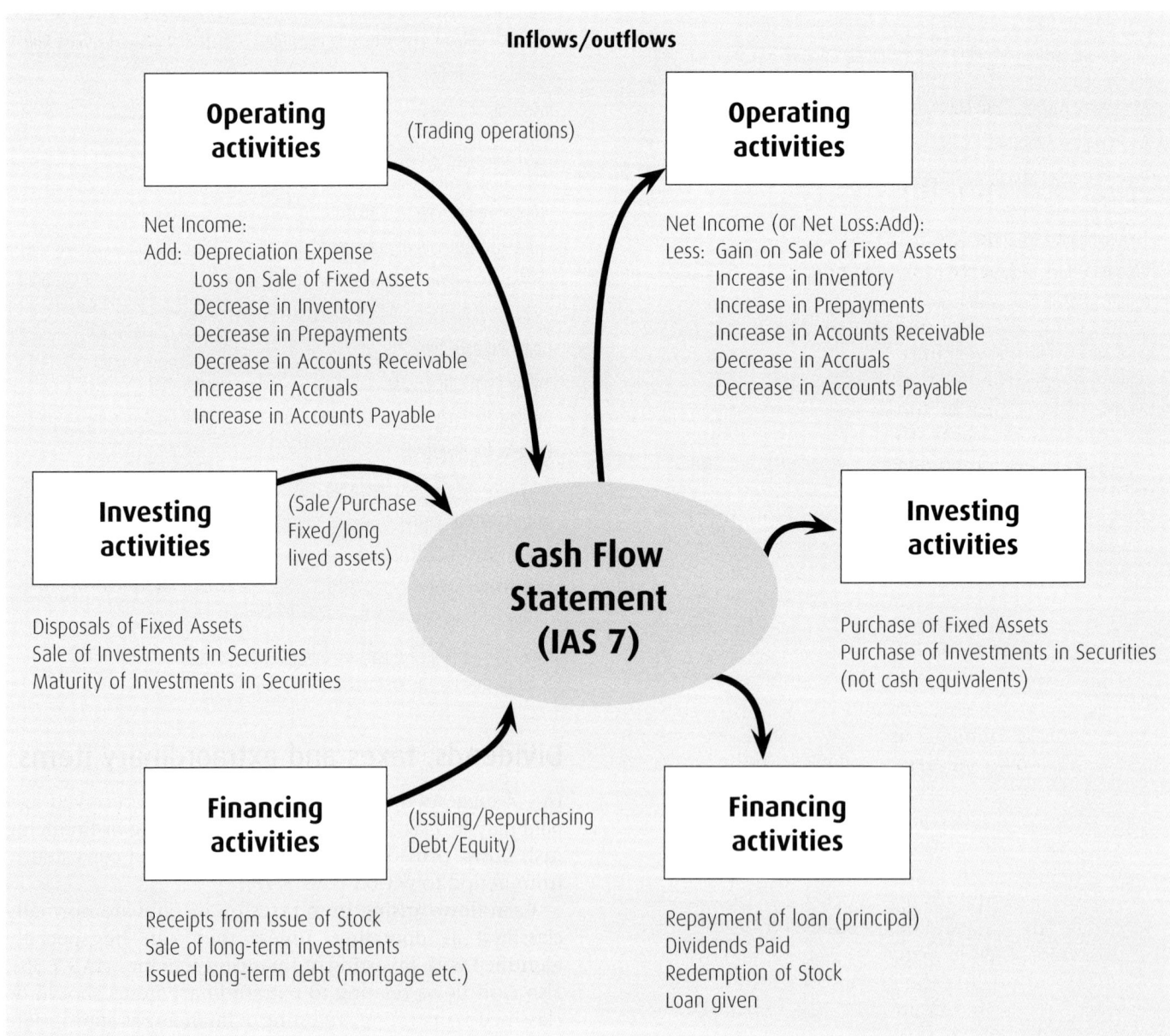

Inflows/outflows

Operating activities

(Trading operations)

Net Income:
Add: Depreciation Expense
      Loss on Sale of Fixed Assets
      Decrease in Inventory
      Decrease in Prepayments
      Decrease in Accounts Receivable
      Increase in Accruals
      Increase in Accounts Payable

Operating activities

Net Income (or Net Loss:Add):
Less: Gain on Sale of Fixed Assets
      Increase in Inventory
      Increase in Prepayments
      Increase in Accounts Receivable
      Decrease in Accruals
      Decrease in Accounts Payable

Investing activities

(Sale/Purchase Fixed/long lived assets)

Disposals of Fixed Assets
Sale of Investments in Securities
Maturity of Investments in Securities

Cash Flow Statement (IAS 7)

Investing activities

Purchase of Fixed Assets
Purchase of Investments in Securities
(not cash equivalents)

Financing activities

(Issuing/Repurchasing Debt/Equity)

Receipts from Issue of Stock
Sale of long-term investments
Issued long-term debt (mortgage etc.)

Financing activities

Repayment of loan (principal)
Dividends Paid
Redemption of Stock
Loan given

19.9 Statement of cash flows

Operating activities

    Net income

    Depreciation expense

    (Gains) losses on sale of assets

    (Increase) decrease in current assets

    Increase (decrease) in current liabilities

Investing activities

    Proceeds from sale of property, plant, and equipment

    Purchase of property, plant, and equipment

Financing activities

    Proceeds from long-term debt

    Repayment of long-term debt

    Issuance of common/preferred stock

    Purchase of treasury stock

    Payment of dividends

19.10 Examination hints

- Memorize the format in which cash flow statements should be prepared for companies, and the items which should be included under each heading.
- Tick each item in the question as you give effect to it, and show your workings.
- All non-cash items in the Profit and Loss Account must be adjusted in the reconciliation of operating profit to net cash flow from operating activities.
- Make sure you understand the effect of changes in stock, debtors and creditors on cash flow.
- Be prepared to draft a cash flow statement for a sole trader or a partnership.
- Get as much practice as you can at preparing cash flow statements.
- Good examination technique starts to earn marks as quickly as possible. Prepare the cash flow statement in outline, leaving plenty of space between the headings for details to be inserted. Start by filling in the easy items such as payments made to purchase fixed assets, proceeds of disposal, issues and redemptions of shares and debentures, movements in stock, debtors and creditors, etc. Then proceed to the items requiring more detailed calculations.
- If the cash flow in your answer in the examination does not equal the change in the cash balance in the question, do not spend time trying to trace the error(s) if this time is better spent tackling the next question. If you have studied the topic thoroughly before the examination, you will probably have done enough to earn useful marks anyway.

19.11 Exercises

1 List four useful purposes of a statement of cash flow.

2 What are the three classifications used in a statement of cash flow?

3 A statement of cash flow explains:

    A How cash moves from the firm to the bank for safe keeping.

    B How a firm obtains and uses cash and cash equivalent during a period.

    C Why cash is in short supply when the firm is expanding.

    D Why cash inflows and cash outflows occur at specific times of the year.

4 IAS7 recommends that:

    A All firms must submit a statement of cash flow.

    B Enterprises which submit income statements and balance sheets need not prepare cash flow statements.

    C Only small corporations need to submit a statement of cash flow.

    D Small corporations and other type of business organizations be encouraged to prepare cash flow statements.

5 When preparing a Statement of Cash Flow, the order of presenting the three activities is:

    A Operating activities, Investing activities, Financial activities

    B Investing activities, Financial activities, Operating activities

    C Financial activities, Operating activities, Investing activities

    D Operating activities, Financial activities, Investing activities.

6 The method which adjusts net income of the firm by eliminating non-cash items to arrive at net cash flows from operating activities is the

    A Direct method

    B Cash inflow method

    C Indirect method

    D Cash outflow method.

7 The method which uses the cash book for receipts and payments of the firm as components of cash flows from operating activities is the

    A Direct method

    B Cash inflow method

    C Indirect method

    D Cash outflow method.

8 In arriving at cash flow from operating activities, which one of the following is not adjusted?

    A Cash purchases

    B Depreciation

    C Loss on sale of equipment

    D Profit on sale of equipment.

9 Identify which activities can be classified as operating, investing and financing.

Activities	Classification
Sale of fixed assets	
Loss on sale of equipment	
Increase in accounts payable	
Repayment of long-term loans	
Issue of common stocks	
Depreciation expense	
Change in inventories	
Purchase of long-term investments	
Change in prepaid expenses	
Net income for the year	
Payment of dividends.	

10 ITSAFACT plc, using the accrual basis, arrived at a Net Income of $24 000. The income statement included depreciation expense of $5000, profit on sale of short term investments $2600 and loss of sale on old machinery $900. The net income on a cash basis will now be:

    A $248 500

    B $245 900

    C $243 300

    D $247 600.

11 In order to arrive at 'Net Cash Flows from Operating Activities', which of the following is incorrect?

    A Increase in current assets: subtract amount from net income

    B Decrease in current liabilities: add the amount to net income

    C Increase in current assets: add the amount to net income

    D Increase in current liabilities: add the amount to net income.

12 Indicate which activities should be added to or subtracted from the Net Income to arrive at Net Cash Flow from Operating Activities. Number one is done for you. (Use + for added and – for subtracted)

Activity	Adjustment
1 Depreciation expense	
2 Profit on sale of equipment	
3 Increase in inventory	
4 Loss on sale of short term investment	
5 Increase in accounts payable	
6 Decrease in accounts receivable	
7 Increase in prepayments	
8 Decrease in accruals	
9 Amortization of patents	
10 Increase in income tax payable.	

13 From the following information, calculate the Net Cash provided by operating activities.

	$
Net income	150 000
Depreciation expense	10 000
Loss on sale of equipment	4 000
Profit on sale of investments	3 000
Increase in inventory	6 000
Decrease in accounts receivable	2 000
Decrease in prepayments	1 000
Increase in accruals	1 500
Decrease in accounts payable	2 500
Increase in income tax payable	2 000

14 An example of a Cash flow from investing activities is:

    A Loss on sale of vehicles

    B Receipt from sale of vehicle

    C Receipt from issue of common stock

    D Outflow to repay long-term debt.

15 Fixed assets paid for through the issue of bonds payable are classified in the statement as cash flow as

    A Operating activities

    B Investing activities

    C Financial activities

    D None of the above.

16 Which of the following cash transactions will not be considered a financing activity?

    A Issuance of capital stock

    B Payment of dividends

    C Sale of building

    D Redemption of bonds.

19.12 Multiple-choice questions

1 The following information is extracted from the accounts of a company.

	Year ended 31 December 2003	Year ended 31 December 2004
	$000	$000
Retained profit at 31 December	50	70
Dividends paid and proposed	40	45
Transferred to General fund	100	100
Taxation	35	38
Interest payable on debentures	30	36

What was the operating profit for the year ended 31 December 2003?

A $194 000   **B** $239 000   **C** $244 000
D $289 000.

2 The following information is extracted from the accounts of a company.

	Year ended	
	30 June 2003	30 June 2004
	$000	$000
Operating profit	100	100
Loss on disposal of fixed assets	16	29
Closing stock	35	41
Debtors	47	49
Creditors	16	20

How much was the cash inflow from operating activities in the year ended 30 June 2004?

A $67 000   **B** $75 000   **C** $125 000
D $133 000.

3 A company acquired an asset worth $5000. In full settlement of the price, the company issued 5000 ordinary shares of $1 as fully paid-up shares to the vendor.

Under which heading in the cash flow statement will this transaction be shown?

A Acquisitions

B Capital expenditure

C Financing

D Not shown under any heading.

4 A company purchased a motor vehicle for $25 000. Settlement was made by a payment of $22 000 and the part exchange of one of the company's own vehicles for $3000. The vehicle given in part exchange had a written down value of $7000, but had a re-sale value of $2000.

Which amount should be shown in the cash flow statement for the acquisition of the vehicle?

A $22 000   **B** $24 000   **C** $25 000
D $29 000.

20 Interpretation and analysis

Objectives
- state the limitations of financial statements
- analyse and interpret financial statements
- calculate ratios
- use ratios
- explain (and how not to explain) ratios

20.1 The limitations of financial statements for shareholders and other interested parties

The purpose of financial statements such as Profit and Loss Accounts and Balance Sheets is to present information in a meaningful way. That is why items in financial statements are placed in groups of similar items: fixed assets, current assets, current liabilities etc. It also explains why you should compile financial statements with every item in its correct place.

Accounting standards are intended to ensure that items included in financial statements and described in similar terms are calculated, as far as possible, on the same bases. The Companies Act and the accounting standards require companies to add numerous notes to their financial statements to throw more light on the items in the accounts.

To be useful, information must be clear, complete, reliable and timely. In spite of the efforts of the Companies Act and the numerous accounting standards to ensure some sort of uniformity in the preparation of financial statements, the published accounts of limited companies have a number of limitations as communicators of information.

- They are not clear to people who have an inadequate knowledge of accounting and finance.
- The information they give is not complete. Legislation and accounting standards recognize that companies are entitled to keep certain information confidential because publication would give competitors an unfair advantage.

- The reliability of financial statements is only relative because companies are permitted to exercise a fair degree of subjectivity in selecting their accounting policies. Depreciation, provisions for doubtful debts, stock valuation and treatment of goodwill are examples of areas where there is no uniformity.
- Companies are allowed to depart from accounting standards if such departure is justified by the nature of their business and will improve the quality of the information provided by the accounting statements.
- By their very nature, published accounts are of historical interest. They may not be published for many months after the end of the financial year they cover. In the meantime, many circumstances may have changed: the economy may have improved or worsened; the political scene may have altered; new technologies may have been developed; fashions may have changed. A company's performance may have improved or worsened between the date of the Balance Sheet and its publication.

The directors' report may help to overcome some of the limitations of the financial statements, but not completely.

Only people with some knowledge of accounting are able to make much sense of the mass of figures in a company's financial statements. Even accountants need to interpret the figures before they are able to understand their significance. As a useful tool for interpreting accounts, accountants calculate ratios that relate certain items in the accounts to other items where there should be some sort of sensible relationship.

20.2 How to calculate and analyse ratios

All the ratios treated can be explained and illustrated with the aid of the following financial statements of Lladnar Ltd.

Lladnar Ltd
Income Statement for the years ended 31 December

	2003		2004	
	$000	$000	$000	$000
Turnover		1200		1600
Cost of sales				
Stock at 1.1.03	42		(1.1.04) 54	
Purchases	800		1166	
	842		1220	
Stock at 31.12. 03	54	788	(31.12.04) 100	1120
Gross profit		412		480
Salaries and wages	102		121	
Rent	66		66	
Electricity	30		32	
Sundry expenses	5		8	
Depreciation	27		37	
Debenture interest	10	240	15	279
Net profit		172		201
General reserve	40		60	
Preference dividend	8		10	
Ordinary dividend	60	108	64	134
Retained profit		64		67

Balance Sheets at 31 December

	2003			2004		
	$000	$000	$000	$000	$000	$000
Fixed assets		670			900	
Current assets						
Stock		54			100	
Accounts receivable		115			200	
Bank		100			29	
		269			329	
Current liabilities						
Accounts payable	101			190		
Dividends	40	141	128	44	234	95
			798			995
Long-term liability						
10% Debentures 2007/2008			100			150
			698			845
Share capital and reserves						
Ordinary shares of $1			400			400
10% Preference shares of $1			80			100
General Reserve			100			160
Retained profit			118			185
			698			845

Most ratios are appropriate for both incorporated and unincorporated businesses. Lladnar Ltd's Income Statement has been prepared in a form which, down to net profit, could apply to any business.

The ratios explained and analysed in §§20.3–20.5 are calculated to three decimal places but rounded to two decimal places. This is the usual requirement in examinations, but the particular requirement of any question must be observed.

20.3 Profitability ratios

The primary ratio: return on capital employed (ROCE)

The test of a good investment is its profitability, that is, the reward it yields on the amount invested in it. (Margin and profitability should not be confused. Margin is expressed as an amount of money: $172 000 for 2003 and $201 000 for 2004 in Lladnar Ltd's case; profitability is a ratio that relates profit to the amount invested.) The **first (or primary) ratio** for investors in a business is the **return on capital employed**. It relates net margin before interest and tax to the capital employed in the business. The formula is

$$\frac{\text{margin before interest and tax}}{\text{capital employed}} \times 100$$

(remember it easily as $\frac{\text{PROBIT}}{\text{capital employed}} \times 100$)

(PROBIT = profit before interest and tax)

Lladnar Ltd's return on capital employed is

2003	2004
$\frac{182}{798} \times 100 = 22.81\%$	$\frac{216}{995} \times 100 = 21.71\%$

Note. Debentures and other long-term loans are included in capital employed.

Comment In 2003, $22.81 of every $100 of turnover was left on the bottom line as net margin. (The net margin is known as the 'bottom line'. Items in accounts may be described as 'above the line' or 'below the line'.) In 2004, the return had decreased by 1.1% to 21.71%. The decrease, although only small, contrasts with the preferred result, which would be an improvement in profitability. Whether or not a rate of return is satisfactory depends upon the return that may be expected on suitable alternative investments.

Margin before interest and tax

Margin before interest and tax is calculated as a percentage of sales. For Lladnar Ltd this is

2003	2004
$\frac{182}{1200} \times 100 = 15.17\%$	$\frac{216}{1600} \times 100 = 13.5\%$

Comment Margin before interest and tax has fallen by 1.67%. When the gross margin percentage is calculated, that ratio will be seen to have fallen even more (by 4.33%). It is not surprising, therefore, to find that the margin before interest and tax has fallen although it should not fall by the same amount as most overheads are more or less fixed and do not vary with turnover.

Net margin percentage

Net margin can be related to sales by the following formula: $\frac{\text{net margin}}{\text{sales}} \times 100$. For Lladnar Ltd this is

2003	2004
$\frac{172}{1200} \times 100 = 14.33\%$	$\frac{201}{1600} \times 100 = 12.56\%$

Comment The net margin percentage has fallen by 1.77% from 14.33% in 2003 to 12.56% in 2004, even though turnover has risen by $33\frac{1}{3}\%$ from $1 200 000 to $1 600 000. The causes for the change in the net margin percentage may be analysed by examining gross margin percentage and the overheads as a percentage of sales.

Gross margin percentage

The formula for gross margin percentage is $\frac{\text{gross margin}}{\text{sales}} \times 100$. For Lladnar Ltd this is

2003	2004
$\frac{412}{1200} \times 100 = 34.33\%$	$\frac{480}{1600} \times 100 = 30.00\%$

Comment Gross margin percentage has decreased by 4.33% from 34.33% to 30.00%. In theory, the gross margin percentage should match the margin the business expects to make on all its sales. In practice, it is not as simple as that because most businesses sell more than one kind of good and a different mark up may be added to each kind. The gross margin percentage is affected by changes in the mix of the different products making up the turnover.

The reduction in the gross margin percentage may be explained by a number of factors:

- a rise in the price of goods purchased may not have been passed on to customers
- it may have been necessary to purchase the goods from a different supplier at a higher price
- the margin on sales may have been cut
  - to increase the volume of sales
  - to fight competition from other businesses
  - as an introductory offer for a new product
  - as a result of seasonal sales
  - to dispose of out-of-date or damaged stocks
  - to increase cash flow when the business is short of cash
- the cost of sales may have been increased by the theft of stock.

Expense to sales ratios

Overheads expressed as percentage of sales are given as follows for Lladnar Ltd:

2003	2004
$\frac{240}{1200} \times 100 = 20\%$	$\frac{279}{1600} \times 100 = 17.44\%$

The overhead percentage is calculated more quickly by finding the difference between the gross and net margin percentages.

Comment Although sales have increased in 2004 by $33\frac{1}{3}\%$, the ratio of overheads to sales has decreased from 20% to 17.44%. Sometimes overheads may increase as a percentage of sales, but the increase should not match the increase in gross margin percentage. The reason is that most overheads, such as rent, do not vary as a result of an increase in sales. Other overheads may vary, but not in proportion to sales. Salespeople's remuneration, for example, may consist of a fixed salary plus a bonus based on sales.

It is possible to analyse overheads further by expressing the individual items as percentages of sales but this is usually of very limited value because of the absence of any direct link between the individual overheads and sales.

20.4 Financial ratios

Current ratio

Current assets are the fund out of which a business should pay its current liabilities; it should never have to sell fixed assets to pay its accounts payable. It follows that there should be a margin of safety between the current assets and the current liabilities. The current ratio expresses the margin in the form of a true ratio:

current assets : current liabilities

Lladnar Ltd's current ratios are

2003	2004
269 : 141 = 1.91 : 1	329 : 234 = 1.41 : 1

The right-hand figure in the ratio should always be expressed as unity (i.e. 1); divide the current liabilities into the current assets.

Comment The ratios show that, although the current assets comfortably exceed the current liabilities, the safety margin has been reduced by 0.5 in 2004. Textbooks often state that the current ratio should be between 1.5 : 1 and 2 : 1 to take account of slow-moving stocks and slow-paying debtors, but much depends upon the kind of business. While a low ratio could signal danger, a high ratio may indicate that a business has resources that are not being used efficiently. High levels of stock, accounts receivable and cash mean that capital is lying idle in the business instead of being used profitably.

The current ratio is sometimes described as an indication of liquidity but that is incorrect. The liquidity of a business depends upon the liquidity of its current assets. A **liquid asset** is one that is in the form of cash (cash and bank balances) or in a form that may become cash in the short term (accounts receivable). Stock is not a liquid asset – no buyer has yet been found for it! The current ratio calculation includes stock, so is not a measure of liquidity. Liquidity is measured by the **liquidity ratio** (or acid test or quick ratio).

Liquidity ratio (acid test or quick ratio)

The liquidity ratio excludes stock from the calculation and shows the proportion of liquid assets (accounts receivable and cash) that is available to pay the current liabilities. The ratio is calculated as

current assets – stock : current liabilities

The liquidity ratios of Lladnar Ltd are

2003	2004
(269 – 54) : 141 = 215 : 141 = 1.52 : 1	(329 – 100) : 234 = 229 : 234 = 0.98 : 1

Comment The liquidity ratio has fallen by 0.54 in 2004 and the cash plus accounts receivable are now less than the current liabilities. Textbooks often state that the liquidity ratio should not fall below 1 : 1, or perhaps 0.9 : 1. This is generally a good guide, but supermarkets' sales are on a cash basis while they enjoy a period of credit before they have to pay for their supplies. In the meantime, they have a constant inflow of cash from sales. Their liquidity ratio may not exceed 0.4 : 1. Without knowing more about Lladnar Ltd's business, further comment may not be helpful. However, it would not appear to be a supermarket.

Accounts receivable, stock and accounts payable may be examined in a little more detail.

Accounts receivable ratio (accounts receivable days)

A business should have set a limit on the amount of time it allows its debtors to pay. Many accounts receivable take longer than the time allowed and the accounts receivable ratio calculates the average time accounts receivable are taking to pay. The formula is

$$\frac{\text{accounts receivable} \times 365}{\text{credit sales}}$$

The accounts receivable days for Lladnar Ltd are

2003	2004
$\frac{115 \times 365}{1200}$ = 34.98 or 35 days	$\frac{200 \times 365}{1600}$ = 45.63 or 46 days

As there is no information about any of Lladnar Ltd's sales being on a cash basis, it has been assumed that all sales were on credit. It is sensible to round all fractions of days up to the next day.

Comment The debtors are taking 11 more days in 2004 to pay their bills. It is usual in many businesses to allow accounts receivable 30 days, or 1 month, to pay. The company seems to be losing control over its accounts receivable payments and to have a deteriorating cash flow. Accounts receivable payments may be affected by a deterioration in the national economy or in the business sector. A business may try to attract new customers by offering more favourable payment terms. When accounts receivable are slow to pay there is an increased risk of incurring bad debts.

$$\text{Accounts receivable turnover} = \frac{\text{Net credit sales}}{\text{Average net receivables}}$$

Stockturn

Stockturn is the rate at which the stock is turned over, or the time that elapses before stock is sold. This ratio is important for the following reasons.

- The more quickly stock is sold, the sooner the profit on it is realized and the more times the profit is earned in the financial year.
- A slow stock turnover may indicate that excessive stocks are held and the risk of obsolete or spoiled stocks increases. Large quantities of slow-moving stocks mean that capital is locked up in the business and is not earning revenue.

However, different trades have their own expected rates of stock turnover. Food shops will expect to have a fast stock turnover if their food is not to deteriorate before it is sold. On the other hand, shops selling furniture, refrigerators, radios and television sets, etc. will have slower stock turnovers, while manufacturers of large items of plant and shipbuilders will have very long stockturns. Generally, fast-moving stocks have lower profit margins than slow-moving stocks. (Compare the profit margin to be expected on the sale of food with that expected on the sale of motor cars.)

The formula for calculating stockturn is

$$\frac{\text{cost of sales}}{\text{average stock}} \quad \text{where average stock} = (\text{opening stock} + \text{closing stock}) \div 2$$

It is important to take average stock because closing stock may not be representative of the normal stock level. If opening stock is not given, use closing stock for the calculation.

It is usual to express stockturn as the number of times a year the stock is turned over, but it is also acceptable to express it as the average number of days stock remains in the business before it is sold.

The stockturns for Lladnar Ltd are

<table>
<tr><td>2003</td><td>2004</td></tr>
<tr><td>$\dfrac{788}{(42+54) \div 2} = 16.4$ times a year</td><td>$\dfrac{1120}{(54+100) \div 2} = 14.55$ times a year</td></tr>
<tr><td>or $\dfrac{365}{16.4} = 23$ days</td><td>$\dfrac{365}{14.55} = 26$ days</td></tr>
</table>

Comment The rate of stockturn has slowed a little in 2004. Without more knowledge about the company's business further comment would only be speculation.

The cash at bank

It is not necessary to make up a formula for a cash ratio; it is sufficient to refer to the balances and, in the case of Lladnar Ltd, to draw attention to the fact that the bank balance has fallen from \$98 000 to \$29 000. When a balance at bank is converted into an overdraft, it may be appropriate to recognize the fact with a suitable comment.

Accounts payable ratio (accounts payable days)

Accounts payable days are calculated using the formula

$$\frac{\text{accounts payable} \times 365}{\text{purchases on credit}}$$

Assuming that all Lladnar Ltd's purchases were made on credit, the accounts payable days are

<table>
<tr><td>2003</td><td>2004</td></tr>
<tr><td>$\dfrac{101 \times 365}{800} = 47$ days</td><td>$\dfrac{190 \times 365}{1166} = 60$ days</td></tr>
</table>

Comment The company is taking 13 days longer to pay its accounts payable and this is beneficial to its cash flow. However, it may be dangerous if it is greatly exceeding the period of credit allowed by suppliers as they may withdraw their credit facilities and require Lladnar Ltd to pay cash with orders in future.

Overtrading

Overtrading may occur when a business increases its turnover rapidly with the result that its stocks, accounts receivable and accounts payable also increase, but to a level that threatens its liquidity. The business may become insolvent and unable to pay its accounts payable as they fall due. The result may be that the business is forced to close.

Lladnar Ltd has increased turnover by $33\frac{1}{3}\%$ in 2004. Stock has increased by \$56 000 (over 100%). Accounts receivable days have increased from 35 to 46 days (31%) suggesting poor credit control by the company. Stockturn has increased, but only slightly. Lladnar Ltd may be overtrading.

The cash operating cycle

The cash operating cycle measures the time it takes for cash to circulate around the working capital system. It calculates the interval that occurs between the time a business has to pay its accounts payable and the time it receives cash from its customers. It is calculated using the following formula:

stockturn in days + accounts receivable days − accounts payable days

The cash operating cycle for Lladnar Ltd is found as follows:

	2003 days	2004 days
Stockturn	23	26
Accounts receivable days	35	46
	58	72
Accounts payable days	47	60
Cash operating cycle	11	12

In both years the company received its money from sales, on average, 11/12 days after it had paid its suppliers. During this time, the company was financing its customers out of its own money!

20.5 Investment (stock exchange) ratios

Investment ratios are of particular interest to people who have invested, or are intending to invest, in a company. These people include shareholders and lenders such as debenture holders and banks.

Gearing

Gearing is fixed-cost capital expressed as a percentage of total capital. Fixed-cost capital is the money that finances a company in return for a fixed return and includes debentures and preference share capital. Total capital includes the equity interests (ordinary share capital and reserves) plus the fixed-cost capital.

The formula is

$$\frac{\text{debentures} + \text{preference share capital}}{\text{ordinary share capital and reserves} + \text{debentures} + \text{preference shares}} \times 100$$

Lladnar Ltd's gearing is

2003
$$\frac{\$100\,000 + \$80\,000}{\$618\,000 + \$100\,000 + \$80\,000} \times 100 = 22.56\%$$

2004
$$\frac{\$150\,000 + 100\,000}{\$745\,000 + £150\,000 + \$100\,000} \times 100 = 25.13\%$$

A company is described as highly geared if the gearing is more than 50%. If it is less than 50%, it is low geared. 50% is neutral gearing. Lladnar Ltd is low geared.

Comment The key word in understanding the importance of gearing is risk. Lenders of money to a company may be concerned if it is highly geared; this may indicate that a large slice of profit is applied in the payment of interest. Risk arises if profits fall and fail to cover the interest payments. Banks approached by a highly geared company will question why, when the company is already heavily dependent upon loans, the shareholders are unwilling to invest more of their own money in their company. Perhaps they lack confidence in the company's future.

The risk to ordinary shareholders is increased in a highly geared company as the following example shows.

	Low geared company	Highly geared company
Gearing	20%	80%
	$	$
Ordinary share capital	800 000	200 000
10% debentures	200 000	800 000
	1 000 000	1 000 000
Year 1		
Profit before interest	100 000	100 000
Debenture interest	20 000	80 000
Profit left for ordinary shareholders	80 000	20 000

Profit as a percentage of ordinary share capital:

$\frac{80\,000}{800\,000}$	10%	$\frac{20\,000}{200\,000}$	10%

Year 2		
Profit before interest	150 000	150 000
Debenture interest	20 000	80 000
Profit left for ordinary shareholders	130 000	70 000

Profit as a percentage of ordinary share capital

$\frac{130\,000}{800\,000}$	16.25%	$\frac{70\,000}{200\,000}$	35%

Year 3		
Profit before interest	50 000	50 000
Debenture interest	20 000	80 000
Profit left for ordinary shareholders	30 000	(30 000)

Profit as a percentage of ordinary share capital

$\frac{30\,000}{800\,000}$	3.75%	$\frac{(30\,000)}{200\,000}$	−15%

The above example shows that if profit varies by ±$50 000 (50%) in the low geared company, the profit left for the ordinary shareholders varies by ±6.25%. In the highly geared company, the variation is ±25%. The swings in the fortunes of ordinary shareholders are greater (more risky) in a highly geared company than in a low geared company.

Debt/equity ratio

The formula for the debt/equity ratio is

$$\frac{\text{debentures} + \text{preference share capital}}{\text{ordinary share capital} + \text{reserves}}$$

Lladnar Ltd's debt/equity ratio is

2003

$$\frac{\$100\,000 + \$80\,000}{\$618\,000} \times 100 = 29.13\%$$

2004

$$\frac{\$150\,000 + \$100\,000}{\$745\,000} \times 100 = 33.56\%$$

Comment This ratio is often taught as an alternative method of calculating the gearing ratio, but it is arguable whether expressing fixed-cost capital as a percentage of equity is as useful as expressing it as a percentage of total capital employed. In contrast to the debt/equity ratio, the gearing ratio is consistent with the formula for return on capital employed.

If the debt/equity ratio is less than 100%, the company is low geared; if it exceeds 100% the company is highly geared; 100% is neutral gearing.

Interest cover

Debenture holders and other lenders to a company need to be sure that the profit before interest adequately covers the interest payments. Interest must be paid even if a company makes a loss, but it is reassuring if the profit before interest covers the interest payments several times; a good cover provides a safety margin against a fall in profits in the future. Shareholders are also concerned to see a good interest cover as their dividends can only be paid if profit is left after charging the interest in the Profit and Loss Account.

The formula for calculating interest cover is

$$\frac{\text{profit before interest}}{\text{interest payable}}$$

The interest cover for Llandar Ltd is

2003	2004
$\frac{182^*}{10} = 18.2$ times	$\frac{216^*}{15} = 14.4$ times
* 172 + 10	* 201 + 15

Comment Lladnar Ltd's interest cover has decreased by 3.8 times in 2004, but is still very satisfactory.

Earnings per share

Earnings are the profit left for the ordinary shareholders after interest, tax and preference dividends have been provided for in the Profit and Loss Account. Ordinary dividends are paid out of earnings, and any earnings not distributed increase the reserves and the Balance Sheet value of the shares. Earnings per share are expressed in cents ($0.00) per share, and are calculated using the formula

$$\frac{\text{earnings}}{\text{the number of ordinary shares issued}}$$

Lladnar Ltd's earnings per share are

2003	2004
$\frac{\$16\,400\,000^*}{400\,000} = \$0.41$ per share	$\frac{\$19\,100\,000^*}{400\,000} = \$0.4775$ per share

* Net profit less the preference dividend × 100

Comment Earnings per share have increased by $0.0675 in 2004 and have allowed an increased dividend to be paid and a small increase in the retained profit for the year (added to the reserves).

Price earnings ratio (PER)

The price earnings ratio calculates the number of times the price being paid for the shares on the market exceeds the earnings per share; it is calculated using the formula

$$\frac{\text{market price per share}}{\text{earnings per share}}$$

The market price of Lladnar Ltd's ordinary shares at 31 December 2003 was $1.80, and at 31 December 2004 it was $2.10. The price earnings ratios are

2003	2004
$\frac{\$1.80}{\$0.41} = 4.39$	$\frac{\$2.10}{\$0.4775} = 4.40$

Comment The price earnings ratio has remained steady over both years. Shareholders have been prepared to pay 4.4 times the earnings per share. This is a measure of confidence in the ability of Lladnar Ltd to maintain its earnings in future. A PER of 4.4 is not particularly good for a long-term investment in a company. PER is an important ratio for investors as it gives a quick and easily understandable indicator of the market's assessment of a company's prospects.

Dividend cover

The formula for dividend cover is

$$\frac{\text{profit after tax and preference dividend}}{\text{dividend on ordinary shares}}$$

Dividend cover is the number of times the profit out of which dividends may be paid covers the dividend. If the cover is too low, a decline in profits may lead to the dividend being restricted or not paid at all. On the other hand, if the cover is high, shareholders may decide that the directors are adopting a mean dividend policy.

Dividend cover for Lladnar Ltd is

2003	2004
$\dfrac{\$164\ 000}{\$60\ 000} = 2.73$ times	$\dfrac{\$191\ 000}{\$64\ 000} = 2.98$ times

Comment A dividend cover of 2 to 3 times may be considered normal and safe.

Dividend yield

Companies usually declare dividends as a certain number of cents per share, representing a certain percentage return based on the nominal value of the share. For example, a dividend of $0.03 per share of $0.50 is a dividend of 6% on the share. Shareholders who have paid the market price for their shares need to know the return based on the price they have paid. This is the dividend yield and is calculated using the following formula:

$$\text{dividend yield} = \text{declared rate of dividend} \times \frac{\text{nominal value of share}}{\text{market price of share}}$$

Lladnar Ltd's declared rates of dividend are

2003	2004
$\dfrac{\$60\ 000}{\$400\ 000} \times 100 = 15\%$	$\dfrac{\$64\ 000}{\$400\ 000} \times 100 = 16\%$

The dividend yields are

2003	2004
$15\% \times \dfrac{\$1}{\$1.80} = 8.33\%$	$16\% \times \dfrac{\$1}{\$2.10} = 7.62\%$

Comment The small decrease in the dividend yield in 2004 is the result of the share price increasing fractionally more than the increase in the dividend. There may be a connection between the increase in the market price and the small increases in the earnings per share and the dividend cover.

Earnings yield

The earnings yield is calculated in a similar manner to the dividend yield. Lladnar Ltd's earnings as a percentage of ordinary share capital are

2003	2004
$\dfrac{\$164\ 000}{\$400\ 000} \times 100 = 41$	$\dfrac{\$191\ 000}{\$400\ 000} \times 100 = 47.75\%$

The earnings yield is calculated using the formula

$$\text{earnings yield} = \text{earnings }\% \times \frac{\text{nominal value of share}}{\text{market price of share}}$$

For Lladnar Ltd, the earnings yields are

2003	2004
$41\% \times \dfrac{\$1}{\$1.80} = 22.78\%$	$47.75\% \times \dfrac{\$1}{\$2.10} = 22.74\%$

Comment The change in the earnings yield in 2004 is not significant.

20.6 Trend analysis and inter-firm comparison

Individual ratios are usually of very limited value. The ratios of a business for past years are necessary if trends in progress or deterioration of performance are to be seen. The examples of Lladnar Ltd have given the results for 2003 and 2004 and some limited trends have been observed. Given the results for, say, four, five or six years, more reliable trends may be discerned.

Trends may signal to investors whether they should stay with their investment, or sell it and re-invest in a more promising venture.

Inter-firm comparison (IFC) is possible when information about the performance of other similar businesses is available. Trade associations collect information from their members and publish the statistics as averages for the trade or industry. It is thus possible to compare the results of one company with the averages for businesses of the same type. Comparisons, however, must be made with care. It is not realistic to compare the statistics of a small trader with results achieved by large companies. Comparison should always be on a like-for-like basis as far as possible.

Inter-firm comparison can inform shareholders whether they have invested their money in the most profitable and stable institutions.

20.7 The limitations of ratios

- To be useful and reliable, ratios must be reasonably accurate. They should be based on information in accounts and notes to the accounts. Some useful information may not be disclosed in the accounts and some account headings may not indicate the contents clearly.

- Information must be timely to be of use. It may not be available until some long time after the end of a company's financial year.
- Ratios do not explain results but may indicate areas of concern; further investigation is usually necessary to discover causes of the concern.
- Ratios usually do not recognize seasonal factors in business:
  - profit margins will be lower than normal during periods of seasonal sales;
  - stock and debtors are unlikely to remain at constant levels throughout the year;
  - Companies, even in the same trade, will have different policies for such matters as providing for depreciation, doubtful debts, profit recognition, transferring profits to reserves, dividend policy, etc.

Such limitations should be borne in mind when making comparisons between businesses.

20.8 How to prepare a Profit and Loss Account and Balance Sheet from given ratios

A Profit and Loss Account and Balance Sheet may be prepared from a list of accounting ratios provided at least one item is given as a numerical term. The method begins with the given numerical term and progresses by steps from that.

Example

Pulchra's stock at 31 December 2004 was $35 000, which was $5000 less than her stock at 1 January 2004. Further information about her business for the year ended 31 December 2004 is as follows:

Stockturn 7 times

Gross profit/sales 44%

Net profit/sales $17\frac{1}{2}$%

Distribution cost to administration expenses 1 : 3

Debtors' days 32 (70% of sales are on credit)

Creditors' days 65 (all purchases were made on credit)

Fixed asset turnover $2\frac{1}{2}$ times

Current ratio 1.8 : 1

Interest cover 12.2 times

The current assets consist of stock, trade debtors and bank balance only.

Pulchra has received a long-term loan on which she pays interest at 10% per annum.

Pulchra has drawn $1000 from the business each week.

Required

Prepare Pulchra's Trading and Profit and Loss Account for the year ended 31 December 2004 and her Balance Sheet at that date in as much detail as possible. Make all calculations to the nearest $.

Answer

The stock at 31 December 2004 is the starting point. Proceed as follows, in the order given by the numbered steps.

Pulchra
Trading and Profit and Loss Account for the year ended 31 December 2004

		$	$
Step 6	Sales (100/56* × 262 500)		468 750
	Cost of sales		
Step 2	Stock at 1.1.04 (35 000 + 5000)	40 000	
Step 5	Purchases (balancing figure)	257 500	
Step 4	(262 500 + 35 000)	297 500	
Step 1	Stock at 31.12.04 (given)	35 000	
Step 3	(cost of sales $\frac{40\,000 + 35\,000}{2} = \times 7$)		262 500
Step 7	Gross profit (468 750 − 262 500)		206 250
Step 10	Distribution costs (124 219 × $\frac{1}{4}$)		31 055
Step 11	Administration expenses (124 219 × $\frac{3}{4}$)		93 164
Step 9	(balancing figure)		124 219
Step 8	Net profit ($17\frac{1}{2}$% of 468 750)		82 031
Step 12	Interest on long-term loan at 10% (82 031 ÷ 12.2)		6 724
Step 13			75 307

*Gross profit/sales = 44%, therefore cost of sales = 56% of sales.

Balance Sheet at 31 December 2004

		$	$
Step 14	Fixed assets (468 750 ÷ $2\frac{1}{2}$)	187 500	
	Current assets		
Step 15	Stock	35 000	
Step 16	Trade debtors (468 750 × $\frac{7}{10}$ × $\frac{32}{365}$)	28 767	
Step 20	Bank (balancing figure)	18 774	
Step 19	(45 856 × 1.8)	82 541	
Step 17	Trade creditors (257 500 × $\frac{65}{365}$)	45 856	
Step 18	(balancing figure)		36 685
Step 21			224 185
Step 22	Less long-term loan at 10% (6724 × 10)		67 240
Step 23			156 945
Step 28	Capital at 1.1.04 (balancing figure)		133 638
Step 24	Profit for the year		75 307
Step 25			208 945
Step 26	Drawings (1000 × 52)		52 000
Step 27			156 945

Note. The steps show the order in which the items should be tackled but the step numbers do not form part of the answer and should not be shown in answers to questions. It is important in examinations to gain as many marks as possible as quickly as possible. It is a good idea to start with an outline for the Trading and Profit and Loss Account and Balance Sheet (leaving spaces to insert additional items if necessary), and to fill in the items as soon as the figures are known. For example, stock in the Balance Sheet can be inserted immediately it has been entered in the Trading Account. Similarly, net profit can be inserted in the Balance Sheet as soon as it has been calculated in the Profit and Loss Account.

Exercise 1

Patience has mislaid her final accounts for the year ended 31 December 2004 but has found the report, which her accountant has prepared, based on those accounts. She has decided to reconstruct the accounts from the information contained in the report.

The accountant's report contained the following data.

At 31 December 2004

Stock $54 000. (This was 20% more than the stock at 1 January 2004.)

For the year ended 31 December 2004

Stockturn	10 times
Gross profit margin	35%
Net profit margin	22%
Fixed asset turnover	4 times
Debtors' days	34 (based on 365 days in the year)
Creditors' days	42 (based on 365 days in the year)
Current ratio	2.5 : 1

The current assets consist of stock, trade debtors and bank balance.

All sales and purchases were made on credit.

Patience drew $140 000 from the business during the year.

Required

(a) Prepare, in as much detail as possible, Patience's Trading and Profit and Loss Account for the year ended 31 December 2004 and the Balance Sheet at that date. Make all calculations to the nearest $.

Virtue carries on a similar business to that of Patience and has the following data for the year ended 31 December 2004.

Stockturn	12 times
Gross profit margin	40%
Net profit margin	20%
Fixed asset turnover	5 times
Debtors' days	31
Creditors' days	36

Required

(b) Compare Virtue's performance with that of Patience and indicate the ratios that show which business is the more efficient.

You should write your answer in sentence form and include supporting figures.

20.9 Report writing and ratios in examination

- Learn the headings under which ratios are shown and which ratios are included under each heading.
- Remember how each ratio is calculated (the model).
- Take care to calculate ratios on the correct figures and check your arithmetic.
- Express every ratio in the correct terms, for example as a percentage, a number of times or days, a true ratio, etc. Marks will not be awarded in an examination if the correct terms are omitted.
- Make sure you understand what each ratio is intended to explain.
- Your comments on ratios should be based on the information you are given and justified by the ratios you have calculated. Do not assume facts you are not given.
- Avoid making definite statements that cannot be supported by the information given. You may *suggest* reasons for the comments you make.
- Your comments should be concise and relevant; avoid repetition of the same point. Rambling answers that stray from the point do not impress the examiner.

20.10 Multiple-choice questions

1 Information about a business is given in the following table:

	year 1	year 2
	$	$
Turnover	200 000	250 000
Cost of sales	125 000	140 000
	75 000	110 000
Operating expenses	32 000	64 000
Profit before interest and taxation	43 000	46 000
Fixed assets	140 000	120 000
Net current assets	60 000	80 000
Long-term loans	(80 000)	(40 000)

Which of the following is true in year 2?

	Gross profit margin	Return on capital employed
A	decreased	decreased
B	increased	decreased
C	decreased	increased
D	increased	increased

2 Extracts from the Profit and Loss Accounts for two years for a business are given in this table:

	Year 1	Year 2
	$	$
Sales	100 000	200 000
Gross profit	30 000	70 000

What might explain the change in the gross profit margin in year 2?

A an increase in sales

B an increase in the sales price

C a reduction in stock

D suppliers offering higher cash discounts.

3 What is the effect on the current ratio and quick ratio of a business if it uses cash to buy stock?

	Current ratio	Quick ratio
A	decrease	decrease
B	decrease	increase
C	no change	decrease
D	no change	increase

4 The quick ratio (acid test) of a business has fallen. What is the reason for the fall?

A a decrease in creditors

B a decrease in stock

C an increase in cash

D an increase in the bank overdraft.

5 The closing stock of a business was $30 000 and the cost of goods sold was $600 000. Stock turnover is based on the average value of the opening and closing stocks.

If the stock turnover was 15 times, what was the opening stock?

A $10 000

B $40 000

C $50 000

D $80 000.

6 The following information is extracted from the final accounts of a business:

	$
Opening stock	6 000
Purchases (all on credit)	220 000
Closing stock	28 000
Creditors at end of year	21 096

What is the period taken to pay the creditors?

A 31 days **B** 32 days **C** 34 days **D** 35 days.

7 The following is an extract from the Profit and Loss Account of a company.

	$
Operating profit	360 000
Debenture interest	24 000
Profit after interest	336 000
Preference dividend	(16 000)
Ordinary dividend	(200 000)
Retained profit	120 000

The company's share capital is as follows:

Authorized: $1 000 000

Issued: 200 000 8% preference shares of $1

800 000 ordinary shares of $1

What is the company's earnings per share?

A $0.32 **B** $0.40 **C** $0.42 **D** $0.45.

8 A company has an authorized share capital of 750 000 ordinary shares of $1 of which it has issued 500 000 shares. The following is an extract from its Profit and Loss Account.

	$
Operating profit	400 000
Debenture interest	(60 000)
	340 000
Transfer to general reserve	(100 000)
Ordinary dividend	(200 000)
Retained profit	40 000

The current market price of the shares is $3.60. What is the price earnings ratio?

A 5.29 **B** 7.5 **C** 8 **D** 11.25.

20.11 Additional exercises

1 On 1 October 2001 Manny Kyoor and his wife formed a limited company, Kyoor Ltd, to run a beautician's business, and each paid in $37 500 as share capital. The bank loaned the company a further $80 000 at 9% interest per annum.

At 30 September 2002 the business's final accounts were drawn up as follows.

Trading and Profit and Loss Account for the year ended 30 September 2002

Sales and fees		$350 000
Less Cost of sales		
Stock bought on 1 October 2001	$31 500	
Purchases	$280 000	
	$311 500	
Stock at 30 September 2002	$66 500	$245 000
Gross Profit		$105 000
Less Expenses		
Rent and Rates	$3 950	
Advertising	$1 750	
Wages	$29 000	
Heat and Light	$5 250	
Interest due	$7 200	
Depreciation	$12 000	$59 150
Net Profit		$45 850

Balance Sheet as at 30 September 2002

Fixed Assets	Cost	Depreciation	NBV
Premises	$124 000		$124 000
Fixtures and fittings	$48 000	$12 000	$36 000
	$172 000	$12 000	$160 000
Current assets			
Stock	$66 500		
Debtors	$21 500	$88 000	
Amounts to be settled within one year			
Creditors	$21 000		
Interest due	$7 200		
Bank	$18 950	$47 150	$40 850
			$200 850
Amounts to be settled after more than one year			
Long-term loan			$80 000
			$120 850
Share Capital and Reserves			
75 000 ordinary shares of $1			$75 000
Retained profit			$45 850
			$120 850

Industry average ratios and other relevant data concerning businesses similar to Kyoor Ltd were as follows:

(i)	Gross Profit percentage	30.00%
(ii)	Net Profit percentage	18.07%
(iii)	Current ratio	2.21 : 1
(iv)	Liquid (Quick) ratio	1.02 : 1
(v)	Stock Turnover ratio	8 times
(vi)	Fixed Assets to Sales	50.18%
(vii)	Return on Total Assets	25.37%
(viii)	Return on Net Assets	34.93%
(ix)	Debtors' Payment period	25 days
(x)	Creditors' Payment period	30 days

(a) Calculate each of the above ratios, to 2 decimal places, for Kyoor Ltd.

(b) Comment on the business's performance in the light of the data for the industry.

Note. It is not sufficient to say that a ratio is 'higher' or 'lower' than the industry average – it must be made clear whether you think it is *better* or *worse* than the industry average and you must give reasons for your comments.

(UCLES, 2002, AS/A Level Accounting, Syllabus 9706/2 (October/November)

2 The following information summarizes the latest set of final accounts of Worky Tout & Co., a partnership.

At 30 April 2001

Stock $45 000. (This was 50% more than the stock at 30 April 2000.)

For the year ended 30 April 2001

Stockturn 12 times

Gross profit margin 40%

Net profit margin 18%

Fixed asset turnover 3 times

Average time taken by debtors to pay: 36 days (based on a year of 365 days).

Average time taken to pay creditors: 40 days (based on a year of 365 days).

The current ratio is 3 : 1.

The only current assets of the firm consist of stock, debtors and balance at bank.

Partners' drawings for the year $125 000.

All sales and purchases were on a credit basis.

(a) Prepare, in as much detail as possible, the Trading and Profit and Loss Account of Worky Tout & Co. for the year ended 30 April 2001 and a Balance Sheet as at that date. (All calculations should be made to the nearest $000.)

The following information is available for Zenapod, a similar business, for the year ended 30 April 2001.

Stockturn 10 times

Gross profit margin 45%

Net profit margin 20%

Fixed asset turnover $3\frac{1}{2}$ times

Time taken by debtors to pay   30 days (based on a year of 365 days)

Time taken to pay creditors   28 days (based on a year of 365 days)

(b) Compare the performance of Worky Tout & Co. with that of Zenapod. Indicate the ratios which show that one business is more efficient than the other. Your answer should be in sentence form with supporting figures.

(UCLES, 2001, AS/A Level Accounting, Syllabus 8427/2, May/June)

3 An extract from Oitar plc's Profit and Loss Account for the year ended 30 April 2002 was as follows:

	$000	$000
Operating profit		1000
Debenture interest ($12\frac{1}{2}$%)		250
		750
Ordinary dividend paid and proposed	350	
Preference dividend paid and proposed	120	
Transfer to General Reserve	200	670
Retained profit for the year		80

Oitar plc's issued share capital and reserves at 30 April 2002 consisted of:

	$000
Ordinary shares of $10	4000
8% preference shares of $5	1500
Capital and revenue reserves	900

The market price of the ordinary shares at 30 April 2002 was $30.

Required

(a) Calculate the following ratios for Oitar plc:
   (i) interest cover
   (ii) dividend cover
   (iii) earnings per share
   (iv) price earnings ratio
   (v) dividend yield
   (vi) gearing.

(b) Explain why each of the ratios in (a) is important for investors in ordinary shares in the company.

Oitar plc's accounting ratios at 30 April 2001 were as follows:

interest cover	5.5 times
dividend cover	2.5 times
price earnings ratio	22
gearing (calculated as a percentage of long term debentures and preference share capital to total long-term capital)	36%

Required

(c) Compare the ratios for 2001 with the same ratios in 2002 as calculated in (a), and comment on the changes that you find.

(d) State, with reasons, any further information you might require and what other documents you might wish to see to enable you to assess the likely future performance of Oitar plc.

(UCLES, 2002, AS/A Level Accounting, Syllabus 9706/4, May/June)

20.12 Exercises

Exercise 1 (Based on the accounts of a sole trader)

Najim wants to analyse the results of his trading for the year ended 31 December 2005 and has prepared his Trading and Profit and Loss Account and Balance Sheet. He compares these with the final accounts for the previous year. The Trading and Profit and Loss Accounts and Balance Sheets for the two years are as follows.

Trading and Profit and Loss Accounts

	for the year ended 31.12.04		for the year ended 31.12.05	
	$	$	$	$
Sales		172 308		187 500
Less cost of sales				
Opening stock	12 000		16 000	
Purchases	116 000		125 500	
	128 000		141 500	
Closing stock	16 000	112 000	14 000	127 500
Gross profit		60 308		60 000
Less expenses		38 769		32 678
Net profit		21 539		27 322

Balance Sheets at

	31.12.04		31.12.05	
	$	$	$	$
Fixed assets (net book values)		78 322		93 750
Current assets				
Stock	16 000		14 000	
Trade debtors	9 914		12 511	
Bank	4 851		7 185	
	30 765		33 696	
Current liabilities				
Trade creditors	13 984	16 781	17 192	16 504
		95 103		110 254
Opening capital		81 176		95 103
Add profit		21 539		27 322
		102 715		122 425
Deduct drawings		7 612		12 171
		95 103		110 254

Further information

1. 60% of Najim's sales are on credit.

2. Najim purchases all his stock of goods on credit.

3. The only current assets are stock, trade debtors and a bank balance.

Required

(a) Calculate the following ratios to *two* decimal places for each of the years ended 31 December 2004 and 2005.
   (i)   gross profit percentage
   (ii) net profit percentage
   (iii) fixed asset turnover
   (iv) stockturn
   (v)   debtors' days
   (vi) creditors' days
   (vii) current ratio
   (viii) liquid (acid test) ratio.

(b) Compare the performance of Najim's business in 2005 with its performance in 2004, using the ratios calculated in (a), and comment on the comparison.

Exercise 2 (Based on the accounts of limited companies)

A financial consultant has been asked by his client for advice on the relative performance of two companies, Dunedin Ltd and Wellington Ltd. Extracts from the Profit and Loss Accounts for the year ended 31 December 2004 and the Balance Sheets at that date of the two companies are as follows:

Profit and Loss Accounts for the year ended 31 December 2004

	Dunedin Ltd	Wellington Ltd
	$000	$000
Operating profit	300	420
Debenture interest	(60)	(120)
	240	300
Transfer to General Reserve	(100)	(50)
Preference dividend	(6)	(60)
Ordinary dividend	(90)	(150)
Retained profit	44	40

Balance Sheet extracts at 31 December 2004

	Dunedin Ltd		Wellington Ltd
	$000		$000
Long-term liabilities		Long-term liabilities	
10% debentures 2007/8	600	12% debentures 2006/7	1 000
Ordinary shares of $1	200	Ordinary shares of $2	1 500
6% preference shares of $1	100	8% preference shares of $1	750
General reserve	120	General reserve	200
Retained profit	80	Retained profit	350
	500		2 800

The market values of the ordinary shares at 31 December 2004 were as follows:

Dunedin Ltd $2.70   Wellington Ltd $3.60

Required

(a) Calculate the following ratios to *two* decimal places for each company:
  (i)   gearing
  (ii)   interest cover
  (iii)   earnings per share (EPS)
  (iv)   dividend per share
  (v)   dividend cover
  (vi)   price earnings ratio (PER)
  (vii)   dividend yield.
(b) Compare and comment on the performance of the two companies in 2004 using the ratios calculated in (a).

A Profit and Loss Account and Balance Sheet may be prepared from a list of accounting ratios provided at least one item is given as a numerical term. The method begins with the given numerical term and progresses by steps from that.

Example

Pulchra's stock at 31 December 2004 was $35 000, which was $5000 less than her stock at 1 January 2004.

Further information about her business for the year ended 31 December 2004 is as follows:

Stockturn 7 times

Gross profit/sales 44%

Net profit/sales $17\frac{1}{2}$%

Distribution cost to administration expenses 1 : 3

Debtors' days 32 (70% of sales are on credit)

Creditors' days 65 (all purchases were made on credit)

Fixed asset turnover $2\frac{1}{2}$ times

Current ratio 1.8 : 1

Interest cover 12.2 times

The current assets consist of stock, trade debtors and bank balance only.

Pulchra has received a long-term loan on which she pays interest at 10% per annum.

Pulchra has drawn $1000 from the business each week.

Required

Prepare Pulchra's Trading and Profit and Loss Account for the year ended 31 December 2004 and her Balance Sheet at that date in as much detail as possible. Make all calculations to the nearest $.

Answer

The stock at 31 December 2004 is the starting point. Proceed as follows, in the order given by the numbered steps:

Pulchra
Trading and Profit and Loss Account for the year ended 31 December 2004

		$	$
Step 6	Sales (100/56* × 262 500)		468 750
	Cost of sales		
Step 2	Stock at 1.1.04 (35 000 + 5000)	40 000	
Step 5	Purchases (balancing figure)	257 500	
Step 4	(262 500 + 35 000)	297 500	
Step 1	Stock at 31.12.04 (given)	35 000	
Step 3	(cost of sales $\frac{40\,000 + 35\,000}{2} = \times 7$)		262 500
Step 7	Gross profit (468 750 − 262 500)		206 250
Step 10	Distribution costs (124 219 × $\frac{1}{4}$)		31 055
Step 11	Administration expenses (124 219 × $\frac{3}{4}$)		93 164
Step 9	(balancing figure)		124 219
Step 8	Net profit ($17\frac{1}{2}$% of 468 750)		82 031
Step 12	Interest on long-term loan at 10% (82 031 ÷ 12.2)		6 724
Step 13			75 307

*Gross profit/sales = 44%, therefore cost of sales = 56% of sales.

Balance Sheet at 31 December 2004

		$	$
Step 14	Fixed assets (468 750 ÷ $2\frac{1}{2}$)	187 500	
	Current assets		
Step 15	Stock	35 000	
Step 16	Trade debtors (468 750 × $\frac{7}{10}$ × $\frac{32}{365}$)	28 767	
Step 20	Bank (balancing figure)	18 774	
Step 19	(45 856 × 1.8)	82 541	
Step 17	Trade creditors (257 500 × $\frac{65}{365}$)	45 856	
Step 18	(balancing figure)		36 685
Step 21			224 185
Step 22	Less long-term loan at 10% (6724 × 10)		67 240
Step 23			156 945
Step 28	Capital at 1.1.04 (balancing figure)		133 638
Step 24	Profit for the year		75 307
Step 25			208 945
Step 26	Drawings (1000 × 52)		52 000
Step 27			156 945

Note. The steps show the order in which the items should be tackled but the step numbers do not form part of the answer and should not be shown in answers to questions. It is important in examinations to gain as many marks as possible as quickly as possible. It is a good idea to start with an outline for the Trading and Profit and Loss Account and Balance Sheet (leaving spaces to insert additional items if necessary), and to fill in the items as soon as the figures are known. For example, stock in the Balance Sheet can be inserted immediately it has been entered in the Trading Account. Similarly, net profit can be inserted in the Balance Sheet as soon as it has been calculated in the Profit and Loss Account.

Exercise 3

Patience has mislaid her final accounts for the year ended 31 December 2004 but has found the report, which her accountant has prepared, based on those accounts. She has decided to reconstruct the accounts from the information contained in the report.

The accountant's report contained the following data.

At 31 December 2004

Stock $54 000. (This was 20% more than the stock at 1 January 2004.)

For the year ended 31 December 2004

Stockturn	10 times
Gross profit margin	35%
Net profit margin	22%
Fixed asset turnover	4 times
Debtors' days	34 (based on 365 days in the year)
Creditors' days	42 (based on 365 days in the year)
Current ratio	2.5 : 1

The current assets consist of stock, trade debtors and bank balance.

All sales and purchases were made on credit.

Patience drew $140 000 from the business during the year.

Required

(a) Prepare, in as much detail as possible, Patience's Trading and Profit and Loss Account for the year ended 31 December 2004 and the Balance Sheet at that date. Make all calculations to the nearest $.

Virtue carries on a similar business to that of Patience and has the following data for the year ended 31 December 2004:

Stockturn	12 times
Gross profit margin	40%
Net profit margin	20%
Fixed asset turnover	5 times
Debtors' days	31
Creditors' days	36

Required

(b) Compare Virtue's performance with that of Patience and indicate the ratios that show which business is the more efficient.

You should write your answer in sentence form and include supporting figures.

21 Impact of inflation on financial statements

Objectives
• explain historical cost accounting
• explain current cost accounting
• state advantages and disadvantages of current cost accounting
• state advantages and disadvantages of constant dollar accounting
• explain the impact of inflation on financial statements

21.1 Historical cost

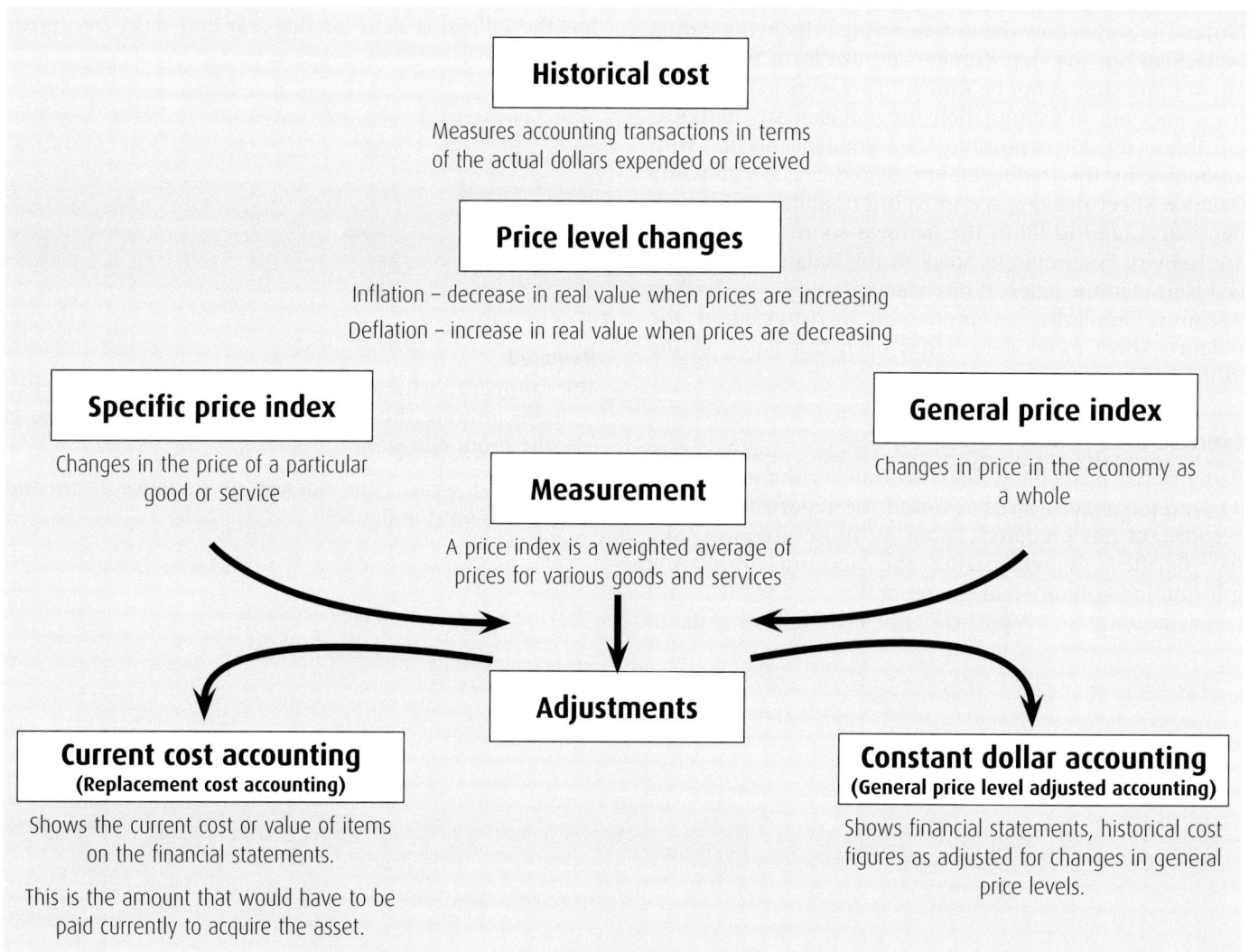

Historical cost

Measures accounting transactions in terms
of the actual dollars expended or received

Price level changes

Inflation – decrease in real value when prices are increasing
Deflation – increase in real value when prices are decreasing

Specific price index

Changes in the price of a particular
good or service

General price index

Changes in price in the economy as
a whole

Measurement

A price index is a weighted average of
prices for various goods and services

Adjustments

Current cost accounting
(Replacement cost accounting)

Shows the current cost or value of items
on the financial statements.

This is the amount that would have to be
paid currently to acquire the asset.

Constant dollar accounting
(General price level adjusted accounting)

Shows financial statements, historical cost
figures as adjusted for changes in general
price levels.

21.2 Consequences of ignoring inflation

1. Misleading information. Fixed assets bought by different companies and sold at later dates can give the wrong impression about management efficiency. Historical cost may make the gain on disposal very high for one company while the other may have experienced higher cost because of inflation resulting in lower profits.

2. Taxes. Income statements may show positive net income values even when the owners' investments have not been maintained because they were recorded at historical costs. When profits are overstated it means that taxes are paid on income when costs have not been covered.

3. Difficult to compare. Comparison across companies is difficult because transactions at different dates exhibit different cost because of inflation. Different amounts of purchasing power expended makes the comparison suspect.

4. Invalid conclusions. Rising prices can give the impression that sales have increased. Whereas the dollar amount of sales may show an increase the volume may have eventually decreased.

5. Individual decision-makers. When financial reports are not adjusted for inflation decisions are taken that may not be in the best interest of a company.

6. Overstated net income. When no adjustment is made for inflation companies with fixed assets recorded at historical cost write-off less depreciation resulting in higher net income.

21.3 Characteristics of historical costs

1. Do not show the impact of changing prices.
2. No provision is made for replacement of materials and assets.
3. Under-costing takes place because current costs are higher.
4. Overstatement of profits because of lower costs.
5. Extra funds needed for working capital.
6. Real capital is not maintained.
7. Working capital increases.

21.4 Advantages and disadvantages of historical cost

Advantages	Disadvantages
1. It's objective and reliable.	1. Overstated profits when prices are rising.
2. Cheap.	2. Subjective – asset life span estimated.
3. Understandable profit concept.	3. Assets undervalued on the balance sheet.
4. Fosters comparability by companies and over periods.	4. Monetary assets/liabilities.
5. Tested and proven.	5. No distinction made between holding gains and operating gains.
	6. It does not reveal the impact of inflation.

21.5 Advantages and disadvantages of current cost accounting

Advantages	Disadvantages
1. Better match of effort and accomplishments because it matches current revenue with current expenses.	1. May be subjective because costs are based on indices or manufacturers' price lists.
2. Capital is maintained if dividend does not exceed current cost income.	2. Difficult and costly to determine if technology changes.
3. Specific current costs incurred by a company are shown.	3. It adjusts the basis of valuing assets and not the measuring unit. It is not a system of inflation accounting.
4. Maintain the same unit of measurement for there is no conversion.	4. It considers only the replacement of assets and not diversification.
5. Realistic asset values are used because current costs and not historical costs are used.	

21.6 Constant dollar accounting

Advantages	Disadvantages
1. It is subjective because the conversion is based on historical costs.	1. The costs of preparing the statements may exceed the benefits.
2. The comparison of financial statements between companies is easy because the procedure and index numbers are the same.	2. It assumes that inflation affects all companies equally.
3. Intra-company comparison of financial statement is easier because the same purchasing power is used.	3. Specific price changes are ignored for only the change in value of the measuring unit is considered.
4. It is cheap to administer because very few additional records need to be kept.	4. There is a degree of subjectivity because of the estimates in historical costs.
5. It is concerned with shareholders' capital.	5. It gives an unrealistic asset value since general prices are adjusted.
6. It deals with inflation by adjusting the measuring unit.	6. It queries whether gains/losses on assets should be considered as profit.
	7. It works with a changing unit of measure.

21.7 Effect on statement

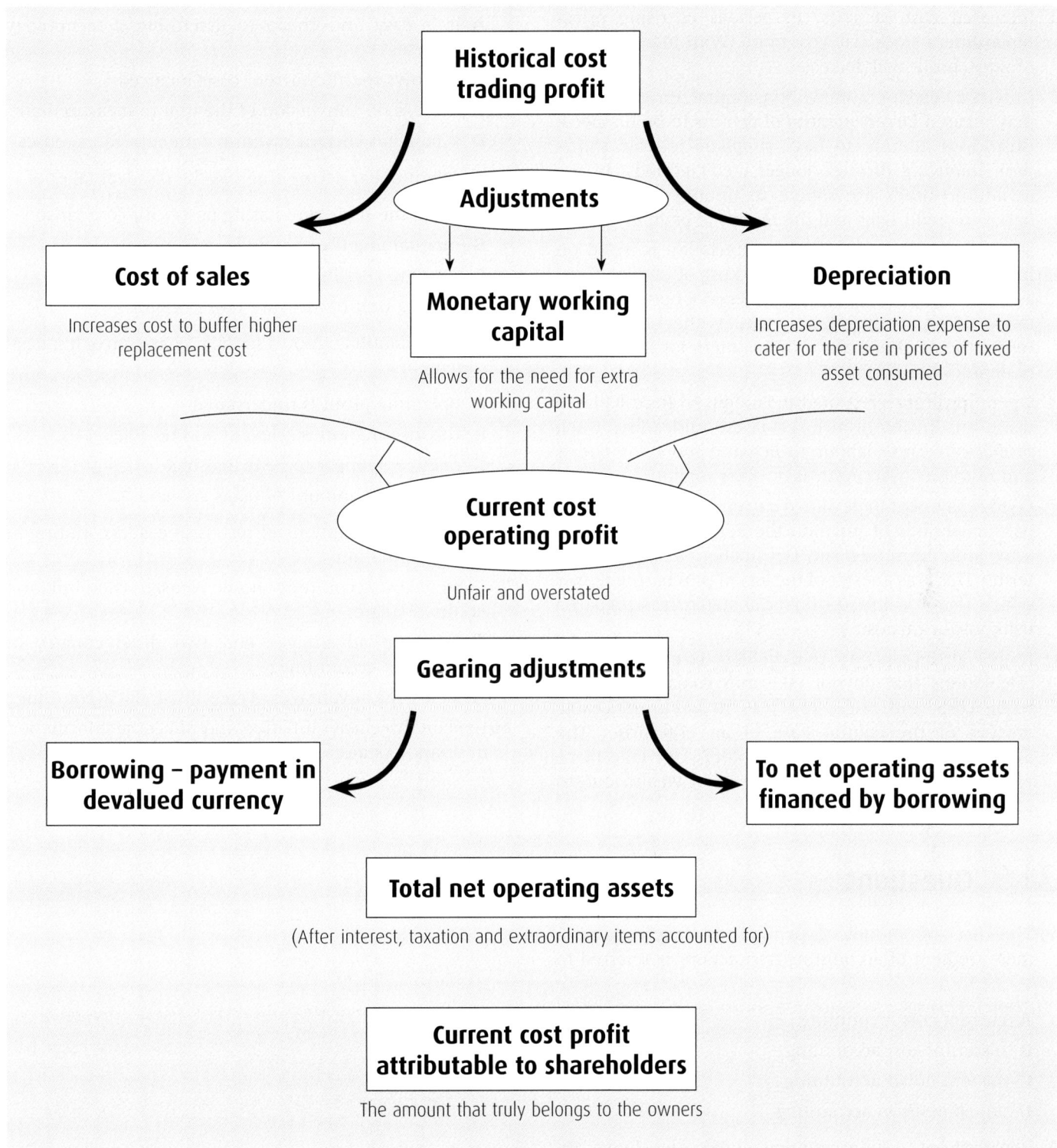

Historical cost trading profit

Adjustments

Cost of sales

Increases cost to buffer higher replacement cost

Monetary working capital

Allows for the need for extra working capital

Depreciation

Increases depreciation expense to cater for the rise in prices of fixed asset consumed

Current cost operating profit

Unfair and overstated

Gearing adjustments

Borrowing – payment in devalued currency

To net operating assets financed by borrowing

Total net operating assets

(After interest, taxation and extraordinary items accounted for)

Current cost profit attributable to shareholders

The amount that truly belongs to the owners

21.8 Impact on financial statements

1. Increased cost of sales. In periods of rising prices replacement stock will cost more. With increased cost of sales, profit will decrease.

2. Creates a need for more working capital. Price increases may mean a larger quantity of debtors to be financed. Businesses attempt to have suppliers provide short-term financing through longer credit periods. In the meantime funds are sought to finance the interval between credit sales and the receipt of payment.

3. Depreciation is understated. Depreciation is based on historical cost. The replacement cost of similar fixed assets will dictate that a higher depreciation charge be made. Under-costing takes place with rising prices. Hence the need to make an adjustment for the backlog of depreciation.

4. Operating profit overstated and unfair. Profits calculated using unadjusted historical data are misleading. Such profits can cause labour to demand more for efforts and investors more returns on their capital.

5. Loan repayment in devalued currency. When loans are paid in periods of inflation the debtor pays back the same amount numerically but smaller amounts in real terms. This is as a result of the loss of purchasing power which is not visible on financial statements prepared using historical cost.

6. Profits attributable to shareholders is eroded. Profit calculations that do not take into consideration the rising costs and prices can lead to an unnoticeable erosion of the central base of an enterprise. The distribution of profits to shareholders can take place when in fact there was no creation of wealth due to inflation.

21.9 Questions

1 The use of money expended or received as a measurement of accounting transactions is referred to as

A current cost accounting

B historical cost accounting

C current dollar accounting

D adjustments in accounting.

2 Replacement cost accounting shows the items on financial statements at

A a mark-up price

B historical cost

C the cost they were acquired

D the cost to acquire them.

3 Which of the following is NOT true about current cost accounting?

A it is easy and cheap to determine if technology changes

B it shows specific current costs incurred

C there is no conversion of the unit of measurement

D it matches current revenue with current expenses.

4 Constant dollar accounting has the disadvantages of

A using the same purchasing power for comparison

B maintaining the shareholders' capital

C needing very little additional records

D using a unit of measure that changes.

5 When inflation is ignored in the preparation of financial statements

A operating profit is understated

B the information is relevant and reliable

C sales can appear to be increasing

D the correct amount of taxes are paid.

6 Explain the limitations of historical cost accounting in times of inflation.

7 Current cost accounting should be used when inflation occurs. Explain.

8 State three advantages and two disadvantages of current cost accounting.

9 What are the advantages of constant dollar accounting?

10 Explain three ways inflation may affect the information in financial statements.

Unit Two

Module One
Costing Principles

22 The nature and scope of cost and management accounting

Objectives
- differentiate between cost and management accounting and financial accounting
- discuss the nature and scope of cost and management accounting
- identify the role of cost and management accounting in manufacturing and service industries
- discuss the similarities between cost and management accounting and financial accounting

Essentially there are two broad types of accounting information: financial accounting and management accounting. Management accounting usually includes cost accounting.

Financial accounting information is geared towards external users of accounting information whilst management accounting is aimed more at internal users of accounting information. Despite the fact that there is a difference in the type of information presented in financial accounts, the underlying objective is the same, that is, to satisfy information needs of the user.

Financial accounting provides management with accurate information on the operational transactions of the firm. Compliance with external reporting bodies such as the International Accounting Standards Board is the focus of financial reports. The firm's performance and financial position at a specific time is a major part of financial reports.

Cost and management accounting is the process of identifying, measuring, accumulating, analysing, preparing, interpreting and communicating information used by management to plan, evaluate and control the organization and to ensure that its resources are used and accounted for appropriately.

Cost and management accounting provides management with financial and non-financial information to effectively manage the organization. Information about productivity, quality and other key success factors can be taken from cost accounting information.

In today's fast-paced and ever-changing production environment it is important for management and cost accounting to provide information that is useful and timely to assist management in decision-making.

22.1 Comparison of financial and management accounting

Financial accounting	Management accounting
• Describes the performance of a business over a specific period of time.	• Helps record, plan and control the activities of the business as well as assist in decision-making.
• The format of reports must comply with International standards even though the level of detail required will reflect the size of the business.	• There is no legal requirement to prepare management accounts.
• Financial accounts concentrate on the business as a whole without analysing separate parts.	• Management accounting has the ability to focus on different business activities and provide information on products, department or even a different country.
• Financial accounting information is measured in monetary terms.	• Management accounting frequently includes non-financial information such as number of employees, sales volume and number of customer transactions.
• Financial accounting information is presented from a historical perspective.	• Management accounting although focusing on historical performance also includes future trends and elements e.g. cash and sales forecast, budgets, etc.

22.2 Role of cost and management accounting in manufacturing and service Industries

Cost and Management Accounting play an important role in Service industries by providing managers with data on the efficient use of company resources and, secondly, computes the cost of providing a service.

Cost deals with data for:	Manufacturing	Servicing
Product costing	Identify weak areas Need to control cost Support price decisions Set inventory values	Cost per service transaction Labour rate per hour
Operating decisions	Response to price questions: Delivery dates Monitor product mix By products/Joint products/further refining or not	Analyse the services provided Review the optimal service mix Include only related services
Current information	Product, planning and scheduling Product line management and development Cash management Capital expenditure Product quality levels Customer satisfaction Selling and distribution	Planning and scheduling attending to large/small customers Improving the quality of service Cash management Maintaining high quality service Attending to the customer in the least possible time
Reporting	External reporting Computing taxes	Upgrading the technology
Budgets	To plan the cost of the product To control/compare actual and budgeted costs	Plan the cost of the service
Profitability	Cost behaviour	Cost behaviour

22.3 Similarities between cost and management accounting and financial accounting

There are similarities between cost and management accounting and financial accounting. Firstly, they provide a performance evaluation of the business for decision-making. Secondly, at times, they share the common practice of reporting economic information and even report some of the same information (accounting system and financial statements used).

22.4 Questions

1 Define the following:
   Cost accounting
   Management accounting
   Financial accounting.

2 List the roles of cost and management accounting in manufacturing and service industries.

3 List the similarities and differences between cost and management accounting and financial accounting.

23 Accounting for manufacturing enterprise

Objectives
- trace or show the flow of cost from raw materials to cost of goods manufactured to cost of goods sold
- prepare a manufacturing account and an income statement

23.1 The flow of cost from raw materials to cost of goods manufactured to cost of goods sold

The charts below show the movement of the flow of manufacturing costs. It depicts the accumulation of costs as

1. raw materials purchased,

2. factory labour costs are incurred and,

3. manufacturing overheads are incurred.

As shown above, these costs are the assigned to

4. the work in process inventory,

5. the finished goods inventory and finally,

6. to the cost of goods sold account.

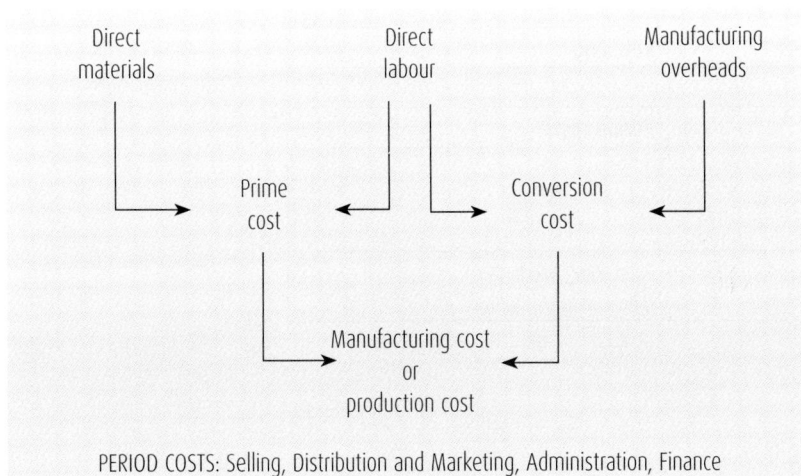

PERIOD COSTS: Selling, Distribution and Marketing, Administration, Finance

23.2 Manufacturing cost flow

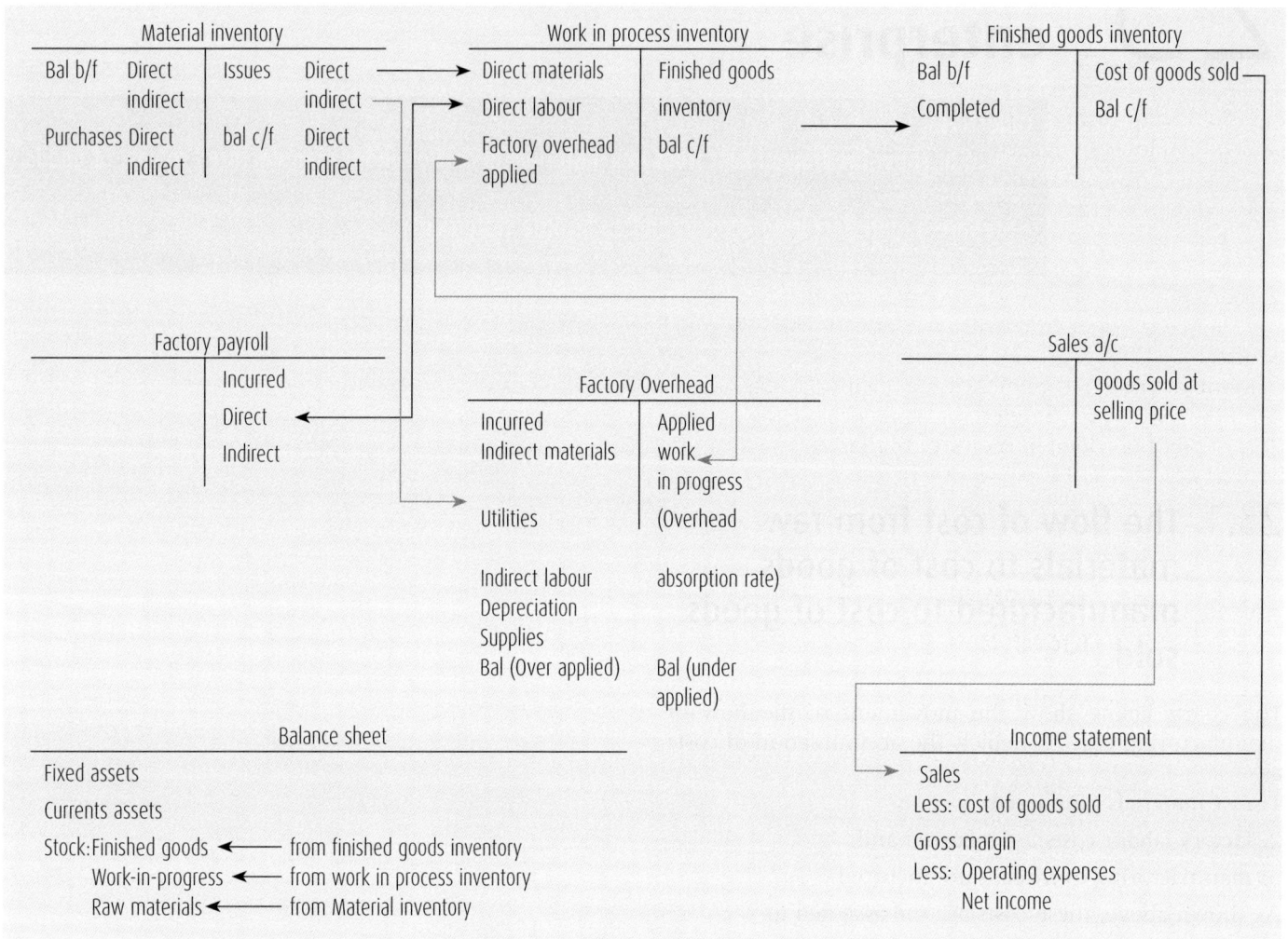

Material inventory			
Bal b/f	Direct indirect	Issues	Direct indirect
Purchases	Direct indirect	bal c/f	Direct indirect

Work in process inventory	
Direct materials	Finished goods
Direct labour	inventory
Factory overhead applied	bal c/f

Finished goods inventory	
Bal b/f	Cost of goods sold
Completed	Bal c/f

Factory payroll	
	Incurred
	Direct
	Indirect

Factory Overhead	
Incurred	Applied
Indirect materials	work
	in progress
Utilities	(Overhead
Indirect labour	absorption rate)
Depreciation	
Supplies	
Bal (Over applied)	Bal (under applied)

Sales a/c	
	goods sold at selling price

Balance sheet
Fixed assets
Currents assets
Stock:Finished goods ← from finished goods inventory
Work-in-progress ← from work in process inventory
Raw materials ← from Material inventory

Income statement
Sales
Less: cost of goods sold
Gross margin
Less: Operating expenses
Net income

23.3 Report on manufacturing

Cost classification	Manufacturing product cost	Retailing
Raw materials	Finished goods	
Items	**Product costs**	**Period costs**
Inventory accounts	Raw materials Work in process Finished goods	Finished goods
Goods source	Cost of goods manufactured finished goods inventory	Purchasing account merchandise inventory

23.4 What is a Manufacturing Account?

Manufacturing Accounts are prepared by manufacturing companies to show the cost of producing goods.

Trading companies purchase finished goods, but a manufacturing company's purchases consist of materials it uses in its manufacturing process. A large part of a manufacturing company's wages will most probably be paid to employees engaged on making goods, and some of the overheads will relate to the manufacturing process. A Manufacturing Account groups all the manufacturing expenses together as factory expenses. If the goods are produced more cheaply than they can be purchased from an outside supplier, the factory may be considered to have made a profit and will be credited with **factory profit**.

Manufacturing companies' stocks include stocks of raw materials, work in progress and finished goods. Any factory profit included in the stock of finished goods must be excluded from the value of the stock shown in the Balance Sheet.

23.5 How to prepare a Manufacturing Account

Select from the trial balance those expenses that relate to the company's manufacturing operation. The expenses are either direct (e.g. the cost of materials from which the goods are made, and the wages of the workers who actually make the goods) or indirect (all other manufacturing expenses).

The following outline shows how expenditure is allocated to Manufacturing Accounts.

Sample Example Ltd
**Manufacturing Account for the year ended
31 December 2004**

	$000	$000
Direct costs		
Direct material[1]		200
Direct labour[2]		380
Other direct expenses[3]		60
Prime cost[4]		640
Factory overheads		
Indirect materials[5]	95	
Indirect wages[6]	120	
Other overheads[7]	330	545
		1185
Work in progress at 1 January 2004[8]	78	
Work in progress at 31 December 2004[9]	(53)	25
Factory cost of finished goods (or cost of production)[10]		1210
Factory profit[11]		242
Cost of goods transferred to Trading Account[12]		1452

1 **Direct material:** material from which goods are made. The cost includes carriage inwards on raw material.

2 **Direct labour:** the wages of the workers who actually make the goods

3 **Direct expenses:** royalties, licence fees, etc. which have to be paid to other persons for the right to produce their products or to use their processes. The payment is a fixed sum for every unit of good produced.

4 **Prime cost:** the total of the direct costs. This description must *always* be shown.

5 **Indirect materials:** all materials purchased for the factory but which do not form part of the goods being produced, for example cleaning materials, lubricating oil for the machinery.

6 **Indirect wages:** the wages of all factory workers who do not actually make the goods, for example factory managers, supervisors, stores staff, cleaners, etc.

7 **Other overheads:** overheads relating exclusively to the factory and production, for example factory rent, heating and lighting, depreciation of the factory building and machinery, etc.

8 **Work in progress:** goods in the process of being made at the end of the previous year but which were not finished are brought into the current year as an input to this year's production.

9 Goods that are not completely finished at the end of the current year must be deducted from the year's costs in order to arrive at the cost of finished goods.

10 **Factory cost of finished goods:** either these words or the alternative, **cost of production**, should be shown at this point in the account.

11 **Factory profit:** the percentage to be added to cost of production as profit. The amount is decided by management and will always be given in questions if necessary. It is debited in the Manufacturing Account and credited in the Profit and Loss Account (see below).

12 The total of the Manufacturing Account is debited in the Trading Account under the heading 'Cost of Sales'.

Example

The following balances have been extracted from Makeit & Co.'s trial balance at 31 December 2004.

	$000	$000
Stocks at 1 January 2004:		
Direct materials	10	
Work in progress	38	
Finished goods	40	
Purchases (direct materials)	140	
Carriage inwards	24	
Direct wages	222	
Direct expenses (patent royalties)	46	
Indirect materials	45	
Indirect labour	72	
Rent: factory	100	
offices	90	
Heating, lighting and power: factory	45	
offices	35	
Sales		1 300
Administration salaries and wages	173	

Further information

1. Stock at 31 December 2004 was as follows.

	$000
Direct materials	18
Work in progress	20
Finished goods	60

2. Depreciation is to be provided on fixed assets as follows.

	$000
Factory building	20
Factory machinery	36
Office equipment	24

3. Factory profit is to be calculated at 15% on cost of production.

Required

Prepare the Manufacturing, Trading and Profit and Loss Account for the year ended 31 December 2004.

Makeit & Co.
Manufacturing, Trading and Profit and Loss Account
for the year ended 31 December 2004

		$000	$000
Direct materials	Stock at 1 January 2004	10	
	Purchases	140	
	Carriage inwards	24	
		174	
	Less Stock at 31 December 2004	18	156
Direct labour			222
Direct expenses			46
Prime cost			424
Indirect materials		45	
Indirect labour		72	
Rent of factory		100	
Heating, lighting and power		45	
Depreciation: factory		20	
machinery		36	318
			742
Work in progress 1 January 2004		38	
Work in progress 31 December 2004		(20)	18
Factory cost of finished goods			760
Factory profit (15%)			114
Transferred to Trading Account			874

	$000	$000
Sales		1300
Cost of sales		
Stock of finished goods at 1 January 2004	40	
Transferred from factory	874	
	914	
Stock of finished goods at 31 December 2004	60	854
Gross profit		446
Wages and salaries	173	
Rent of offices	90	
Heating and lighting	35	
Depreciation of office equipment	24	322
Net profit on trading[1]		124
Add factory profit[2]	114	
Less Unrealized profit on closing stock of finished goods[3]	8	106
Net profit		230

1 Net profit on trading is the profit that has been made from the trading activity and does not include factory profit.

2 Factory profit (after deducting unrealized profit) is added to the net profit on trading to show Makeit & Co.'s total profit.

Note. The Trading and Profit and Loss Account follows on from the Manufacturing Account without a break. It is included in the heading to the Manufacturing Account.

Unrealized profit included in stocks of finished goods

The figure of closing stock in Makeit & Co.'s Trading Account includes factory profit. This profit will not be realized until the stock is sold and must be excluded to arrive at the realized factory profit. (The concept of realization must be applied.) Makeit & Co.'s unrealized profit is calculated as follows. The stock of $60 000 is 115% of the cost of manufacture and the unrealized profit is $60 000 x $\frac{15}{115}$ = $8000 (rounded). The double entry for unrealized profit, $8000, debited in the Profit and Loss Account is completed by a credit to a Provision for Unrealized Profit.

In future years, it will be necessary only to adjust the Provision for Unrealized Profit for increases or decreases in closing stocks. For example, if Makeit & Co.'s finished goods stock one year later, at 31 December 2005, is $85 000, the provision required for unrealized profit will be $85 000 x $\frac{15}{115}$ = $11 000. Only the increase of $3000 in the provision will be debited in the Profit and Loss Account and credited to the Provision for Unrealized Profit.

An increase in the provision is recorded as follows.

> **Debit** Profit and Loss Account
>> **Credit** Provision for Unrealized Profit
> With the amount of the increase

A decrease in the provision is recorded as follows.

> **Debit** Provision for Unrealized Profit
>> **Credit** Profit and Loss Account
> With the amount of the decrease

23.6 Manufacturing Balance Sheet

The Balance Sheet of a manufacturing business includes the stocks of materials, work in progress and finished goods at cost.

The stocks appear in Makeit & Co.'s Balance Sheet at 31 December 2004 as follows:

Current assets		$000	$000
Stock:	materials		18
	work in progress		20
	finished goods	60	
	Less unrealized profit	8	52
			90

Exercise 1

The Fabricating Company carries on a manufacturing business. Information extracted from its trial balance at 31 March 2004 is as follows:

		$000	$000
Sales			700
Stocks at 1.4.03	Raw materials	10	
	Work in progress	12	
	Finished goods	24	
Purchase of raw materials		130	
Carriage inwards		14	
Direct labour		170	
Other direct expenses		16	
Factory overheads		128	
Office overheads		96	

The following further information is given:

		$000
Stocks at 31.3.04	Raw materials	20
	Work in progress	22
	Finished goods	36
Depreciation charges for the year:		
	Factory	12
	Office	3

Completed production is transferred to the warehouse at a mark-up on factory cost of 20%.

Required

Prepare a Manufacturing, Trading and Profit and Loss Account for the year ended 31 March 2004.

Exercise 2

The following balances have been extracted from the books of Glupersoo at 30 April 2004:

	$
Sales	800 000
Purchase of raw materials	132 000
Direct wages	146 250
Indirect wages	19 500
Rent	45 000
Heating and lighting	42 300
Insurance	3 150
Office salaries	51 450
Carriage inwards	11 505
Carriage outwards	2 520
Advertising	7 000
Motor van expenses	6 000
Stocks at 1 May 2003: Raw materials	11 250
Work in progress	18 000
Finished goods	27 000

Further information

1. Stocks at 30 April 2004:

	$
Raw materials	13 125
Work in progress	15 750
Finished goods	24 000

2. The following expenses must be accrued at 30 April 2004:

	$
Rent	3750
Heating and lighting	2700

3. The following expenses have been prepaid at 3 April 2004:

	$
Insurance	900
Advertising	3500

4. Expenses are to be apportioned as follows:

Rent: Factory 75%; Offices 25%

Heating and lighting: Factory $\frac{2}{3}$, Offices $\frac{1}{3}$

Insurance: Factory $\frac{9}{10}$; Offices $\frac{1}{10}$

Motor costs: Factory 50%

5. Provision for depreciation is to be made as follows:

	$
Factory building	3 000
Factory machinery	10 000
Office machinery and equipment	4 000
Motor vans	8 000

Required

Prepare a Manufacturing, Trading and Profit and Loss Account for the year ended 30 April 2004.
(Make all calculations to the nearest $.)

23.7 Schedules

Manufacturing income statements can be prepared in schedules, namely cost of goods manufactured and cost of goods sold.

Example

Tryit Company had the following balances as at December 31, 2002:

	$
Sales	300 000
Raw materials inventory, January 1	10 000
Raw materials purchased	100 000
Raw materials inventory, December 31	20 000
Direct labour	20 000
Depreciation – factory	4 000
Insurance – factory	1 000
Indirect labour	3 000
Maintenance – factory	1 000
Work in process, January 1	20 000
Work in process, December 31	8 000
Finished goods, January 1	40 000
Finished goods, December 31	50 000
Selling and administrative expenses:	
Advertising	2 000
Salaries	3 000
Telephone	2 000
Salaries	30 000

Prepare the following:
(a) Cost of goods manufactured schedule
(b) Cost of goods schedule
(c) Income statement.

Solution I

TRYIT
Schedule of cost of goods manufactured
for the year ended December, 2002

(a)

	$	$
Direct materials:		
Raw materials, inventory January 1	10 000	
Add: Purchases of raw materials	100 000	
Raw materials available for use	110 000	
Deduct: Raw materials, inventory December 31	20 000	
Raw materials used in production		90 000
Direct labour		20 000
Manufacturing overheads:		
Depreciation – factory	4 000	
Insurance – factory	1 000	
Indirect labour	3 000	
Maintenance – factory	1 000	
Total overhead costs		9 000
Total manufacturing costs		119 000
Add work in process, January 1		20 000
		139 000
Deduct work in process, December 31		8 000
Cost of goods manufactured		131 000

Cost of goods sold schedule

(b)

	$
Finished goods, January 1	40 000
Add: Cost of goods manufactured	131 000
Goods available for sale	171 000
Less: Finished goods, December 31	50 000
Cost of goods sold	121 000

Income statement

(c)

	$	$
Sales		300 000
Cost of goods sold		121 000
Gross margin		179 000
Less selling and administrative expenses		
Advertising	2 000	
Salaries	30 000	
Telephone	2 000	34 000
Net income		145 000

Solution II (Another format of Cost of Goods Manufactured)

	$	$	$
TRYIT			
Cost of goods manufactured			
for the year ended December, 2002			
Work in process, January 1			20 000
Direct materials:			
Raw materials, January 1	10 000		
Raw materials purchased	100 000		
Total raw materials purchased	110 000		
Less raw materials, December 31	20 000		
Raw materials used		90 000	
Direct labour		20 000	
Manufacturing overheads:			
Depreciation – factory	4 000		
Insurance – factory	1 000		
Indirect labour	3 000		
Maintenance – factory	1 000		
Total manufacturing overheads		9 000	
Total manufacturing costs			119 000
Total cost of work in process			139 000
Less work in process, December 31			8 000
Cost of good manufactured			131 000

23.8 Multiple-choice questions

1 Goods are transferred from the Manufacturing Account to the Trading Account at factory cost of production plus a mark-up of 20%.

The transfer prices of the closing stocks of finished goods were as follows:

Year 1 $39 600

Year 2 $42 000

Year 3 $45 600

What was the provision for unrealized profit charged against the profit for Year 3?

A $400

B $600

C $720

D $1200

2 Goods are transferred from the factory to the warehouse at a mark-up of $33\frac{1}{3}$%. At 1 April 2003, the balance on the Provision for Unrealized Profit was $17 000. At 31 March 2004, the closing stock of finished goods was $60 000.

What was the effect on profit of the entry in the Provision for Unrealized Profit on 31 March 2004?

A decrease of $2000

B decrease of $3000

C increase of $2000

D increase of $3000

3 The following items appear in the accounts of a manufacturing company:

(i)   Carriage inwards

(ii)   Carriage outwards

(iii) Depreciation of warehouse machinery

(iv) Provision for unrealized profit.

Which items will be included in the Manufacturing Account?

A (i) and (ii)

B (i) and (iii)

C (ii) and (iii)

D (ii) and (iv)

4 A manufacturing company adds a factory profit of 25% to its cost of production. The following information is available:

	$
Stock of finished goods at 1 April 2003 (per Balance Sheet at that date)	30 000
Cost of goods produced (per Manufacturing Account for the year ended 31 March 2004)	300 000
Closing stock of finished goods (per Trading Account for the year end 31 March 2004)	60 000

How much will be credited as factory profit in the Profit and Loss Account for the year ended 31 March 2004?

A $67 500

B $69 000

C $70 500

D $71 500

23.9 Additional exercises

1 The following balances have been extracted from the books of Spinners & Co. at 31 December 2003.

	$
Stocks at 1 January 2003:	
Raw materials	8 000
Work in progress	12 000
Factory expenses	
Direct wages	40 000
Indirect wages	28 000
Patent fees paid to patent holder	16 000
Heating and lighting	5 000
General factory expenses	14 000
Insurance of plant and machinery	6 000
Purchases of raw materials	140 000
Plant and machinery at cost	70 000

Further information

1. Stocks at 31 December 2003:

	$
Raw materials	10 000
Work in progress	9 700

2. Expenses owing at 31 December 2003:

	$
Direct wages	600
Indirect wages	400
General expenses	300

3. Expenses prepaid at 31 December 2003:

	$
Insurance	400
Heating and lighting	180

4. Plant and machinery are to be depreciated at the rate of 10% on cost.

5. A factory profit of 10% is added to the factory cost of goods produced.

Required

Prepare the Manufacturing Account for the year ended 31 December 2003.

2 The following balances have been extracted from the books of the Uggle Box Manufacturing Company at 30 April 2004.

	$
Premises at cost	250 000
Plant and machinery (net book value)	70 000
Motor vehicles at cost	40 000
Stocks at 1 May 2003	
Raw materials	42 000
Work in progress	50 000
Finished goods	48 000
Factory wages (direct)	280 000
Royalties based on production	40 000
Factory expenses	20 000
Selling expenses	42 000
Administrative expenses	62 000
Sales	1 240 000
Purchases of raw materials	390 000
Carriage inwards	26 000

Further information

1. Stocks at 30 April 2004:

	$
Raw materials	36 000
Work in progress	46 000
Finished goods	62 400

2. Finished goods are transferred to the Trading Account at factory cost plus a mark-up of 20%.

3. Depreciation is to be provided as follows:

Premises: 5% per annum on cost

Plant and machinery: 20% per annum on the written down value

Motor vehicles: 20% per annum on cost

4. Depreciation charges are to be apportioned as follows:

Premises:	Factory	50%
	Administration	50%
Plant and machinery:	Factory	80%
	Administration	20%
Motor vehicles:	Factory	90%
	Administration	10%

Required

Prepare a Manufacturing, Trading and Profit and Loss Account for the year ended 30 April 2004.

3 The following balances have been extracted from Yendor's books at 31 March 2004.

		$000	$000
Stocks at 1 April 2003:	Raw materials	450	
	Work in progress	375	
	Finished goods	390	
Factory wages	Direct	900	
	Indirect	90	
Purchases	Direct materials	2250	
	Indirect materials	45	
Carriage inwards		162	
Other factory overheads		245	
Sales			6075
Office salaries		391	
Other administration expenses		675	
Provision for Unrealized Profit			65
Freehold premises at cost		1000	
Provision for Depreciation of Freehold Premises			160
Manufacturing Plant and Machinery at cost		600	
Provision for Depreciation of Manufacturing Plant and Machinery at 31 March 2003			350
Office equipment at cost		300	
Provision for Depreciation of Office Equipment at 31 March 2003			100

Further information

1. Stocks at 31 March 2004 were as follows (in $000s): raw materials $440; work in progress $562; finished goods $594.

2. Carriage inwards relates wholly to the purchase of raw materials.

3. Finished goods are transferred from the factory to the warehouse at a mark-up of 20%.

4. The factory occupies $\frac{3}{4}$ of the freehold premises; the administrative offices occupy the remainder.

5. Depreciation should be provided as follows:

Freehold premises 4% per annum on cost

Plant and machinery 30% per annum on net book value

Office equipment 15% per annum on net book value

Required

Prepare Yendor's Manufacturing, Trading and Profit and Loss Account for the year ended 31 March 2004.

4 Anyhow Inc. balances for the year ended December 31, 2005 are as follows:

	$
Purchases of raw materials	90 000
Raw materials inventory, January 1	10 000
Raw materials inventory, December 31	17 000
Depreciation – factory	42 000
Insurance – factory	8 000
Direct labour	60 000
Maintenance – factory	30 000
Administrative expenses	70 000
Sales	400 000
Supplies – factory	1 000
Indirect labour	60 000
Work in process inventory, January 1	7 000
Work in process inventory, December 31	30 000
Finished goods inventory, January 1	100 000
Finished goods inventory, December 31	40 000

Required

1. Prepare a schedule of cost of goods manufactured.
2. Prepare a schedule of cost of goods sold and an income statement.

24 Costing for raw materials

24.1 Principles of procurement function (material control)

Since businesses must keep stock, it is necessary that there be near-perfect timing between usage and delivery of material. There are costs involved in holding too much stock as well as losses incurred in keeping too little stock. The mere exercise of holding stock is costly and certain principles should be followed to keep such costs at a minimum. To ensure timing and control, the following guidelines should be adhered to:

1. Keep a general stock list with quantity, description and other technical data.

2. Determine the requirements to meet planned production.

3. Decide on the materials to be stocked.

4. Ensure that the quantity and quality of materials are available when needed.

5. Inform the purchasing department of future requirements and the dates delivery is expected.

6. Record materials issued and used for each order.

7. Record materials moving in and out of stores.

8. Take advantage of bulk purchases.

9. Minimize ordering cost.

10. Keep storage cost at a minimum.

24.2 Principles of inventory valuation

The value placed on closing inventory is of utmost importance for reporting purposes. The valuation affects cost of sales and by extension, the gross profit. There are a number of methods for valuing inventory. However, the standard specifies that:

1. Inventory must be valued at the lower of cost or net realizable value.

2. Whichever policy is used for valuing inventory must be applied consistently over the life of the business.

When the principles are followed and the purchase price of inventory is higher than the net realizable value, the loss is matched to the period it occurred and prudently recognized.

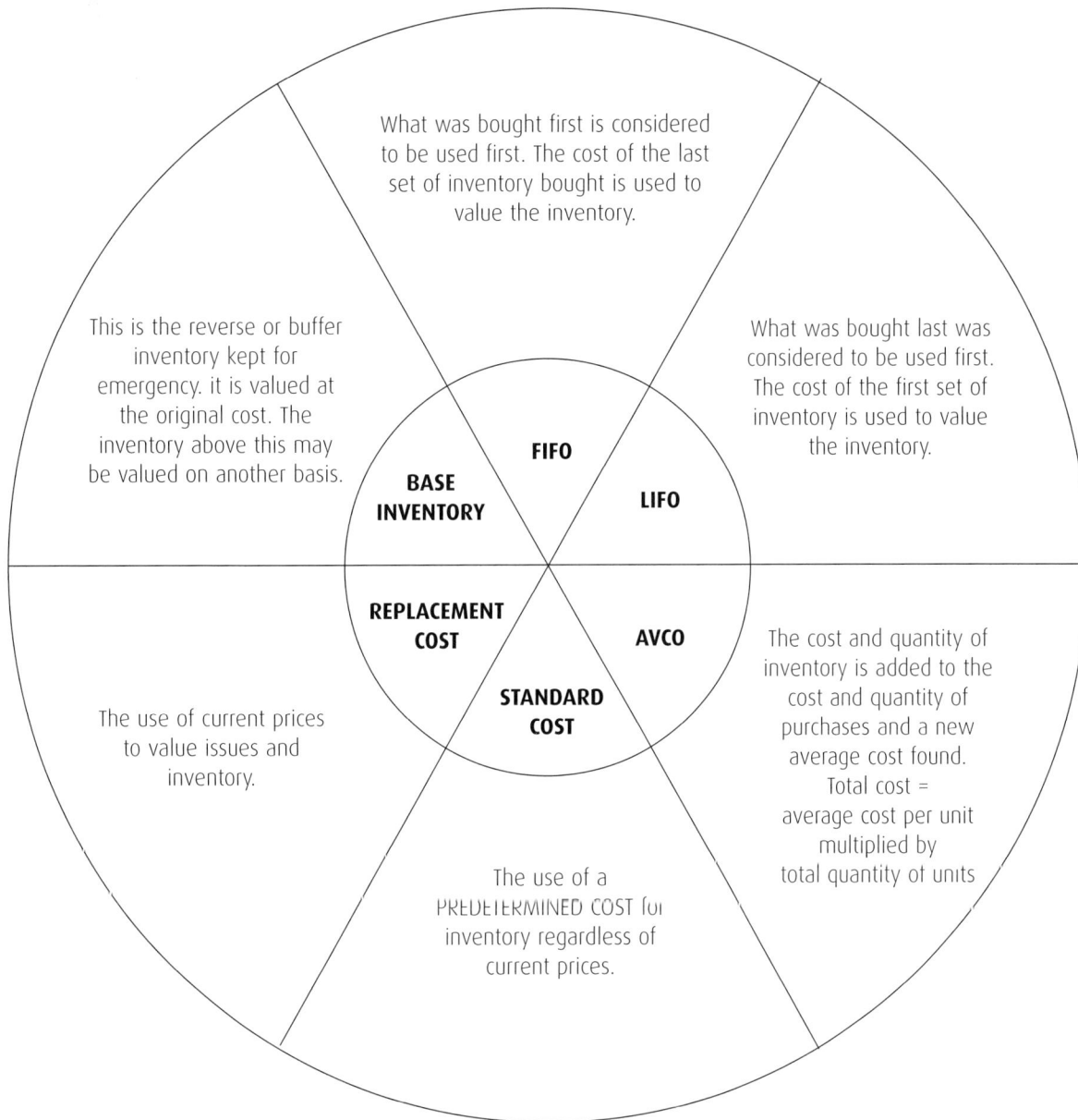

The diagram shows a circular chart with six segments. The inner circle contains the labels, and the outer ring contains descriptions:

- **FIFO** — What was bought first is considered to be used first. The cost of the last set of inventory bought is used to value the inventory.
- **LIFO** — What was bought last was considered to be used first. The cost of the first set of inventory is used to value the inventory.
- **AVCO** — The cost and quantity of inventory is added to the cost and quantity of purchases and a new average cost found. Total cost = average cost per unit multiplied by total quantity of units
- **STANDARD COST** — The use of a PREDETERMINED COST for inventory regardless of current prices.
- **REPLACEMENT COST** — The use of current prices to value issues and inventory.
- **BASE INVENTORY** — This is the reverse or buffer inventory kept for emergency. it is valued at the original cost. The inventory above this may be valued on another basis.

24.3 Introduction to the Economic Order Quantity concept

Procurement function: economic order quantity

This concept is concerned with timely acquisition of inventory so as to limit the cost of 'holding' or 'storing' an excessive amount, or reduce the additional cost involved in late or last minute inventory purchases.

Economic Order Quantity is the quantity of inventories which should be ordered so as to minimize the costs of both ordering and holding inventories over a given period of time. Some firms attempt to minimize holding cost (sometimes called carrying cost) by ordering small quantities of inventory at regular intervals. This may result in loss of revenue associated with bulk buying. Other firms prefer to benefit from bulk purchasing and accept the costs associated with additional storage space and time.

The appropriate reorder quantity is therefore usually determined by applying a qualitative formula after certain assumptions are considered. Thus, Economic Order Quantity calculation proceeds as follows.

Economic Order Quantity (EOQ) is the size of the order which provides the lowest holding cost per item purchased –

This is influenced by (1) storage space

                        (2) order placement cost

                        (3) cost of storage

$$EOQ = \sqrt{\frac{2CO}{S}}$$

C – annual consumption or usage in units

O – cost of planning one order.

S – storage and holding of one unit for one year (usually expressed as a percentage of the cost per unit) or carrying cost.

Carrying Cost – warehouse staff, equipment maintenance and running costs.

Example

Annual consumption	6000 units
Cost re-ordering	$10.00
Storage + holding cost	25%
Unit cost price	$ 4.00

$$EOQ = \sqrt{\frac{2CO}{S}}$$

$$= \sqrt{\frac{2 \times 6000 \times 10}{\frac{25}{100} \times 4}}$$

$$= \sqrt{\frac{120000}{1}}$$

$$= \quad 346.4 \ (\ 17.3 \text{ orders per annum })$$

Formula to calculate other components of EOQ:

(1) Ordering cost = $\dfrac{C}{EOQ}$

(2) Carrying cost = $\dfrac{EOQ}{2}$

(3) Reorder point = Average units per day × days to place and receive order

The most commonly used methods of inventory valuation are

1. Last in First Out (LIFO)

2. First in First Out (FIFO)

3. Average inventory.

The following examples highlight inventory valuation using each of the methods.

Inventory valuation: LIFO

Date	Units	Unit cost	Issue at the cost price Units	Unit cost	Balance at the cost price Units	Unit cost $
May 1st B/F	100	2.00	NIL	NIL	100	2.00
May 3rd B/F	100	2.00			100	2.00
Bought	400	3.00	NIL	NIL	400	3.00
May 4th B/F	100	2.00	NIL	–	100	2.00
Bought	400	3.00	200	3.00	200	3.00
May 9th B/F	100	2.00			100	2.00
Bought	200	3.00			200	3.00
	300	4.00	NIL	NIL	300	4.00
May 11th B/F	100	2.00	NIL	–	100	2.00
	200	3.00	100	3.00	100	3.00
	300	4.00	300	4.00	NIL	–
May 18th B/F	100	2.00			100	2.00
Bought	100	3.00			100	3.00
	100	5.00	NIL	–	100	5.00
May 20th B/F	100	2.00	NIL	–	100	2.00
	100	3.00	NIL	–	100	3.00
	100	5.00	100	5.00	NIL	–

Issues at cost price: $(200 \times 3) + (100 \times 3) + (300 \times 4) + (100 \times 5) = \$2600$

Closing inventory: $(100 \times 2) + (100 \times 3) = \$500.00$

In periods of inflation there is a tendency with LIFO for

1. materials to be issued at a cost that approximates to current market value;
2. closing inventory to be valued below current market value.

Inventory valuation: FIFO

Date	Units	Unit cost	Issue at the cost price Units	Unit cost	Balance at the cost price Units	Unit cost $
May 1st B/F	100	2.00	NIL	NIL	100	2.00
May 3rd B/F	100	2.00			100	2.00
Bought	400	3.00	NIL	NIL	400	3.00
May 4th B/F	100	2.00	100	2.00	NIL	–
Bought	400	3.00	100	3.00	300	3.00
May 9th B/F	300	3.00			300	3.00
Bought	300	4.00	NIL	NIL	300	4.00
May 11th B/F	300	3.00	300	3.00	NIL	–
	300	4.00	100	4.00	200	4.00
May 18th B/F	200	4.00	NIL	–	200	4.00
Bought	100	5.00	NIL	–	100	5.00
May 20th B/F	200	4.00	100	4.00	100	4.00
	100	5.00			100	5.00

Issues at cost price: $(100 \times 2) + (100 \times 3) + (300 \times 3) + (100 \times 4) + (100 \times 4) = \$2200$

Closing inventory: $(100 \times 4) + (100 \times 5) = \$900$

In periods of inflation there is a tendency for

1. materials to be issued at a cost lower than the current market value;
2. closing inventory to be valued at a cost approximately to current value.

Inventory valuation: weighted average method (AVCO)

Date		Total cost	Unit cost	Issue at the cost price Units	Total cost	Balance at the cost price Units	Total cost $
May 1st	100 × 2	200	2.00	NIL	NIL	100 x 2.00	200
May 3rd	b/f 100 × 2 bought 400 × 3 500	200 1200 1400	2.80	NIL	NIL	500 x 2.80	1400
May 4th	b/f 500 × 2.80	1400		200 x 2.80	560	300 x 2.80	840
May 9th	b/f 300 × 2.80 bought 300 × 4.00 600	840 1200 2040	3.40	NIL	NIL	600 x 3.40	2040
May 11th	b/f 600 × 3.40	2040	3.40	400 x 3.40	1360	200 x 3.40	680
May 18th	b/f 200 × 3.40 bought 100 × 5 300	680 500 1180	3.93	NIL	NIL	300 x 3.93	1180
May 20th	b/f 300 × 3.93	1180		100 x 3.93	393	200 x 3.93	787

Issues at cost price: (560 + 1360 + 393) = $2 313

Closing inventory: = $ 787

In periods of inflation there is a tendency for
1. materials to be issued at a cost that lags behind the current market value;
2. closing inventory to be valued at a cost slightly below current market value.

Cost classification/ascertainment

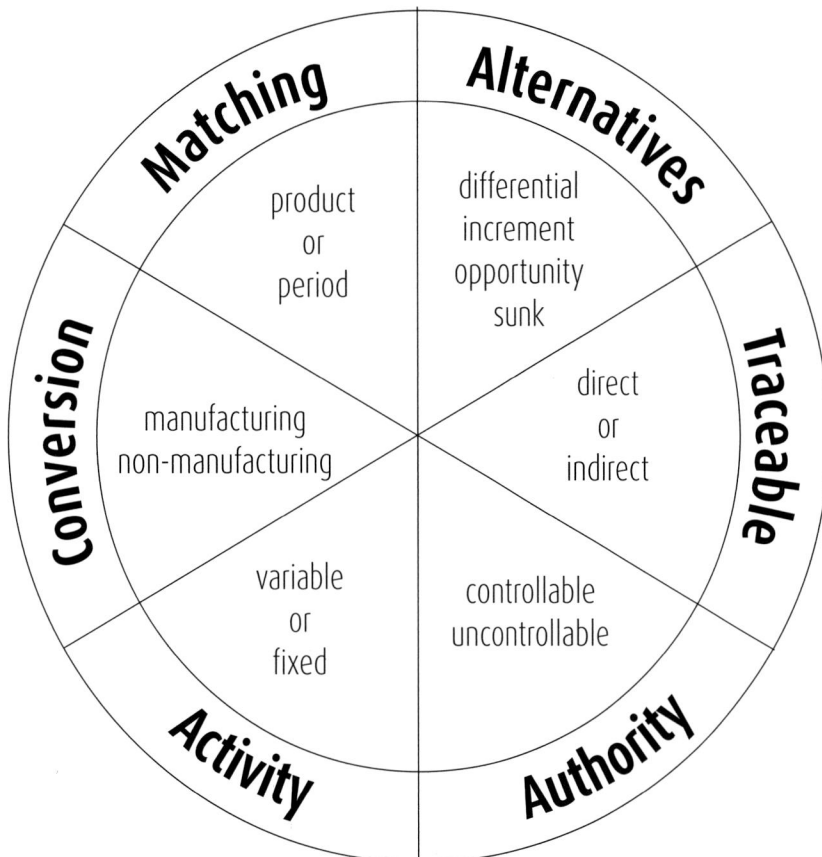

24.4 Cost classification

Inventory valuation

Product cost (inventoriable cost) – All cost that is involved in the purchase or manufacture of goods: e.g. direct materials, indirect labour, manufacturing, overheads.

Period cost – All cost matched against revenue on a time period basis e.g. selling, administrative.

Carrying cost – A cost that increases with the number of units of inventory:

(a) out of pocket – Insurance of inventory; inventory, taxes, annual inspection and licence etc.

(b) cost of capital – The opportunity cost of having funds in inventory rather than in other earning assets.

Decision making (alternatives)

Differential cost – Any cost that is present under one alternative but is absent in whole or part under another alternative in a decision-making situation. Also see *Incremental cost.*

Incremental cost – An increase in cost between two alternatives. Also see *Differential cost.*

Opportunity cost – The potential benefit that is lost or sacrificed when the selection of one course of action makes it necessary to give up a competing course of action.

Avoidable costs – A cost that can be escaped by choosing an alternative.

Sunk cost – An expenditure made in the past that cannot be changed by present or future decisions.

Relevant cost – a cost that will have a bearing on which alternative is selected.

Activity

Fixed – A cost that remains constant in total, regardless of changes in the level of activity. If a cost is expressed on a per unit basis, it varies inversely with the level of activity. It is also called period or policy cost.

Variable – A cost that is expressed in total, in direct proportion to changes in the level of activity. A variable cost is constant per unit.

Mixed – Both variable and fixed costs are charged to the same general ledger: e.g. repairs, maintenance, are full time workers (fixed), and helpers (variable) as they are hired depending on the amount of work.

Semi-variable – A cost that has variable and fixed components: e.g. telephone expenses, electricity.

Conversion

Direct labour combined with manufacturing overhead to change to raw materials.

Manufacturing – The conversion of raw materials into finished products through the efforts of factory workers and the use of production equipment.

Manufacturing overhead (non-manufacturing cost) – All costs associated with the manufacturing process except direct materials and direct labour.

Traceable

Direct cost – A cost that can be obviously and physically traced to a unit of product or other organizational segment.

Indirect cost – A cost that must be allocated in order to be assigned to a unit of product or some other organizational segment. An indirect cost is also known as a common cost.

Authority

Controllable cost – A cost is controllable at a particular level of management when the designated person has the power to authorize the cost.

24.5 Hazardous materials management

Hazardous materials are substances that have hazardous characteristics, such as: flammable, corrosive, reactive, radioactive, poisonous, carcinogenic or infectious. In a general sense, these materials are considered hazardous because they present a potential risk to humans and/or the environment. A waste is basically any discarded material. By law, a hazardous waste is defined as a waste or combination of wastes. Its quantity, concentration or physical, chemical or infectious characteristics may cause or significantly contribute to an increase in serious irreversible or incapacitating reversible illness or pose a substantial present or potential hazard to human health, safety or welfare or to the environment when improperly treated, stored, transported, used or disposed of or otherwise managed. Hazardous waste management plans generally separate waste into three broad groups: radioactive, chemical and biological.

Hazardous waste includes a wide range of material such as discarded commercial chemical products, process wastes and wastewater. Some chemicals and chemical mixtures are hazardous wastes because they are specifically listed by the Environmental Protection Agency (EPA). Most of the common laboratory solvents are listed wastes. A chemical waste that is not listed by the EPA is still a hazardous waste if it has one or more of EPA's four hazardous characteristics: ignitability, corrosivity, reactivity or toxicity.

There is a hierarchy of options when choosing a disposal option for material that is waste at a particular site.

1. Re-use or return. If the material cannot be used at the facility where it is waste, it may be useful at a nearby federal facility. Alternatively, the manufacturer may accept return of unused product.

2. Recycle. Can the waste be returned to the manufacturers for recycle?

3. Reject. Waste may be properly disposed of at provincially licensed landfills or by licensed haulers at licensed waste facilities.

A series of 'handling and disposal advice' sheets are being developed to recommend alternatives for disposal of hazardous and other waste from federal facilities in Atlantic Canada. These sheets will not tell you how to manage your site to create less waste. These sheets will recommend a disposal practice.

24.6 Examination hints

- Read questions carefully to see which method or methods of stock valuation are required.
- Some questions are about the value of stock-on-hand, but others are concerned with the cost of stock issued to production or sold. Make sure you understand the point of the question or you may provide the wrong answer.
- Perform all calculations with the utmost care.
- Be prepared to answer questions on the principles governing stock valuation and the advantages and disadvantages of each method.
- Questions on stock valuation may require you to use techniques and knowledge gained from your studies on any part of the syllabus.

24.7 Multiple-choice questions

1 How should stock be valued in a Balance Sheet?

A at the lower of net realizable value and selling price

B at the lower of replacement cost and net realizable value

C at lower of cost and replacement cost

D at lower of cost and net realizable value

2 A company bought and sold goods as follows.

	Bought		Sold
	Units	Unit price ($)	Units
March 1	20	2.00	
3	10	2.50	
4			12
5	20	3.00	
6			16

What is the value of the stock at 6 March based on FIFO?

A $44

B $45

C $65

D $66

3 A company had the following stock transactions in June.

June	1 Purchased 50 units of stock at $3 per unit
	14 Purchased 100 units at $4.50 per unit
	23 Sold 70 units
	30 Purchased 62 units at $5 per unit

What is the value of stock at 30 June based on AVCO?

A $4.292

B $4.437

C $4.50

D $5.00

4 A trader has valued his opening and closing stocks using LIFO. He has now heard that LIFO is not acceptable under current accounting standards and has amended his accounts to value the stocks on FIFO. His stocks valued at FIFO and LIFO are as follows.

	FIFO	LIFO
Opening stock	$2000	$1500
Closing stock	$4000	$3200

What effect will this amendment make to the trader's gross and net profits?

	Gross profit	Net profit
A	decrease $300	decrease $300
B	decrease $300	no change
C	increase $300	increase $300
D	increase $300	no change

24.8 Additional exercises

1 Discuss how the concept of prudence might be relevant when considering the valuation of Stock in Trade. (UCLES, 2001, AS/A Level Accounting, Syllabus 8706/2, October/November)

2 Janice Jersey's first 6 months of trading showed the following purchases and sales of stock.

1990	Purchases	Sales
January	280 @ $65 each	
February		140 @ $82 each
March	100 @ $69 each	
April		190 @ $85 each
May	220 @ $72 each	
June		200 @ $90 each

Calculate Janice's profit for the 6 months ended 30 June 1990 using the following methods of stock valuation:

(a) FIFO (First In First Out)

(b) LIFO (Last In First Out)

(c) AVCO (Weighted Average Cost). Calculate to 2 decimal places.

(UCLES, 2002, AS/A Level Accounting, Syllabus 9706/2, May/June)

3 Because of illness, Achmed's annual stocktaking, which should have taken place on 31 March 2001, was not completed until 7 April 2001, and was undertaken by an inexperienced member of the staff. Achmed felt that the stock figure of $92050 was too low and ordered an investigation. It was discovered that the following had occurred during the week ended 7 April 2001 and had not been accounted for in the closing stock calculation:

1. Goods with a selling price of $1040 had been sent to a customer on approval.

2. Goods costing $9400 were received and invoiced.

3. Sales of $18760 had been made and invoiced to customers.

   These sales included

   (i) an overcharge of $160;

   (ii) sales of $6000 on special offer at a margin of 10%;

   (iii) damaged goods which had cost $2500 and were sold for $2800.

Achmed's standard rate of gross profit is 25% of sales.

Calculate the correct value of closing stock at 31 March 2001.

(UCLES, 2001, AS/A Level Accounting, Syllabus 9366/2, May/June)

4 A company purchases raw materials at a cost of $20 per unit. The annual demand for the raw material is 10 000 units. The holding cost per unit is $5 and the cost of placing an order is $25. Calculate the economic order quantity.

5 Classify the following costs into the following: variable cost, fixed cost, period cost and product cost.
General office salaries
Factory manager salary
Sales commissions
Depreciation, factory building
Depreciation, office equipment
Indirect materials, factory
Factory labour
Advertising
Insurance, factory
General office supplies

6 IDID Steel Mill Company uses 10 000 units of a particular part each year. To get better control over its inventory, the company is anxious to determine the economic order quantity for this part. The company has determined that it costs $50 to place an order for the part from the supplier and $5 to carry one part in the inventory each year.

Required

Compute the EOQ for the part.

25 Cost classification and identification

Objectives
- distinguish between direct and indirect labour
- identify methods of remuneration
- discuss and apply the appropriateness of the methods to situations
- identify fixed and semi-fixed overhead costs
- apply the bases for apportionment
- allocate overhead and service department costs – direct method, reciprocal method (direct and step down methods and the highest percentage concept)
- apportion service department costs to production departments
- calculate predetermined overhead recovery rate using direct labour cost and machine hours
- state why department costs are absorbed by products
- illustrate cost behaviour using graphics

25.1 Comparison of direct and indirect labour

	Direct labour	Indirect labour
Involvement	Works on altering or construction.	The effort cannot be identified with the specific item. It is not involved in changing the form.
Importance	Performs the main task or service.	Provides a supporting service.
Cost centre	The effort is changed to a unit cost.	The effort is charged to a general a/c as Department Expenses.
Cost absorption	Produces for stock or a particular customer.	Aids the entire business or the department.
Accounts used	Wages charged to a stock order or number or customer order number.	The wage/salary is classified as an overhead expense.

25.2 Methods of remuneration

Remuneration is the reward for labour and service.
Incentive is the stimulation of effort and effectiveness by
offering monetary inducement or enhanced facilities.

Methods	Definition	Appreciation
1. Time rates Ordinary level	Payment for time spent rather than production rate per hrs worked.	Suitable: worker learning a job or trade. Unsuitable: processing, high degree of skill needed.
High level	High rate paid for high performance and productivity.	Suitable: selecting good workers, organized supervision, higher level of performance and output, lowering overhead and unit cost. Unsuitable: for cutting cost
Measured day work	Payment for efficiency and performance (over time all at a higher than ordinary rate).	Suitable: reducing paperwork, everyone rewarded accordingly, equity in job allocation.
2. Piece rates	Payment for effort and incentives offered (to increase output). The previous period is received and the rate adjusted.	
Straight piece rate	Payment of fixed sum per fixed unit. (Produced regardless of time taken).	Suitable: reducing unit cost increasing output through incentives, determining individual output easily and quickly. Unsuitable: no allowance made for unsuitable materials and tools, solving labour troubles as output rates vary.
Guaranteed day rates		Suitable: where the incentive scheme is affected by tutors outside the employer's control.
Differential piece rate	Ties a standard piece or time for doing a job, but there are two piece rates, a low rate for output standard and a high rate worker for production safe standard.	Suitable: regarding fast workers, attracting the best workers, penalizing the beginner or slow. Unsuitable: quality may fall to reach high outcome.
3. Bonus systems Premium bonus schemes	Allows for the payment of a day rate plus a proportion of the time saved when production is completed in a shorter time.	Suitable: sharing the gains from increased output between employer and employee. Employee protected against high rate fixing. Diminishing labour cost. Increasing hourly rate not in direct proportion to output to get the employer to improve methods and equipment.
Group bonus schemes	An incentive paid to a group for savings in cost or for output above an agreed minimum.	Suitable: encouraging team effort.

25.3 Overhead costs

Fixed	Variable	Semi-variable
Unchanged in the short-run, not related to activity:	Related to activity:	Part changed in the short run and part related to activity:
Depreciation Insurance Rates Rent Salaries	Compressed air Fuel Lubricants Power Royalties Spoilage	Clerical labour Cost of supervision Electricity Gas Telephone charges

Definitions

Allocation: The distribution of costs to cost centres when these costs are traceable to these entities.

Apportionment: The distribution of cost to cost centres when these costs were undertaken for the benefit of the business as a whole.

Absorption: This is the addition of overhead costs to prime or direct cost to arrive at the cost of production.

Cost centre: A cost centre is an entity to which costs can be attributed.

Cost unit: It is a unit of production.

25.4 Bases of apportionment

Base	Overhead costs
Floor area/volume	Building: Rent, insurance, rates, maintenance, depreciation, heating, lighting.
Cost or Book value	Depreciation: Plant, machinery, equipment.
Replacement value	Insurance: Plant, machinery, equipment.
Stores requisition	Cost of store keeping.
Number of employees or Direct labour hours	Cost of canteen, personnel department, administration.

Overhead Absorption Rate (OAR): This is the predetermined amount of overhead in a cost centre that is added to each cost unit passing through that cost centre.

The rate is calculated as follows:

$$\text{OAR} = \frac{\text{Predetermined overhead expenditure}}{\text{Budgeted (estimated) production or activity level}}$$

Bases	When appropriate
Machine hours	Capital intensive operations
Direct labour hours	Labour intensive operations
Direct wages	Production related to direct wages
Direct material cost	Production related to material cost
Units of output: Cost unit	One product produced and processed

Budgeted/estimated

	Mixing $	Baking $	Finishing $
Predetermined overhead expenditure	91 000	40 000	25 000
Base: Machine hours	Capital intensive 13 000	Capital intensive 5 000	—
Base: Labour hours	—	—	Labour intensive 8 000
Overhead absorption rate	$\dfrac{91\ 000}{13\ 000}$ = $7	$\dfrac{40\ 000}{5\ 000}$ = $8	$\dfrac{25\ 000}{8\ 000}$ = $3.125

Interpretation:

In the Mixing department, overhead is added to prime cost at the rate of $7 per machine hour.

In the Baking department, overhead is added to Prime Cost at the rate of $8 per machine hour.

In the Finishing department, overhead is added at the rate of $3.125 per direct labour hour.

25.5 Overhead absorption

Departments	Overhead absorption rate
Mixing	$7 per machine hour
Baking	$8 per machine hour
Finishing	$3.125 per direct labour hour

Direct materials cost per unit $7.50
Direct wages cost per hour $25

Departments	Production units	Direct Labour Hours per Unit	Machine Hours per Unit
Mixing	6000	2.5	4.0
Baking	5800	1.0	3.0
Finishing	5500	3.0	.5

Calculate for each department:

(a) The direct materials cost.   (b) The direct wages cost.   (c) The overhead absorbed.

(a) Direct materials cost:

      Mixing   6000 × 7.50 = $45 000

      Baking   5800 × 7.50 = $43 500

      Finishing 5500 × 7.50 = $41 250

(b) Direct wages cost:

      Mixing   6000 × 2.50 × 25 = $375 000

      Baking   5800 × 1.0 × 25 = $145 000

      Finishing 5500 × 3.0 × 25 = $412 500

(c) Overhead absorbed:

      Mixing   6000 × 4.0 × 7 = $168 000

      Baking   5800 × 3.0 × 8 = $139 200

      Finishing 5500 × .5 × 3.125 = $8593.75

25.6 Cost allocation, apportionment and absorption

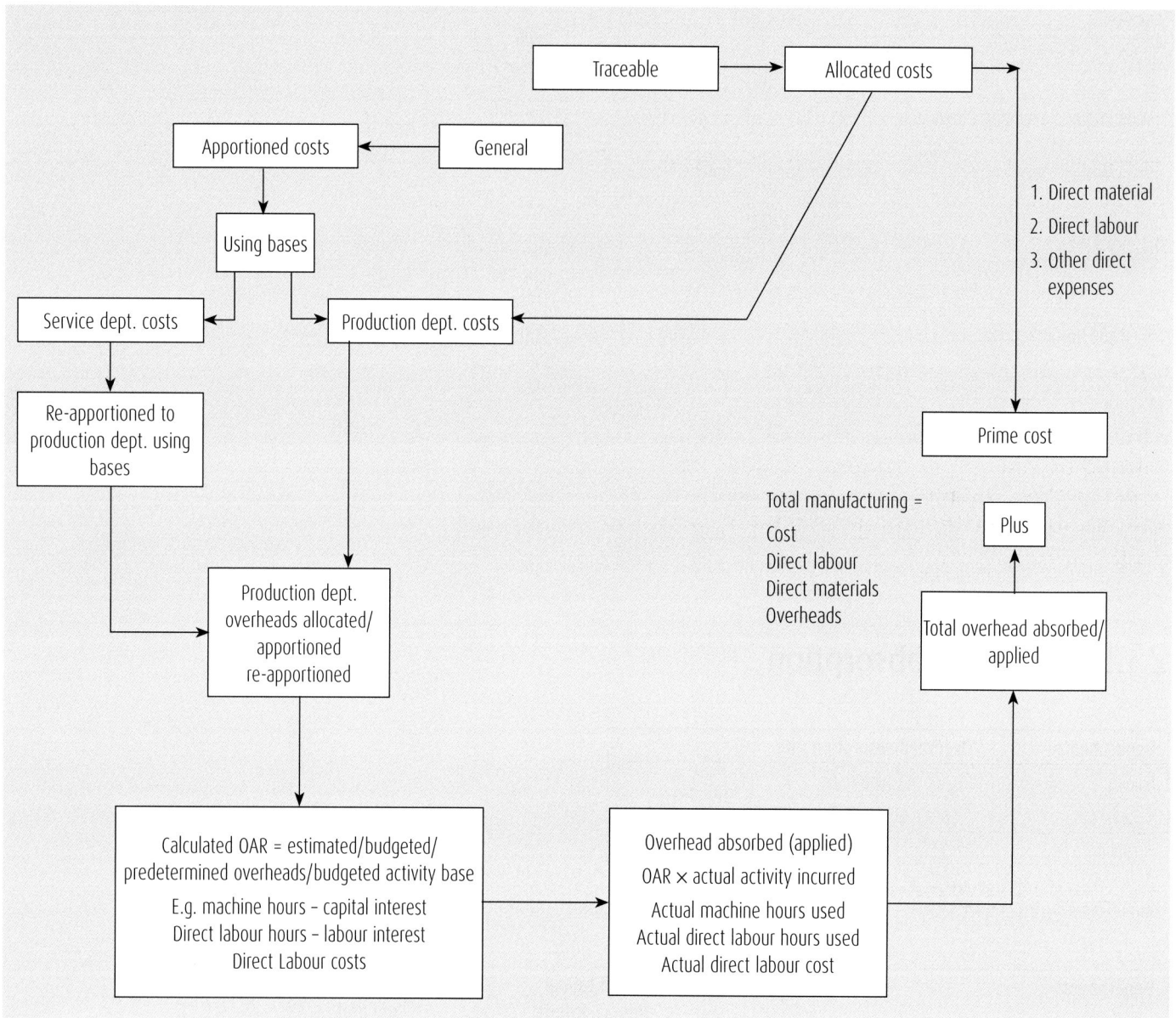

25.7 How to apportion overheads to cost centres

Cost centres

A **cost centre** is any location in a business to which costs may be attributed. A cost centre is usually a department or process, but may be an item of equipment (a machine) or even a person (e.g. a marketing manager). **Production cost centres** are directly involved in producing goods, for example moulding or shaping raw material, assembling components, painting, etc. **Service cost centres** are not involved in the production of goods, but provide services for the production cost centres, for example stores, building and plant maintenance, canteen, etc. The service costs are charged to operating departments by a process of reapportionment.

Some of the typical cost units used in service costing are:

Service	Cost units
Materials handling	Hours of service, volume handled
Transport	Miles travelled, tonne-mile, passenger mile
Medical institutions	Number of employees, hours worked, patient days, number of operations, cases handled
Electricity	Kilowatt hours used, capacity of machines
Hotels	Occupied bed-nights
Restaurants	Meals served
Colleges	Full time equivalent student
Airport services	Number of flights
Maintenance	Machine hours, total labour hours
Product planning and control	Services rendered, direct labour hours

The three methods of reapportionment of the service departments cost are the **Direct method**, the **Step down method (Elimination/step method)** and the **Reciprocal method (Repeated distribution method)**. The three methods differ in how they deal with service flows among other service departments

25.8 Direct method

The service cost is reapportioned to production **only** ignoring all other reciprocal services, determining **each** production department's share of that service.

Example 1

Allocated costs – to be charged directly to the appropriate cost centres

	Mixing	Baking	Finishing
Production materials	11 900	5 200	4 500
Direct labour	40 000	25 000	14 000
Indirect labour	13 500	4 000	2 500
	65 400	34 200	21 000

Apportioned costs – to be charged to the production departments as overhead using appropriate bases.

	Total	Bases	Mixing	Baking	Finishing
Insurance	6 000	Floor area (000m²)	10	9	11
Rent	9 000	Floor area (000m²)	10	9	11
Plant depreciation	8 000	Plant cost ($ 000)	26	8	6
Canteen	4 000	Personnel	650	250	100
Store keeping	7 500	Stores requisition	20	9	11
	34 500				

25.9 Direct allocation & apportionment analysis sheet

Example 2

Cost	Basis of change	Total $	Mixing $	Baking $	Finishing $
Direct materials	Allocation	21 600	11 900	5 200	4 500
Direct labour	Allocation	79 000	40 000	25 000	14 000
Indirect labour	Allocation	20 000	13 500	4 000	2 500
Total allocated costs		120 600	65 400	34 200	21 000
To be apportioned					
Insurance	Floor area	6 000	2 000	1 800	2 200
Rent	Floor area	9 000	3 000	2 700	3 300
Depreciation (plant)	Cost	8 000	5 200	1 600	1 200
Canteen	personnel	4 000	2 000	900	1 100
Store keeping	No. of requisition	7 500	4 875	1 875	750
Total apportionment		34 500	17 075	8 875	8 550
Total cost per department		$155 100	$82 475	$43 075	$29 550

25.10 Step down method (step method/elimination method)

This method uses a sequence of steps in the allocation of service departments to production departments. The service department providing the greatest service to the other departments is allocated first.

Apportionment of service cost centre overheads to production cost centres

The total cost of goods produced includes all overhead expenditure, including the overheads of service departments; these must be apportioned to the production departments on suitable bases. The bases usually adopted are:

Service cost centre	Apportioned on
Stores	number or value of stores requisitions raised by production cost centre
Canteen	number of persons in each production cost centre
Building maintenance	area occupied by each production cost centre*
Plant and machinery maintenance	number or value of machines in each cost centre*

*However, records of actual maintenance costs may be kept and the costs allocated accordingly.

There are a number of ways of apportioning service cost centre overheads to production cost centres and they all usually produce very similar results. The simplest, and quickest, way is the step down method.

Example of step down

Sammy Company has three service departments and two operating departments. The costs and other data relating to the departments are as follows:

	Service Departments		Operating Departments		
	Janitorial	Canteen	Engineering	Assembly	Finishing
Overhead costs	$80 000	$60 000	$90 000	$300 000	$400 000
Square feet	1 000	2 000	1 500	4 000	2 000
Number of employees	20	15	60	300	500

Janitorial costs are allocated on the basis of square feet. The Cafeteria and Engineering costs are allocated on the basis of the number of employees.

Note. The company makes no distinction between variable and fixed service departments.

Required

Allocate service department costs to the operating departments using the step method (Sammy allocates service department costs in the following order: Janitorial, Cafeteria, then Engineering).

Answer

	Service Departments		Operating Departments		
	Janitorial	Canteen	Engineering	Assembly	Finishing
	$80 000	$60 000	$90 000	$300 000	$400 000
Allocations:					
Janitorial (W1)	(80 000)	16 840	12 360	33 680	16 840
Cafeteria (W2)		(76 840)	5 361	26 805	44 675
Engineering (W3)	——	——	(107 991)	40 497	67 495
Total	– 0 –	– 0 –	– 0 –	400 982	529 010

(W1) $\dfrac{\text{Janitorial cost}}{\text{Total square feet}} = \dfrac{80\ 000}{9\ 500} = \$8.42 \text{ per square feet}$

(W2) $\dfrac{\text{Cafeteria cost}}{\text{Number of employees}} = \dfrac{76\ 840}{800}$ (60 000 + 16 840) = $89.35 per employee

(W3) $\dfrac{\text{Engineering cost}}{\text{Number of employees}} = \dfrac{107\ 991}{800}$ (90 000 + 12 630 + 5 361) = $134.99 per employee

25.11 Reciprocal method (repeated distribution)

This method takes into account **all** the flows (forward and backward) between service departments.

Example 3

Reciprocal or continuous allotment

	Production departments			Service departments	
	Mixing	Baking	Finishing	Repairs	Canteen
	$	$	$	$	$
Costs	70 000	36 500	19 100	10 000	7 000
First apportionment (Canteen)	2 800	2 100	1 575	525	(7 000)
				10 525	–
Second apportionment (Repairs)	4 953	2 477	1 238	(10 525)	1 857
				–	
Third apportionment (Canteen)	743	557	418	139	(1857)
				139	–
Fourth apportionment (Repairs)	65	33	16	139	25
Fifth apportionment (Canteen)	10	8	5	2 2	5
	75 571	41 675	22 352	–	–

It is assumed that the service departments provide reciprocal services for each other.

25.12 Allocation and apportionment of costs Production & service departments

Example 4

Cost allocation

	Production departments			Service departments	
	Mixing	Baking	Finishing	Repairs	Canteen
Direct materials	11 900	4 600	3 500	–	–
Direct labour	40 000	25 000	14 000	–	–
Indirect labour	13 500	4 400	1 500	9 500	4 600
Indirect materials	4 600	2 500	100	500	2 400
	70 000	36 500	19 100	10 000	7 000

Apportionment of service department costs

Departments	Bases	
	Floor Area (000 m^2)	No. of Meals
Mixing	40	800
Baking	20	600
Packing	10	450
Repairs	15	150
Canteen	15	–

25.13 Elimination method

Example 5

	Mixing $	Baking $	Finishing $	Repairs $	Canteen $
	Production departments			Service departments	
Costs	70 000	36 500	17 100	10 000	7 000
First apportionment (Canteen) Meals	2 800	2 100	1 575	525	(7 000)
				10 525	
Second apportionment (Repairs)	6 014	3 007	1 504	(10 525)	–
	78 814	41 607	22 179	–	–

Assumption: The services provided by the repairs department and the canteen are not reciprocal.

25.14 Other bases for calculating OARs

The following bases for calculating overhead absorption rates are generally unsatisfactory, for the reasons stated, and are seldom used.

Direct material cost Overhead absorption is not related to the cost of material. A product which is made of expensive material would be charged with a greater share of overheads than one which is made of cheap material but which requires the same time to make.

Direct labour cost The labour cost incurred in making a product depends partly on the rate paid to the workers engaged on making it. A product made by highly skilled workers would be charged with a greater share of overheads than one which is made by unskilled workers but which takes the same time to make.

Prime cost This method combines the disadvantages of the direct material cost and the direct labour cost.

Cost unit This method is restricted to the production of one type of good which is made by a common process.

25.15 Under/over-absorption of overheads

As explained above, overhead absorption rates are calculated on planned levels of production and budgeted overhead expenditure. It is most likely that the actual volume of goods produced and the actual overhead expenditure will turn out to differ from the forecasts. The result will be that overhead expenditure will be either under absorbed or over absorbed.

Under-absorption occurs when actual expenditure is more than budget and/or production is less than the planned level.

Over-absorption occurs when actual expenditure is less than budget and/or actual production is more than the planned level.

Example

A company calculated its overhead absorption rates for the six months to 30 June and the next six months to 31 December as follows.

	6 months to 30 June	6 months to 31 December
Budgeted overhead expenditure	$200 000	$240 000
Planned production in units	80 000	100 000
Actual results were: expenditure	$215 000	$230 000
goods produced	76 000	106 000
OAR	$\dfrac{\$200\ 000}{80\ 000} = \$2.50$	$\dfrac{\$240\ 000}{100\ 000} = \$2.40$
Overhead recovered	76 000 × $2.50 $190 000	106 000 × $2.40 $254 400
(Under-)/Over-absorption	$(215 000 – 190 000) ($25 000)	(230 000 – 254 400) $24 400

Exercise 1

Upandown Ltd has provided the following information about its overhead expenditure for four quarterly periods ended 31 December.

	3 months to 31 March	3 months to 30 June	3 months to 30 September	3 months to 31 December
Budgeted overhead	$124 000	$128 000	$130 000	$131 000
Planned productions (units)	1 000	1 000	1 000	1 000
Actual overhead	$128 000	$125 000	$129 500	$132 800
Actual output (units)	900	1 050	1 100	980

Required

Calculate the under-absorption or over-absorption of overhead in each of the four quarterly periods. State clearly in each case whether the overhead was under- or over-absorbed.

25.16 Cost behaviour illustrated in graphs

In all of the graphs illustrated the horizontal axis represents different levels of activity, and the vertical axis represents total cost.

Fixed costs

Figure 1 shows fixed cost at various levels of output. It is in the form of a horizontal straight line, indicating that total fixed cost is the same throughout all levels of output plotted on that graph.

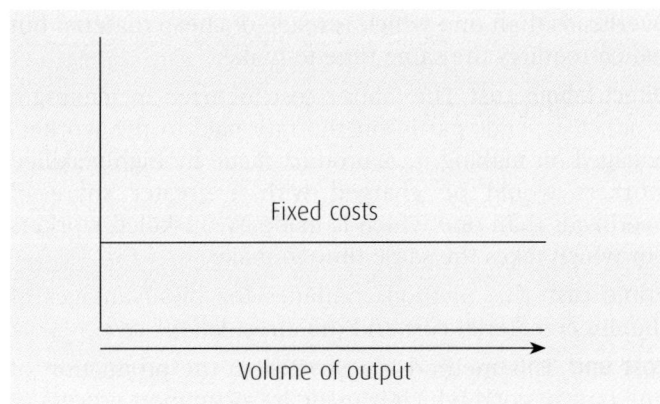

Figure 1. Cost behaviour pattern: Fixed costs

Variable costs

Figure 2 shows that the total variable cost increases in a straight line as output increases, i.e. the cost is completely variable in the sense that there is a direct relationship between increases output and increases in cost.

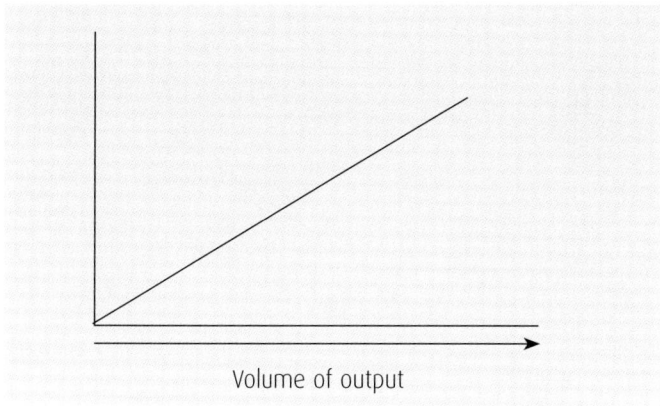

Figure 2. Cost behaviour pattern: Variable costs

Variable cost of raw materials

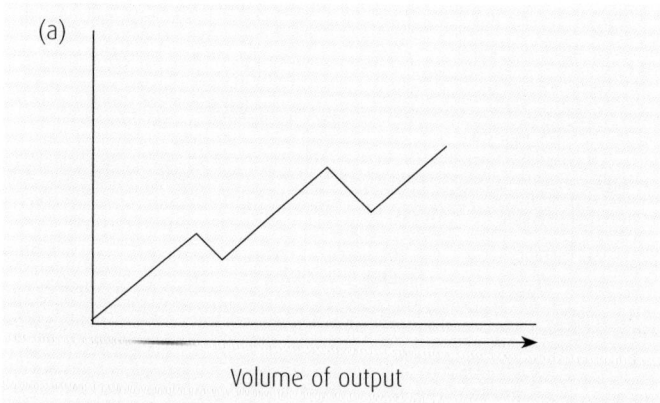

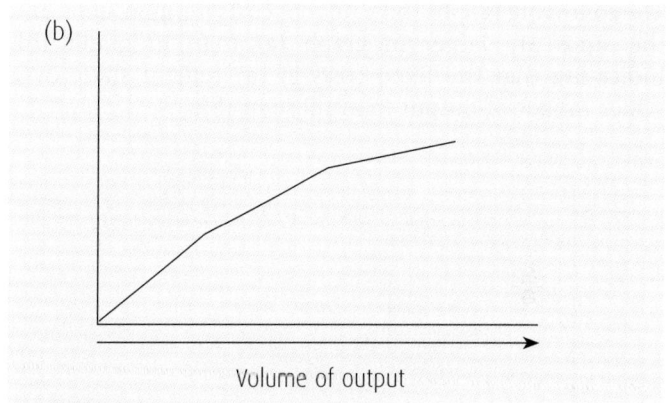

Figure 3. Cost behaviour patterns: change in variable cost at discrete levels of output

Cost of direct labour

Figure 4 illustrates the behaviour of costs relative to the method of remuneration.

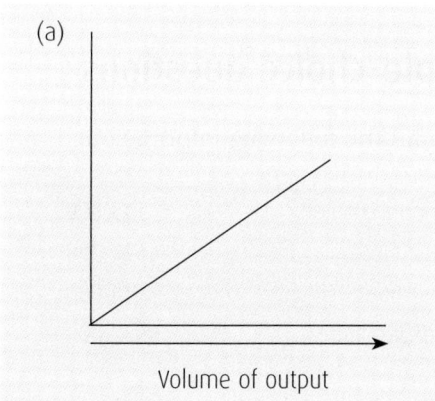

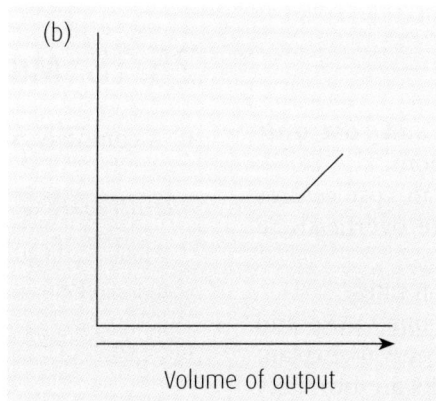

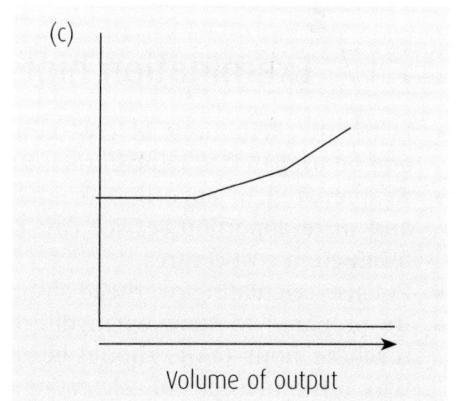

Figure 4. Cost behaviour patterns: labour

Semi-variable cost (Semi-fixed or mixed cost)

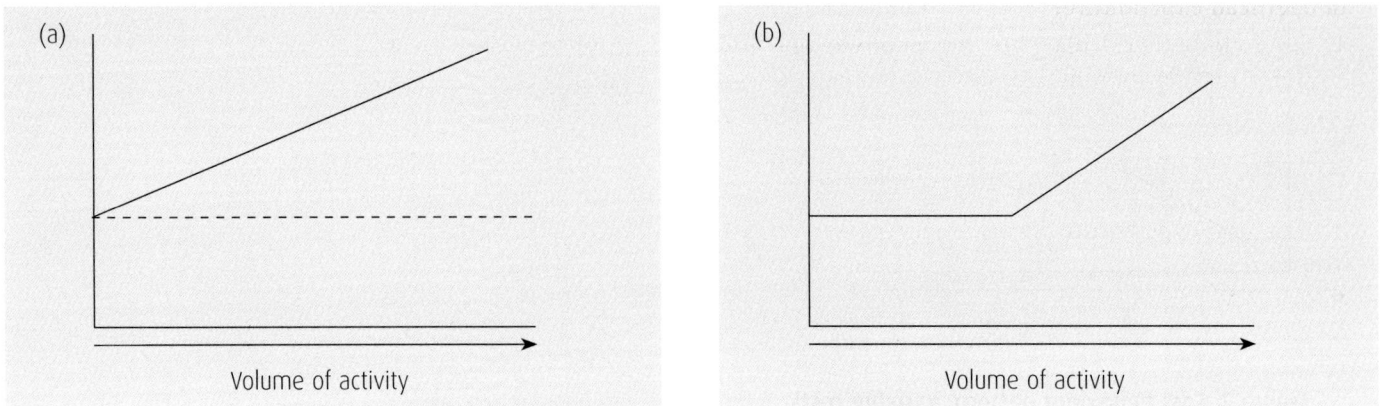

Figure 5. Cost behaviour pattern: semi-variable costs

Step costs

The following graphs indicate that costs jump in steps, but the steps are larger in graph (a) than in graph (b), indicating that the fixed costs in (a) remain static over wider ranges of output than those in (b).

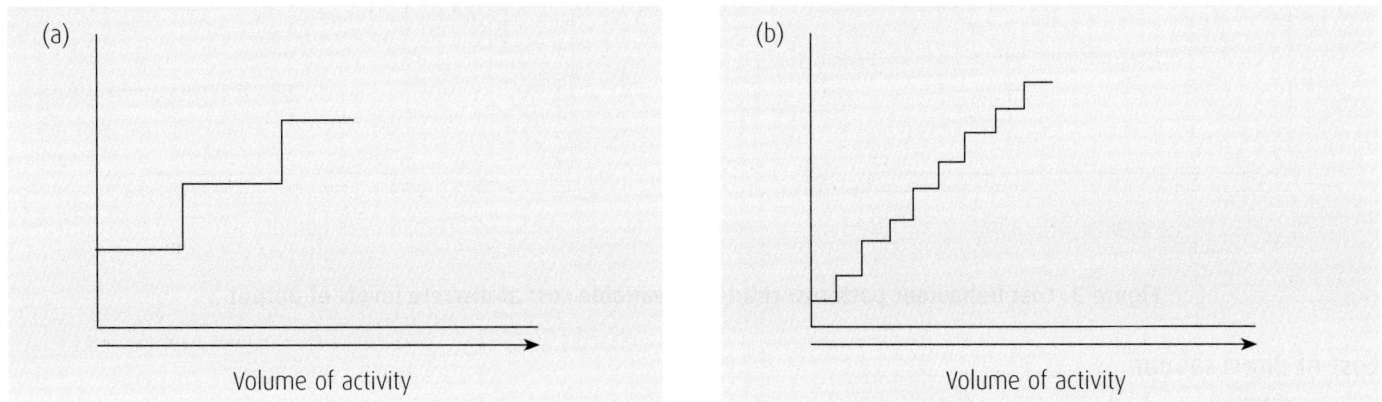

Figure 6. Cost behaviour pattern: step costs

25.17 Examination hints

- Learn the definitions of **cost centre** and **cost unit** and be prepared to explain their functions.
- Be prepared to apportion overheads to cost centres and to re-apportion service cost centre overheads to production cost centres.
- Practise calculating overhead absorption rates.
- Be prepared to state when direct labour OARs and machine hour OARs should be used and to explain why other methods of calculating OARs are normally unsuitable.
- Learn how to calculate under-absorption and over-absorption of overheads.
- Check all calculations carefully; arithmetical mistakes cost marks.
- Make sure you understand the causes of under-absorption and over-absorption. This is a weak spot for many candidates in examinations.

25.18 Multiple-choice questions

1 A company provides the following information:

Actual direct labour hours worked	13 000
Actual overhead expenditure	$520 000
Budgeted direct labour hours	14 000
Budgeted overhead expenditure	$532 000

What is the overhead absorption rate based on direct labour hours?

A $37.14
B $38
C $40
D $40.42

2 Which of the following could cause an under-absorption of overhead expenditure?

1. absorption rate calculated on actual production and actual number of units produced

2. units produced exceeding the budgeted production

3. units produced being less than the planned production

4. overhead expenditure exceeding budget

A 1 and 2
B 1 and 3
C 2 and 4
D 3 and 4

3 The following information is provided by a company.

Actual direct labour hours	12 400
Actual overhead expenditure	$198 400
Budgeted direct labour hours	11 000
Budgeted overhead expenditure	$170 500

Which of the following correctly describes the overhead absorbed?

	Under-absorbed	Over-absorbed
A	$6 200	
B		$6 200
C	$21 700	
D		$21 700

25.19 Additional exercises

1 (a) Explain the following terms:

(i) Cost Centre

(ii) Cost Unit

(b) Julie and Cleary Ltd manufactures toy soldiers. The company has three production departments – Moulding, Sanding and Painting – and two service departments – Canteen and Maintenance. Estimated indirect overheads for the year ended 30 April 2002 are as follows:

Overhead	Cost or Calculation	Basis of Apportionment or Allocation
Administration	$104 000	Number of employees
Electricity	$70 000	Kilowatt hours used
Depreciation	10%	Cost of Fixed Asset
Indirect wages	$360 000	Allocated
Rent	$80 500	Floor area (square metres)

Relevant information on the five departments is as follows:

	Moulding	Sanding	Painting	Canteen	Maintenance
No. of employees	40	50	40	38	40
Power (kW hours)	1400	1600	150	160	190
Cost of Fixed Asset	$162 000	$175 000	$40 000	$43 000	$80 000
Floor area (sq m)	625	475	500	300	400
Indirect wages	$6 000	$11 250	$6 375	$18 750	$36 190
Direct Labour hours	8 000	7 800	7 500		
Direct Machine hours	7 750	5 625	1 250		

Canteen costs are shared among all the other departments on the basis of number of employees. Maintenance costs are shared among the three production departments on the basis of floor area.

(i) Prepare an overhead analysis sheet for the year ending 30 April 2002 detailing the total overheads for Moulding, Sanding and Painting.

(ii) Moulding and Sanding department overhead rates are calculated on a Direct Machine hour basis. Painting department overhead rate is calculated on a Direct Labour hour basis. Calculate the Overhead absorption rate for each of the three production departments for the year ending 30 April 2002. Calculations should be shown to two decimal places.

(UCLES, 2001, A/AS Level Accounting, Syllabus 8706/2, May/June)

2 Auckland (Manufacturers) Ltd has two manufacturing departments: (i) Machining and (ii) Assembly. It also has two service departments: (i) Maintenance and (ii) Power house. The information in the table below is available for the coming year.

Required

(a) Analyse the above indirect costs between the four departments showing the bases of apportionment you have used.

(b) Re-apportion the costs of the service departments over the two production departments using appropriate bases.

(c) Calculate an overhead absorption rate for the machining department based on machine hours and an overhead absorption rate for the assembly department based on direct labour hours.

3 (a) Define the term 'overhead expenses'.

(b) Explain the meaning of the following terms as they relate to overhead expenditure:
  (i) allocation
  (ii) apportionment.

(c) Explain the meaning of the terms:
  (i) overhead absorption
  (ii) overhead under-absorption
  (iii) overhead over-absorption.

(d) State reasons why a company might recover more in overheads than the amount spent on overheads in the period.

(e) Explain why estimated figures are used to calculate overhead absorption rates.

	Machining	Assembly	Maintenance	Power house	Total
	$000	$000	$000	$000	$000
Indirect materials	298	482	132	152	1064
Indirect labour	706	918	282	672	2578
Rent and local taxes					1426
Supervision					660
Plant depreciation					1650
					7378

Further information is available as follows:

	Machining	Assembly	Maintenance	Power house
No. of employees	40	80	20	10
Area (metres²)	3 000	5000	1000	200
Plant valuation ($000s)	13 000	5000	2400	1600
Direct labour hours	3 200	4800		
Machine hours	11 080	2320		
Maintenance hours	1 800	600		
Units of power used	4 200	1200	600	

26 Absorption costing (total costing) and marginal costing (variable costing)

Objectives
- state the purpose and nature of total (absorption) costing
- define marginal cost and how it is used
- explain how variable costing differs from absorption costing and compute the unit product cost under each method
- explain the process for dealing with fixed manufacturing overheads and inventory in total costing
- prepare income statements using variable and absorption costing, and reconcile the two income figures
- state the advantages of each method

26.1 The purpose and nature of total (absorption) costing

Cost accounting is one of the management tools included in a number of systems of accounting known as **management accounting**. Management accounting provides management with information which is not obtainable from the financial accounts of a business. Consider the following example.

Makeit & Co.
Manufacturing Account for the year ended
30 June 2004

		$000	$000
Direct materials	Stock at 1 July 2003	10	
	Purchases	140	
	Carriage inwards	24	
		174	
Less	Stock at 30 June 2004	18	156
Direct labour			222
Direct expenses			46
Prime cost			424
Indirect materials		45	
Indirect labour		72	
Rent of factory		100	
Heating, lighting and power		45	
Depreciation:	factory	20	
	machinery	36	318
			742
Work in progress 1 July 2003		38	
Work in progress 30 June 2004		(20)	18
Factory cost of finished goods			760

This manufacturing account has been prepared as part of the company's financial accounting system. It provides us with information about prime cost, overheads and the cost of producing goods. If only one type of good has been produced, the unit cost can easily be found by dividing the factory cost by the number of units produced. The selling price for the good is fixed by adding the required amount of profit per unit. So far, so good, but it does not go far enough to help management make important decisions.

Assuming that Makeit & Co. manufactures only one type of product and that the output for the year was 1000 units of that product, each unit has cost $760. If the managers want to find the cost of producing 1001 units, the answer will not be $760\,000 \times \frac{1001}{1000} = \$760\,760$, that is $(760\,000 + 760)$. The additional unit will not result in additional costs of $760 because not all costs (rent and depreciation, for example) will be affected by the addition of one unit of output; they are fixed costs, which do not vary with the number of units produced. The effect on costs of increasing numbers of units produced is covered in chapter 33 on marginal costing.

The problem is even more complicated if Makeit & Co. manufactures more than one type of product, and each type requires different types and quantities of materials, different numbers of labour hours and different processes. Management must know how much it costs to make a single unit of each product if they are to fix selling prices. This problem is considered now.

26.2 Marginal cost

We have seen how total costing can be used to determine price and profit but, beyond that, its uses are limited. For many management decisions it is necessary to know the **marginal cost** of a unit of production (variable unit cost of production). Marginal cost can be described as the cost of making one extra unit of an item. It is based on the principle that an additional unit of production will only entail an increase in the variable costs and that the fixed costs will not be affected. **Marginal cost of production** is the total of the variable costs of manufacture.

26.3 Comparison of classification of cost per unit of product

Absorption costing method	Variable costing method
Direct materials	Direct materials
Direct labour	Direct labour
Variable manufacturing overheads	Variable manufacturing overheads
Fixed manufacturing overheads	

The absorption costing allocates a part of the fixed manufacturing costs to each unit of product along with the variable manufacturing costs. These costs are called **product costs**.

Fixed manufacturing overheads are not treated as a product cost in variable costing. It is treated as a **period cost** and charged as an expense in the income statement. Therefore, the cost of unit of product in inventory (cost of goods sold) contains no element of fixed overhead cost.

Format for the calculation of unit product cost for absorption costing and variable costing.

Absorption costing	
Direct materials	X
Direct labour	X
Variable manufacturing overheads	X
Fixed manufacturing overheads	X
Unit product cost	X
Variable costing	
Direct materials	X
Direct labour	X
Variable manufacturing overheads	X
Unit product cost	X

Example

The cost of producing 1000 units of a good are shown in the table on this page (with the unit cost shown in the second column).

The marginal cost of production for 1000 units is $150\,000 (or $150 for a single unit). The difference between the total cost of production (i.e. including fixed overheads) and the selling price gives the profit of $40\,000 (or $40 per unit – not shown). Fixed overheads + profit = $90\,000, or $90 per unit. This is called the **contribution** because it is the contribution that each unit of production makes towards covering the overheads and providing a profit. The contribution per unit is calculated as follows: selling price per unit less the total of the variable costs per unit or SP – VC (per unit).

	Cost for 1000 units $	Cost per unit $
Variable costs		
Direct material	30 000	30
Direct labour	100 000	100
Direct expenses	5 000	5
Prime cost	135 000	135
Variable overheads	15 000	15
Marginal cost of production	150 000	150
Fixed overheads	50 000	
Total cost of production	200 000	
Profit (20% of total cost)	40 000	
Contribution		90
Selling price	240 000	240

The cost of making 1001 units will be $(240 000 + 150) = $240 150, not $240 240 as it might seem if we only had a total cost statement.

The ratio of the contribution to the selling price is known as the **C/S ratio**. In this example the C/S ratio is $\frac{90}{240} \times 100 = 37.5\%$. This is a very useful ratio that can be used to calculate the answers to many problems. The use of the C/S ratio can avoid the need to spend valuable time calculating marginal cost.

Answer

	$
Variable costs	
Absorption costing	
Direct materials	30
Direct labour	100
Direct expenses	5
Variable manufacturing overheads	15
Total variable product cost	150
Fixed manufacturing overheads (40 000 ÷ 1000)	40
Unit product cost	190
Variable costing	
Direct materials	30
Direct labour	100
Direct expenses	5
Variable manufacturing overheads	15
Unit product cost	150

Example

Idley provided the following information	
Units in beginning inventory	NIL
Units produced	10 000
Units sold	8 000
Units in ending inventory	2 000
Selling price per unit	$50
Unit product cost:	
Direct material	$20
Direct labour	$10
Variable manufacturing overheads	$5
Selling and administrative expenses:	
Variable expenses per unit	$5
Fixed selling and administrative	$10 000
Fixed manufacturing overheads	$30 000

Required

(a) Calculate total unit product cost for each method.
(b) Prepare income statements for each method (showing calculations for closing inventory and net income).

Solution

(a) Calculation of total unit product.

	Absorption Costing	Variable Costing
	$	$
Direct materials	20	20
Direct labour	10	10
Variable manufacturing expenses	5	5
Fixed manufacturing cost		
(30 000 ÷ 10 000)	3	–
Unit product cost	38	35

(b)

IDLEY
Income Statement
(Absorption Costing)

	$	$
Sales (8 000 × $50)		400 000
Less cost of goods sold		
Opening inventory	0	
Add cost of goods manufactured		
(10 000 × $38)	380 000	
Goods available for sale	380 000	
Less ending inventory		
(2 000 × $38)	76 000	
Cost of goods sold		304 000
Gross margin		96 000
Less selling and administrative expenses:		
Variable (8 000 × $5)	40 000	
Fixed manufacturing overheads	10 000	50 000
Net income		46 000

IDLEY
Income Statement
(Variable Costing)

	$	$
Sales (8 000 × $50)		400 000
Less variable cost of goods sold		
Opening inventory	0	
Add variable manufacturing cost		
(10 000 × $35)	350 000	
Goods available for sale	350 000	
Less ending inventory		
(2 000 × $35)	70 000	
Variable cost of goods sold	280 000	
Variable selling and administrative expenses:		
(8 000 × $5)	40 000	320 000
Contribution margin		80 000
Less fixed expenses:		
Fixed manufacturing overheads	30 000	
Fixed selling and administrative expenses	10 000	40 000
Net income		40 000

	$
Variable costing income	40 000
Add fixed manufacturing overheads	
cost c/f in inventory under absorption	
costing (2000 × $3)	6 000
Absorption costing net income	46 000

26.5 Advantages of each method

Variable	Absorption
Suitable for cost volume analysis	Adheres to Generally Accepted Accounting Policies (GAAP)
Changes in inventories does not affect net income	Good for financial reporting
Fixed costs are identified	Useful for the preparation of income taxes
Profitability can be easily estimated	
Good for variance analysis and flexible budgets	

26.6 Questions

1 Zoey operations for 2005 are as follows:

Units produced	80 000
Units sold	60 000
Units in ending inventory	20 000
Selling price per unit	$150
Variable costs per unit:	
Direct materials	$ 40
Direct labour	$ 30
Direct expenses	$ 10
Variable manufacturing overhead	$ 8
Variable and administrative expenses	$ 8
Fixed costs:	
Fixed manufacturing overhead	$ 160 000
Fixed selling and administrative	$ 40 000

26.4 Income comparison of absorption costing and the handling of fixed manufacturing cost in inventory

In the absorption costing method, all productions are variable and fixed whereas under the variable costing method only variable production costs are included, thus causing the ending inventory to be different.

When we examine IDLEY's absorption costing income statements, of the $30 000 in the fixed manufacturing overhead cost incurred during the period only $24 000 (8000 units sold × $3) has been included in the cost of goods sold. The remaining $6000 (2000 not sold × $3) has been deferred as inventory to the next accounting period.

Under variable costing, the entire $30 000 in fixed manufacturing overhead cost has been treated as an expense of the current period.

The inventory figure under variable is $6000 lower than absorption costing thus causing the absorption costing income to be $6000 higher.

The variable costing statement classifies costs by behaviour whereas the absorption costing statement makes no distinction between fixed and variable costs.
To check the reconciliation of the net incomes using the two methods for Idley:

Required

Using the two methods:
(a) Compute the unit product cost
(b) Determine the value of the ending inventory
(c) Prepare the income statements
(d) Reconcile the net incomes

Answer

(a) Unit Product Cost

Absorption	$
Direct materials	40
Direct labour	30
Direct expenses	10
Variable manufacturing overheads	8
Total variable product cost	88
Fixed manufacturing overhead	
(160 000 ÷ 80 000)	2
Unit product cost	90

Variable	$
Direct materials	40
Direct labour	30
Direct expenses	10
Variable manufacturing overheads	8
Total variable product cost	88

(b)

Ending Inventory

    Absorption   20 000 × $90 = $1800 000

    Variable   20 000 × $88 = $1760 000

(c)

Income statement

Absorption costing

	$	$
Sales (60 000 × $150)		9000 000
Less cost of goods sold:		
Opening inventory	0	
Add cost of goods manufactured		
(80000 × $90)	7200 000	
Goods available for sale	7200 000	
Less ending inventory	1800 000	5400 000
Gross margin		3600 000
Less selling and administrative expenses:		
Variable (60 000 × $8)	480 000	
Fixed	40 000	520 000
Net income		3080 000

Variable costing

	$	$
Sales (60 000 × $150)		9000 000
Less variable expenses		
Variable cost of goods sold:		
Opening inventory	0	
Add variable manufacturing costs		
(80 000 × $88)	7040 000	
Goods available for sale	7040 000	
Less ending inventory	1760 000	
Variable cost of goods sold	5280 000	
Variable selling and administrative		
(60 000 × $8)	480 000	5760 000
		3240 000
Less fixed expenses:		
Fixed manufacturing overhead	160 000	
Fixed selling and administrative	40 000	200 000
Net income		3040 000

(d) Reconcile the net income

	$
Variable costing net income	3040 000
Add fixed manufacturing overhead cost c/f	
in inventory under absorption costing (20000 × $2)	40 000
Absorption costing net income	3080 000

2 Brasen Company manufactures a single product and has the following costs:

Variable cost per unit:	
Direct materials	$8
Direct labour	$12
Variable manufacturing overhead	$4
Variable selling and administrative expense	$3
Fixed manufacturing overhead	$150 000
Fixed selling and administrative expenses	$50 000

The company produces 25 000 units each month.

Required

(a) Calculate unit product cost using absorption costing
(b) Calculate unit product cost using variable costing
(c) Calculate the net incomes for each method using the information as follows:

    Beginning inventory   0

    Units sold   20 000 units

    Unit selling price $40

(d) Reconcile net incomes for the two methods.

Module Two
Costing Systems

27 Job costing

Objectives
- describe the features of job costing
- identify the elements of costs associated with job costing
- explain the flow of costs in a job costing system
- complete job cost sheets for job costing
- apply predetermined overhead rates to a job costing system
- calculate and treat over and under absorption of overheads

27.1 Costing

Cost accounting includes the collection, measuring and reporting of the costs of a product. The product may be an item or batch of anything produced, a job performed or a service provided.

A costing system is the method used in identifying, collecting and presenting the costs associated with manufacturing the product, performing the job or providing the service.

Although many types of product costing practices may exist, there are two common systems of product costing which are most prevalent:

1. Job order costing,
2. Process costing.

27.2 Job order costing

Job order costing is a system of allocating costs to a particular job or batch of products. An example of a job would be building a 1000 gallon water tank or manufacturing 100 identical desks for a school (batch).

27.3 Features of job costing or batch costing

1. Job costing is used when the finished product is separate and readily identifiable as a unit or as batches.

2. The key elements of costs collected are direct material, direct labour and manufacturing overheads.

3. The source documents used are material requisition forms, labour time tickets or time cards and predetermined overhead rates.

4. The summary of job costs is collected in a job cost sheet.

5. Job costing flows through a series of accounts: From manufacturing costs – work in process inventory – finished goods inventory – cost of goods sold inventory.

27.4 Elements of costs

Job order costing for a manufacturing concern, categorizes cost into direct material, direct labour and manufacturing overheads. These categories of costs are incurred as the physical elements of these costs are converted into the finished products.

For accounting purposes these costs are accumulated into

1. the raw materials inventory account

2. the direct labour account

3. the manufacturing overheads account.

Example

(1)

Raw materials inventory

Balance b/f	300	Material used	3 500
Material purchases	3 700	Balance c/f	500
	4 000		4 000
Bal c/d	500		

(2)

Direct labour

Direct labour	8 000	Factory labour used	8 000

(3)

Manufacturing overheads

Factory supplies	400	Overheads applied	3 000
Indirect labour	700		
Power/Rates/Depreciation	1 200		
	2 300		
Over applied	700		
	3 000		3 000

Costs are then transferred to the Work In Process Inventory as depicted by the journal entry:

Work in process inventory	Dr. 14 500
Raw material inventory	Cr. 3 500
Direct labour	Cr. 8 000
Manufacturing overheads	Cr. 3 000

(4)

Work in process inventory

Direct material	3 500	Completed	14 100
Direct labour	8 000	Unfinished	400
Factory overheads	3 000		
	14 500		14 500

From the work in process inventory, job costs are then transferred on completion to the finished goods inventory, and finally to the cost of goods sold inventory when the product or batch of goods is sold.

(5)

Finished goods inventory

Work in process	14 100	Cost of goods sold	13 800

Cost of goods sold

Finished goods	13 800	

27.5 Job cost flow

A job cost flow chart follows the movement of costs through different stages of production. It depicts the accumulation of costs as

1. raw materials are purchased,
2. factor labour costs are incurred and
3. manufacturing overheads are incurred.

As shown above these costs are then assigned to

4. the Work in process inventory
5. the Finished goods inventory and finally,
6. to the Cost of goods sold account.

27.6 Job cost sheet

The job cost sheet or job cost record is a form used to record all the costs associated with a particular job, product, batch of products or service. It summarizes the costs information derived from the source documents, i.e. material requisition forms for direct material costs; labour time ticket or time card for the time and direct labour costs for each job, and predetermined overhead rates for manufacturing overhead costs.

Job cost sheet

Job No. 41
Item: wooden desks
For: Ace Summer School

Quantity   50
Date started: Jan 5
Date completed: Jan 31

Date	Direct Material $	Direct Labour $	Manufacturing Overhead $
Jan. 4	3 500		
Jan. 8		4 000	
Jan. 14		4 000	
Jan. 21			3 000
	3 500	8 000	3 000

Cost of completed Job: $

Direct materials   3 500

Direct labour   8 000

Manufacturing overheads   3 000

Total cost   14 500

Unit cost $14 500 ÷ 50 = $290

Calculation of Prime Cost and Factory Cost

DM + DL = PC

27.7 Predetermined overhead rates

A predetermined overhead rate is an accounting method used to allocate portions of total manufacturing overhead costs of a department to the products which created costs while being processed in the department. The formula for predetermined overhead rate is

Estimated annual overhead costs ÷ estimated level of activities.

The estimated figures are calculated at the beginning of the period based on the figures of previous years. The level of activity is usually stated in terms of unit drivers which will provide an equitable basis for applying overheads to products or jobs. The most frequently used units are

1. direct labour hours;

2. direct machine hours;

3. direct labour costs.

These units are referred to as cost drivers. Thus if it is estimated that the department will incur overhead costs for the year of $24 000 and products serviced by the department will use an estimated 16 000 hours of machine time for the year, the predetermined overhead rate will be $24 000 ÷ 16 000 = $1.50 per machine hour.

Assuming that for this particular job (No. 41) 2000 machine hours were used, then the overhead costs assigned to this job will be 2000 × $1.50 = $3000 as manufacturing overhead cost.

27.8 Over- and under-absorption of overheads

A predetermined overhead rate is an *estimated* figure calculated at the beginning of the year based on

1. an *estimated* overhead cost figure for the year, e.g. $24 000 and

2. an *estimated* level of activity of e.g. 16 000 machine hours.

The estimated predetermined overhead rate is thus $1.50. It is highly unlikely that at the end of the year, the actual overhead costs will be equal to the estimated cost of $24 000, it may be more or less. Similarly the actual machine hours used by the end of the year will be either more than or less than 16 000 hours.

Suppose the actual overheads absorbed were $26 000 for the year and 16 200 machine hours were used. Then applying the rate of $1.50 per machine hour calculated earlier to the 16 200 machine hours (16 200 × $1.50) means that $24 300 worth of overheads were absorbed into production instead of $26 000. Thus there was an *under-absorption* of $1 700 i.e. ($26 000 – $24 300).

If on the other hand the **actual** overhead costs at the end of the year were $23,000, and 16 100 machine hours were used, the amount of overheads absorbed would be (16 100 × $1.50) $24 150. This means that there was an over-absorption of $1,150 (i.e. $24 150 – $23 000) into production.

An over- or under-absorption of overheads occurs when the **actual** figures for overhead costs and level of activities are different from the estimated figures used at the beginning of the year.

27.9 Treatment of under- or over-absorption

Prime costs (Direct Material plus Direct Labour) as well as manufacturing overhead costs will influence the net income of the firm. It is the **actual** costs and not estimated costs which determine an accurate total production cost of the enterprise. Thus adjustment must be made to include an over- or under-absorption of manufacturing overheads in the process.

If there is an under-absorption of $200 for example, it should be added to the production cost at the end of the year:

Actual Direct Material		Actual Direct Labour		Actual Prime Cost		Absorbed Overheads		Under Absorption		Total Costs of Production
$3500	+	$8000	=	$11 500	+	$3000	+	$200	=	$14 700

On the other hand, if there is an over-absorption of $150 for example, it would be deducted from production cost at the end of the year:

								(over absorption)		
$3500	+	$8000	=	$11 500	+	$3000	–	$150	=	$14 350

27.10 Questions

1 A costing system in which costs are applied to each batch of custom-produced goods is

 A process costing system

 B activity based costing system

 C job order costing system

 D overhead absorption costing system.

2 The objective of job order costing is

 A to compute the cost per job

 B to accumulate costs for a period of time

 C to order raw material for a specific job

 D to compute the final overhead cost per job.

3 The flow of costs in a job order costing system is

 A work in process inventory → manufacturing costs → cost of goods sold → finished goods inventory

 B work in process inventory → finished goods inventory → manufacturing cost → cost of goods sold

C manufacturing costs → work in process inventory → cost of goods sold → finished goods inventory

D manufacturing costs → work in process inventory → finished goods inventory → cost of good sold.

4 When manufacturing costs are assigned to work in process, the journal entries are

  A raw materials inventory – Dr; work in process – Dr; factory labour – Cr; manufacturing overheads – Cr

  B manufacturing overheads – Dr; raw material inventory – Cr; work in process – Cr; factory labour – Cr

  C work in process – Dr; raw materials inventory – Cr; factory labour – Cr; manufacturing overheads – Cr

  D factory labour – Dr; manufacturing overheads – Dr; work in process – Cr; raw material inventory – Cr.

5 When costs are assigned to jobs, the costs are summarized and recorded in

  A production cost reports

  B a job report schedule

  C a job cost performance analysis

  D a job cost sheet.

6 The formula for computing a predetermined overhead rate is

  A estimate overhead cost divided by expected level of activity

  B expected level of activity times estimated overhead cost

  C expected level of activity divided by estimated overhead cost

  D estimated overhead cost times total direct labour hours.

7 A predetermined overhead rate is used to

  A allocate overhead costs to service departments

  B allocate direct costs to products which created those costs

  C allocate overhead costs to products which created those costs

  D allocate total overhead costs to productive departments.

8 VETO Ltd has two departments, moulding and assembling. A job order costing system is used and a predetermined overhead rate is determined for each department. The moulding department uses a machine hour rate, while the assembling department uses a rate based on direct labour hours. At the beginning of the year 2006, the company made the following estimates:

	Department	
	Moulding	Assembling
Direct labour hours	8 000	18 000
Machine hours	36 000	4 000
Manufacturing overhead cost	$540 000	$460 000
Direct labour cost	$40 000	$240 000

Required

(a) Calculate the predetermined overhead rate to be used by each department in 2006.

The job cost sheet from Job no. 105, which was started and completed during the year, revealed the following information:

	Department	
	Moulding	Assembling
Direct labour hours	10	42
Machine hours	60	12
Manufacturing overhead cost	$450	$360
Direct labour cost	$50	$120

(b) Calculate the total overhead cost of Job no. 105

Answer

(a) Moulding department

$$\frac{\$540\ 000}{36\ 000} = \$15 \text{ per machine hour}$$

Assembling department

$$\frac{\$460\ 000}{28\ 000} = \$25.56 \text{ per direct labour hour}$$

(b) Overhead cost of Job no. 105

Moulding department 60 @ $15 per hour = $900
Assembling department 42 @ $25.56 per hour = $1 073.52
Total overhead cost =$1 973.52

9 Evermore Ltd started production on 1 June 2006 using a job order costing system and applied manufacturing overheads on the basis of direct labour cost to work in process.

The work in process activity at the end of June was as follows:

Work in process			
Direct materials	$70 000	To finished goods	$500 000
Direct labour	105 000		
Manufacturing overheads	252 000		

Required

(a) Calculate the predetermined overhead rate used by Evermore Ltd in the month of June

At the end of June only one job (210) was still in process and was charged with direct labour cost of $16 000.

Required

(b) Complete the following job cost sheet for the partially completed Job no. 210:

```
                    Job cost sheet – No. 210
Direct materials            $
Direct labour               $
Manufacturing overhead      $ _____
TOTAL COST                  $ _____
```

Answer

(a) Predetermined overhead rate = $\dfrac{252000}{105\ 000}$ = 240% or 2.4

(b) Cost assigned to unfinished job is

$500\ 000 - $427\ 000 = $73\ 000

```
                    Job cost sheet
Direct labour                       $16 000
Manufacturing overheads (240% * 16 000)   38 000
Direct material (balancing figure)    18 600
Total cost                          $73 000
```

28 Process costing

Objectives
- describe the features of process costing
- compare job costing with process costing
- identify the elements of costs associated with process costing
- explain the flow of cost in a process costing system
- complete the production cost report for process costing

28.1 Process costing

Process costing is a method used to allocate cost to products which cannot be identified when produced, as separate units of production, or jobs. These products usually go through a series of processes before the product is completed. Examples of such products are paint, drinks, textiles, oil.

28.2 Features of process costing system

1. Process costing accumulates cost of products produced for a time period at the end of each process, rather than for a job.

2. The elements of costs collected are direct material, direct labour, manufacturing overheads and work in process.

3. Like job costing, the source documents are material requisition forms, labour time tickets and memorandum of predetermined overhead rates.

4. In the process cost system, costs are summarized in a production cost report.

5. Process costing system has more than one work in process inventory, i.e. one for each process.

6. Completed goods and incomplete goods are completed in terms of equivalent units.

28.3 Process costing and job costing compared

Process costing is an accounting system that applies cost to **identical products** which are **mass produced** in a **continuous manner**, through a **series of production** processes. Examples of products which lend themselves to process costing include oil, paint, soft drinks, cornflakes, soap, paper.

Process costing is an alternative to job costing. Job costing is used when the finished products are readily identifiable as separate or individual units, or batches, with each unit requiring separate attention, such as furniture, cars, computers, houses etc.

The basic distinction between a job costing system and a process costing system is how each method determines or measures product costs.

Job costing applies costs to each individual physical unit produced, or specific job done such as a car, or a few similar items – a batch – such as a dozen chairs.

Process costing, on the other hand, deals with a great mass of identical items which cannot be individualized and costed. Costing is usually applied by dividing the *cost* of producing a quantity of the product over a period of time, e.g. one month, by the amount of the product produced over the same period. The amount or quantity of product may be measured in terms of thousands of pounds, or hundreds of gallons, or hundreds of barrels, etc.

28.4 Elements of costs and cost flows

Like job costing, process costing uses direct material, direct labour and manufacturing overhead costs as the fundamental elements of cost.

The flow of costs is also similar except that in the process costing system there are usually more than one work in process account: one for each department or for each process. A comparison of their flow of costs will look like this:

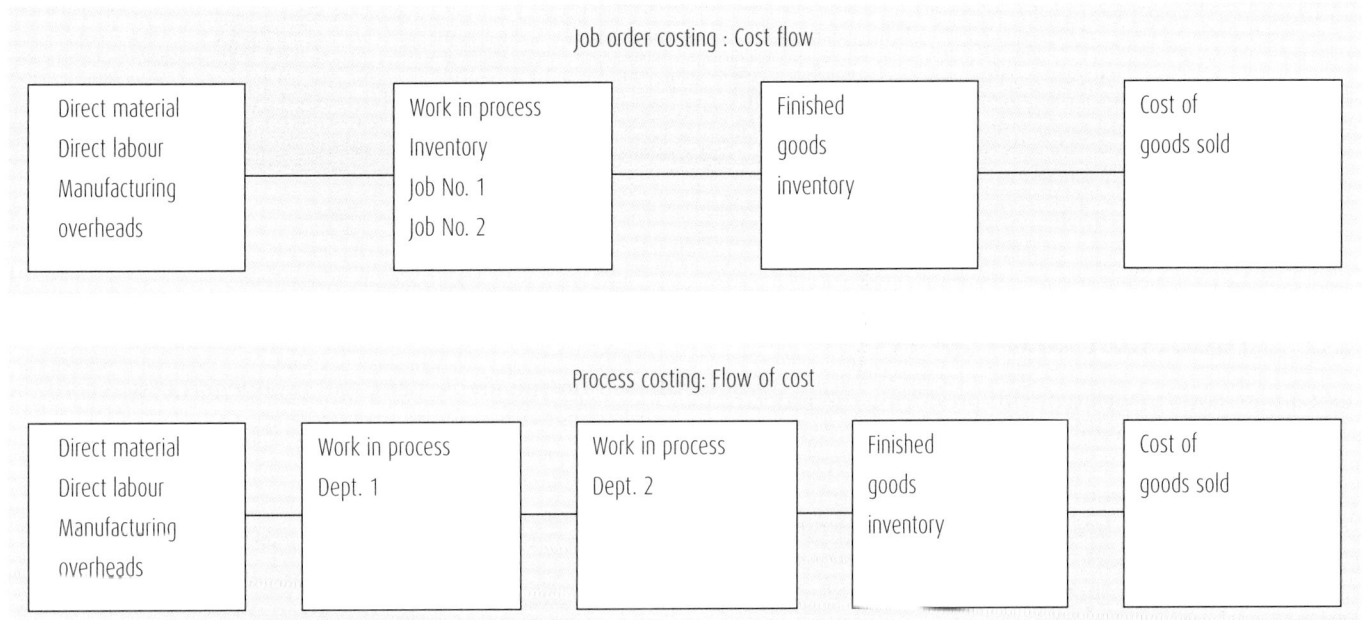

Job order costing : Cost flow

Direct material	Work in process	Finished	Cost of
Direct labour	Inventory	goods	goods sold
Manufacturing	Job No. 1	inventory	
overheads	Job No. 2		

Process costing: Flow of cost

Direct material	Work in process	Work in process	Finished	Cost of
Direct labour	Dept. 1	Dept. 2	goods	goods sold
Manufacturing			inventory	
overheads				

In the process costing system, direct materials, direct labour and manufacturing overheads are added at each stage or process, and the unfinished goods are transferred from stage to stage or from department to department until they are completed and transferred to the finished goods inventory.

28.5 Equivalent units of production

At the end of an accounting period there will be completed and partly completed units in each department. Costs must be applied to these incomplete units as well as the completed ones. In order to spread costs equitably over partly completed and fully completed units, a concept called equivalent units is applied. Equivalent units are the sum of units both *completed* and *incompleted* at the end of a process. For example, two units half-completed are considered as one equivalent unit. Four units half-completed together count for two equivalent units. Equivalent units are determined by multiplying physical units by the percentage of completion. In so doing a weighted average is applied to them.

If in a period of production 4000 units were completed and 200 were 60% completed, total equivalent units will be {4000 + (60% of 200)} = 4000 + 120 = 4120 equivalent units.

Thus cost per unit of production = Total cost / Total number of equivalent units.

Equivalent units is a measure of both complete and incomplete work done during a period, expressed in fully complete units.

28.6 Conversion cost

This term is used to describe the cost of converting materials from one stage of manufacture to the next. This cost involves a combination of direct labour and manufacturing overhead costs, and is incurred uniformly during the process.

For example, if the boxing and sealing department of a cornflakes manufacturer completed 20 000 identical boxes during May, its costs for that month were

		$
Direct materials		12 000
Conversion costs:		$
Direct labour	8 000	
Factory overheads	3 000	11 000
Costs to account for		23 000

The unit cost of goods completed will be $23 000 / 20 000 = \$1.15$.

If shown separately:

Direct materials	$12 000 / 20 000 = $	$ 0.60
Conversion costs	17 000 / 20 000 =	0.55
Unit cost of 1 completed box of cornflakes		1.15

28.7 Production cost report

When all the costs associated with producing the product for a process are collected, i.e. direct material costs and conversion costs (direct labour + manufacturing overhead), together with the percentage completion of unfinished work in process, they are summarized in a production cost report. This report shows both the production quantity and costs for a period of a department.

In preparing the production cost report, five sequential steps are usually followed:

Step 1. Show the flow of physical units.
Step 2. Calculate output in terms of equivalent units.
Step 3. Calculate total costs to account for.
Step 4. Calculate unit costs.
Step 5. Prepare a cost reconciliation schedule.

A production cost report can be prepared from the following information of an assembling department:

Physical units		
Work in Process: Jan. 1		
100% complete: Direct material		
60% complete: Conversion costs	80 000	Units
Units started during January	400 000	
Units completed and transferred out of assembly dept.	420 000	
Work in Process: Jan. 31		
100% complete: Direct material		
50% complete: Conversion cost	60 000	Units
Costs		
Work in process: Jan. 1		$
Direct materials		18 000
Conversion cost		16 000
Cost of work in process		34 000
Cost added during the period of January		
Direct materials		126 000
Conversion costs		74 000
Total costs to account for		200 000

Based on the above data, the production cost record on worksheet can now be prepared.

Production cost report (weighted average method)

Units				Equivalent units		
Flow of production		Physical units		Materials		Conversion Costs
Jan 1	Work in process	80 000				
	Started during Jan.	400 000				
	Units to account for	480 000				
	Completed & transferred out	420 000		420 000		420 000
Jan 31	Ending work in process	60 000		60 000	(50%)	30 000
		480 000		480 000		450 000

Costs

		Materials	Conversion Costs	Total
		$	$	$
Jan 1	Work in process	18 000	16 000	34 000
	Added costs in Jan.	126 000	74 000	200 000
	Total cost to account for	144 000	90 000	234 000
Divided by number of Equivalent units		480 000	450 000	
	Unit cost	.30	.20	.50

Application of costs to:	
Completed goods (420 000 × 0.50)	210 000
Work in progress:	
Material (60 000 × 0.30)	18 000
Conversion cost (30 000 × 0.20)	6 000
Total Work in Process	234 000

28.8 Production report: weighted average and FIFO methods

Two methods are usually considered when treating with units of opening inventory of work in process in a production cost report.

Weighted average method

In this method seen above, no distinction is made between opening inventory units of work in process and units started during the current period. Both unit costs are merged into one, or added together to arrive at one **average cost** per equivalent unit for completed units.

FIFO method

This method of production cost presentation treats beginning inventory units of work in process separate and apart from units started and completed during the current period. The assumption under the FIFO method is that work started first will be completed first. Therefore the beginning work in process inventory will be completed before the batch which was started during the month.

Using the previous information, the production cost report using FIFO will be as follows:

Production cost report (FIFO)

Units			Equivalent units	
Flow of production	Physical units	Materials		Conversion costs
Jan 1 Work in process	80 000			
Started during January	400 000			
Units to account for	480 000			

Units completed:				
Jan 1 Work in process	80 000		(40%)	32 000
Units started and completed in Jan.	340 000	340 000		340 000
Ending work in process	60 000	60 000	(50%)	30 000
Units accounted for	480 000	400 000		402 000

Costs

	Materials $	Conversion Costs $	Total $
Jan 1 Work in process			34 000
Added costs	126 000	74 000	200 000
Total costs to account for			234 000
Cost per equivalent unit:	$126 000 ÷ 400 000 = $0.315	$74 000 ÷ 402 000 = $0.1841	

Application of cost: Completed goods: valued at 1 Jan. ($18 000 + 16 000) $34 000

Added conversion (32 000 @ $0.1841)   5 891

$39 891

Started and completed

Materials	340 000 @ $0.315 = $107 100	
Conversion	340 000 @ $0.1841 = $ 62 594	169 694

Closing work in process

Materials	60 000 @ $0.315 = $ 18 900	
Conversion	30 000 @ $0.1841 = $ 5 523	24 423
		234 008

The difference between the totals of $0.008 is due to decimal places.

28.9 Questions

1 What are the two main inventory methods used in process costing? What are the differences between these methods?

2 This information refers to units processed in a Guyana's Printers binding department for the month of September:

	Units of product	Percentage of labour added
Beginning goods in process inventory	250 000	60%
Goods started and compeleted	300 000	100
Ending goods in process inventory	120 000	25

Required

(a) Compute the total equivalent units of production with respect to labour for September using the FIFO inventory method

(b) Compute the total equivalent units of production with respect to labour for September using the weighted-average inventory method.

3 Honda Company's assembly department shows the following data for the month of January 2007:

Units started	2500
Units transferred to finishing department	2000
Units in hand at January 31, 2007	500 (20% labour and overhead)
Costs: materials	$40 000
labour	$32 000
overhead	$16 000

Required

Prepare a production cost report for the month of January.

29 Activity-based costing

Objectives
- explain activity based costing (ABC)
- compare ABC techniques with traditional approaches
- compute unit cost using ABC
- explain terms related to ABC

29.1 Activity-based costing

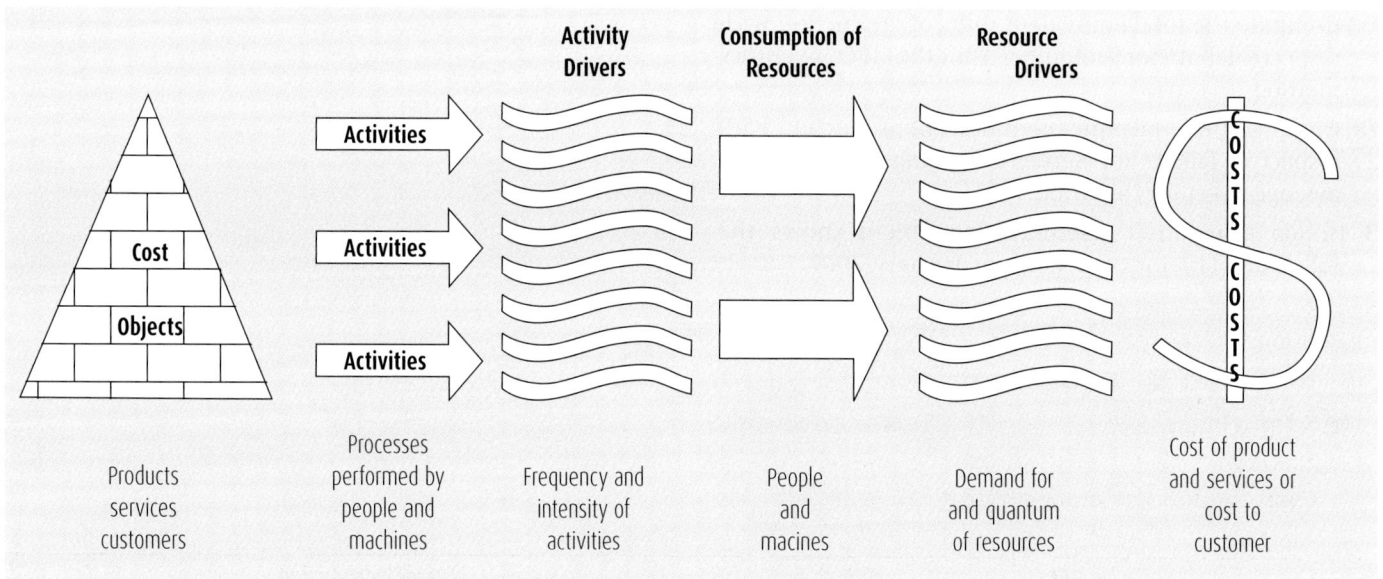

	Activity Drivers	Consumption of Resources	Resource Drivers	
Products services customers	Processes performed by people and machines	Frequency and intensity of activities	People and macines	Demand for and quantum of resources

Cost of product and services or cost to customer

Activity-based costing (ABC) is an accounting technique that allows the determination of the actual cost associated with each product and service produced by a business based on activities. It focuses on the activities of a production cycle. It is based on a premise that outputs require activities to produce and that activities consume resources. This two-stage costing method creates cost pools for each major activity in an organization and determines what drives (cost driver) those activities. Examples of activities are purchase orders, set-ups required, or number of inspections completed.

Cost objects

This may be a customer, product, service or project for which a separate cost measurement is desired.

Activity

This is any work or process done by people or machines in an enterprise to make a product, provide a service or satisfy a customer.

Activity driver

This is a measure of how often activities are demanded to achieve a particular cost objective.

Resources

These are the skills of people, capacity of machines or the elements of land used to perform activities.

Resource driver

This is a measure of the amount of materials, skills and capacity used up by an entity.

Costs

These are the resources consumed in pursuing activities expressed in monetary terms and attached to the cost objects.

29.2 Benefits and limitations of ABC

ABC as a costing system, even though it is an improvement on the traditional way of costing products and services, is plagued by many limitations.

Benefits	Limitations
There is a better allocation of resources.	Organization sustaining costs and cost of idle capacity are not assigned to products.
It improves cost visibility.	The benefits of increased accuracy may not exceed the additional costs.
Output is geared towards satisfying consumer requirements.	Managers may find it difficult to adjust to the information provided.
Cost comparison is possible over periods.	Caution must be exercised in the use of the data generated.
It's easy to allocate costs.	It does not conform to GAAP.
Total production costs are paced to output.	Activities are not always well defined.
It identifies efficient and inefficient areas.	Allocation may sometimes appear to be subjective.
It encourages the use of alternative methods of production.	
It identifies areas that may benefit from process improvement.	

29.3 Comparison of ABC and traditional costing

Compared with the traditional approach to overhead allocation, apportionment, and absorption
- ABC generates more accurate product costs.
- It also provides managers with a wider understanding of the economies of production and those resource-consuming activities that provide the wealth we know as 'value added'.
- ABC aligns costs to outputs thereby increasing cost visibility and its usefulness in forecasting.

	ABC	Traditional costing
Implementation cost	Expensive to start up and maintain.	Inexpensive to start up and to maintain.
Decision-making	Cost alignment to activities allows for more accurate information.	Cost generalization leads to over/under costing.
Cost control	Activities are monitored and combined to control costs.	Cost is controlled by departments reducing functions.
Cost objects	Costs are accumulated by activities and resources.	A unit of product or service is cost object.
Cost behaviour	Recognizes that costs are driven by the frequency of activities and cost of resources used.	Assumes that costs are driven by volume.
Allocation bases	Activity and resource drivers are used to allocate costs.	Volume is used as the basis for cost allocation.
Cost accumulation	A single factor is responsible for each cost.	A cost is incurred by a number of different factors.
Idle capacity	Only the cost of capacity used is changed to products.	Unused and idle capacity are charged to products through the predetermined overhead rate.

29.4 Computing unit cost

The application of ABC involves a set procedure:
1. **Collect overhead** via control accounts.
2. Allocate overhead to form cost pools.
3. **Identify cost drivers and cost driver volume**.
4. Calculate cost driver rates, i.e. pool/driver volume.
5. Charge overhead to product/service based upon the demand for the activity.

Example 1

Allocation of overheads to cost pools, computation of total overhead costs and preparation of income statements.

Cool Welding Company use the ABC method. The company has 4 activity cost pools which are listed below:

Activity cost pool	Annual activity
Producing units	8000 machine hours
Processing orders	1500 orders
Customer support	2000 customers
Other	Not applicable

The 'other' activity cost pool consists of idle capacity costs. The company traces the cost of direct materials and direct labour to jobs. Overheads both manufacturing and non-manufacturing are allocated to jobs using the ABC system. The company's overhead costs for the year are listed below:

Annual overhead costs	
Indirect factory wages	150 000
Other factory overhead	200 000
Selling and administrative overhead	450 000
Total overhead cost	800 000

For allocations the distribution to the 4 activity cost pools will be as follows:

	Producing units	Processing orders	Customer support	Other	Total
Indirect factory wages	40%	30%	10%	20%	100%
Other factory overhead	30%	10%	0%	60%	100%
Selling and administrative overhead	0%	25%	40%	35%	100%

Required

Compute:

(a) The first-stage allocation to the activity cost pools.

(b) The activity rates for each activity of the cost pools (use the results from the first stage allocations).

(c) The total amount of overhead cost that would be allocated to an order that requires 10 machine hours.

(d) Prepare a report from the activity in part (c) to show the margin. The revenue from the job is $3500, the direct materials is $985 and the direct labour cost is $1075.

Answer

(a) First-stage allocation (steps 1 and 2):

	Producing Units	Processing Orders	Customer Support	Other	Total
Indirect factory wages	60 000 *(40% × 150 000)	45 000 (30% × 150 000)	15 000 (10% × 150 000)	30 000 (20% × 150 000)	150 000
Other factory overhead	60 000 *(30% × 200 000)	20 000 (10% × 200 000)	NIL	120 000 (60% × 200 000)	200 000
Selling and administrative overhead	NIL	112 500 *(25% × 450 000)	180 000 (40% × 450 000)	157 500 (35% × 450 000)	450 000

*Calculation of allocations

(b) Computation of activity rates (steps 3 and 4):

Total activity	Producing Units 8000 machine hours	Processing Orders 1500 orders	Customer Support 2000 customers
Indirect factory wages	(60 000 ÷ 8000) $7.50	(45 000 ÷ 1500) $30	(15 000 ÷ 2000) $7.50
Other factory overhead	(60 000 ÷ 8000) $7.50	(20 000 ÷ 1500) $13.33	NIL
Selling and administrative overhead	NIL	(112 500 ÷ 1500) $75	(180 000 ÷ 2000) $90
TOTAL OVERHEAD COST	$15	$118.33	$97.50

(c) Total overhead cost of an order requiring 10 machine hours:

Total Activity	Producing Units 10 machine hours	Processing Orders 1 order	Total
Indirect factory wages	$75	$30	$105
Other factory overhead	$75	$13.33	$88.33
Selling and administrative overhead	NIL	$75	$75
TOTAL OVERHEAD COST	$150	$118.33	$268.33

(d)

Report	$	$
Revenue		3500.00
Costs:		
Direct materials	985.00	
Direct labour	1075.00	
Producing units	150.00	
Processing orders	118.33	2328.33
Margin		1171.67

Example 2

Citar Design Company had a total of $66 000 overhead.
Purchases department spent $33 000 comprising 10 purchase orders: 4 for Customer A and 6 for Customer B.

Warehousing overhead: $11 000 comprising 90% of the space occupied for machinery held for Customer A and 10% for Customer B.

General administration: $22 000 was spent equally on the two jobs.

Materials purchased for the jobs, $24 000: $\frac{2}{3}$ for Customer A and $\frac{1}{3}$ for Customer B.

Labour cost amounted to $12 000 for a total of 600 hours: $\frac{1}{3}$ for Job A and $\frac{2}{3}$ for Job B.

Required

Determine the total cost for each job using the activity-based costing method for the allocation of overhead and cost per unit. (Number of units produced 10 000.)

Answer

	Customer A		Customer B		Total
Materials	($\frac{2}{3}$ × 24 000)	16 000	($\frac{1}{3}$ × 24 000)	8 000	24 000
Labour	($\frac{1}{3}$ × 12 000)	4 000	($\frac{2}{3}$ × 12 000)	8 000	12 000
Purchasing	($\frac{4}{10}$ × 33 000)	13 200	($\frac{6}{10}$ × 33 000)	19 800	33 000
Warehousing	(90% × 11 000)	9 900	(10% × 11 000)	1 100	11 000
Administration	(22 000 ÷ 2)	11 000	(22 000 ÷ 2)	11 000	22 000
		54 100		47 900	102 000
Total no. of units		10 000		10 000	10 000
Cost per unit	(54 100 ÷ 10 000)$5.4		(47 900 ÷ 10 000)$4.79		(102 000 ÷ 10 000)$10.20

29.5 Questions

Comfort Fabricating Company uses activity-based costing. The company has four activity cost pools which are listed below:

Activity cost pool	Annual activity
Producing units	8000 machine hours
Processing orders	2000 orders
Customer support	500 customers
Other	Not applicable

The 'other' activity cost pool consists of idle capacity and organization sustaining costs. The company traces the costs of direct materials and direct labour to jobs. Overhead costs both manufacturing and non-manufacturing are allocated to jobs using the ABC system. The company's overhead costs for the year are listed below:

Annual overhead costs	
Indirect factory wages	300 000
Other factory overhead	400 000
Selling and administrative overhead	500 000
	1200 000

The four activity cost pools are

	Other	Producing units	Processing orders	Customer support	Total
Indirect factory wages	10%	40%	40%	10%	100%
Other factory overhead	40%	30%	30%	Nil	100%
Selling and administrative overhead	30%	Nil	30%	40%	100%

Required

(a) Compute the first-stage collection of costs to the activity cost pools.

(b) Compute activity rates for each of the activity pools.

(c) Compare the total amount of overhead cost that would be allocated to an order that requires 25 machine hours.

30 Service sector costing

30.1 Service sector costing

Service sector costing is accounting for special services, departments or functions. These businesses may offer **any** one of the following services:

- The use of personal skills, for example, dental services or beauty supplies.
- A financier may use his skill to offer cash or other range of services.
- Make available to customers the use of fixed assets, the use of rooms or transport services.

Whatever the nature of the business it will either:

- Carry out specific and separate jobs for clients, or
- Provide a continuous sequence of services of a similar nature.

30.2 How is the service sector different from the manufacturing sector?

1. There is no physical product to deal with.
2. The products cannot be stored, instead they are perishable.
3. Cost component: Direct professional labour.
   Service overhead.
4. Direct materials are relatively small compared to total cost.
5. The nature of the service determines how materials, labour and other expenses are recorded.

6. If the service is not profit-oriented, its costing is used to estimate future costs and control service department costs.
7. It cannot be inspected for quality in advance.
8. The service may vary each time with the situation.

30.3 Why is service sector costing difficult?

An attempt to provide answers to the following questions will reveal the extent of the problem of service sector costing.

1. Are there one or several cost units to choose from?
2. How is the output to be measured for management purposes?
3. What scope is there for cost control? Are the costs controllable or apportioned?
4. How should costs be compared by departments, by periods or budgeted against actual?
5. Does comparable unit cost reflect management efficiency?
6. Should total cost or unit cost be compared?
7. What costing method should be used, job or continuous?

30.4 Types of services

A service company can use service costing at two levels. A costing method can be used to determine the cost of providing a service to a party **external** to itself and an application can be made to determine the cost of one department providing services to other departments (**internal services**). The reasons for costing services provided externally to customers are the same for costing a product. On the other hand, costing services provided internally serve to help departments control their costs and to prevent abuse of such services.

30.5 Service sector activities

	External service				Internal service		
	Hotel	Hospital	School	Transport	Canteen	Maintenance	Computer
Possible cost units	Rooms Bed-nights Meals	Bed days Per operation Per visit	Student hour Per student Part/Full time Short course	Ton mile Passenger mile Miles travelled Type of vehicle used	Meals Staff	Hours to user Machine hrs per user	Hours provided per user
Costing system	Terminal (Job type) or Continuous (Average cost)				Direct method or Reciprocal step method		
Example for hotel	Special functions Marginal or Standard		Normal customers Absorption		Advantages: Discourages wastage Discourages abuse Profit centre analysis		

Service sector costing

Internal

Examples	Canteen	Maintenance	Computer	Transport	Postal
Cost Unit	Meals Staff	Hours to user Machine hours per user	Hours provided per user	Passenger miles Miles travelled Tonne miles Type of vehicle used	

Cost allocation

1. Trace direct costs and allocate indirect costs.
2. Allocate service department costs to production departments.
3. Allocate production costs to products.

Cost accumulation

Direct method: A method of cost allocation that charges costs of service departments to user departments and ignores any services used by other service departments.

Step method: This method of service department cost allocation recognizes some inter-departmental services.

(Start with the greatest server or the greatest server of service departments.)

Reciprocal method (simultaneous solution method): This method of service department cost allocation recognizes all services provided by any service department, including services provided to other service department.

External

Examples	Law firms	Movie studios	Repair shops	Hospitals	Accounting
The job	Client	Picture	Items	Patient	Tax payer
Direct materials	Stationery	Costumes Props Films	Parts Materials	Medication	Stationery
Labour (time expended)	Attorney	Actor Director	Technician	Doctors Nurses	Accountant
Overhead	Clerical Secretaries Rent Depreciation	Utilities Salaries Depreciation	Utilities Salaries Depreciation	Clerical Utilities Salaries	Meetings trainings
Overhead application	Attorney's time	Actor's time	Technician's time	Consultation time	Accountant's time
Cost unit	A case	Motion picture	Item for repair	Bed days Per visit Per operation	Audit job

30.6 Analysis of service costs

Service costs should be analysed so as to achieve the following objectives:

1. Analyse expenses by type.

2. Distinguish between fixed, variable and semi-variable expenses.

3. Analyse expenses over cost centres.

4. Compare actual cost centre expense with budgeted or previous period actual costs (for control).

5. Measure cost per unit for each service provided.

6. Measure cost per unit to charge customer (or another centre).

7. Unit cost helps to determine the use of the service internally or externally.

This application can be used to determine cost in a hotel in the following way:

Hotel

1. Possible cost units – bed available; bed occupied; meals; functions.

2. What is the most meaningful measurement for management purposes?

3. What are the peculiar circumstances for each activity? E.g. meals for resident/non-resident; expensive/cheap etc.

4. Why measure the output?

5. Are most of the costs controllable or apportioned fixed expenses?

6. What is the ratio of variable or fixed expenses? (Variable – laundry, cleaning, wages, meals.)

7. How does the unit cost per period compare? Example, use cost per room, per occupancy level, high or low occupancy level?

8. Is unit cost affected by peaks and troughs in the use of the service or by cost reductions?

9. Does the comparable unit cost reflect efficiency or inefficiency?

10. How to use cost comparison to measure efficiency? Use total cost or cost unit per centre?

11. What cost system should be used? Continuous or job?

The data obtained can be placed in a format to display total cost and unit cost.

	HOTEL COST CENTRES		
	Laundry	Restaurant	Cleaning

Variable: Overtime wages
         Food
         Power			

Fixed: Basic Wage
       Power
      Apportioned:
         Rent and rates
         General office
         Laundry
         Canteen			

Total cost			
Unit cost per bed occupied			

Worked example

Accounting firm Jackson and Saunders worked for clients and provided the following information:

D. Quarry Ltd   800 hours
N. Transport Ltd   1200 hours
Tax auditor's rate per hour $75
Total hours worked for the period 2200, of which 200 were spent in meetings
Overhead cost for the period $11 000
Overhead is assigned proportionately based on direct labour hours
Administrative expenses $8000
The firm's billing rate for an accountant is $125 per hour (all transactions are on credit).

Solution

JOURNAL ENTRIES

1. Direct labour cost

			Dr. Direct labour:	
D. Quarry Ltd	800 × $75		D. Quarry Ltd.	60 000
N. Transport Ltd.	1 200 × $75		N. Transport Ltd.	90 000
Other	200 × $75		Other	15 000
			Cr. Wages payable	165 000

2. Accumulate total overhead

($11 000)		Dr. Unassigned overhead	11 000
		Cr. Accounts payable	11 000

3. Assign overhead

Rate 11 000 ÷ 2 200 = $5 per hour

D.Q. Ltd 800 × $5;		Dr. D. Quarry Ltd.	4 000
N.T. Ltd. 1200 × $5;		N. Transport Ltd.	6 000
Other 200 × $5		Other	1 000
		Cr. Unassigned overhead	11 000

4. Accumulate marketing and administrative cost

| | ($8 000) | Dr. Marketing and admin. | 8 000 |
| | | Cr. Accounts payable | 8 000 |

5. Billing the client for services rendered

		Dr. Accounts receivable	250 000
		Cr. Revenue:	
D. Quarry Ltd.	800 × $125	D. Quarry Ltd.	100 000
N. Transport Ltd.	1 200 × $125	N. Transport Ltd.	150 000

The Ledger

Wages payable A/C
Direct labour:

D. Quarry	60 000
N. Transport Ltd.	90 000
Other	15 000

D.Quarry Ltd. A/C

| Direct labour | 60 000 |
| Overhead | 4 000 |

Accounts payable A/C
Overhead:

D. Quarry Ltd.	4 000
N. Transport Ltd.	6 000
Other	1 000
Marketing & admin.	8 000

N. Transport Ltd.

| Direct labour | 90 000 |
| Overhead | 6 000 |

Accounts receivable A/C
Revenue:

| D. Quarry Ltd. | 4 000 |
| N. Transport Ltd. | 150 000 |

Jack and Saunders
Income Statement for the period ended

	$	$
Revenue from services to clients		250 000
Less: Cost of services:		
Labour (60 000 + 90 000)	150 000	
Overhead (4000 + 6000)	10 000	
Cost of services		160 000
Gross margin		90 000
Less other costs:		
Labour (165 000 – 150 000)	15 000	
Overhead (11 000 – 10 000)	1 000	
Marketing & administration	8 000	
Total other costs		24 000
Operating profit		16 000

The methods used to allocate department costs to other service departments (and production departments) can be found in Chapter 25 with accompanying examples.

30.7 Questions

1 XY Hospital keeps a record for all their patients. The ante-natal room and delivery room had budgeted allocation bases of 3000 nursing hours and 2000 nursing hours respectively. The budgeted nursing overhead costs for each department for the month were $200 000 and $100 000 respectively. The nursery and recovery room for post-natal had budgeted overhead costs of $1500 000 and 20 000 nursing hours for the month. Amy Roberts, a patient, incurred 5 hours in the ante-natal room and 6 hours in the delivery room. She spent 5 days (100 hours) in the hospital. Other related costs to Roberts were

	Ante-natal costs	Delivery room	In-room costs
Patient medicine	$300	$400	$3000
Direct nursing time	$2000	$3000	$4080

Required

What was the total cost of Amy Roberts' stay as a patient in XY Hospital?

2 Choose an industry with which you are familiar and list five to seven major production support or service departments in the business. What is the output of each of these support and service departments?

3 A university has an annual running cost of $3 million with the following students on roll:

Classification	Number of students on roll	Attendance (weeks per annum)	Hours per week
3 year	2700	30	28
4 year	1500	35	20
Diploma	1900	30	25

Required

Calculate the cost per unit for the university to the nearest dollar.

Module Three
Planning and Decision Making

31 Budgeting

Objectives
- state the objectives of budgeting
- state the role of the budget committee
- explain the rationale for the use of budgets in planning, decision-making and controlling
- state the difference between a static budget and a flexible budget

31.1 Objectives of budgeting

1. Forecasting – to forecast financial and non-financial transactions.
2. Communicating – to foster horizontal and vertical communication to ensure data agreement on plans and to provide accurate and meaningful information to the recipient.
3. Planning – to force management to look ahead and plan goals and events and to allocate resources internally.
4. Co-ordinating – to encourage co-operation among management teams and departments.
5. Evaluating performance – to review performance by comparing budgeted with actual results.
6. Behavioural – to identify roles and allocation of responsibilities.
7. Participative – to ensure that goals are congruent with the mission of the organization and to motivate labour.

31.2 Role of the budget committee

1. Objectives – to establish key objectives to form the basis of the budget.
2. Instructions – to give adequate instructions to all levels of management on budget preparation procedure.
3. Submissions – to ensure that all levels of management make submissions of subsidiary budgets.
4. Compatibility – to ensure that subsidiary budgets are compatible with overall company objectives.
5. Co-ordinate – to put the subsidiary budgets together.
6. Supervision – to supervise the preparation of the master budget and forecast cash flows.
7. Report (Monitoring) – to prepare control reports to monitor results.

31.3 Rationale for budgets in planning (resource allocation)

1. Long-range plans – look at product quality; market share; growth rate.
2. Short-range plans/strategies – plan product lines and profit; designs a specific timetable.
3. Personnel – defines responsibilities and interaction; identifies a director who is to participate, and the communication necessary.
4. In-house principles – ensures realism; strict deadlines and flexibility.
5. Monitor – periodic review; periodic performance reports; review of problems.

31.4 Rationale for budgets in decision-making

1. How much market share, growth rate percentage.
2. Sales; profit of product lines; personnel needs and expected changes.
3. Coordinator and staff selection; level of participation and communication.
4. Realism – organization before department; deadline important to all.
5. Frequent checking and correcting.

31.5 Rationale for budgets in controlling

1. Procedures – to help in establishing procedures to achieve planned revenues and costs.
2. Plans – to aid in co-ordinating and communicating plans to all concerned.
3. To formulate a basis for effective revenue and cost control.
4. Results – to compare results, budgeting is actual.

31.6 Differences between flexible and static budgets

Static	Flexible
Geared towards one level of activity	Geared towards all levels of activity in the relevant range
Actual results vs budgeted costs at the original budgeted activity level	The actual level attained is compared to what costs should have been

31.7 The difference between a forecast and a budget

A business **forecast** is an estimate of the likely position of a business in the future, based on past or present conditions. For example, Cindy's sales over the past five years have been $100 000, $105 000, $110 250, $115 750 and $121 500; the sales have been increasing at the rate of about 5% each year. Based on this information, and assuming that trading conditions will continue unchanged, the forecast sales for the next year might be about $127 600.

A **budget** is a statement of *planned* future results which are expected to follow from actions taken by management to change the present circumstances. Cindy may want sales to grow by 10% each year in future by introducing new products, or by increasing advertising, or by offering improved terms of trading. Her budgeted sales for next year will then be $133 650 ($121 500 × 110%), and $147 000 and $161 700 for the following two years. A budget expresses management's plans for the future of a business in money terms.

31.8 Budgets as tools for planning and control

Planning

Managers are responsible for planning and controlling a business for the benefit of its owners, and budgets are essential tools for planning and controlling. Well-managed businesses have short-term budgets for, say, the year ahead. Small businesses may function well enough with these, but larger businesses need to plan further ahead and may prepare long-term budgets, in addition to the short-term ones, for the next five, ten or even more years ahead. These plans are often known as **rolling budgets** because, as each year passes, it is deleted from the budget and a budget for another year is added. A budget for one year ahead will be detailed, but budgets for the following years may be less precise because of uncertainty about future trading conditions.

The manager of each department or function in a business is responsible for the performance of his or her department or function. Separate operational, or functional, budgets must be prepared for each department or activity detailing the department's revenue (if any) and expenses for a given period. The budgets will be prepared for sales, production, purchasing, personnel, administration, treasury (cash and banking), etc. Opinions differ as to who should prepare these budgets.

Top-down budgets are prepared by top management and handed down to departmental managers, who are responsible for putting them into effect. Such budgets usually have the merit of being well co-ordinated so that they all fit together as a logical and consistent plan for the whole business. However, departmental managers may not feel committed to keeping to these budgets as they have had little or no say in their preparation and may be of the opinion that the budgets are unrealistic.

Bottom-up budgets are prepared by departmental managers and may be unsatisfactory because:

- they may not fit together with all the other departmental budgets to make a logical and consistent overall plan for the business;

- managers tend to base their own budgets on easily achievable targets to avoid being criticized for failing to meet them; this will result in departments performing below their maximum level of efficiency and be bad for the business as a whole.

A budget committee, which should include the accountant, should coordinate the departmental budgets to ensure that they achieve top management's plans for the business.

The benefits of budgets may be summarized as follows.

1. They are formal statements in quantitative and financial terms of management plans.

2. Their preparation ensures the coordination of all the activities of a business.

3. Budgets identify limiting factors (shortages of demand or resources).

4. When managers are involved in the preparation of their budgets, they are committed to meeting them.

5. Budgets are a form of responsibility accounting as they identify the managers who are responsible for implementing the various aspects of the overall plan for the business.

6. Budgets avoid 'management by crisis', which describes situations in which managers have not foreseen problems before they arise and prepared for them in advance. These managers spend their time grappling with problems that should never have arisen had they been foreseen. The managers are sometimes described as 'fire fighters' when they should be 'fire preventers'.

Control

Control involves measuring actual performance, comparing it with the budget and taking corrective action to bring actual performance into line with the budget. It is important that deviations from budget are discovered early before serious situations arise. Annual departmental budgets are broken down into four-weekly or monthly, or even weekly, periods, and departmental management accounts are prepared for those periods. These management accounts compare actual performance with budget and must be prepared promptly after the end of each period if they are to be useful. If actual revenue and expenditure are better than budget, the differences (or variances) are described as **favourable** because they increase profit. On the other hand, if 'actual' is worse than budget, the variance is described as **adverse**.

Departmental management accounts usually contain many items of revenue and expenditure with a mixture of favourable and adverse variances. Managers should concentrate their attention on items with adverse variances and, to help managers focus their attention on these, management accounts may report only the items

with adverse variances. This is known as **management by exception** or **exception reporting**.

Flexible budgets Experience shows that sales and costs rarely conform to the patterns anticipated by management when they prepare a 'fixed' budget, that is, one that does not allow for different levels of activity and changing conditions. Fixed budgets may lose their usefulness as management tools as a result. Invariably, the number of units produced and sold is more or less than the number in a fixed budget. To overcome this, budgets may be 'flexed' to reflect various levels of activity and costs. Flexing budgets makes use of marginal costing and is an important process when standard costing techniques are employed.

31.9 How to flex budgets

The actual volume of goods produced is seldom the same as the volume on which a budget has been based. Sensible comparisons can only be made if 'like is compared with like', and the budget is based on the actual volume of output. This is done by **flexing** the budget.

The variable expenses in the budget must be adjusted to take account of the actual volume of goods produced.

Example 1

Variable Grommets Ltd produced the following budget for the production and sale of 10 000 grommets for the six months ending June 2005.

Budget for 10 000 grommets Six months ending June 2005	
	$
Variable expenses	
Direct materials	50 000
Direct labour	100 000
Production overheads	40 000
Selling and distribution	8 000
	198 000
Fixed expenses	
Production overheads	78 000
Selling and distribution	43 000
Administration	91 000
Total cost	410 000

The output for the six months ended 30 June was 12 000 grommets. The budget is flexed by multiplying the variable expenses by $\frac{12\,000}{10\,000}$, that is by 1.2.

Flexed budget for 12 000 grommets
Six months ended June 2005

	$
Variable expenses	
Direct materials	60 000
Direct labour	120 000
Production overheads	48 000
Selling and distribution	9 600
	237 600
Fixed expenses	
Production overheads	78 000
Selling and distribution	43 000
Administration	91 000
Total cost	449 600

The fixed expenses have not changed. The flexed budget is the one that would have been prepared as the original budget if it had been known that the output would be 12 000 grommets.

Exercise 1

Brekkifoods Ltd's budget for the production of 100 000 packets of Barleynuts in the year ending 31 December 2005 was as follows.

		$
Variable expenses		
Direct materials		20 000
Direct labour		15 000
Production expenses		6 000
		41 000
Fixed expenses		
Production expenses	13 000	
Administration		29 000
		83 000

The actual output for the year ended 31 December 2005 was 110 000 packets of Barleynuts.

Required

Prepare a flexed budget for the production of 110 000 packets of Barleynuts.

Flexing budgets with semi-variable expenses

Budgets may not show a distinction between fixed and variable expenses. In these cases, the distinction must be found by inspection.

Example 2

Obskure Ltd has prepared flexed budgets for the production of (i) 5000 and (ii) 6000 pairs of sunglasses.

	5000 pairs of glasses	6000 pairs of glasses
	$	$
Direct materials	10 000	12 000
Direct labour	15 000	18 000
Production overheads	16 000	18 000
Selling and distribution	19 000	22 000
Administration	12 000	12 000
	72 000	82 000

8000 pairs of glasses were produced and a flexed budget for that output is required.

Answer

Some expenses vary directly with output: direct materials are $2 per pair of spectacles, and direct labour is $3 per pair. The cost of these items for 8000 pairs of glasses will be: direct materials $16 000; direct labour $24 000.

Production overheads and selling and distribution expenses have not increased proportionately with the increased production. Each of these items contains a fixed element. To find the variable elements of these costs, deduct the costs for 5000 units from the costs for 6000 units to find the variable costs for 1000 units

Production overheads

Production overheads for 1000 units = $(18 000 – 16 000) = $2000, or $2 per unit.

Fixed production costs are now found by deducting the variable cost for 5000 units from the total production cost: $(16 000 – 10 000) = $6000.

Production cost for 8000 pairs of spectacles is $6000 + (8000 × $2) = $22 000.

Selling and distribution

Selling and distribution for 1000 units = $(22 000 – 19 000) = $3000, or $3 per unit.

Fixed selling and distribution cost is found by deducting the variable cost for 5000 units from the total selling and distribution cost: $(19 000 – 15 000) = $4000.

Selling and distribution cost for 8000 pairs of spectacles is $4000 + (8000 × $3) = $28 000.

The flexed budget for 8000 pairs of spectacles is

	$
Direct materials	16 000
Direct labour	24 000
Production overheads	22 000
Selling and distribution	28 000
Administration	12 000
	102 000

Exercise 2

Flexers Ltd has prepared the following budgets for the production of time locks.

No. of locks	6000	8000
	$	$
Direct materials	15 000	20 000
Direct labour	36 000	48 000
Production overhead	25 000	31 000
Selling and distribution	24 000	28 000
Administration	80 000	80 000
	180 000	207 000

Required

Prepare a flexed budget for the production of 9000 time locks.

31.10 Limiting (or principal budget) factors

Limiting factors, sometimes called **principal budget factors**, are circumstances which restrict the activities of a business. Examples are:

- limited demand for a product
- shortage of materials, which limits production
- shortage of labour, which also limits production.

Limiting factors must be identified in order to decide the order in which the departmental budgets are prepared. If the limiting factor is one of demand for the product, a sales budget will be prepared first. The other budgets will then be prepared to fit in with the sales budget. If the limiting factor is the availability of materials or labour, the production budget will be prepared first and the sales budget will then be based on the production budget.

31.11 How to prepare a sales budget

Sales budgets are based on the budgeted volume of sales. The volume is then multiplied by the selling price per unit of production to produce the sales revenue. For the sake of simplicity, the examples which follow assume that only one type of product is being sold.

Example

Xsel Ltd's sales for the six months from January to June 2005 are budgeted in units as follows:
January 1000; February 800; March 1100; April 1300; May 1500; June 1400.
The current price per unit is $15 but the company plans to increase the price by 5% on 1 May.

The sales budget will be prepared as follows:

	January	February	March	April	May	June	Total
				2005			
Units	1000	800	1100	1300	1500	1400	7100
Price	$15	$15	$15	$15	$15.75	$15.75	
Sales	$15 000	$12 000	$16 500	$19 500	$23 625	$22 050	$108 675

Exercise 3

Flannel and Flounder Ltd's sales budget in units for six months ending 30 June 2005 is as follows:
January 1000; February 1200; March 1300; April 1500; May 1700; June 1800.
The price per unit will be $20 for the three months to 31 March but will be increased to $22 from 1 April.

Required

Prepare Flannel and Flounder Ltd's sales budget for the new product for the six months ending 30 June 2005. (Keep your answer; it will be needed later.)

31.12 Schedule of cash collections

This should accompany the sales budget. It shows the anticipated cash inflow from Sales and collections of accounts receivable for the budget period.

31.13 How to prepare a production budget

Manufacturing companies require production budgets to show the volume of production required monthly to meet the demand for sales. It is important to check that production is allocated to the correct months.

Example

Xsel Ltd (see the example in §31.11) manufactures its goods one month before they are sold. Monthly production is 105% of the following month's sales to provide goods for stock and for free samples to be given away to promote sales. Budgeted sales for July 2005 are for 1800 units.

Required

Prepare Xsel Ltd's monthly production budget for the period from December 2004 to December 2005.

Answer

	2004	2005					
	December	January	February	March	April	May	June
Production for sales (units)	1000	800	1100	1300	1500	1400	1800
Add 5% for stock and samples	50	40	55	65	75	70	90
Monthly production	1050	840	1155	1365	1575	1470	1890

Exercise 4

Flannel and Flounder Ltd (see exercise 3, §31.11) manufacture their goods one month before the goods are sold. Monthly production is 110% of the following month's sales. Budgeted sales for July 2005 are 2000 units.

Required

Prepare Flannel and Flounder Ltd's production budget. (Keep your answer; it will be needed later.)

31.14 How to prepare a purchases budget

A purchases budget may be prepared for either

1. raw materials purchased by a manufacturer, or
2. goods purchased by a trader.

A manufacturing company's purchases budget is prepared from the production budget while a trader's purchases budget is prepared from the sales budget. The purchases budget is calculated as follows:

Units produced per production budget × quantity of material per unit produced × price per unit of material

Take care to ensure that the purchases are made in the correct month.

Example

Xsel Ltd (see the example in §31.13) purchases its raw materials one month before production. Each unit of production requires 3 kg of material, which costs $2 per kg.

Required

Prepare the purchases budget for the materials to be used in the production of goods for the period from December 2004 to June 2005.

Answer

	2004		2005				
	November	December	January	February	March	April	May
No. of units	1050	840	1155	1365	1575	1470	1890
Material required (kg)	3150	2520	3465	4095	4725	4410	5670
Purchases ($2 per litre)	6300	5040	6930	8190	9450	8820	11 340

Exercise 5

Flannel and Flounder Ltd (see exercise 4, §31.13) use 2.5 litres of material in each unit of their product. The price of the material is currently $4.10 per litre, but the company has learned that the price will be increased to $4.25 in March 2005. The raw materials are purchased one month before production; 2100 units are budgeted to be produced in August 2005.

Required

Prepare Flannel and Flounder Ltd's purchases budget based on its production budget for the seven months from December 2004 to June 2005. (Make all calculations to the nearest $.)

31.15 Schedule of expected cash disbursement

This should accompany the raw materials budget. It shows the cash disbursements for raw materials and accounts payable.

31.16 How to prepare an expenditure budget

An expenditure budget includes payments for purchased materials (from the purchases budget) plus all other expenditure in the period covered by the budget. Take care to ensure that

- purchased materials are paid for in the correct month
- all other expenses are included in the budget in accordance with the given information.

Example

Xsel Ltd pays for its raw materials two months after the month of purchase (see §31.14). Its other expenses are as follows.

1. Monthly wages of $4000 are paid in the month in which they are due.

2. The staff are paid a commission of 5% on all monthly sales exceeding $15 000. The commission is paid in the month following that in which it is earned (see §31.10).

3. General expenses are paid in the month in which they are incurred and are to be budgeted as follows: January $6600; February $7100; March $6900; April $7000; May $7300; June $7500.

4. Xsel Ltd pays interest of 8% on a loan of $20 000 in four annual instalments on 31 March, 30 June, 30 September and 31 December.

5. A final dividend of $2000 for the year ended 31 December 2004 is payable in March 2005.

Required

Prepare an expenditure budget for Xsel Ltd for the six months ending 30 June 2005. All amounts should be shown to the nearest $.

Answer

	2005					
	January	February	March	April	May	June
	$	$	$	$	$	$
Purchases	6 300	5 040	6 930	8 190	9 450	8 820
Wages	4 000	4 000	4 000	4 000	4 000	4 000
Commission	–	–	–	75	225	431
General expenses	6 600	7 100	6 900	7 000	7 300	7 500
Loan interest	–	–	400	–	–	400
Dividend	–	–	2 000	–	–	–
Total expenditure	16 900	16 140	20 230	19 265	20 975	21 151

Exercise 6

Flannel and Flounder Ltd's overheads and other expenses for six months to 30 June 2005 are budgeted as follows.

1. Purchases are paid for in the following month.

2. Wages of $4000 per month are paid in the same month as they are earned.

3. Staff are paid a bonus equal to 4% of the amount by which monthly sales exceed $20 000. The bonus is paid in the month following that in which it is earned.

4. Electricity bills are expected to be received in January 2005, for $2400, and in April for $1800. The bills will be paid in the month following their receipt.

5. Other expenses are expected to amount to $6000 per month. From April 2005 they are expected to increase by 10%. They are paid in the month they are incurred.

6. Flannel and Flounder Ltd have a loan of $20 000 on which interest at 10% is payable in four quarterly instalments on 31 March, 30 June, 30 September and 31 December.

7. The company will purchase a machine in May 2005 for $15 000.

8. A final dividend of $4000 for the year ended 31 December 2004 will be paid in April 2005.

Required

Prepare Flannel and Flounder Ltd's expenditure budget for the six months ending 30 June 2005. Save your answer; it will be needed later.

31.17 How to prepare a cash budget

Cash budgets are prepared from the sales and expenses budgets. Special care must be taken with respect to the following.

- Sales revenue must be allocated to the correct months. Receipts from credit customers who are allowed cash discounts must be shown at the amounts after deduction of the discounts. The discounts should not be shown separately as an expense.
- Payments to suppliers (purchases) must be shown in the correct months; read the question carefully.

Example

Xsel Ltd's sales in November 2004 were $18 000, and in December 2004 were $17 600.

Of total sales, 40% are on a cash basis; 50% are to credit customers who pay within one month and receive a cash discount of 2%. The remaining 10% of customers pay within two months.

$10 000 was received from the sale of a fixed asset in March 2005. The balance at bank on 31 December 2004 was $12 400.

Required

Prepare Xsel Ltd's cash budget for the six months ending 30 June 2005. All amounts should be shown to the nearest $.

Answer

		2005				
	January	February	March	April	May	June
	$	$	$	$	$	$
Receipts						
Cash sales[1]	6 000	4 800	6 600	7 800	9 450	8 820
Debtors – 1 month[2]	8 624	7 350	5 880	8 085	9 555	11 576
Debtors – 2 months[3]	1 800	1 760	1 500	1 200	1 650	1 950
Sales of fixed asset	–	–	10 000	–	–	–
	16 424	13 910	23 980	17 085	20 655	22 346
Expenditure						
	January	February	March	April	May	June
	$	$	$	$	$	$
Purchases	6 300	5 040	6 930	8 190	9 450	8 820
Wages	4 000	4 000	4 000	4 000	4 000	4 000
Commission	–	–	–	75	225	431
General expenses	6 600	7 100	6 900	7 000	7 300	7 500
Loan interest	–	–	400	–	–	400
Dividend	–	–	2 000	–	–	–
	16 900	16 140	20 230	19 265	20 975	21 151
Net receipts/(payments)	(476)	(2 230)	3 750	(2 180)	(320)	1195
Balance brought forward	12 400	11 924	9 694	13 444	11 264	10 944
Balance carried forward	11 924	9 694	13 444	11 264	10 944	12 139

1 Cash sales = 40% of sales for month.

2 Cash received from debtors after one month = sales for previous month × 50% × 98%.

3 Cash received from debtors after two months = 10% of sales for two months previously.

Note. At 30 June 2005:

Debtors for sales:	$
10% of May sales ($23 625)	2 362.50
98% of 50% of June sales ($22 050)	10 804.50
10% of June sales	2 205.00
	15 372.00

Creditors for supplies: May purchases (paid for in July) = $11 340 + June purchases for production in July.

Accrued expenses: staff commission, 4% of $2050 = $82

Stock: If information for July and August had been available the following would be known:

> raw materials – purchased in June
>
> finished goods – made in June

Exercise 7

Flannel and Flounder Ltd's sales in November 2004 were $18 000 and in December 2004 were $17 600.

Of total sales revenue, 50% is on a cash basis, 40% is received one month after sale. Cash discount of $2\frac{1}{2}\%$ is allowed to customers who pay within one month. 10% of sales revenue is received two months after sale.

The company sold plant and equipment for $12 000 in February 2005. The balance at bank on 31 December 2004 was $31 750.

Required

(a) Prepare Flannel and Flounder Ltd's cash budget for the six months ending June 2005. Make all calculations to the nearest $.

(b) State the amount of Flannel and Flounder Ltd's trade debtors and creditors, and expense creditors at 30 June 2005.

31.18 How to prepare a master budget

A **master budget** is a budgeted Profit and Loss Account and Balance Sheet prepared from sales, purchases, expense and cash budgets. The purpose of the master budget is to reveal to management the profit or loss to be expected if management's plans for the business are implemented, and the state of the business at the end of the budget period.

It is important to remember that the Profit and Loss Account must be prepared on an accruals basis, and the information in the functional budgets must be adjusted for accruals and prepayments; it is advisable to identify these when preparing the cash budget. Much information additional to that required for the functional budgets mentioned above will usually be given. Details of fixed assets which are to be sold or purchased will often be supplied; this information will usually be included in a **capital budget**.

Example

Meadowlands Ltd's Balance Sheet at 31 December 2004 was as follows.

Fixed assets	Cost	Depreciation	Net
	$	$	$
Equipment	13 000	6 000	7 000
Motor vehicles	11 000	7 000	4 000
	24 000	13 000	11 000
Current assets			
Stock		9 600	
Trade debtors		33 600	
Cash at bank		15 000	
		58 200	
Current liabilities			
Trade creditors		6 200	52 000
			63 000
Share capital and reserves			
Ordinary shares of $1			40 000
Profit and Loss Account			23 000
			63 000

Further information

1. Goods are purchased one month before the month of sale.

2. Budgeted quarterly purchases and sales for the year ending 31 December 2005 are as follows:

	Purchases	Sales
	$	$
January – March	72 000	132 000
April – June	96 000	156 000
July – September	84 000	168 000
October – December	96 000	144 000

3. Meadowlands Ltd receives one month's credit on all purchases and allows one month's credit on all sales.

4. The following expenses will be incurred in the year ending 31 December 2005:

   (i)   rent of $1600 per quarter paid in advance on 1 January, 1 April, 1 July, and 1 October

   (ii) wages of $7200 payable each month

   (iii) an insurance premium of $3000 for 15 months to 31 March 2006 paid on 1 January 2005

   (iv) other expenses of $20 000 paid quarterly.

5. The company will purchase additional equipment costing $15 000 on 1 April 2005.

6. A new motor vehicle will be purchased on 1 April 2005 for $12 000.

7. A motor vehicle which cost $6000 and has a written down value of $3000 at 31 December 2004 will be sold for $2000 on 1 July 2005.

8. The company depreciates equipment at 10% per annum on cost. It depreciates motor vehicles at $12\frac{1}{2}\%$ per annum on cost.

9. The company's stock at 31 December 2005 will be valued at $32 000.

Required

(a) Prepare a cash budget for the year ending 31 December 2005.

(b) Prepare Meadowlands Ltd's budgeted Profit and Loss Account for the year ending 31 December 2005 and a budgeted Balance Sheet as at that date.

Answer

Meadowlands Ltd Cash budget for the year ending 31 December 2005

	Jan/Mar $	Apr/Jun $	Jul/Sept $	Oct/Dec $
Receipts				
Sales	121 600[1]	148 000[2]	164 000[2]	152 000[2]
Proceeds from sale of van	–	–	2 000	–
	121 600	148 000	166 000	152 000
Payments				
Purchases	54 200[3]	88 000[4]	88 000[4]	92 000[4]
Rent	1 600	1 600	1 600	1 600
Wages	21 600	21 600	21 600	21 600
Insurance	3 000	–	–	–
Other expenses	20 000	20 000	20 000	20 000
Purchase of equipment	–	15 000	–	–
Purchase of motor vehicle	–	12 000	–	–
	100 400	158 200	131 200	135 200
Net receipts/(payments)	21 200	(10 200)	34 800	16 800
Balance brought forward	15 000	36 200	26 000	60 800
Balance carried forward	36 200	26 000	60 800	77 600

1 Debtors at 31 December 2004 + $\frac{2}{3}$ of sales for January/March.

2 $\frac{1}{3}$ of previous quarter's sales + $\frac{2}{3}$ of current quarter's sales.

3 Creditors at 31 December 2004 + $\frac{2}{3}$ of purchases for January/March

4 $\frac{1}{3}$ of previous quarter's purchases + $\frac{2}{3}$ of current quarter's purchases.

Budgeted Profit and Loss Account for the year ending 31 December 2005

	$	$	$
Sales			600 000
Less Cost of sales:			
Stock at 1.1.05		9 600	
Purchases		348 000	
		357 600	
Stock at 31.12.05		32 000[5]	325 600
Gross profit			274 400
Less expenditure			
Wages		86 400	
Rent		6 400	
Insurance ($\frac{12}{15} \times \$3000$)		2 400	
Other expenses		80 000	
Loss on sale of motor vehicle		1 000	
Depreciation: equipment	2800[6]		
motor vehicles	2125[6]	4 925	181 125
Net profit			93 275

5 Stock purchased in December 2005 for sale in January 2006 ($\frac{1}{3}$ of $96 000).

6 See fixed assets in Balance Sheet.

Budgeted Balance Sheet at 31 December 2005

Fixed assets	Cost $	Depreciation $	Net $
Equipment	28 000	8 800	19 200
Motor vehicles	17 000	6 125	10 875
	45 000	14 925	30 075
Current assets			
Stock		32 000	
Trade debtors		48 000[7]	
Prepaid insurance		600	
Balance at bank		77 600	
		158 200	
Current liabilities			
Trade creditors		32 000[8]	126 200
			156 275
Share capital and reserves			
Ordinary shares of $1			40 000
Profit and Loss Account (23 000 + 93 275)			116 275
			156 275

7 December sales.

8 December purchases.

Exercise 8

The directors of Greenfields Ltd have prepared functional budgets for the four months ending 30 April 2005. To discover the effect that the budgets will have on the company at the end of the four months, they require the accountant to prepare master budgets. The accountant is provided with the following data.

Greenfields Ltd Balance Sheet at 31 December 2004

Fixed assets	Cost	Depreciation	Net
	$	$	$
Freehold premises	50 000	10 000	40 000
Plant and machinery	37 500	22 500	15 000
	87 500	32 500	55 000
Current assets			
Stock		30 000	
Trade debtors		42 500	
Balance at bank		20 750	
		93 250	
Current liabilities			
Trade creditors		22 500	70 750
			125 750
Long-term liability			
12% debentures 2009/10			25 000
			100 750
Share capital and reserves			
Ordinary shares of $1			65 000
General reserve			30 000
Retained profit			5 750
			100 750

Further information

1. Sales and purchases for the four months from January to April 2005 are budgeted to be

	Sales	Purchases
	$	$
January	62 500	25 000
February	70 000	20 000
March	75 000	30 000
April	82 500	37 500

2. 40% of sales are to cash customers; one month's credit is allowed on the remainder.
3. The company pays for its purchases in the month following purchase.
4. Selling and distribution expenses amount to 10% of sales and are paid in the month in which they are incurred.

5. Administration expenses amount to $20 000 per month and are paid in the month in which they are incurred.
6. Stock at the 30 April 2005 is estimated to be valued at $22 500.
7. Additional plant and machinery costing $60 000 will be purchased on 1 March 2005.
8. Annual depreciation of fixed assets is based on cost as follows: Freehold premises 3%; plant and machinery 20%. 50% of all depreciation is to be charged to selling and distribution expenses, and the balance to administration expenses.
9. Debenture interest is payable half-yearly on 30 June and 31 December.
10. A dividend of $0.10 per share will be paid on the ordinary shares on 30 April 2005.
11. $25 000 will be transferred to the General Reserve on 30 April 2005.

Required

(a) Prepare a cash budget for each of the four months from January 2005 to 30 April 2005.
(b) Prepare a budgeted Profit and Loss Account for the four months ending 30 April 2005 in as much detail as possible.
(c) Prepare a budgeted Balance Sheet as at 30 April 2005 in as much detail as possible.

31.19 Examination hints

- Practise the preparation of the functional and master budgets. They are not too difficult provided you read questions carefully to ascertain exactly when transactions are to take place. Failure to allocate sales, purchases, receipts and payments to the correct periods is a common cause of the loss of valuable marks.
- Preparation of budgets is often an exercise in arithmetic, so be accurate; but note if the question states the degree of accuracy required (e.g. to nearest $ or nearest $000).

31.20 Multiple-choice questions

1 A bedside table is made from 4 kg of raw material. Production for six months is based on the following data.

Budgeted sales	5000 tables
Budgeted decrease in stock of raw material	1200 kg
Budgeted increase in stock of tables	800 tables

How many kilograms of raw material will be purchased for the six months?

A 18 000 kg

B 18 800 kg

C 22 000 kg

D 23 200 kg

2 Debtors at the year-end are $40 000. It is planned to double turnover in the next year and to reduce the debtors' collection period from 45 days to 30 days.

What will the debtors be at the end of the next year?

A $26 667

B $53 334

C $60 000

D $80 000

3 The sales budget for four months from January to April is as follows.

January $80 000

February $100 000

March $110 000

April $130 000

The cost of the raw material used in the goods is 40% of sales. The material is purchased one month before the goods are made, and manufacture takes place one month before sale. 50% of the material is paid for one month after purchase and the balance is paid for two months after purchase.

How much will be paid for raw materials in March?

A $40 000

B $42 000

C $46 000

D $48 000

4 A company plans to purchase a new machine costing $40 000. It will part exchange one of its existing machines for the new one. The existing machine has a net book value of $4000 and the part exchange will result in a loss on disposal of the machine of $1000. The company will pay the balance due on the new machine by cheque.

How will the transaction be recorded in the cash budget?

A payment for new machine $37 000

B payment for new machine $40 000

C payment for new machine $40 000; cash received for old machine $3000

D payment for new machine $40 000; cash received for old machine $4000

31.21 Additional exercises

1 The sales budget for Roh Ltd for the six months to 30 November 2003 is as follows:

	Units
June	600
July	800
August	1000
September	900
October	980
November	1020

Further information is as follows:

1. All units are sold for $60. Customers are allowed 1 month's credit.

2. Monthly production of the units is equal to the following month's sales plus 10% for stock.

3. Costs per unit are as follows:

Material	3 kilos
Cost of material	$4.00 per kilo
Labour	2 hours
Labour rate of pay	$8.00 per hour
Absorption rates	
Variable overhead	$14.00
Fixed overhead	$3.50

4. Materials are purchased one month before they are needed for production and are paid for two months after purchase.

5. Wages and variable overheads are paid in the current month.

6. Fixed overheads are paid in the following month.

7. The following information is to be taken into account:
   (i) cash book balance at 30 June 2003: $16 000;
   (ii) stock of finished goods at 31 July 2003: $56 420.

Required

(a) The following budgets for the month of August 2003 *only*.
   (i) Production budget (in units only)
   (ii) Purchases budget
   (iii) Sales budget.
(b) Calculate the cash book balance at 31 July 2003.
(c) A cash budget for the month of August 2003 *only*.
(d) (i) Explain the advantages and uses of budgets.
   (ii) Explain how principal budget factors affect the preparation of budgets.

(UCLES, 2003, AS/A Level Accounting, Syllabus 9706/04, May/June)

2 Banner Ltd's budget for the four months from January to April includes the following data.

1.

Month	Sales $000	Materials $000	Wages $000	Overheads $000
January	615	114.4	30	360
February	636	118.8	33	390
March	690	132.0	36	412
April	684	128.0	39	420

2. One-third of sales revenue is received one month after sale and the remainder is received two months after sale. The sales in the previous two months were: November $600 000; December $540 000.

3. One-quarter of purchases of materials are paid for in the month of purchase. The remainder are paid for two months later. Purchases in the previous two months were: November $108 000; December $106 000.

4. Two-thirds of the wages are paid in the month in which they are earned, and the balance is paid in the following month. The wages for the previous December amounted to $30 000.

5. One-half of the overhead expenditure is paid in the month in which it is incurred, and the balance is paid in the following month. The overheads for the previous December were $380 000.

6. Old machinery will be sold for $4000 in April. New machinery will be purchased in March for $90 000 but only one-half of the price will be paid in that month. The balance will be paid in August.

7. Banner Ltd has an overdraft $63 000 at the bank at 31 December.

Required

(a) Prepare Banner Ltd's cash budget for each of the four months from January to April. The budget should be prepared in columnar form.

(b) Prepare a statement to show the accruals in part (a) which would appear in a Balance Sheet at 30 April.

32 Standard costing

Objectives
- explain the concept of standard costing
- differentiate between standards and budgets
- apply standards to cost elements of direct material, labour and manufacturing overheads
- explain the standard setting process
- distinguish between ideal standards and attainable standards
- compute material, labour and overhead variances
- state reasons for variances

32.1 Standard costing

A standard is a predetermined acceptable level of performance, which is used as a benchmark by which other performances are judged or measured. Standards are common and widely used by everyone.

Cost accounting standards are usually associated with standard costing or standard cost. Standard costing involves setting a cost target for a job or product or service, which should be attained. Standard costs are predetermined *unit costs* of a product or job.

Standard costing is an accounting technique which establishes predetermined estimates of products or jobs and compares these estimates with actual costs as they are incurred.

32.2 Standards and budgets

Standards and budgets are similar in nature in that both involve estimates of costs. They both set target levels to be achieved in order to assess the performance of a department or cost centre. They are both used as important strategic elements of management control and planning.

Standards however are concerned with units. It is a unit amount. Budgets on the other hand are concerned with totals. For example the **standard** material cost for manufacturing one chair is $20. The **standard** direct labour cost for that chair is $30. If 100 chairs are to be manufactured for the month, the **budgeted** cost (total) is $5 000. The standard costs (units) are $20 and $30. A standard is therefore concerned with the individual cost components that make up the entire budget. Budget data do not form part of the accounting process. They are not journalized. The information serves as a memorandum. In contrast, standards are incorporated in the cost accounting system process and form part of the double entry process.

32.3 Standards and elements of cost

Standard costing focuses on setting standards for the three cost elements: material, labour and manufacturing overheads. Standards are set for quantity and cost (price) for each element. Direct material for a product will be analysed in terms of its **standard quantity** i.e. how much of the material should be used to make one unit of the product, as well as its **standard price** i.e. the price that should be paid for the material used to make one unit of the product.

32.4 Direct material standards

In producing wooden chairs for example, a manufacturer's direct material standard quantity could be 4 feet (board) per chair. The standard price could be $5.00 per foot of board. The standard direct material cost per chair will be $20.00 i.e. standard quantity (4 feet) × standard price ($5.00).

32.5 Direct labour standards

The standard direct labour cost per chair will also be analysed in terms of quantity and price. Standard quantity is the time that would be required to make one unit of the product e.g. 3 hours. The standard price for labour is sometimes called standard rate. It is the rate per hour that should be incurred for direct labour. If it is determined that the direct labour rate per hour be $10.00, then the direct labour cost per unit (chair) will be $30.00 i.e. standard direct labour hours (3hrs.) × standard direct labour rate $10.00. The direct labour quantity standard is also referred to as the direct labour efficiency standard.

32.6 Manufacturing overhead standards

Standards for manufacturing overheads are calculated for both variable and fixed overhead components. An appropriate activity index, labour hours or machine hours, is used with a budgeted overhead cost to arrive at the predetermined overhead rate to be used in setting the standard. Supposing, for example, a budgeted overhead cost of $225 000 is identified for the year, comprising $135 000 variable cost and $90 000 fixed cost. Also suppose 15 000 chairs are to be manufactured. When we apply direct labour hours as the basis of activity, which as indicated before was 3 hours per chair, the level of activity becomes 45 000 direct hours (15 000 × 3). We can now determine the overhead rate as follows:

Budgeted overhead costs	Amount	Standard direct labour hours	Overhead rate per direct labour hour
Variable	$135 000	45 000	$3.00
Fixed	$ 90 000	45 000	$2.00
Total	$ 225 000	45 000	$5.00

The standard manufacturing overhead rate per unit =

$$\underset{\$5}{\text{Predetermined overhead rate}} \times \underset{\text{3 hours}}{\text{Activity index quantity}} = \$15 \text{ per unit}$$

32.7 Total standard cost per unit

Having established the budgeted standard cost for direct material, direct labour and manufacturing overheads, we can now summarize them to determine the standard cost per unit (chair).

Element of cost	Standard quantity	x Standard price	= Standard cost
Direct material	4 feet	$ 5	$20
Direct labour	3 hours	$ 10	$30
Manufacturing overheads	3 hours	$ 5	$15
Total standard cost per unit			$65

32.8 The standard setting process

Setting cost standards requires the active participation and input from all persons in the organization who are responsible for costs and quantities. It also requires the involvement of technical experts. A wide cross-section of personnel such as production supervisors, purchasing agents, management accountants, quality control supervisors, labour supervisors, trade union representatives and department supervisors will form part of the teams required to set standards for product cost quantity and quality.

Data of past costs and activities are gathered, organized and analysed for various levels of operation in the past. The data is then adjusted to cater for anticipated future conditions such as demand and supply, varying economic trends and changing technologies. Standard-setting will also involve analysing manufacturing processes with the use of production engineers to expertly determine how much direct material, labour and manufacturing overhead costs are required in the production process.

32.9 Ideal standards

In setting standards a distinction is usually made between ideal standards and attainable standards. Ideal standards are standards which can only be attained under perfect operating conditions. Ideal standards do not cater for waste, spoilage, machine breakdowns or other forms of interruptions. In reality ideal standards are usually unattainable, and the few firms that use them do so for motivational purposes for their workers. It is argued however that workers may become disenchanted and discouraged on realizing that they cannot achieve maximum efficiency.

Attainable standards These standards are levels of performances that can be achieved with a realistic amount of effort. They cater for realistic work stoppages, rest periods, material wastage, spoilage and other acceptable levels of inefficiencies. However they also anticipate a high level of worker's performance so that its achievement is possible. Once workers know the standards are attainable, they can be sufficiently motivated to achieve them.

32.10 Variances

The actual amount of material and time used in producing products by the end of the period is seldom ever equal to the amount of material and time estimated to be used. In other words total actual cost is usually never equal to total standard cost.

A variance is the difference between total actual costs and total standard costs. This can be explained by looking at the previously calculated standard costs:

Cost element	Standard costs	Actual costs	Variances
Direct material	$2 000	$2 250	$250 Unfavourable
Direct labour	$3 000	$3 120	$120 Unfavourable
Variable manufacturing overheads	$900	$940	$40 Unfavourable
Fixed manufacturing overheads	$90 000	$86 000	$4 000 Unfavourable

Element of cost	Standard quantity	x	Standard price	=	Standard cost
Direct material	4 ft		$5		$20
Direct labour	3 hrs		$10		$30
Variable manufacturing overheads	3 hrs		$3		$9
Fixed manufacturing overheads	3 hrs		$2		$6
Total standard cost per unit					$65

32.11 Total material variance

Standard costs

Example: Assuming that 100 chairs are to be produced, the following budgets can be determined for the period:

Cost element	Standard costs	Amount	Total
Direct material	$20	100	$2 000
Direct labour	$30	100	$3 000
Variable manufacturing overheads	$9	100	$900
Fixed manufacturing overheads			$90 000

Actual costs

Example: Assuming that the 100 chairs produced for the period actually used 500 feet of material at $4.50 per foot, the total standard cost would be: $100 \times 4ft \times \$5.00 = \$2\ 000$. However, the actual cost is $500ft. \times \$4.50 = \$2\ 250$.

Total material variance is $250 unfavourable because the actual cost of making 100 units was $250 more than the amount budgeted.

The actual cost will be determined at the end of the period and compared with the standard cost to determine the variance.

32.12 Analysing elements of variances

The material, labour and variable manufacturing overhead variances calculated above are all unfavourable and must now be analysed.

Each element of cost is generally divided between quantity and price as follows:

	Quantity	Price
Direct material	Usage	Price
Direct labour	Efficiency	Rate
Fixed overheads	Efficiency	Expenditure
Variable overheads	Volume	Efficiency

The total material variance of $250 unfavourable can now be analysed in terms of usage (quantity used) and price. This distinction helps to identify the person or department responsible for the unfavourable variance. If the usage variance is unfavourable, better management and control may be required in the production department. If the price variance is unfavourable, attention needs to be paid to the purchasing department.

32.13 Usage and price variance for materials

The total materials variance for the production of 100 units can be determined by the formula

$$
\begin{array}{cccc}
\text{Actual quantity} \times \text{Actual price} & - & \text{Standard quantity} \times \text{Standard price} \\
\text{i.e.} \qquad (500 \times \$4.50) & - & (400 \times \$5) \\
\$2250 & - & \$2000 & = \$250 \text{ unfavourable}
\end{array}
$$

The **material usage** variance for the production of a 100 units can be determined by the formula

$$
\begin{array}{cccc}
\text{Actual quantity} \times \text{Standard price} & - & \text{Standard quantity} \times \text{Standard price} \\
AQ \times SP & - & SQ \times SP \\
(500 \times \$5) & - & (400 \times \$5) \\
\$2500 & - & \$2000 & = \$500 \text{ unfavourable}
\end{array}
$$

In this analysis, more material was actually used (500 ft) than budgeted for (400 ft). That is 100 ft more at $5 per foot, which means that $500 more was spent on material, than planned.

The **material price** variance for the production of 100 units can be determined by the formula

$$
\begin{array}{cccc}
\text{Actual quantity} \times \text{Actual price} & - & \text{Actual quantity} \times \text{Standard price} \\
AQ \times AP & - & AQ \times SP \\
(500 \times \$4.50) & - & (500 \times \$5.00) & = \$250 \text{ favourable} \\
\$2250 & - & \$2500
\end{array}
$$

In this analysis the actual price of material was less than the budgeted price by $0.50. Thus the amount spent to purchase material will be less by $250 (500 × $0.50).

The general variance formula can be redefined as follows:

$$
\left.\begin{array}{l}
\text{Standard quantity} \times \text{Standard price} \\
\text{Actual quantity} \times \text{Standard price}
\end{array}\right\} \text{Quantity variance}
$$

$$
\left.\begin{array}{l}
\text{Actual quantity} \times \text{Standard price} \\
\text{Actual quantity} \times \text{Actual price}
\end{array}\right\} \text{Price variance}
$$

The material quantity variance can be written in the alternative form

$$
\begin{array}{ll}
SP \times (AQ - SQ) & = MQV \\
\$5.00 \times (500 - 400) & = \$500 \text{ unfavourable}
\end{array}
$$

The material price variance can be written as

$$
\begin{array}{ll}
AQ \times (AP - SP) & = MPV \\
500 \times (\$4.50 - \$5.00) & = \$250 \text{ favourable}
\end{array}
$$

32.14 Total labour variance

The same model can be used to analyse direct labour variances. The two sub-variances involved will be **efficiency** for quantity and **rate** for price. In the previous example, the direct labour cost is 3 hours at $10 per hour. Assuming that the 100 chairs produced actually used 260 hours at $12 per hour, the total labour variance will be calculated as follows:

$$
\begin{array}{cccccc}
\text{Actual hours} \times \text{Actual rate} & - & \text{Standard hours} \times \text{Standard rate} \\
(260 \times \$12) & - & (300 \times \$10) \\
\$3120 & - & \$3000 & = \$120 \text{ unfavourable}
\end{array}
$$

The total labour variance is $120 unfavourable because the actual labour cost of making 100 units was $120 more than was budgeted for.

The labour efficiency variance for the production of 100 units can be determined by the formula

Actual hours × Standard rate − Standard hours × Standard rate
(260 hrs   × $10)   −   (300 hrs   × $10)
        $2600   − $3000   = $400 favourable

The efficiency variance is favourable because less hours were actually used than budgeted for in the production of 100 units.

Labour rate variance

The formula used for the calculation of the labour rate variance will be:

Actual hours × Standard rate − Actual hours × Actual rate
(260 hrs   × $10)   −   (260   × $12)
        $2600   − $3120   = $520 unfavourable

The variable is unfavourable because the actual cost of labour $12 is more than cost budgeted, i.e. $10.

Using the model indicated previously, the above variance can be summarized as follows:

Standard quantity × Standard price = 300 × 10 = 3000
LESS Actual quantity × Standard price = 260 × 10 = 2600   } 400 F Efficiency

Actual quantity × Standard price = 260 × 10 = 2600
LESS Actual quantity × Actual price = 260 × 12 = 3120   } 520 U Rate

Total labour variance is 120 U

This summary can also be applied to direct material variance.

32.15 Manufacturing overhead variances

Overhead variances are analysed separately as variable and fixed overhead variances.

32.16 Variable overhead variances

These variances are determined in a similar manner to direct material and direct labour, since variable overhead costs change with a change in the level of activity, just like direct materials and direct labour. The variable overhead variances are usually analysed in terms of efficiency and expenditure.

In an earlier example, it was shown that the budgeted variable overhead costs was $135 000 and the budgeted number of direct labour hours was 45 000 hours. It was also earlier indicated that each unit took 3 hours to be produced. Assuming that 100 units were actually produced, actual hours worked were 260 hours and variable overheads actually incurred were $940, the time taken for 100 units will be 300 hours (100 × 3 hrs).

Variable overhead total variance

The standard variable overhead cost of 300 hours at $3 per hour is	$900
Actual cost was	$940
The total variance is therefore	$40 Unfavourable

This variance is unfavourable because the actual cost exceeds the standard cost by $40 and profits will therefore be lower than expected.

Variable overhead efficiency and expenditure variances

We can now use the summary formula to analyse the variance into efficiency and expenditure.

Standard quantity × Standard price = 300 × $3 = $900
LESS Actual quantity × Standard price = 260 × $3 = $780 } 120 F Efficiency

Actual quantity × Standard price = 260 × $3 = $780
LESS Actual quantity × Actual price = $940 } 160 U Expenditure

In this analysis, we see that the variable overhead efficiency variance is $120 favourable since less direct labour hours were used than expected in the production of 100 units. The expenditure variance however is $160 unfavourable since the actual variable overhead cost per hour was greater than expected for 100 units.

32.17 Fixed overhead cost variances

These variances show the effect on profit caused by a difference between actual and budgeted fixed overhead costs. Usually an absorption costing system is assumed, thereby explaining the variances in terms of over absorption or under absorption of overheads.

Fixed overhead total variance

In the earlier example, the budgeted data was as follows:

Budgeted fixed overheads $90 000
Budgeted direct labour hours 45 000 hrs
Budgeted production 15 000 units

Assuming that 14 500 units were actually produced using 42 000 hours and the actual fixed overhead cost was $86 000.

Utilizing an absorption costing system, the pre-determined overhead absorption rate (OAR) will be $2 per direct labour hour, i.e. 90 000 hrs ÷ 45 000 units.

Also, the budgeted time to complete 1 unit is 3 hours, i.e. 45 000 hrs ÷ 15 000 units.

Thus, 14 500 units at 3 hrs per unit will use 43 500 hours.

43 500 hrs at an OAR of $2 per direct labour hour will absorb $87 000 of overheads.

Using absorption costing, this $87 000 is the standard cost of the actual production of 14 500 units. When compared to the actual cost:

Standard cost	$87 000	
Actual cost	$86 000	
Total fixed overhead variance	1 000	Favourable

This favourable variance represents an over-absorption.

Fixed overhead volume variance

This volume variance measures the difference between the amount actually absorbed based on actual production and the amount budgeted to be absorbed (all based on standard hours). Thus,

Budgeted production (standard labour hours)	45 000 hrs	
Actual production (standard labour hours)	43 500 hrs	
Difference	1 500 hrs	Unfavourable
1500 Standard hours valued at an OAR of $2 per hour = $3000		

This variance is unfavourable because the actual output is less than the expected output.

32.18 Expenditure variance

This variance shows the effect on profit of the actual fixed overhead expenditure as compared to the budgeted amount. Thus,

Budgeted expenditure	90 000	
Actual expenditure	86 000	
	4 000	F

The variance is favourable because the actual expenditure is less than the expected expenditure.

32.19 Reasons for variances

Variances	Sub-variances	Causes
Total direct material	Price	1. Unforeseen price changes 2. Use of different materials at different prices 3. Discount available 4. Delivery method used 5. Using substitute materials because planned ones unavailable
	Usage	1. Substituting different quality materials 2. Reduced or increased efficiency 3. Faulty machines 4. Untrained labour 5. Poor supervision 6. Different material yield than planned
Total direct labour	Rate	1. Untrained labour doing skilled work 2. Highly paid doing lowly paid job 3. Payment and unplanned overtime on hours
	Efficiency	1. Employing better in lower paid labour 2. Better or poorer quality of materials 3. Greater/lesser motivation 4. Machine problems
Total variable overhead This is the over or under absorption of overheads Actual variable overhead incurred vs Variable overhead absorbed	Expenditure (Actual variable overhead increased vs Allowed variable overhead based on actual hours worked)	1. Increases or reductions in charges from suppliers 2. Wastage
Total fixed overhead variance Actual variable overhead vs variable overhead absorbed by the actual production, i.e. over/under-absorption of overhead variance	Budgeted Actual fixed overhead vs Allowed fixed overhead (Budgeted fixed overhead)	1. Increase or reduction of charges by suppliers
	Volume Fixed overhead absorbed by the actual production vs Budgeted fixed overhead Efficiency – Standard hours of actual production vs Actual hours valued at Fixed overhead actual rate Capacity – Budgeted hours vs Actual hours at fixed overhead actual rate	1. Excess actual hours worked 2. Variation in efficiency 3. Variation in activity level

32.20 Questions

Exercise 1

Brekkifoods Ltd's budget for the production of 100 000 packets of Barleynuts in the year ending 31 December 2005 was as follows:

		$
Variable expenses		
Direct materials		20 000
Direct labour		15 000
Production expenses		6 000
		41 000
Fixed expenses		
Production expenses	13 000	
Administration		29 000
		83 000

The actual output for the year ended 31 December 2005 was 110 000 packets of Barleynuts.

Required
Prepare a flexed budget for the production of 110 000 packets of Barleynuts.

Exercise 2

Flexers Ltd has prepared the following budgets for the production of time locks:

No. of locks	6000	8000
	$	$
Direct materials	15 000	20 000
Direct labour	36 000	48 000
Production overhead	25 000	31 000
Selling and distribution	24 000	28 000
Administration	80 000	80 000
	180 000	207 000

Required
Prepare a flexed budget for the production of 9000 time locks.

Exercise 3

Enigma Ltd has prepared a budget based on standard costs. It is shown below together with the actual results.

	Budget	Actual
No. of units	4000	4250
	$	$
Direct material	20 000	23 400
Direct labour	46 000	47 236
Variable overhead	10 000	10 500
Fixed overhead	50 000	50 000
Total costs	126 000	131 136

Required
(a) Prepare a flexed budget for 4250 units.
(b) Calculate:
   (i) total cost variance
   (ii) expenditure variance
   (iii) direct material variance
   (iv) direct labour variance.
(c) Reconcile the actual cost incurred with the budgeted costs, using the variances calculated in (b).

Exercise 4

Underpar Ltd has prepared a budget based on standard costs. It is shown below together with the actual results.

	Budget	Actual
No. of units	7000	6300
	$	$
Direct material	23 800	20 890
Direct labour	47 250	44 065
Variable overhead	3 500	3 250
Fixed overhead	62 000	62 000
Total costs	136 550	130 205

Required
(a) Prepare a flexed budget for 6300 units.
(b) Calculate:
   (i) total cost variance
   (ii) expenditure variance
   (iii) direct material variance
   (iv) direct labour variance.
(c) Reconcile the actual cost incurred with the budgeted costs, using the variances calculated in (b).

Exercise 5

Dandelion Ltd manufactures a health food known as 'Pickup'. The standard material cost of a packet of Pickup is as follows: 3 litres at $5 per litre. In one month Dandelion Ltd produced 12 000 packets of Pickup using 2.8 litres of material per packet at a total cost of $4.80 per litre.

Required

Calculate the direct material usage and price variances for 12 000 packets of Pickup.

Direct labour efficiency variance This variance is calculated using the formula $(SH - AH)SR$ where SH is the standard hours, AH is the actual hours taken and SR is the standard rate of pay.

> Acrobat Ltd's standard hours were 40 minutes per Caper, or a total of $\frac{40}{60} \times 23\ 000 = 15\ 333.33$ hours
>
> The actual time taken was 45 minutes per Caper, or a total of $\frac{45}{60} \times 23\ 000 = 17\ 250.00$ hours
>
> Variance = 1916.67 hours (A)
>
> 1916.67 hours × Standard rate at $12 = $23 000 (A)

Direct labour rate variance This is calculated using the formula $(SR - AR)AH$ where AR is the actual hourly rate of pay.

Acrobat Ltd's actual hourly rate of pay was $10 and the rate variance is $(12 - 10)17\ 250 = \$34\ 500$ (F).
Check: Efficiency variance – rate variance = total labour variance: $23 000 (A) – 34 500 (F) = $11 500 (F) (See p.281.)

Exercise 6

Dandelion Ltd has a standard direct labour cost for the production of one packet of Pickup based on 1 labour hour at $10 per hour. The production of 12 000 packets of Pickup required 1.25 hours paid at $8.50 per hour.

Required

Calculate the direct labour efficiency and rate variances for 12 000 packets of Pickup.

Exercise 7

Larabee Ltd prepared a budget for the production of 300 units in April 2004 as follows:

	$
Direct materials (4 kg per unit)	7200
Direct labour ($11 per hour)	6600

The production for the month was 400 units and the costs were as follows:

	$
Direct materials ($6.25 per kg)	9 000
Direct labour (2.25 hours per unit)	10 890

Required

(a) Calculate the following variances for April 2004:
  (i)   direct material usage
  (ii) direct material price
  (iii) direct labour efficiency
  (iv) direct labour rate.
(b) Comment on the variances in (a) and suggest possible causes.

Exercise 8

Cantab Ltd's standard costing records provide the following information for three month's production and sales:

	$
Master budget profit	98 970
Variances	
Quantity	17 009 (A)
Sales volume	6 210 (F)
Sales price	3 730 (A)
Material usage	6 280 (A)
Material price	9 635 (F)
Labour efficiency	10 500 (F)
Labour rate	7 840 (A)
Overhead expenditure	5 760 (A)

Required

Prepare a statement to show the actual profit made by Cantab Ltd in the three months covered by the given information.

32.21 Multiple-choice questions

1 A company manufactures a product which requires 2 hours of direct labour per unit. Normal output is 1400 units and the standard labour rate is $6.50 per hour.

In one month the company manufactured 1300 units of the product in 2500 direct labour hours costing $17 550.

What is the direct labour efficiency variance?

A $650 (favourable)   **B** $675 (favourable)
C $1300 (favourable)   **D** $1350 (favourable)

2 A company makes a single product which requires two types of raw material: ionium and zetonium. The standard cost of materials to produce one unit of the product is shown:

Material	kg	Standard cost ($ per kg)
Ionium	30	2
Zetonium	45	3

100 units of the product have been made using 3100 kg of ionium and 4400 kg of zetonium.
What is the total material usage variance?

A $100 (adverse)   **B** $100 (favourable)

C $500 (adverse)   **D** $500 (favourable)

3 A company's standard cost statement shows the following variances (F favourable; A adverse):

		$
1	Sales total variance	1300 (A)
2	Sales volume variance	1500 (A)
3	Sales price variance	?
4	Materials total variance	950 (A)
5	Materials usage variance	670 (F)
6	Materials price variance	?
7	Labour total variance	660 (F)
8	Labour efficiency variance	415 (F)
9	Labour rate variance	?

What is the effect *in total* of variances 3, 6 and 9 on the profit of the company?

A $1175 (A)   **B** $1175 (F)   **C** $1575 (A)

D $1665 (A)

4 The following information is available about a product.

Standard selling price per unit	$17
Budgeted sales (units)	45 000
Actual sales (units)	48 000
Total sales revenue	$744 000

What is the sales price variance?

A $51 000 (A)   **B** $51 000 (F)   **C** $72 000 (A)

D $72 000 (F)

5 Details of direct material costs are as follows.

Budget	Actual
41 500 kg at $12 per kg	44 000 kg at £13.20 per kg

What is the direct material price variance?

A $49 500 (A)   **B** $49 500 (F)   **C** $52 800 (A)

D $52 800 (F)

6 A company's cost of production is made up of the cost of direct materials and the cost of direct labour. The following variances have been calculated at the end of three month's production:

	$	
Direct materials usage	1600	adverse
Direct materials price	1300	favourable
Direct labour efficiency	820	favourable
Direct labour rate	900	adverse

The actual cost of production was $23 440.
What was the standard cost of production?

A $22 220   **B** $23 020   **C** $23 060

D $24 580

32.22 Additional exercises

1 Kings Ltd makes an electronic device for finding lost keys, which it has patented under the trademark 'Gonkeys'. The product passes through two processes and the budget for the production of 10 000 Gonkeys is as follows:

	Process 1	Process 2
Costs per Gonkey		
Material	2 kg	4 litres
Cost of material per kg/litre	$8	$6
Labour hours per Gonkey	2	4
Labour rate per hour	$10	$12
Production overhead absorption	$20 per labour/hour	$23 per labour/hour

Required

(a) Prepare budgeted accounts for processes 1 and 2 to show the cost of producing 10 000 Gonkeys.

The actual production for process 1 was 10 000 Gonkeys. In process 2, completed production was 9000 Gonkeys, and 1000 Gonkeys were completed as to 50% of material and wages.

Required

(b) Prepare a flexed budget for process 2 based on actual production.

Actual costs per Gonkey were as follows:

	Process 1	Process 2
Material	2.22 kg	3.75 litres
Cost of material per kg/litre	$8.25	$6.2
Labour hours per Gonkey	2.25	4.5
Labour rate per hour	$11.50	$11.50
Production overhead absorption	$20 per labour/hour	$23 per labour/hour

Required

(c) Prepare ledger accounts for processes 1 and 2 based on actual expenditure

(d) Calculate the following variances for process 1
  (i)   material price
  (ii) material usage
  and the following variances for process 2
  (iii) labour efficiency
  (iv) labour rate.

(e) State *four* advantages of using a system of standard costs.

2 Pembroke Ltd makes an item of furniture known as a Tripos. The standard cost per Tripos is as follows:

Direct material: 2 kg at $7 per kg

Direct labour: 3 hours at $10 per hour

Production overhead: direct (variable) $14 per direct labour hour

indirect (fixed) based on overhead absorption rate of $30 per direct labour hour

Further information for the three months ending 30 June 2005:

1. The budgeted amount for direct labour: $120 000.

2. Administration and selling overheads for three months ending 30 June 2005: $32 000.

3. Factory profit is 20% of cost of production.

4. The budgeted selling price per Tripos: $250.

5. No stocks of raw materials, work in progress or finished goods arc held.

Required

(a) Prepare a budgeted Manufacturing, Trading and Profit and Loss Account for the three months ending 30 June 2005 to show the budgeted net profit or loss.

(b) Calculate, using the information in (a), the break-even point and margin of safety. The margin of safety should be shown as a percentage.

The actual production of Tripos and the related revenue and costs for the three months ended 30 June 2005 were as follows:

No. of Tripos produced	4180
Materials used	8990 kg
Cost of materials	$61 132
Direct labour hours	14 630
Direct labour cost	$138 985
Fixed overhead expenditure:	
Production	$372 000
Administration and selling	$42 000
Selling price per Tripos	$248

The overhead absorption rate for variable production overhead was not affected. All Tripos produced were sold.

Required

(c) Prepare
  (i)   a flexed budget based on the actual number of Tripos produced and sold and
  (ii) a financial statement based on actual results.

(d) Calculate the following variances:
  (i)   quantity (the additional profit arising from increased production)
  (ii)   sales volume
  (iii) sales price
  (iv)   direct materials usage
  (v)   direct materials price
  (vi)   direct labour efficiency
  (vii) direct labour rate.

(e) Calculate the break-even point based on actual revenue and expenditure. (Show your workings.)

(f) Prepare a financial statement to reconcile the original budgeted profit with the actual profit.

32.23 Questions

1 A standard cost is

   A always equal to actual cost

   B the cost of a product obtained at the end of the period

   C a predetermined unit cost of a product or service

   D only used to determine overhead expenses.

2 Standards and budgets are similar except that

   A standards involve estimates of costs but budgets do not

   B standards are unit amounts while budgets are total amounts

   C standards set targets to be achieved but budgets do not

   D standards are used for management control but budgets are used for planning.

3 Standards represent an expected level of performance which is

   A expressed on a per unit basis

   B expressed on a total basis

   C determined by the workers

   D always attained.

4 Standard costing focuses on setting standards for all except

   A material

   B fixed assets

   C overheads

   D labour.

5 Standards for the three cost elements are usually analysed in terms of

   A price and demand

   B quantity and reliability

   C direct and indirect

   D quantity and price.

6 Standard direct material or labour cost is calculated by

   A standard overheads times standard quantity

   B standard price times standard overheads

   C standard quantity times standard price

   D standard overhead times standard material.

7 In producing one unit of a product 5 kilos of direct material costing $3 per kilo are to be used. If 4 units of the product were made, the standard direct material costs for the units produced will be

   A $60

   B $15

   C $20

   D $12.

8 In manufacturing metal beds, 3 hours of direct labour at a rate of $15 per hour are to be used. If 6 beds are to be produced in the period, the standard direct labour cost will be

   A $45

   B $90

   C $270

   D $18.

9 The direct labour quantity standard is also referred to as the

   A labour efficiency standard

   B labour rate standard

   C labour usage standard

   D labour price standard.

33 Short-term decision making

Objectives
- explain how changes in activities affect contribution margin and net income.
- compute the contribution margin ratio
- calculate break-even point by both the equation method and contribution margin method
- prepare a break-even chart (cost volume graph) and explain the significance of each of its components
- state the limitations of break-even charts
- compute the margin of safety and explain its significance
- define relevant cost
- outline steps in the decision-making process

33.1 Cost volume analysis

Cost volume analysis is used by managers for decision-making. It shows the relationship between cost, volume and profit in an organization. Questions to be answered by the analysis:

1. What are the products to sell or manufacture?

2. What are the productive resources to be acquired?

3. What are the marketing strategies to adopt?

Contribution margin is the amount remaining after deducting variable expenses after sales. Therefore one can safely say that it is the amount available to cover the expenses and the rest to be retained as profits.

Unit contribution margin – calculation	
Selling price	X
Less variable expenses	X
Unit contribution margin	X

Contribution margin ratio expresses the contribution as a percentage of sales. There are two formulas to calculate these ratios. They are

1. $\dfrac{\text{Contribution margin}}{\text{Sales}}$

2. $\dfrac{\text{Unit contribution margin}}{\text{Unit selling price}}$

Contribution margin ratio can be used to predict the change in the total contribution margin.

To calculate the change in dollar sales: change in dollar sales × contribution margin ratio.

There are two types of analysis used by managers for making day to day decisions, namely break-even analysis and target profit analysis.

33.2 Break-even analysis

The break-even point can be completed either using the equation method or the contribution margin method.

33.3 Contribution margin method

The point at which a business or a product makes neither a profit nor a loss is the **break-even point**. Managers need to know the break-even point of a product when making decisions about pricing, production levels and other matters.

Break-even occurs when contribution equals fixed costs. It is found by dividing the total fixed costs by the contribution per unit. The calculation gives the number of units that have to be produced and sold before the fixed costs are covered.

Example

The following information relates to the production of a chemical:

	$
Marginal cost per litre	26
Selling price per litre	50
Total of fixed costs	72 000

The contribution per litre is $(50 - 26) = 24.

Break-even point $= \dfrac{\$72\,000}{\$24} = 3000$ litres.

The sales revenue at which the product will break even is $3000 \times \$50 = \$150\,000$. This may also be found as follows:

$$\dfrac{\text{total fixed costs}}{\text{contribution per \$ of selling price}} = \dfrac{\$72\,000}{0.48} = \$150\,000$$

(contribution per \$ of selling price $= \$24 \div 50 = \$0.48$).

When the calculation of break-even point results in a fraction of a unit of production, the answer should be rounded up to the next complete unit, for example: Contribution per unit of product \$23; total fixed costs \$32 000.

Break-even $= \dfrac{\$32\,000}{\$23} = 1391.304$, shown as 1392 units.

Answer

Sales	=	Variable expenses	+	Fixed expenses	+	Profits
50x	=	26x	+	$72 000	+	0
24x	=	$72 000				
x	=	$72 000 ÷ 24				
x	=	3000 litres				

33.4 Break-even charts

A **break-even chart** is a diagrammatic representation of the profit or loss to be expected from the sale of a product at various levels of activity. The chart is prepared by plotting the revenue from the sale of various volumes of a product against the total cost of production. The break-even point occurs where the sales curve bisects the total cost curve and there is neither profit nor loss.

Example

The marginal cost of product X is $10 per litre. It is sold for $22.50 per litre. Fixed costs are $50 000.

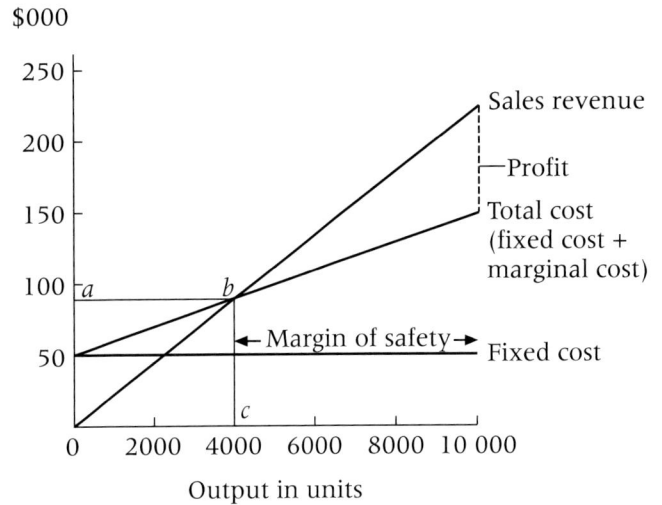

Break-even chart for product X

The line ab shows the revenue at break-even point ($90 000). The line bc shows the output in units at break-even point (4000). At 10 000 units, the sales revenue is $225 000 and total cost is $150 000. The distance between those two lines shows the profit of $75 000.

The area between the sales revenue line and the total cost line *before* the break-even point represents the loss that will be made if the output falls below 4000 units. The area *beyond* the break-even point represents profit.

The difference between the break-even point and 10 000 units is the **margin of safety**, or the amount by which output can fall short of 10 000 units before the business risks making a loss on product X. It may be expressed as a number of units, 6000, or as a percentage,

$\dfrac{6000}{10\,000} \times 100 = 60\%$.

The break-even charts of two products, A and B, will now be compared. Both products have similar total costs and revenues, but product A has high fixed costs while product B has low fixed costs.

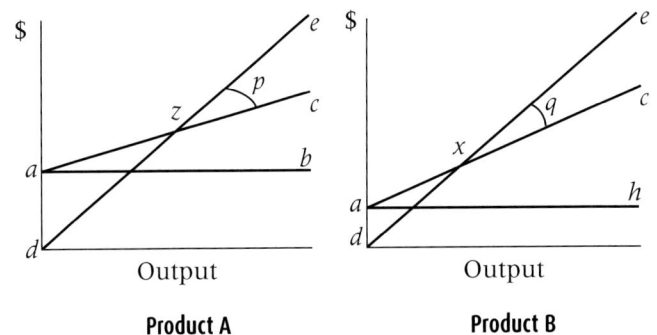

Product A

Product B

In each case, line *ab* represents fixed costs, line *ac* represents total cost, and line *de* represents sales revenue. The break-even point *x* for product A occurs further to the right of the chart (i.e. later) than that for product B. This shows that high fixed costs tend to result in high break-even points. Product B with a low fixed cost has a lower break-even point even though the marginal cost is greater.

The angle *p* at which the revenue line *de* intersects the total cost line *ac* for product A is greater than the angle *q* for product B. The size of the angle of intersection is an indication of the **sensitivity** of a product to variations in the level of activity. It can be seen that, as output increases for the two products, the profitability of product A increases at a faster rate than the profitability of product B. On the other hand, if output decreases for both products, the profitability of A decreases at a faster rate than for B. Product A is more sensitive to changes in output than product B. When the proportion of fixed cost to total cost is high, the risk to profitability is also high. Profit and break-even points are said to be sensitive to changes in prices and cost. This aspect will be considered later.

The calculation for margin of safety without the use of the graph:

a. Margin of safety in dollars

Total budgeted (or actual sales)	X
Less break even sales	X
Margin of safety	X

b. Margin of safety in percentage = $\dfrac{\text{Margin of safety}}{\text{Total break even (actual) sales}} \times 100$

Profit/volume charts

Break-even charts may also be drawn to show only the profit or loss at each level of output. The cost and revenue lines are omitted. The break-even chart for product X given in the example above could be drawn as a profit/volume chart:

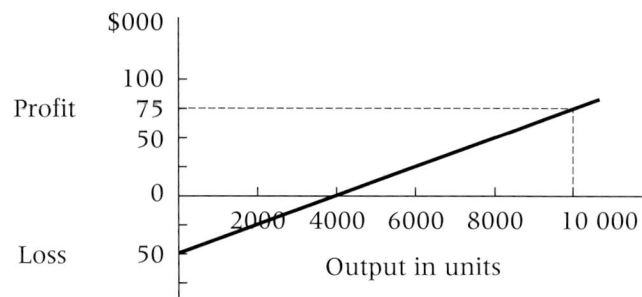

Profit/volume chart for product X

At zero output, the loss equals the total of the fixed costs, £50 000. At 10 000 units, the profit is equal to $75 000. A straight line joining the two points intersects the output line at the break-even point.

33.5 The limitations of break-even charts

Break-even charts are useful visual aids for the study of the effect of changes in output, costs and revenues on the break-even point, especially for managers with little accounting knowledge. The charts, however, have their limitations.

- Some costs are not easily classified as fixed or variable.
- Many fixed costs are fixed only within certain limits and may increase with the level of activity; they are 'stepped' costs.
- If sales revenue and costs are represented by straight lines they may be misleading. Maximum sales revenue may only be achieved if customers are given attractive discounts, while variable costs may be affected by quantity discounts when output is increased. These factors would be more accurately represented on charts by curves than straight lines.

The charts may mislead people whose accounting knowledge is limited, but trained accountants will know when to make allowances for the charts' limitations.

33.6 Target profit

This is used when a manager would like to know how much the company would have to sell to attain a specific target profit. Calculations used to calculate target profit are

1. Sales = Variable expenses + Fixed expenses + Target profit
2. Units sold to attain target profit = $\dfrac{\text{Fixed expenses + Target profit}}{\text{Unit contribution margin}}$
3. Dollars sales to attain target profit = $\dfrac{\text{Fixed expenses + Target profit}}{\text{Contribution margin ratio}}$

Short-term decisions are operating decisions made by a manager. He makes a choice between alternatives (incremental analysis) utilizing both quantitative (financial) and qualitative (non-financial) in order to determine change in output levels, pricing and inventory levels. The decisions made are routine and repetitive by nature. They involve the commitment and use of funds to the receipt of benefits. As the decisions are short-term, they receive priority over others due to their volume of output and, in addition, their ability to show results in a shorter period of time.

33.7 Relevant cost

Relevant costs are costs to be incurred at some future time and differ for each option available to the decision-maker.

Cost is an important factor, therefore, managers must have the tool to distinguish a particular cost that is relevant in one situation but may be irrelevant in another (direct and indirect cost). The important point to note is that relevant cost represents those future costs (incremental cash flow) which will be changed by a particular decision, while irrelevant cost will not be affected by the decision. Relevant cost is crucial for short-term decisions.

33.8 Incremental analysis (differential analysis)

Incremental analysis is the difference between costs and revenues generated over an alternative choice of action.

33.9 Types of incremental analysis

The price at which a good may be sold is usually decided by a number of factors:

- the need to make a profit
- market demand
- a requirement to increase market share for a product
- maximum utilisation of resources
- competition from other firms
- economic conditions
- political factors (price regulation etc.).

Marginal costing can help management to decide on pricing policy but first it is necessary to understand that some expenses, such as selling expenses, may be variable. An example is salesperson's commission based on the number of units sold. When variable selling expenses are included in marginal cost, the result is the **marginal cost of sales**:

	$000
Direct materials	100
Direct wages	80
Direct expenses	30
Marginal cost of production	210
Variable selling expenses	15
Marginal cost of sales	225
Other fixed expenses	175
Total cost	400

It is important to use the correct marginal cost when using marginal costing for decision making.

Example (Increasing market share)

The Larabee Gamebusters Company produces and sells a computer game that sells at $30 per game.

Each year 6000 of the games are sold. The marketing director suggests that, if the price is reduced to $28, sales will increase to 8000 games. The sales manager thinks that sales will increase to 11 000 games if the price is reduced to $25.

The following information is available for 6000 computer games:

	$
Direct materials	48 000
Direct labour	66 000
Variable selling expenses (commission)	12 000
Fixed expenses	48 000

Required

Calculate the profit or loss from the sale of (i) 6000 (ii) 8000 (iii) 11 000 units and recommend which option should be adopted.

Answer

Every unit sold incurs a variable selling expense (commission) and the marginal cost of sales is used:

Per unit:	$	$	$
Selling price	30	28	25
Direct material	8		
Direct labour	11		
Variable selling expense	2		
Marginal cost of sales	21	21	21
Contribution	9	7	4

	6000 units	8000 units	11 000 units
	$	$	$
Total contribution	54 000	56 000	44 000
Fixed expenses	48 000	48 000	48 000
Profit/(loss)	6 000	8 000	(4 000)

The Larabee Gamebusters Company should reduce the price of the game to $28.

33.10 Acceptance of orders below normal selling price

There are occasions when orders may be accepted below the normal selling price. These may be considered when there is spare manufacturing capacity and in the following circumstances:

- when the order will result in further contribution to cover fixed expenses and add to profit
- to maintain production and avoid laying off a skilled workforce during a period of poor trading
- to promote a new product
- to dispose of slow-moving or redundant stock.

The selling price must exceed the marginal cost of production.

Example

K2 Altimeters Ltd makes altimeters that it sells at $80 each. It has received orders for
(i)   1000 altimeters for which the buyer is prepared to pay $60 per altimeter,
(ii) 2000 altimeters at $48 each.
The following information is available:

	$
Direct material per altimeter	21
Direct labour per altimeter	32

Fixed expenses will not be affected by the additional production.

Required

State whether K2 Altimeters Ltd should accept either of the orders.

Answer

Order for 1000 altimeters at $60 each:

Contribution per altimeter $(60 − 53) = $7
Additional contribution from order: $7000

K2 Altimeters Ltd should accept the order.
   Order for 2000 altimeters at $48 each:

Contribution per altimeter $(48 − 53) = $(5)

K2 Altimeters Ltd would make a loss of $10 000 on the order and should not accept it.

33.11 Make or buy decisions

We have already seen in §23.4 that a Manufacturing Account may suggest that it would be more profitable for a business to buy goods from another supplier than make the goods itself. This involves a **'make or buy' decision**. It may be relevant for goods that are already being produced, or to the introduction of a new product.

The decision will be based primarily on whether the cost of buying the goods from another supplier is more or less than the marginal cost of production. Notice that the marginal cost of sales is not relevant to this type of decision as any variable selling costs will have to be incurred whether the goods are manufactured or purchased.

Example

Uggle Boxes Ltd makes and sells uggle boxes for which the following information is available:

Per box	$
Selling price	25
Direct material	9
Direct labour	6
Variable selling expenses	7

Uggle Boxes Ltd's fixed overheads amount to $60 500.

The variable selling expenses are ignored as they will have to be incurred anyway. The marginal cost of production is $(9 + 6) = $15. The contribution per unit is $(25 − 22) = $3. The current break-even point is $\frac{\$60\,500}{\$3}$ = 20 167 boxes.

Uggle boxes may be bought from Ockle Cockle Boxes Ltd for $13 per box, and from Jiggle Boxes Ltd for $16 per box.

Purchase of the boxes from Jiggle Boxes Ltd will increase the marginal cost to $23 and reduce the contribution to $2. Profit will be reduced and the break-even point will increase to $\frac{\$60\,500}{\$2}$ or 30 250 boxes. This option should not be considered.

If the boxes are bought from Ockle Cockle Boxes Ltd, the marginal cost will be $20 and the contribution will increase to $5. Profit will be increased and the break-even point will reduce to $\frac{\$60\,500}{\$5}$ or 12 100 boxes. This appears to be a good option.

Note. There are other matters which Uggle Boxes Ltd should consider before finally deciding to buy the boxes from another supplier:

- How certain is it that Ockle Cockle Boxes Ltd will not increase the price above $13? If the price is increased to more than $15 it may not be easy for Uggle Boxes Ltd to recommence manufacturing the boxes if it has rid itself of its workers and other resources.

- Will Ockle Cockle Boxes Ltd supply boxes of the proper quality?
- Will Ockle Cockle Boxes Ltd deliver the boxes promptly? Uggle Boxes Ltd cannot afford to keep its customers waiting because it is out of stock.
- Has Uggle Boxes Ltd an alternative use for the resources which will become free when it ceases to make the boxes? Unless it can utilize the resources profitably to make another product it will either have to shed the resources (labour, machines, etc.) or increase its unproductive costs.
- Can Uggle Boxes Ltd afford to lose the services of a skilled and loyal workforce which it may be difficult to replace at a later date when the need arises?

As we shall see again in chapter 34 on capital investment appraisal, managers often need to take non-financial factors into account before deciding which course of action to take.

33.12 Making the most profitable use of limited resources

Anything which limits the quantity of goods that a business may produce is known as a **limiting factor**. Limiting factors include

- shortage of materials
- shortage of labour
- shortage of demand for a particular product.

When faced with limited resources, a company making several different products should use the limited resources in a way that produces the most profit. The products must be ranked according to the amount of contribution they make from each unit of the scarce resource. Production will then be planned to ensure that the scarce resource is concentrated on the highest-ranking products.

Example 1 (Shortage of material)

Hillbilly Ltd makes three products: Hillies, Billies and Millies. All three products are made from a material called Dilly. Planned production is as follows: Hillies 2000 units; Billies 3000 units; Millies 4000 units. The following information is given for the products.

	Hillies	Billies	Millies
Selling price per unit	$54	$50	$105
Direct material per unit	2 kg	4 kg	5 kg
Direct labour hours per unit	3	2	6

Direct material costs $6 per kg; direct labour is paid at $10 per hour.

Fixed expenses amount to $72 000.

Hillbilly Ltd has discovered that the material Dilly is in short supply and only 30 000 kg can be obtained.

Required

Prepare a production plan that will make the most profit from the available material.

Answer

Calculation of contributions per kg of Dilly:

	Hillies	Billies	Millies
	$	$	$
Direct material per unit	12	24	30
Direct labour per unit	30	20	60
Marginal cost per unit	42	44	90
Selling price per unit	54	50	105
Contribution per unit	12	6	15
Contribution per kg of material	6	1.5	3
Ranking	1	3	2

Revised plan of production:

	Units	Direct material	Contribution
		kg	$
Hillies	2000	4 000	24 000
Millies	4000	20 000	60 000
Billies	1500	6 000	9 000
		30 000	93 000
Deduct fixed expenses			72 000
Profit			21 000

Example 2 (Shortage of direct labour hours)

The data for the manufacture of Hillies, Billies and Millies is as given for example 1 but the number of direct labour hours available is limited to 33 000. There is no shortage of material.

Required

Prepare a production plan that will make the most profit from the available labour hours.

Answer

Calculation of contributions per direct labour hour:

	Hillies	Billies	Millies
	$	$	$
Contribution per unit (as above)	12	6	15
Contribution per direct labour hour	4	3	2.5
Ranking	1	2	3

Revised plan of production:

	Units	Direct labour hours	Contribution
			$
Hillies	2000	6 000	24 000
Billies	3000	6 000	18 000
Millies	3500	21 000	52 500
		33 000	94 500
Deduct fixed expenses			72 000
Profit			22 500

33.13 Determine whether a product line or department in a business should be dropped or retained

The loss of contribution is considered from the viewpoint of savings in specific costs (avoidable/escapable expenses) from closure (such as redundancy and compensation to customers) alternative use for resources released also, and non-quantifiable effects. Expenses (unavoidable/inescapable) must be included as (costs) will continue even if the product line/department were eliminated. The rule of thumb to determine elimination: if the revenue is less than the avoidable expense, the product line/department should be eliminated.

Example

Bootleg is considering dropping its Slippers department because its total expenses of $32 700 are higher than its sales of $20 400. These are the expenses:

Cost of goods sold	$20 000	
Direct expenses	5 000	
Depreciation-equipment	200	
Indirect expenses:		
Rent	2 000	
Advertising	500	
Breakdown of service cost		
Office	3 000	(avoidable $2000; unavoidable $1000)
Purchasing	2 000	(avoidable $500; unavoidable $1000)

Do you think Bootleg should eliminate the slippers department?

Analysis

	Total	Avoidable	Unavoidable
Cost of goods sold	$20 000	$20 000	$ -0-
Direct expenses	5 000	5 000	-0-
Depreciation-equipment	200		200
Rent	2 000		000
Advertising	500	500	-0-
Office	3 000	2 000	1 000
Purchasing	2 000	500	1 000
Total	$32 700	$28 000	$ 4 200

To determine the profit/loss from the elimination of the department: Find the difference between the sales and the avoidable expenses:

$20400 - $28 000 = $7600

From the calculation the avoidable expenses is $7600 more than the revenue, therefore the department should be eliminated.

33.14 Sell joint product at a split off point or process

Problems of concern arise for the correct product mix when there are two or more products, as there may be a constraint (limiting factor) in production. In a case as this, it is better to produce and sell as much as possible of the product that has the highest margin per unit of time on the constrained activity.

Rule of thumb: the process can continue once the incremental revenue from the processing exceeds the incremental processing costs.

Example

Interior Doors makes doors. The cost to manufacture an unfinished door is $60. The total manufacturing cost per unit is made of the following:

Direct material	$24
Direct labour	18
Variable manufacturing overhead	12
Fixed manufacturing overhead	6
Manufacturing cost per unit	$60

Selling price per unfinished unit is $150.00. Interior Doors has unused production capacity and has decided to use the capacity to finish the doors and sell them at

$200.00 per unit. In order to complete the door, direct materials will increase by $6 and direct labour cost will increase by $12. Variable manufacturing overhead costs will increase by 50% of direct labour.

Determine whether Interior Doors should sell or process further.

Analysis

	Sell	Process further	Net income increase/ decrease
Sales	$150.00	$200.00	$50.00
Cost per unit:			
Direct materials	24	30	(6)
Direct labour	18	30	(12)
Variable manufacturing overhead	12	21	(9)
Fixed manufacturing overhead	6	6	-0-
Total	60	87	(27)
Net income per unit	90	113	23

Interior doors should continue to process (will make an incremental revenue of $50.00; additional processing cost of $27.00 will be covered from it).

33.15 Scrap or rework product

Consider cost of reworking the product or sell as scrap?

Example

Well Doctor machine company has 5000 defective units of a product that initially cost $1 per unit to manufacture. These units can be sold as it is now for $0.30 each (as scrap) or they can be reworked for $0.60 each per unit and then sold for $1.50 each.

Should Well Doctor sell the units as scrap or rework them?

Sunk cost Sunk costs are costs that are committed or were incurred.

Well Doctor must recognize that $1 per unit is manufacturing cost (sunk cost) already incurred. Therefore the costs are irrelevant for decision-making. Only costs for reworking defects and those that affect normal operation would be included.

For reworking defects Well Doctor is unable to manufacture 5000 new units with an incremental cost of $1 per unit and a selling price of $1.50 per unit.

Opportunity cost Opportunity cost is the amount of a benefit being sacrificed for an alternative course of action. It can be the loss of revenue.

The firm incurs an opportunity cost of $2500 (5000 × $1) − (5000 × $1.50).

Analysis

	Scrap	Rework
Sale of scrapped/reworked units		
(5 000 × .30)	$1500	
(5 000 × $1.50)		$7500
Less costs to rework defects		
(5000 × .60)		(3000)
Less opportunity costs of not making units		(2500)
Incremental net income	$1500	$2000

Well Doctor should rework the 5000 defective units as they will make an incremental income of $2000.

33.16 Steps that can be used to analyse cost for decision making

1. Associate costs with the options considered.
2. Ignore sunk costs, only relevant costs especially materials and labour (not committed and historical costs or cash flows and non-cash charges). All costs should be forward looking.
3. Omit costs that do not differ between alternatives (that is fixed costs, not all of stepped costs).
4. Make decisions on the remaining costs (these costs are known as differential/relevant/avoidable).

33.17 Quantitative and qualitative factors that can be used for decision making

- Alternative use of resources
- Obligations to employees
- Other source of supply available
- Effect on customer relations
- Spare productive capacity available
- Image of the company
- The environment.

33.18 Examination hints

- Make sure you are able to distinguish between variable and fixed costs.
- Learn the definition of 'marginal cost'.
- The C/S ratio is most important and is certain to be required in marginal cost questions. Make sure you know how to calculate the ratio and when to use it.
- Learn how to calculate the break-even point and the margin of safety. Break-even point is calculated by dividing the total fixed costs by the contribution per unit. If you are given the fixed cost per unit, multiply it by the number of units to find the total fixed costs.
- Practise drawing break-even charts. Choose as large a scale as possible for the chart to achieve a good degree of accuracy. Give every chart a proper heading and label the x and y axes clearly. Indicate the break-even point and other features. Take a ruler, pencil and rubber to the exam.
- Make sure you know how to use limited resources most profitably. Products should be ranked according to the contribution per unit of the limited resource.

33.19 Multiple-choice questions

1 The following information relates to product Q:

	$
Sales revenue at break even point	72 000
Unit sales price	24
Fixed costs	18 000

What is the marginal cost of each unit of product Q?

A $4.00   **B** $6.00   **C** $10.00   **D** $18.00

2 The annual results of a company with three departments are as follows:

Department	X	Y	Z
	$	$	$
Sales	210 000	100 000	140 000
Less: variable costs	100 000	80 000	90 000
head office fixed costs	75 000	35 000	50 000
Net profit (loss)	35 000	(15 000)	0

Head office fixed costs have been apportioned on the basis of the respective sales of the departments and will not be reduced if any department is closed. Which action should the company take, based on these results?

A close department Y

B close departments Y and Z

C close department Z

D keep all the departments open

3 A company makes three products, X, Y and Z, all of which require the use of the same material. Information about the products is as follows:

	Product X	Product Y	Product Z
	$	$	$
Per unit:			
Selling price	260	200	240
Direct material	96	80	90
Direct labour	50	40	50
Variable overhead	40	30	36
Fixed overhead	54	36	36
Profit	12	14	27

The material is in short supply. Which order of priority should the company give to the products to maximize profit?

	Order of priority		
	1	2	3
A	Y	X	Z
B	Y	Z	X
C	X	Y	Z
D	X	Z	Y

4 Barkis & Co. Ltd manufacture specialized containers for use under water. The business uses two machines. These machines have different levels of efficiency. The following information applies to production and costs.

Machine	X	Y
Hourly rate of production	160	250
Material cost per unit	$5.00	$4.60
Hourly labour rate	$10	$10
Number of operatives	4	5
Fixed costs per order	$200	$500
Variable costs per order	$2.40	$2.60

Orders have been received from different customers for (a) 800 and (b) 1000 containers. Which machine should be used for each order, in order to minimize cost? Orders may not be split between machines, but the same machine may be used for more than one order.

(a) Order 123/P for 800 containers.

(b) Order 382/Q for 1000 containers.

(c) Calculate the contribution to be made for order 123/P to make a profit of 25% on total cost, using each machine.

(d) Barkis & Co. Ltd require more funds to purchase an additional machine to complete further orders.

Three methods of doing so have been discussed:

(i) a rights issue;

(ii) an issue of shares to the public;

(iii) an issue of debentures.

Give *one* advantage and *one* disadvantage of each method.

(UCLES, 2002, AS/A Level Accounting, Syllabus 9706/2, May/June)

33.20 Exercises

Exercise 1

Veerich Ardson Ltd makes and sells mobile phones. The following information is given.

Per phone:	$
Selling price	50
Direct materials	18
Direct labour	20
Variable selling expenses	3

Fixed overheads amount to $70 000.

Required

Calculate the profit or loss from the sale of (i) 10 000 phones at $50 each (ii) 15 000 phones at $48 each, (iii) 20 000 phones at $42 each.

Exercise 2

El Dugar Peach Ltd sells canned fruit for which the following information is given.

Per 1000 cans of fruit:	$
Direct materials	5500
Direct labour	8750

The company has received orders for:
(i) 5000 cans of fruit at $16 000 per 1000 cans
(ii) 3000 cans of fruit at $14 100 per 1000 cans.
The additional production will not require any additional fixed expenses.

Required

State which of the two orders, if any, El Dugar Peach Ltd should accept.

Exercise 3

Canterbury Planes Ltd supplies the following information for the production of 15 000 tools.

	$
Direct materials	45 000
Direct labour	37 500
Other direct expenses	15 000
Variable selling expenses	30 000

Fixed expenses total $74 000. The tools sell for $16 each.

Canterbury Planes Ltd has received the following quotations for the supply of the tools:

North Island Tool Co.	$6000 per 1000 tools
South Island Tool Co.	$6800 per 1000 tools

Required

(a) Calculate the effect on profit and the break-even point of the quotations of
(i) North Island Tool Co.
(ii) South Island Tool Co.
if either was awarded the contract to supply the tools to Canterbury Planes Ltd.

(b) State whether Canterbury Planes Ltd should continue to produce the tools or whether it should buy them, and if so, from whom. Support your answer with figures.

Exercise 4

Castries Ltd makes three products: Gimie, Gros and Petit. The budgeted production for three months is as follows.

	Gimie	Gros	Petit
No. of units	1000	2000	800
Selling price per unit	$14	$25	$20
Direct material per unit (litres)	2.5	3.25	4
Direct labour per unit (hours)	0.5	1.4	0.6

Direct material costs $2 per litre. Direct labour is paid at $10 per hour.

Fixed expenses are $10 000.

Castries Ltd has been informed that only 10 575 litres of material are available.

Required

Prepare a revised production budget that will produce the most profit from the available materials.

34 Long-term decision making

Objectives
- define investment appraisal
- non-discounting methods to evaluate investment decisions
- use financial (quantitative) or time value applications to evaluate investment decisions
- state the advantages and disadvantages of the methods of investment appraisal

34.1 What is investment appraisal?

Investment appraisal is a process of assessing whether it is worthwhile to invest funds in a project. The project may be replacement of an existing asset, acquiring an additional asset, introducing a new product, opening a new branch of a business, etc. Funds invested in a project may include additional working capital as well as expenditure on fixed assets. These projects always involve making choices, including whether or not to proceed with the project, which assets to buy, which new products to introduce, and so on.

Accounting techniques are essential tools when these decisions have to be made. However, projects must sometimes be undertaken even when the accounting techniques appear to advise against them. For example, a business that is causing an environmental nuisance may face being closed down by health and safety inspectors unless it spends a considerable sum of money to abate the nuisance. It is well to remember that investment decisions should only be made after all relevant matters, economic, political, environmental, social, etc. have been considered.

This chapter is concerned principally with the financial techniques of appraisal:

- accounting rate of return (ARR)
- payback period
- net present value (NPV)
- internal rate of return (IRR).

These techniques are designed to assess the quality of projects, benefits arising from them, and degrees of risk involved. Only accounting rate of return is concerned with profitability; the others are based on cash flows. The net present value and internal rate of return take the time value of money into account They are all based on additional benefits and costs which will arise from a project. These are referred to **incremental** profits and cash flows. Existing profit and cash flows are ignored as being irrelevant because they will continue whether the new project is undertaken or not. There are two new terms to learn.

- **Sunk costs** consist of expenditure that has been incurred before a new project has been considered. For example, a company plans to introduce a new product that will require the use of a machine it acquired some years ago and has used in the production of an existing product. The cost of the machine is a sunk cost because it has already been incurred and is not *incremental*. Its cost is a historical fact and cannot have any bearing on future decisions.
- **Opportunity costs** are the values of benefits that will be sacrificed if resources are diverted from their present uses to other applications. For example, if a machine that has been earning annual net revenue of $50 000 is to be used exclusively for another operation, it will cease to earn the $50 000. The lost revenue is an opportunity cost. If the machine will earn net revenue of $70 000 in its new capacity, the incremental net revenue will be $20 000 ($70 000 − $50 000).

34.2 Long-term decision making

Methods of capital appraisal

Financial:

<u>Non-discounting methods</u>

Payback period – This is the length of time required to recover the investment.

Simple rate of return – It uses accounting profits and calculates the average annual profit as a percentage of the cost of the project.

<u>Discounting methods</u>

Discounted payback period.

Net present value. It is the future cash flows converted to present value and the total matched with the cost of the investment.

Internal rate of return. It is the rate of interest an investment is expected to yield over its useful life.

Non-financial: Environmental

Ethical

Social

Typical cash inflows

Incremental revenue

Reduction in costs (Savings)

Salvage value

Release of working capital

Typical cash outflows

Initial investment

Increased working capital needs

Repairs and maintenance

Incremental operating costs

34.3 Profitability index

This is a technology used in the allocation of scarce resources or limited funds. It ranks competing alternative investment projects based on their desirability.

Calculation

Profitability index = $\dfrac{\text{Present value of net cash inflows}}{\text{Investment required}}$

The present value of net cash inflows will be the difference between the discounted inflows and outflows.

The investment required will be the initial investment plus working capital needed less the salvage value of the project.

Acceptance

The profitability index is a means of rating projects in order of priority.

The higher the index, the more desirable the project.

Example

	Projects		
	Weatherbed	Thunder	Fawn
Present value of cash inflows	140 000	310 000	240 000
Present value of cash outflows	20 000	90 000	40 000
Initial investment	60 000	75 000	80 000
Working capital needed	30 000	60 000	55 000
Salvage value	10 000	36 000	30 000

Solution

Profitability index = $\dfrac{\text{Present value of net cash inflows}}{\text{Investment required}}$

	$\frac{120\,000}{80\,000}$	$\frac{220\,000}{99\,000}$	$\frac{200\,000}{105\,000}$
=	1.5	2.2	1.9

Ranking

1st – Project Thunder

2nd – Project Fawn

3rd – Project Weatherbed

34.4 Computing non-discounting methods

Payback period

This is the time span needed for the cash flows to be equal to the investment.

Calculation

Match cash flows against
(a) the investment
(b) the running costs/operating expenses.

Acceptance

(a) A project is acceptable if it is within the stated payback period.
(b) A project is selected if it pays back first.

Example 1: Uneven cash flows

Year	Cash Flows	Cumulative Cash Flows
0	<100 000>	<100 000>
1	20 000	<80 000>
2	15 000	<65 000>
3	26 000	<39 000>
4	30 000	<9 000>
5	36 000	27 000

Explanations:

Year '0' – The beginning of the investment period.

Cash flows <100 000> – this is the amount of the initial investment or outlay of cash.

Cash flow $20 000; $15 000 etc. – these represent inflows of cash.

Cumulative cash flows are the sum of the difference between the inflows and outflows of cash.

The cumulative cash flows became positive only in the 5th year.

Up to that point the payback period is four (4) years.

In the 5th year cash flow per month is $\frac{36\,000}{12}$ = $3 000

Payback period of $9 000 is 3 months.

Therefore, payback period = 4 years 3 months.

Example 2: Uneven cash flows

When the net annual cash inflows are uneven the average is found and payback period is calculated thus:

$$\text{Payback period} = \frac{\text{Cost of investment}}{\text{Average annual net cash inflows}}$$

$$= \frac{100\,000}{\frac{127\,000}{5}}$$

$$= \frac{100\,000}{25\,400}$$

$$= 3.93 \text{ years}$$

Note: Averages tend to be misleading so this formula should be used only in the absence of details.

Example 3: Even cash flows

When the net annual cash inflows is the same each year:

$$\text{Payback period} = \frac{\text{Net investment outlay}}{\text{Average annual net cash inflows}}$$

Year	Cash flows	Operating expenses	Net cash inflows	Cumulative cash flows
0	<100 000>	–	<100 000>	<100 000>
1	20 000	2000	18 000	< 82 000>
2	15 000	2000	13 000	< 69 000>
3	26 000	3000	23 000	< 46 000>
4	30 000	5000	25 000	< 21 000>
5	36 000	5000	31 000	< 10 000>

Solution (a)

$$\text{Payback period} = \frac{\text{Net investment outlay}}{\text{Average annual net cash inflows}}$$

$$= \frac{100\,000}{22\,000}$$

$$= 4.5 \text{ years}$$

Solution (b)

Fours years plus

average monthly inflow year 5 $= \frac{31\,000}{12}$

$= 2\,583$

Time to payback $10 000 $= \frac{10\,000}{2\,583}$

Payback period $= 4$ years 4 months

Accounting rate of return

Profit as calculated by the accountant is expressed as a percentage of the cost of the investment.

It is also called by other names:
Simple rate of return (ROR)
Unadjusted rate of return
Return on investment (ROI)
Return on capital employed (ROCE)
Financial statement method.

Calculation

It is best done using the formula

$$\text{Return on capital employed} = \frac{\text{Average annual profits}}{\text{Average investment} + \text{Working capital}}$$

Acceptance

(a) A project is acceptable if it yields a profit.
(b) A project is selected if it yields the highest profit.

Example 4

Capital expenditure	$200 000
Residual value	$ 18 000
Useful economic life	7 years

Solution

Annual depreciation =

$$= \frac{\text{Cost} - \text{Residual value}}{\text{Life span}}$$

$$= \frac{200\,000 - 18\,000}{7}$$

$$= \$26\,000$$

Year	Profit before depreciation	Depreciation expense	Profit after depreciation
0	<200 000>		
1	66 000	26 000	40 000
2	71 000	26 000	45 000
3	64 000	26 000	38 000
4	61 000	26 000	35 000
5	1 000	26 000	<25 000>
6	36 000	26 000	10 000
7	46 100	26 000	20 100
			$163 100

Average annual profits

$$= \frac{163\,100}{7}$$

$$= \$23\,300$$

Average investment

$$= \frac{\text{Beginning} + \text{End}}{2}$$

$$= \frac{\text{Initial investment} + \text{Residual value}}{2}$$

$$= \frac{200\,000 + 18\,000}{2}$$

$$= \frac{218\,000}{2}$$

$$= \$109\,000$$

ROCE

$$= \frac{23\,300}{109\,000} \times \frac{100}{1}$$

$$= 21.4\,\%$$

34.5 Time value of money

Money generates money over time. A loan accrues expenses to the debtor (interest expense) and revenue to the creditor (interest received). The use of money for a specific period of time has a cost associated with it.

Money not utilized forgoes returns that could have been earned if invested. The cost for using money is calculated using either simple interest or compound interest.

Calculation of future value

The information needed to calculate the interest cost would be the principal, the rate of interest and the period of the investment or the usage of the funds.

Simple interest

If the principal is the same each period the interest will also remain the same.

Example: If the same $100 is invested at 10% each year over a five year period the yield will be $50 in interest and the total value of the investment after 5 years will be $150, calculated as follows:

Years	Re-Investment	Interest Calculation
1	$100	$100 \times \frac{10}{100} \times 1 = 10$
2	$100	$100 \times \frac{10}{100} \times 1 = 10$
3	$100	$100 \times \frac{10}{100} \times 1 = 10$
4	$100	$100 \times \frac{10}{100} \times 1 = 10$
5	$100	$100 \times \frac{10}{100} \times 1 = \underline{10}$
	Total interest	$\underline{\$50}$

$$\text{Value of the investment} = \text{Principal} + \text{Interest}$$
$$= 100 + 50$$
$$= \$150$$

This can be done alternatively using the formula

$$\text{Simple Interest} = \text{Principal} \times \text{Rate} \times \text{Time}$$
$$= 100 \times \frac{10}{100} \times 5$$
$$= \$50$$

Compound interest

In order to compound the interest, add the interest of each single period to the principal. This will cause the principal and interest of each period to increase.

Example

What would be the future value of $100 invested at 10% annually for 5 years with the interest compounded over that period and reinvested?

Year	Interest Calculation	Principal at Beginning Of Next Period
1	$100 \times \frac{10}{100} \times 1 = 10$	$100 + 10 = 110$
2	$110 \times \frac{10}{100} \times 1 = 11$	$110 + 11 = 121$
3	$121 \times \frac{10}{100} \times 1 = 12.10$	$121 + 12.10 = 133.10$
4	$133.10 \times \frac{10}{100} \times 1 = 13.31$	$133.10 + 13.1 = 146.41$
5	$146.41 \times \frac{10}{100} \times 1 = 14.64$	$146.41 + 14.64 = 161.05$

$$\text{Total Interest} = \text{Principal at end} - \text{Principal at beginning}$$
$$= 161.05 \quad - \quad 100$$
$$= \$61.05$$
$$\text{Value of the investment} = \$161.05$$

This can be done alternatively using the formula

$$\text{Future value (n)} = \text{Principal} (1 + \text{Rate})^n, \text{where } ^n \text{ is the investment period.}$$
$$= 100 (1 + .10)^5$$
$$= 100 (1.6105)$$
$$= \$161.05$$

This calculation can be simplified using tables indicating the future value of $1 after a given number of time periods.

Procedure

1. Locate 10% at the top of the table.
2. Read down that column to the 5 period line.
3. The factor is 1.611.
4. Multiply the principal by the factor.

$$\begin{array}{c} \text{Principal} \times \text{Factor} \\ \$100 \times 1.611 \end{array} = \$161.10 \text{ approximately.}$$

Since investments are seldom a one-period scenario, a series of equal instalments made at the end of equal intervals of time (called annuities) and the cost calculated using compound interest will differ slightly.

Example

What is the future value of $100 invested annually for five years at the rate of 10%?

Procedure

1. Consult a table for future value of $1.00 paid at the end of each period (Ordinary Annuity) for a given number of periods.
2. Locate 10% at the top of the table.
3. Read down that column to the five periods line.
4. The factor is 6.105
5. Multiply the periodic payment by the factor

$$\begin{array}{ccc} \text{Periodic payment} & \times & \text{Factor} \\ \$100 & \times & 6.105 \end{array} = \$610.50.$$

The value of the investment after five years is $610.50.

Calculation of present value

The future value of an investment can be calculated if given the present value of the investment the time period and the rate of return.

Similarly, the present value of the amount to be invested can be calculated from data on the future value of the investment, the life span and the rate of return.

Since it is a cost associated with the passage of time an amount that can be received now is worth more than the same amount received later. Future values must then be discounted to find present values.

Example

What is the value of a single sum to be invested now in order to receive a future value of $161.05 after five years at the rate of 10% annually?

Procedure

1. Consult the table in the Appendix for present value of $1 to be received at the end of a given number of periods.

2. Locate 10% at the top of the table.

3. Read down that column to the five-period line.

4. The factor is 0.621

5. Multiply the future value by the factor:

Future value × Factor
  161.05   × 0.621   = $100

the present value of the investment.

If the receipts from the investment are equal over the life of the investment, tables can be used again to calculate the present value of what should be invested.

Example

How much should be invested now at 10% for five years so that it will have a future value of $610.50 received annually as $122.10?

Procedure

1. Consult a table of present value of an ordinary annuity of $1 received at the end of each period.

2. Locate the 10% column.

3. Locate the five periods line.

4. Determine the factor, 3.791.

5. Multiply the periodic receipts by the factor.

Periodic receipts × Factor
    $122.10   × 3.791   = $462.88

The present value of the investment can be done alternatively as follows:

Year	Receipts	Factors	Present Value
1	122.10	.909	110.99
2	122.10	.826	100.86
3	122.10	.751	91.70
4	122.10	.683	83.40
5	122.10	.621	75.83
	610.50		$462.78

34.6 Computing net present value (NPV)

Future cash flows are discounted back to the present using present value tables.

Calculation

The present value of all the future net cash inflows is matched against the current investment. If the former is greater than the latter there is a positive net present value and vice versa.

Acceptance

(a) A project is considered if at the chosen discount rate the total discounted cash inflows exceed the cost of the investment.

(b) A project is selected if it has the highest net present value among projects and the non-financial benefits do not outweigh the financial benefits.

Example

Heavy Investments Ltd is considering a project that entails buying heavy equipment.

The initial outlay is $300 000 and the project will last five years.

Because of the shortage of funds the money will have to be borrowed at an interest rate (cost of capital) of 12%.

The expected future cash inflows are

Year   1 100 000
       2 125 000
       3 180 000
       4 175 000
       5 200 000

Advise Heavy Investments Ltd on the project.

Solution

Year	Cash inflows	Discount factor 12%	Present values
0	<300 000>	1.000	<300 000>
1	100 000	0.893	89 300
2	125 000	0.797	99 625
3	180 000	0.712	128 160
4	175 000	0.636	111 300
5	200 000	0.567	113 400
* Positive net present value			$241 785
* Total discounted cash inflows			541 785
Less: Cost of the investment			300 000
			$241 785

Procedure

1. Locate table showing the present value of $1.00.
2. Read across the percentages at the top until you come to the discount percentage 12%.
3. Read vertically under 12% to get the discount factors for years 1, 2, 3, 4 and 5.
4. To calculate the present value of an inflow multiply the inflow for that year by the corresponding factor. An amount spent at the beginning of the period (Year 0) maintains its value since no time has elapsed (hence the factor 1.000).
5. Tally all the present values ($541 785) except the investment. Find the difference between the investment ($300 000) and the total discounted cash inflows.
6. If the investment exceeds the total discounted cash inflows then the net present value is negative and vice versa.
7. This project is acceptable because it has a positive net present value.
8. This project will be selected if it has the highest NPV among alternative projects.

34.7 Computing internal rate of return

The individual rate of return is the rate of earnings a project promises over its useful life.

Calculation

It is computed by finding the discount rate at which the net present value is zero. Alternatively this discount rate makes the discounted receipts equal to the cost of the project.

Present value outflows = Present value inflows

or

Cost of the project = Present value inflows

or

Net present value = 0.

Acceptance

(a) A project is desirable if the rate of return is higher than the cost of capital.
(b) The project with the highest IRR compared with the cost of capital is selected.
(c) The net present value method is usually considered the most reliable method for selecting projects.

There are a number of methods to calculate the internal rate of return. The most common is the trial and error technique performed as follows, using the assumptions that there are

(a) Constant cash flows (annuities)
(b) Variations in cash flows (interpolation).

Constant cash flows (annuities)

Example

Investment	$29 502
Life span	6 years
Annual savings	$ 6000

Solution

1. Calculate the factor

$$\frac{\text{Investment}}{\text{Annual cash inflows}} = \frac{29\ 502}{6000}$$

$$= 4.917.$$

2. Locate the factor in the present value tables for annuities.

   Found under 6% in the 6th year.
3. The rate of return promised by the project is 6%.
4. Test accuracy: 6 year/6%

   $= 4.9170 \times 6\ 000 = 29\ 502$

   $=$ initial investment.

Variations in cash flows (interpolation)

Example

Cost of the investment	$12 000
Average annual savings	3500
Life span of project	4 years

Solution

1. Calculate the factor:

$$\frac{\text{Investment}}{\text{Average annual cash inflows}} = \frac{12\ 000}{3\ 500}$$

$$= 3.429.$$

2. Locate the factor in the annuity table:

   Scan 4 years in the range 6–8%
3. Need to interpolate (apply formula).

Lower %: 6% factor	3.465	3.465
Calculated: true factor	3.429	
Higher %: 8% factor		3.312
Difference	0.037	0.153

$$\text{Internal rate of return} = \text{Lower factor} + \left(\frac{\text{Lower factor} - \text{True factor}}{\text{Lower factor} - \text{Higher factor}}\right) \times (\text{Higher \%} - \text{Lower \%})$$

$$= 6\% + \left(\frac{3.465 - 3.428}{3.465 - 3.312}\right) \times (8 - 6)$$

$$= 6\% + \left(\frac{0.037}{0.153}\right) \times 2$$

$$= 6\% + 0.483$$

$$= 6.483\%$$

OR

$$\text{Internal rate of return} = 6\% + \left\{\frac{\text{PV Using lower factor} - \text{PV using true factor}}{\text{PV Using lower factor} - \text{PV using higher factor}}\right\} \times \begin{array}{l}\text{Difference}\\\text{in discount rate}\end{array}$$

$$= 6\% + \left\{\frac{(3.465 \times 3500) - (3.428 \times 3500)}{(3.465 \times 3500) - (3.312 \times 3500)}\right\} \times 8 - 6\%$$

$$= 6\% + \left(\frac{12\ 128 - 11\ 998}{12\ 128 - 11\ 592}\right) \times 2\%$$

$$= 6 + \frac{130}{536} \times 2\%$$

$$= 6 + 0.485$$

$$= 6.485\%$$

Computing discounted payback period

Example

Should this project be accepted given that the cash flow stated below will be discounted at 15% over its life span of four years?

Solution

Year	Cash flows	Discount factors at 15%	Present values	Cumulative cash flows
0	<100 000>	1.000	<100 000>	<100 000>
1	20 000	.870	17 400	< 82 600>
2	15 000	.756	11 340	< 71 260>
3	26 000	.658	17 108	< 54 152>
4	30 000	.572	17 160	< 36 992>
5	36 000	.497	17 892	< 19 100>
Negative net present value			(19 100)	

The total discounted cash flows do not exceed the investment in four years.

The project is unacceptable.

Use the application and methods to accept/reject projects

Example

Using the information in example 3, which project should be accepted given the data on project R and project T:

Net present value

Year	Project R	Project T	Discount factor at 12%	Project R present value	Project T present value
0	<300 000>	<800 000>	1.000	–	–
1	100 000	200 000	.893	89 300	178 600
2	125 000	300 000	.797	99 625	239 100
3	180 000	400 000	.712	128 160	284 800
4	175 000	250 000	.636	111 300	159 000
5	200 000	300 000	.567	113 400	170 100

Total					
Inflows	780 000	1450 000	Total discounted cash flows	541 785	1031 600
			less initial investment	300 000	800 000
			net present value	241 785	31 600

Discounted payback

Year	Discounted cash flow Project R	Cumulative	Discounted cash flows Project T	Cumulative
0	<300 000>	<200 000>	<800 000>	<800 000>
1	89 300	<110 700>	178 600	<621 400>
2	99 625	< 11 075>	239 100	<382 300>
3	128 160	117 085	284 800	< 97 500>
4	111 300		159 000	61 500
5	113 400		170 100	

Project R	Project T
In year 3	In year 4
Cash flow per month	Cash flow per month
$= \dfrac{128\ 160}{12}$	$= \dfrac{159\ 000}{12}$
= 10 680	= 13 250.
Discounted payback period approx. 2 years 1 month 1 week.	Discounted payback period approx. 3 years 5 months.

Accounting rate of return

		Project R	Project T
Total in flows		780 000	1 450 000
Less depreciation		300 000	800 000
Total profits		480 000	650 000
Average annual profits		$\dfrac{480\ 000}{5}$	$\dfrac{650\ 000}{5}$
	=	$96 000	$130 000
Average investment	=	$\dfrac{300\ 000 + 0}{2}$	$\dfrac{800\ 000 + 0}{2}$
	=	$150 000	$400 000
Return on capital employed (ARR or ROI)	=	$\dfrac{96\ 000 \times 100}{150\ 000}$	$\dfrac{130\ 000 \times 100}{400\ 000}$
	=	64%	32.5%

Decision with reasons

Project R should be selected because

(1) it has a higher NPV $241,785;

(2) the investment is recovered in a shorter time: 2 years 1 month 1 week;

(3) it yields a higher return on investment 64%.

34.8 Evaluating investment decisions

Quantitative	Qualitative
(Financial)	(Non-Financial)

Screening

Internal rate of return
Cost of capital
Corporate return on investment
Industry average return on investment
Bank interest rate

Contributing to improvement in product/process quality
Decrease in waste of resources and time
Decrease in production and delivery time
Increase in customer satisfaction

Preference

Discounted accounting rate of return
Discounted payback period
Net present value

Ethical Environmental Social
Corporate short-term objectives
Corporate long term objectives
Corporate social objectives
Current economic system
Economic system

34.9 Capital appraisal methods: advantages and disadvantages

	Advantages	Disadvantages
Payback period	1. Simple to use and understand 2. Useful when liquidity is important 3. Promotes caution	1. Disregards total contribution 2. Cash flow after payback period ignored 3. Does not consider the value of money 4. Disregards the size of the cash flow in the payback period 5. Focuses on short-term returns
Accounting rate of returning	1. Uses readily available accounting data 2. Understood by managers 3. Easy to calculate	1. Deals with accounting profit rather than cash flow 2. Methods of depreciation and stock valuation make a difference 3. Ignores the value of money 4. Disregards the size of the initial investments 5. Average profits distort high and low points
Net present value	1. Uses cash flow data 2. Considers time and size of cash flow 3. Maximizes shareholders wealth 4. Takes into account interest lost 5. Recognizes risks and uncertainty of future cash flows	1. May not be cost effective to collect data 2. May conflict with what IRR recommends 3. Concept difficult to grasp
Internal rate of return	1. Considers both timing and size of cash flows	1. May conflict with what NPV recommends There may be numerous IRR if outflows and inflows are separated by periods

Assumption of capital appraisal

1. Investments occur at the beginning of the respective period.
2. Cash flows occur evenly throughout any one period.
3. Cash flows occur at the end of the period.
4. Economic conditions remain the same.
5. The only economic change takes place in the value of money.

34.10 Questions

Exercise 1

Baseball Ltd intends to introduce a new product that is expected to produce the following profits over a period of six years.

	$		$
Year 1	23 000	Year 4	26 000
2	24 000	Year 5	29 000
3	25 000	Year 6	23 000

The project will require the use of a machine that was purchased some years ago at a cost of $16 000 and the use of a second machine that will have to be purchased for $120 000. It is estimated that stock held will increase by $10 000, and debtors will increase by $15 000.

Required
Calculate the accounting rate of return that will be earned from the new product.

Exercise 2

Mapleduck Ltd is planning to replace one of its machines. It has two choices of replacements: Duckbill and Kwak, each costing $90 000.

The following information is available for the machines.

	Duckbill		Kwak	
	Cash inflow	Cash outflow	Cash inflow	Cash outflow
	$	$	$	$
Year 0	–	90 000	–	90 000
1	80 000	50 000	60 000	20 000
2	90 000	54 000	68 000	28 000
3	100 000	60 000	72 000	32 000

Required
Calculate the payback periods for Duckbill and Kwak and state, with reasons, which machine Mapleduck Ltd should purchase.

Exercise 3

Nomen Ltd is considering buying a machine and has three options, machine A, B or C, only one of which it will buy. Each machine costs $135 000 and will have a five-year life with no residual value at the end of that time.

The net receipts for each machine over the five-year period are as follows.

	Machine A	Machine B	Machine C
	$	$	$
Year 1	50 000	38 000	26 000
2	50 000	38 000	26 000
3	38 000	38 000	38 000
4	26 000	38 000	50 000
5	26 000	38 000	50 000

Nomen Ltd's cost of capital is 12%.

The discounting factors at 12% are: year 1, 0.893; year 2, 0.797; year 3, 0.712; year 4, 0.636; year 5, 0.567.

Required
Calculate the net present value of each option and state which machine Nomen Ltd should choose.

Exercise 4

The information is given as for Nomen Ltd in exercise 3, with the addition of the discounting factors for 20%: year 1, 0.833; year 2, 0.694; year 3, 0.579; year 4, 0.482; year 5, 0.402.

Required
Calculate the internal rate of return for machines A and B.

Notes
- IRR can be calculated from two positive net present values but will be less accurate. The denominator of the fraction in the formula must be amended as follows: $P + [(P - N) \times (\frac{P}{p - n})]$. If the discounting factors in a question produce only positive net present values, do *not* try to find another discounting rate; the examiner expects you to use the ones supplied in the question.
- When the receipts are constant for a number of consecutive years, the net present value of those receipts may be calculated quickly if the annual amount is multiplied by the sum of the factors for the years concerned. For example, if net receipts are $25 000 in each of the first five years and the cost of capital is 10%, the NPV for the five years is $25 000 × (0.909 + 0.826 + 0.751 + 0.683 + 0.621) = $25 000 × 3.790 = $94 750.

Exercise 5

Baxter Ltd requires a new machine to use in the manufacture of a new product. Two machines are available: Big Gee and Maxi-Shadbolt. Baxter Ltd depreciates machinery using the straight-line method. Baxter Ltd will obtain a bank loan at interest of 10% per annum to buy the machine.

Further information

	Big Gee	Maxi-Shadbolt
Cost of machine	$140 000	$180 000
	$	$
Additional receipts Year 1	98 000	101 000
2	112 000	118 000
3	126 000	126 000
4	126 000	140 000
5	100 000	110 000

Additional costs (including depreciation and bank interest):

	$	$
Year 1	70 000	84 000
2	84 000	98 000
3	91 000	105 000
4	98 000	112 000
5	95 000	100 000
Useful life of machine	5 years	5 years
Estimated proceeds of disposal		
after 5 years	$20 000	$30 000
Present value of $1	10%	40%
Year 1	0.909	0.714
2	0.826	0.510
3	0.751	0.364
4	0.683	0.260
5	0.621	0.186

Required

(a) Calculate for each machine:
   (i)   the accounting rate of return (ARR)
   (ii) the payback period
   (iii) the net present value
   (iv) the internal rate of return (IRR).
(b) State, with reasons, which machine Baxter Ltd should purchase.

Exercise 6

A company proposes to replace an existing machine with a new one costing $150 000. It is estimated that the use of the new machine will result in net savings over the next four years of $50 000 per annum. The company will borrow $150 000 at an interest rate of 10% per annum to pay for the machine.

Required

Calculate the degrees of sensitivity as regards the cost of the machine and the annual operational savings.

34.11 Multiple-choice questions

1 The net present value of a project has been calculated as follows:

	NPV ($)
at 10%	30 000
at 20%	(8 000)

What is the internal rate of return on the project?

A 10%

B 12.1%

C 17.9%

D 20%

2 Why are cash flows discounted for investment appraisal?

  A $1 now is more useful than $1 receivable at a future time.

  B It is prudent to state future cash flows at a realistic value.

  C Money loses its value because of inflation.

  D The risk of not receiving money increases with time.

3 Which method of investment appraisal may be based on either actual cash flows or discounted cash flows?

  A accounting rate of return

  B internal rate of return

  C net present value

  D payback

4 A company has $4 million to invest. Its investment opportunities are as follows.

Amount of investment for a period of 5 years	NPV($)
1. $3 mill.	600 000
2. $2.5 mill.	350 000
3. $1.5 mill.	280 000
4. $1 mill.	50 000

In which opportunities should the company invest?

A 1 and 3

B 1 and 4

C 2 and 3

D 2 and 4

34.12 Additional exercises

1 The directors of Joloss plc intend to purchase an additional machine to manufacture one of their new products. Two machines are being considered: Milligan and Bentine. The company depreciates its machinery using the straight-line method.

Joloss plc will borrow the money required to purchase the machine and pay interest of 10% per annum on the loan.

Estimates for the machines are as follows:

		Milligan $	Bentine $
Cost of machine		100 000	130 000
Additional receipts	Year 1	70 000	72 000
	2	80 000	84 000
	3	90 000	90 000
	4	90 000	100 000
Additional costs	Year 1	50 000	60 000
(see note)	2	60 000	70 000
	3	65 000	75 000
	4	70 000	80 000

Note. These costs include the charges for depreciation and interest on the loans.

	4 years	4 years
Useful life of the machine	4 years	4 years
Value at end of useful life	nil	nil

Present value of $1	10%	20%
Year 1	0.909	0.833
2	0.826	0.694
3	0.751	0.579
4	0.683	0.482

Required

(i) Calculate the net present value of each machine. (Base your calculations on the cost of capital.)

(ii) State, with your reason, which machine Joloss plc should purchase.

The directors require the machine to produce a return on outlay of not less than 25%.

(iii) Calculate the internal rate of return on the machine you have selected in (ii) to see if it meets the required return on outlay.

(UCLES, 2002, AS/A Level Accounting, Syllabus 9706/4, May/June)

2 Jane Pannell Ltd proposes to purchase a new machine costing $120 000. It will be sold at the end of four years for $20 000. The company depreciates machinery using the straight-line method.

The machine will earn revenue of $80 000 per annum and involve additional expenditure of $46 000 each year. The company's cost of capital is 10%.

The present value of $1 is as follows:

	10%	15%
Year 1	0.909	0.870
2	0.826	0.756
3	0.751	0.658
4	0.683	0.572

Required

Calculate

(a) the accounting rate of return

(b) the net present value

(c) the internal rate of return.

Appendix. Table showing net present value of $1

Present value of $1

Years	5%	6%	7%	8%	9%	10%	11%	12%	13%	14%	15%	16%	17%
1	0.952	0.943	0.935	0.926	0.917	0.909	0.901	0.893	0.885	0.877	0.870	0.862	0.855
2	0 907	0.890	0.873	0.857	0.842	0.826	0.812	0.797	0.783	0.769	0.756	0.743	0.731
3	0.864	0.840	0.816	0.794	0.772	0.751	0.731	0.712	0.693	0.675	0.658	0.641	0.624
4	0.823	0.792	0.763	0.735	0.708	0.683	0.659	0.636	0.613	0.592	0.572	0.552	0.534
5	0.784	0.747	0.713	0.681	0.650	0.621	0.593	0.567	0.543	0.519	0.497	0.476	0.456
6	0.746	0.705	0.666	0.630	0.596	0.564	0.535	0.507	0.480	0.456	0.432	0.410	0.390
7	0.711	0.665	0.623	0.583	0.547	0.513	0.482	0.452	0.425	0.400	0.376	0.354	0.333
8	0.677	0.627	0.582	0.540	0.502	0.467	0.434	0.404	0.376	0.351	0.327	0.305	0.285
9	0.645	0.592	0.544	0.500	0.460	0.424	0.391	0.361	0.333	0.308	0.284	0.263	0.243
10	0.614	0.558	0.508	0.463	0.422	0.386	0.352	0.322	0.295	0.270	0.247	0.227	0.208

Years	18%	19%	20%	21%	22%	23%	24%	25%
1	0.847	0.840	0.833	0.826	0.820	0.813	0.806	0.800
2	0.718	0.706	0.694	0.683	0.672	0.661	0.650	0.640
3	0.609	0.593	0.579	0.564	0.551	0.537	0.524	0.512
4	0.516	0.499	0.482	0.466	0.451	0.437	0.423	0.410
5	0.437	0.419	0.402	0.386	0.370	0.355	0.341	0.328
6	0.370	0.352	0.335	0.319	0.303	0.289	0.275	0.262
7	0.314	0.296	0.279	0.263	0.249	0.235	0.222	0.210
8	0.266	0.249	0.233	0.218	0.204	0.191	0.179	0.168
9	0.225	0.209	0.194	0.180	0.167	0.155	0.144	0.134
10	0.191	0.176	0.162	0.149	0.137	0.126	0.116	0.107

Appendix. Present value of an annuity of $1 in arrears

Periods	4%	5%	6%	8%	10%	12%	14%	16%	18%	20%	22%	24%	26%	28%	30%	40%
1	0.962	0.952	0.943	0.926	0.909	0.893	0.877	0.862	0.847	0.833	0.820	0.806	0.794	0.781	0.769	0.714
2	1.886	1.859	1.833	1.783	1.736	1.690	1.647	1.605	1.566	1.528	1.492	1.457	1.424	1.392	1.361	1.224
3	2.775	2.723	2.673	2.577	2.487	2.402	2.322	2.246	2.174	2.106	2.042	1.981	1.923	1.868	1.816	1.589
4	3.630	3.546	3.465	3.312	3.170	3.037	2.914	2.798	2.690	2.589	2.494	2.404	2.320	2.241	2.166	1.879
5	4.452	4.330	4.212	3.993	3.791	3.605	3.433	3.274	3.127	2.991	2.864	2.745	2.635	2.532	2.436	2.035
6	5.242	5.076	4.917	4.623	4.355	4.111	3.889	3.685	3.498	3.326	3.167	3.020	2.885	2.759	2.643	2.168
7	6.002	5.786	5.582	5.206	4.868	4.564	4.288	4.039	3.812	3.605	3.416	3.242	3.083	2.937	2.802	2.263
8	6.733	6.463	6.210	5.747	5.335	4.968	4.639	4.344	4.078	3.837	3.619	3.421	3.241	3.076	2.925	2.331
9	7.435	7.108	6.802	6.247	5.759	5.328	4.946	4.607	4.303	4.031	3.786	3.566	3.366	3.184	3.019	2.379
10	8.111	7.722	7.360	6.710	6.145	5.650	5.216	4.833	4.494	4.192	3.923	3.682	3.465	3.269	3.092	2.414
11	8.760	8.306	7.887	7.139	6.495	5.988	5.453	5.029	4.656	4.327	4.035	3.776	3.544	3.335	3.147	2.438
12	9.385	8.863	8.384	7.536	6.814	6.194	5.660	5.197	4.793	4.439	4.127	3.851	3.606	3.387	3.190	2.456
13	9.986	9.394	8.853	7.904	7.103	6.424	5.842	5.342	4.910	4.533	4.203	3.912	3.656	3.427	3.223	2.468
14	10.563	9.899	9.295	8.244	7.367	6.628	6.002	5.468	5.008	4.611	4.265	3.962	3.695	3.459	3.249	2.477
15	11.118	10.380	9.712	8.559	7.606	6.811	6.142	5.575	5.092	4.675	4.315	4.001	3.726	3.483	3.268	2.484
16	11.652	10.838	10.106	8.851	7.824	6.974	6.265	5.669	5.162	4.730	4.357	4.033	3.751	3.503	3.283	2.489
17	12.166	11.274	10.477	9.122	8.022	7.120	6.373	5.749	5.222	4.775	4.391	4.059	3.771	3.518	3.295	2.492
18	12.659	11.690	10.828	9.372	8.201	7.250	6.467	5.818	5.273	4.812	4.419	4.080	3.786	3.529	3.304	2.494
19	13.134	12.085	11.158	9.604	8.365	7.366	6.550	5.877	5.316	4.844	4.442	4.097	3.799	3.539	3.311	2.496
20	13.590	12.462	11.470	9.818	8.514	7.469	6.623	5.929	5.353	4.870	4.460	4.110	3.808	3.546	3.316	2.497
21	14.029	12.821	11.764	10.017	8.649	7.562	6.687	5.973	5.384	4.891	4.476	4.121	3.816	3.551	3.320	2.498
22	14.451	13.163	12.042	10.201	8.772	7.645	6.743	6.011	5.410	4.909	4.488	4.130	3.822	3.556	3.323	2.498
23	14.857	13.489	12.303	10.371	8.883	7.718	6.792	6.044	5.432	4.925	4.499	4.137	3.827	3.559	3.325	2.499
24	15.247	13.799	12.550	10.529	8.985	7.784	6.835	6.073	5.451	4.937	4.507	4.143	3.831	3.562	3.327	2.499
25	15.622	14.094	12.783	10.675	9.077	7.843	6.873	6.097	5.467	4.948	4.514	4.147	3.834	3.564	3.329	2.499
26	15.983	14.375	13.003	10.810	9.161	7.896	6.906	6.118	5.480	4.956	4.520	4.151	3.837	3.566	3.330	2.500
27	16.330	14.643	13.211	10.935	9.237	7.943	6.935	6.136	5.492	4.964	4.525	4.154	3.839	3.567	3.331	2.500
28	16.663	14.898	13.406	11.051	9.307	7.984	6.961	6.152	5.502	4.970	4.528	4.157	3.840	3.568	3.331	2.500
29	16.984	15.141	13.591	11.158	9.370	8.022	6.983	6.166	5.510	4.975	4.531	4.159	3.841	3.569	3.332	2.500
30	17.292	15.373	13.765	11.258	9.427	8.055	7.003	6.177	5.517	4.979	4.534	4.160	3.842	3.569	3.332	2.500
40	19.793	17.159	15.046	11.925	9.779	8.244	7.105	6.234	5.548	4.997	4.544	4.166	3.846	3.571	3.333	2.500

Index